DEBRAHMANISING HISTORY
Dominance and Resistance in Indian Society

Egalitarianism is neither alien to India nor the gift of the West. Marginalised people everywhere have always aspired to build an egalitarian world. Espousing the perspective of the non-elites, this book brings out the beauty and resilience of a counter-tradition by visiting some of the major sites of resistance and creativity from below. Ranged against caste and brahmanism, this rational-liberating tradition is to be found in the heterodoxies of various inclinations, particularly Buddhism, the movements of subaltern saint-poets, Sufism and Sikhism.

This legacy was carried forward in modern India by, more than anybody else, Phule, Iyothee Thass, Narayana Guru, Periyar, and Ambedkar. Recognising the power of culture in the politics of transformation, they had emancipatory visions that embraced the whole of Indian experience, and stand firmly as an alternative to Tilak-Savarkarite, Gandhian, and Nehruvian visions. Their determined, but diverse and resourceless struggles, fought in the teeth of opposition from the caste elites, could not arrest the neo-brahmanism which under colonial patronage and the archaeology of knowledge derived from Orientalism went on to reincarnate – and nationalise – itself into octopus-like Hinduism. Their sublime failure adds to their enduring appeal to the marginalised as old forms of hierarchy and hegemony menacingly morph into new structures of inequality in post-1947 India.

In some studies, the egalitarian orientation of this tradition is belatedly being recognised, but it is seldom integrated with macro-level theoretical studies on Indian culture and society. An attempt in that direction, this searing critique of caste and dominant historiography is meant for all those who are – or want to be – part of the ongoing struggle of human liberation.

Braj Ranjan Mani writes on Indian society and culture from the perspective of the marginalised majority. His publications include *Resurgent Buddhism: Ambedkar's Predecessors in Modern India*, and *A Forgotten Liberator: The Life and Struggle of Savitribai Phule*. Earlier associated with *The Times of India*, Mani is currently a Fellow, Indian Institute of Advanced Study, Shimla. Reach him at brajrmani@gmail.com

DEBRAHMANISING HISTORY
Dominance and Resistance in Indian Society

BRAJ RANJAN MANI

MANOHAR
2011

First published 2005
Reprinted 2007, 2008, 2011

© Braj Ranjan Mani, 2005

All rights reserved. No part of this publication may be reproduced or transmitted, in any form or by any means, without prior permission of the author and the publisher.

ISBN 81-7304-640-9 (Hb)
ISBN 81-7304-648-4 (Pb)

Published by
Ajay Kumar Jain *for*
Manohar Publishers & Distributors
4753/23 Ansari Road, Daryaganj
New Delhi 110002

Printed at
Salasar Imaging Systems
Delhi 110035

Do not believe in hearsay; do not believe in what is handed down through generations; do not believe in anything because it is accepted by many; do not believe because some revered sage or elder makes a statement; do not believe in truths to which you have become attached by habit; do not believe merely on the authority of your traditional teachings. Have deliberation and analyse, and when the result accords with reason and conduces to the good of one and all, accept it and live up to it.

GAUTAM BUDDHA
The *Anguttara Nikaya*, I, 188,
see Woodward and Hare, 1932

. . . I have the audacity to believe that peoples everywhere can have three meals a day for their bodies, education and culture for their minds, and dignity, equality and freedom for their spirits. I believe that what self-centred men have torn down men other-centred can build up. . . . I still believe that we shall overcome. This faith can give us courage to face the uncertainties of the future. It will give our tired feet new strength as we continue our forward stride toward the city of freedom. When our days become dreary with low-hovering clouds and our nights become darker than a thousand midnights, we will know that we are living in the creative turmoil of a genuine civilisation struggling to be born.

MARTIN LUTHER KING, JR.
Nobel acceptance statement, 1964

Contents

Preface   11

Introduction   13

1. **Historical Roots of Brahmanic Dominance and Shramanic Resistance**   45
   Violence and domination underpin Vedic ideology – caste indoctrination – brahmanical pseudo-religion as engine of oppression – caste, karmayoga and swadharma in the Gita – *Dandaniti* central to brahmanical polity and state – shramanic counter-tradition of resistance and equity – popular heterodoxies debunk elite historiography.

2. **Buddhist India: Against Caste and Brahmanism**   85
   Buddha's humanitarian synthesis of mind and matter – Buddhist dialectics an antithesis of Upanishadic absolutism – searing indictment of caste – paradigm of human liberation – alternative vision of social and political institutions – Buddhist ascendancy and India's past greatness – counter-revolution and brahmanical revivalism – forgeries to recast Indian culture in the brahmanical mould.

3. **Medieval Mukti Movements of the Subaltern Saint-Poets**   134
   Social resistance in religious idiom – Kabir and monotheistic radicalism in the north – Siddha rebellion in Tamil Nadu – Virashaiva socialism in Karnataka – Varakari movement in Maharashtra – social dimension of bhakti and the brahman backlash.

Contents

4. **Colonialism, and Birth of Vedic-Brahmanic Nationalism** — 188
   Orientalism, Aryan race theory and Neo-Hinduism – Roy, reforms, renaissance: fact against fiction – Dayananda's valorisation of Aryan race and Vedic culture – self-strengthening modernisation of brahmanism – 'Nationalist' vindication of caste ideology – Vivekananda's polemics – monolithic and hegemonic cultural nationalism – symbiosis of cultural chauvinism and communal politics.
   Appendix: *Parallel Fascist thinking in East and West: Manu's 'brahman' and Nietzsche's 'superman'*

5. **Phule's Struggle against Brahmanical Colonialism** — 251
   Brahman power and oppression of the time – emergence of anti-caste radicalism – Satyashodhak Samaj: vision of a new society – the rewriting of history and mythology – education as emancipation and empowerment – gender inequality and women's subordination – agriculture, peasantry and labour – critique of nation and nationalism.

6. **Guru, Iyothee, Periyar, Acchutanand: Different Strategies, One Goal** — 291
   Dynamics and dimension of egalitarian emergence – Narayana Guru and Kerala's liberation struggle – Dravidian upsurgence: Iyothee Thass and the Justice Party – Periyar and the Self-Respect movement – the battle in the north: Acchutanand and Mangoo Ram – movements from below signal the end of colonialism.

7. **Nationalist Power Politics, Excluded Masses and the Gandhi-Ambedkar Debate** — 343
   The myth of the Mahatma – Ambedkar's revolt – the Machiavelli in the Mahatma: the true story of Poona Pact – the anatomy of Gandhian paternalism – grime behind the glamour – varna swaraj: obscurantist critique of modernity – Nehru and Ambedkar

on Gandhism – vision of the nation as social democracy – radical realism amidst euphoria of freedom: the Constitution and the Hindu Code Bill

8. Epilogue: Institutionalised Discrimination from the Past to the 'Democratic' Present — 406

Notes — 416

Bibliography — 427

Index — 445

Preface

Ostentatious use of exquisitely lovely words — and lovelier ideals — such as harmony and peace is neither new nor confined to any particular society. Dominant classes the world over invoke harmony without snapping their ties with the oppressive structures of class, caste, and gender hierarchies. Hollow, hypocritical advocacy of justice and equity becomes necessary for the power elites, especially in the democratic times in which we live. Therefore, those who aspire to build a more humane, more inclusive society have per force to take off the elitist mask of generosity and solidarity in the name of seamless cultural unity or nationalism. Such deconstruction for an egalitarian reconstruction runs the risk of gross misconceptions and distortions at the hands of the entrenched interests and 'embedded' scholars. I would like to make it clear, therefore, that this work is not intended to target any castes or groups but to present the historical wrongs in a perspective that pitches for the greater good. As Thomas Szasz (1974: 20) says, 'In the animal kingdom, the rule is, eat or be eaten; in the human kingdom, define or be defined', I had no choice but to write this book.

This work reflects the creativity not of one author but of many engaged social scientists. My thanks go first to all the people whose perspectives — articulated here in indigenous terms — militate against the colonisation of minds and bodies. I am also grateful to friends who read parts of the manuscript and offered their suggestions. I owe a special debt to G. Aloysius. Also in the debt department are Gail Omvedt, Arun Kumar, Namrata, and Anil.

My thanks to Mr Ramesh Jain who went against the conventional academic wisdom and decided to publish the work.

No words can express my gratitude to my parents, brothers and sister. This work would not have happened without their love and support. I dedicate *Debrahmanising History* to my mother.

New Delhi
January 2005

BRAJ RANJAN MANI

Introduction

> The impulse to oppose cultural norms appears as inarticulate revolt, as social criticism, as vision, as ideology, as completed revolution; it may spring from logic, disillusionment, or the experience of oppression. In short, it is part of the continuing dialectic of history, as much our cultural heritage as what it opposes. What I mean, then, by 'counter-tradition' is not 'that which opposes tradition', but, 'the tradition which opposes'.
>
> LOUIS KAMPF
> in Sheila Delany, ed., *Counter-Tradition: The Literature of Dissent and Alternatives*, 1971: 4

In any society dominant and subordinated classes, as well as their ideologies and narratives of the past and present, do not exist in isolation but in conflict. The perpetrators and the victims of injustice seldom escape tension and confrontation, for privilege is enjoyed at the expense of the other. Oppressors cannot be with the oppressed, as being against the oppressed is the essence of oppression. Thus the ideology that serves the interests of one group subverts the interests of the others (Freire 1996). Not surprisingly, subordinated classes everywhere do not share the dominant ideology and history doled out by elites, and in fact have traditions and ideologies of resistance. Master narratives and dominant ideologies, however, often inhibit and confuse the construction of the traditions and ideologies of resistance. Since social scientists are mostly associated with power elite, they tend to view the social world from the top, constructing and interpreting events or evidence in ways that marginalise or ignore the role of non-elites. When they recognise resistance, they do so reluctantly – even grudgingly – and only when it attacks the formal institutions of power. On the whole social scientists do not take notice of the protests erupting in one form or another in everyday life without the fanfare of open defiance in the public realm. Studies of popular protest, of revolution, and rebellion are distorted in several 'scholarly' ways and often misrepresent events as instances of token or misguided resistance (MacGuire and Paynter 1991: 10-13).

In other words, dominant ideologies unify the elite and subvert their subordinates by denying the latter a critical understanding or any ideology of protest that can enable them to change their submission into a transforming force that would reconstruct the world and make it more egalitarian. The general design is to obscure the whole situation of social, economic, and political domination that perpetuates ignorance, disunity, and lethargy among the suppressed. Dominant ideologies ensure that the subordinate classes do not see through the hegemonic ideology and strategy, lest they unite and engage in a struggle for liberation (Freire 1996: 126-7).

Marx correctly said, 'The ruling ideas of society are the ideas of the ruling class.' But his overemphasis on 'material forces' somewhat subjects the realm of ideas and ideals to the dominion of all-powerful economic base and the social relations of production that anchor the ideological superstructure. A relatively independent role of ideology is seminally expounded by Gramsci through what he terms the phenomenon of hegemony. Not just a system of domination (whether of ideas or political power) hegemony, he says, is the process whereby the dominant class indoctrinates the masses and manufactures a consensus in civil society through largely peaceful means. Elite-controlled agencies and apparatuses – religious institutions, political parties, academia, the media, art, and literature – 'sell' the status quo by presenting it as natural and good and generate 'expressions of respect for the established order [that] serve to create around the exploited person an atmosphere of submission and of inhibition which lightens the task of policing' (Fanon 63: 38). Ideological indoctrination or thought-policing from the top not only produces docile subjects, it also helps the ruling elite to mask or mystify its repressive machinery – police, law courts, the military. In a famous essay Althusser (1971: 121-73) establishes that ideology is the fulcrum of the state mechanism through which the dominant class is able to reproduce its class domination. Moulded into subjects through ideological state apparatuses, succeeding generations continue to conform to the norms of the existing class relations. However, the crux of the Marxist-Gramscian dialectic is that the dominant ideas are never fully accepted. Ultimately they are challenged by the deprived and degraded.

On the other hand, those intellectuals who are a part of the power elite play a major role in the scheme of domination. They try to conceal – or at least minimise – the existence of social cleavages, and the concomitant conflicts of interest and values between masters and slaves, capitalists and workers, oppressors and oppressed in class, race, and gender. Class conflict, as Freire's work exemplifies, is a concept that upsets the elite since they do not see themselves as oppressive even though they cannot outrightly deny the existence of huge social divides. Injustice and oppression, whatever its form or colour, is a threat to peace and harmony. Not surprisingly, struggle, in multifarious forms throughout history, against the exploitative system are as old as oppression. The co-existence of domination and defiance is increasingly being accepted in many theories of society, culture, knowledge, and history. As Foucault in his analysis of power (1990: 90-7) and many others have shown, domination and resistance often go hand in hand.

Ideology as an instrument of domination, of ensuring that the common people thought and behaved as the ruling elite want them to, finds an archetypical expression in brahmanism. Named after those at the top of the caste hierarchy, brahmanism is the main exploiting system of traditional Indian society. It stands for the aggregate of the sacerdotal literature, social structure and religio-political institutions that have been masterminded by the elite with the primary aim of keeping the masses ignorant, servile and disunited (Dharma Theertha 1992). Brahmanism uses the ideology of caste as a crucial instrument to dehumanise, divide and dominate the productive majority. Ambedkar, in his preface to *The Untouchables*, put it as 'a diabolical contrivance to suppress and enslave humanity' (*BAWS*, vol. 7: 239).

In the classical sense, the caste system is a form of social stratification in which castes are hierarchised, occupationally specialised and separated from each other (in matter of marriage, physical contact, food) by rules of purity and pollution. The birth-based segregation is reinforced by rigorous endogamy and strict control over women's sexuality. Hierarchy – along with purity and power – culminates in the brahman. Says Manu, the ancient lawgiver of brahmanical tradition, 'When a brahman is born he springs to light above the world; he is the chief of all creatures, entitled by eminence of birth to the wealth of the world' (*Manusmriti* I.99-100, see Doniger et al., eds., 1991). The brahman's anti-thesis is the shudra, under which category come all the labouring masses – peasants, artisans and workers. The shudra is the most impure, born in sin. Caste-and-order, theorised and made sacred and sacrosanct as varnashrama-dharma by its beneficiaries, is an institutional arrangement of social closure in which knowledge, wealth, and human dignity are denied to the 'impure' groups who are pushed down the ladder of graded hierarchy.

In other words, the characteristic attribute of the caste system is not only 'hereditarily appointed work' but also 'unequally divided rights' (Bougle 1991: 64). Berreman aptly describes it as 'institutionalised inequality' that guarantees 'differential access to valued things in life'. Not merely a system of interdependence, inhuman hierarchy of caste implies the concentration of power, privilege, affluence, and security at the top, and humiliation, deprivation, want, and anxiety at the bottom (Berreman 1991: 84-92; Mencher 1991: 93-109).

Caste is also a highly patriarchal system where all women of all castes are treated like chattel. Malicious, misogynist expressions such as *na stri swaatantryamarhati* (women should not be given freedom) and *striyo hi mool doshaanaam* (woman is the root cause of all evils) abound in the caste canon. There are frequent co-references to woman and shudra in the brahmanical literature – both are lifelong slaves from birth to death. Manu and Yajnavalkya, the premier law-givers, hold that even when released from slavery they are not emancipated because slavery is inborn in them (Sharma 1983: 45-8). As we shall see in Chapter 1, the anti-woman, anti-shudra epistemology is enshrined in the brahmanical sacred texts.

Brahmanism/casteism is a hegemonic ideology, sustained through a cleverly designed socio-religious structure, which works, to use Antonio Gramsci's phrase, as a 'permanently organised force'. Mere economism – reflected in the history-as-study-of-succession-of (advancing)-modes-of-production approach – does not help us to understand the complex and highly resilient character of brahmanism. It works at several levels in a multiplicity of forms – all of which empower the brahman and allied castes, and disempower the rest, legitimising gross inequalities, human rights abuse, gender discrimination, mass illiteracy, untouchability, etc. Traditionally, it is propelled by the ruthless pursuit to self-aggrandisement based on caste, priest-craft and false philosophy – caste representing the scheme of domination, priest-craft the means of exploitation, and false philosophy a justification for both (Dharma Theertha 1992). Ambedkar and many others have compellingly argued that brahmanism has never stood for any consistent philosophy, doctrine or ethics, but has adjusted its hegemonic methods and principles to changing situations.

Power politics, thus, is at the heart of brahmanism. The exercise of power necessarily involves conflict and resistance. The contestation for economic, cultural, and intellectual resources between the powerful and the powerless involves both dominance and resistance. This conflict – obviously multi-faceted – takes place at different levels. There are many forms and faces of domination, which is equally true of resistance. There is heterogeneity of resistance as there is heterogeneity of domination. As Turner (1983: 78) says, 'Each mode of production will give rise to at least two significantly separate ideologies corresponding to the class position of subordinate and superordinate classes.' In other words, since no dominant ideology goes unchallenged, it is never absolute, never all pervasive.

If Indian society is not an exception to this, it means that there has been a tradition and ideology of anti-brahmanism and anti-casteism. Resistance to the caste ideology, in sharp contrast to the brahmanical presentation of the past, actually began as soon as it came into existence. In fact, the history of Indian society from the Aryan immigration around the middle of the second millennium BC to the present era has been a history of conflict and contestation over land, resources, and cultural practices between the Aryans or Indo-Aryans who later glorified themselves as brahmans on the one hand and the various communities of indigenous people who were denigrated and dehumanised as rakshasas, dasas, shudras and chandalas on the other.

As the knowledge-system and socio-religious world-view developed by the caste elites were intended to exploit and enslave the majority 'low castes', there has been a long tradition of resistance from below against the discriminatory system. If Indian society has been a caste society as postulated by sociological gurus of diverse hues such as Dumont, Ghurye, and Srinivas, it has also been an anti-caste society. This becomes clear when we see what the 'lower castes' – actually *lowered* castes, as Arun Kumar eloquently phrases them – think of their social position and of the caste system as a whole. Peasants, artisans and workers who have been humiliated and brutalised as dasa-shudras, chandalas and ati-shudras, who now call themselves dalit-bahujan or the 'oppressed majority', have never had a stake in keeping caste alive. As it was in the interest of the brahmans and brahmanised castes to preserve and promote it, it was in the interest of the lowered castes to smash the prison-house of caste. At any rate, they did not become slaves and clogs in the caste machine of their own volition – they were forced into servility by the deadly combination of brahmanic socio-religious mechanism and kingly-feudal coercion. Nevertheless, through the ages protests in one form or another were registered against oppression. As the relatively powerless groups more often express their resistance in less overt forms, deliberately avoiding direct confrontation with authority or with elite norms, 'their resistance includes a wider range of actions than massive, confrontational, political resistance' (MacGuire and Paynter 1991: 12). Underlining the importance of understanding social psychology of collective behaviour, Georges Lefebvre, the French historian who first used the term 'history from below', has argued that 'social history cannot be limited to describing the external aspects of antagonistic classes. It must also come to understand the mental outlook of each class' (cited in Kaye in his Foreword to Rude 1995: xi).

The Dharmashastras are crammed with the choicest abuse, and recommendations of stringent injunctions and punishment to make the toiling people fall in the caste system. Elites destroyed the records of their opponents, especially of the Buddhists, but the anti-caste views and attitudes are still discernible in the tradition of Buddhism and in various popular heterodoxies, strands of regional cultures, and in Pali and Prakrit literature. The views expressed in these sources are sharply antagonistic to the brahmanic caste culture. The resistance to caste is also apparent from the fact that 'when the

Sanskrit literature, whether the Dharmashastras, the epics, or any other, refers to varna and caste, the attempt is not to realistically *describe* the society but to *prescribe* for it. The references represent projections; the brahmanic texts are an attempt to delineate an ideal model and impose it on the society. They are a manifesto for a particular form of social inequality' (Omvedt 2003: 133). Not surprisingly, contending with the conventional – and falsified – history of caste, Omvedt has come to the conclusion that the 'real history of caste in India is still to be written!' (ibid.: 134).

These are the views of a social scientist who is sympathetic to the struggle of the caste-oppressed. Dalit-bahujan writers and thinkers, who have themselves suffered pain and humiliation due to their caste, know the history of caste from their own experience. Breaking the 'culture of silence' imposed on them, they have started telling their stories in their own language and idiom, and refute the conventional representation of themselves in history and culture. Dalit-bahujan ideology, popularly referred to as Phule-Ambedkarism, heroes of the social justice movement in modern India, rejects the brahmanic version of caste and culture. The imperative for the dalit-bahujan deconstruction and construction of history is increasingly being felt by their organic intellectuals. Emphasising the need for the oppressed to construct their own narratives and texts, Kancha Ilaiah, for instance, suggests that all that has been written by 'brahmanical thinkers, writers, politicians, everything in every field – must be reexamined thoroughly' for the simple reason that they cannot be at once judge and party to the lawsuit:

. . . *the life-world of the Dalit-bahujans of India has hardly anything in common with the socio-cultural and political environment of Hindu-Brahmanism. The Dalit-bahujans live together with the Hindus in the civil society of Indian villages and urban centres, but the two cultural worlds are not merely different, they are opposed to each other. Hindu thinking is set against the interests of Dalit-bahujan castes; Hindu mythology is built by destroying the Dalit-bahujan cultural ethos. Dalit-bahujan castes were never allowed to develop into modernity and equality. The violent, hegemonic, brahmanical culture sought to destroy Dalit-bahujan productive structures, culture, economy and its positive political institutions. Everything was attacked and undermined. This process continues in post-Independence India.* (1996: 114)

Ilaiah's understanding of the past and present is shared by other dalit-bahujan scholars. This is understandable because the upper caste subordination of the dalit-bahujan people was carried active during the anti-colonial struggle. The national leadership, contrary to the official depiction, did not strive to build a casteless, equalitarian ideology. Instead, brahmanical ideologues eulogised the caste culture and structure of ancient India in the name of nationalism. From Rammohun Roy, Dayananda and Vivekananda to Tilak and Savarkar, Gandhi and Nehru, they all defined the nation and nationalism in hegemonic cultural terms. This strengthened the brahmanical forces in order to reestablish their domination in the modern time. Those who criticised brahmanism and the caste system and demanded socio-cultural reconstruction were accused of mounting an attack on Indian custom and tradition. It was argued that the fabric of 'spiritual' India was being torn apart by low-caste leaders and their illiterate followers. The subaltern leaders indeed had a different vision of the past and present. Ambedkar's unfinished work *The Revolution and Counter-Revolution in Ancient India* (*BAWS*, vol. 3) made the 'mortal conflict' between Buddhism and brahmanism the cornerstone of reconstructing the past.

As Aloysius (1997) and others have shown, eulogisation of varna ideology, in fact, became the standard by which one's patriotic credentials were to be judged. Those who excelled in the art of selling caste to India and the rest of the world were lionised as national heroes. No wonder that varna ideology was found splendid and worthy of export to all cultures of the globe in the nationalist discourse of Vivekananda, Tilak, and Gandhi. Even Jawaharlal Nehru was so enamoured of caste that he saw caste as a solution to the problem of organising the coexistence of different races. He feared therefore that its abolition 'may well lead to a complete disruption of social life, resulting in the absence of cohesion, mass suffering and the development on a vast scale of abnormalities in individual behaviour . . .' (Nehru 1996: 247). Thus, despite differences in modes of expression, the high caste nationalist trajectory on caste was unambiguously clear – caste had kept us alive as a nation.

Not surprisingly, the brave new India that emerged from the anti-colonial struggle retains the exclusivist and casteist structure of the past. The basic substance of the past, contends Barbara Joshi, is sustained, even when the environment appears to change dramatically:

Belief in the inherent inferiority of an hereditary population has dangerous economic and psychological advantages for all individuals in the dominant society: a vast pool of cheap, legitimately degraded labour; limits on competition for the goods and positions that shape modern prestige and power – land, white-collar professions, political leadership; limits on competition for scarce loans to marginal farmers and scarce jobs for industrial labour; an automatic boost to the self-esteem of all in the dominant society.
(Joshi 1986: 6)

Ilaiah makes the same point.

After 1947, in the name of democracy, the brahmans, the baniyas and the neo-kshatriyas have come to power. Post-colonial development in its entirety has been systematically cornered by these forces. The brahmans have focussed their attention on politico-bureaucratic power, the baniyas established their hegemony on capitalist markets and the neo-kshatriyas established their control over the agrarian economy. This modern triumvirate restructured the state and society to affirm and reproduce their hegemonic control.
(Ilaiah 1996: 114-15)

However, the social scientists who dominate academia preach in the 'national' style of their modern masters, Gandhi-Nehru or Tilak-Savarkar, the implausible theory of harmony between the high caste oppressor minority and lowered caste oppressed majority. R. S. Sharma contends, 'The main trend noticeable in the works of recent Indian writers such as Ketkar, [R. C.] Dutt, and Ghurye is to present the caste system in such a way as may help to recast it in response to present requirements. Works on the position of women in ancient India display the same tendency' (1983: 12). This Sanskritising trend is carried forward in the works of scholars like Radhakrishnan, Srinivas and Madan. In fact, blocking the understanding of dehumanising, dividing, and patriarchal face of caste is crucial and common among elites of all hues because only then can they valorise in different idioms the brahmanical tradition as the shaper and saviour of national unity and harmony. Their innumerable analyses and interpretations, based on a selective and sectarian reading of the past and present, and clothed in clever abstractness or ambiguities, if not validating the caste directly, at least appear to endorse the view that the brahmanical socio-religious system, which has over the centuries institutionalised the subjugation of toiling men and women, cease to be odious because it has survived for so long!

In the elitist construction and interpretation of Indian culture, the destroyers of social unity who equate the ascriptive socio-religious order with cultural nationalism are hailed as builders of modern India, while the real unifiers and builders who demand the annihilation of the caste order and struggle for the reconstruction of society are accused – in earlier times directly, today with a lot of sugarcoating – of destructive and anti-national politics. Such a perspective finds favour not only with scholars openly aligned with the hegemonic, communal brahmanism, which has been refurbished and recast as 'Hindu nationalism', but also with many self-styled liberal-secularists who have started celebrating the 'tolerance', 'harmony' and 'magnanimity' of the Hindu tradition. Belated in their recognition of the glorious traditions of Hinduism, the elitist secularists now constantly invoke images from the Hindu pantheon and wield the names of superstars of hegemonic nationalist project, to ward off the rampaging menace of communalism. Like them, many liberal-democrats do not want to see that communalism in India is not confined to strife between Hindus and Muslims but actually has its genesis in the dominant ideology of caste.

The pedigree of hate and communalism in India goes back to a time when a class of people with claims of high birth and purity of blood attempted to accord divine sanction to the system and to the brahmans therein, a position of pre-eminence. Simultaneously there were concerted efforts to dehumanise and demonise the other, particularly the shudras, ati-shudras and those outside the pale of varna society, who either did not observe or refused to conform to the rules of caste laid down in the Dharmashastras. The term coined to demonise the other, apart from *rakshasa* and *asura*, was *mleccha*, the 'unclean, unwashed other', which has a history, according to Romila Thapar, going back to around 800 BC and occurs originally in a Vedic text (1999: 17). Contrary to the Hindutva claim that the term was essentially one of the contempt for the invading, barbarous foreigners, especially Muslims, it was used originally and frequently by the upper castes to refer to shudras and ati-shudras, considered the enemy. Thapar contends that demonisation/*rakshasisation* of the enemy – irrespective of who the enemy was – has been a constant factor with reference to many pre-Islamic enemies and going back to earlier time:

Sayana's commentary of the fourteenth century AD *refers to the dasas of the Rigveda as rakshasas and asuras. Inscriptions of this period freely use the terms rakshasas and Ravana for enemies who are Hindu. In later centuries, the reference to some Muslims as mlecchas was an extension of the term to include them among the many others who were denied varna status. This usage is more common in sources which come from the upper castes, such as Sanskrit texts and inscriptions, and was more easily used for the lower castes who were, even without being Muslim, marginalised, moved to the fringes of society and treated with contempt.* (ibid.: 17-18)

The commoner or the shudra, in brahmanic phraseology 'born in sin' and 'the untruth itself', was demonised so much and saddled by so many disabilities as to be virtually relegated to a condition where he lost his human status. 'The sight of mere possession of wealth by a shudra injures the brahman', says Manu, who also declares that an attempt made by the common man to acquire knowledge is a crime. If he listens to a recitation of the Vedas his ears are to be filled with molten lead; if he recites the sacred texts his tongue is to be torn out; and if he remembers them, his body is to be split. The brahman was divinely entitled to insult, beat, and enslave a shudra but let the latter murmur a protest and he would have a red hot iron thrust into his mouth. According to the law-givers, the killing of a shudra by a brahman was equivalent to the killing of a cat, frog, lizard, owl, or crow. Similar animal similes for Jews were used by Adolf Hitler in his autobiography, *Mein Kampf*. The Nazis, it may be recalled, appropriated Nietzsche – the progenitor of the concepts of the 'master race' and 'superman' – as their patron-philosopher. Nietzsche, for his part, was greatly inspired by Manu's ideology. In fact, his 'superman' was modelled on Manu's 'brahman'. (See the Appendix to Chapter 4.)

Other societies and religions have in the past perpetrated atrocities against their own people, but no society or religion can match the record of upper caste hatred and bigotry against their co-religionists, which was maintained for centuries and buttressed by every resource of religious force and social sanction. No religion other than Hinduism discriminates – socially, culturally and educationally – against the majority of its own co-religionists, that too on scriptural authority. The infringement of the rights and dignity of the common man on religious grounds is unique to Hinduism. In a stinging assessment of Hinduism, born out of real life experiences, Ilaiah writes:

> ... *this religion, from its very inception, has a fascist nature, which can be experienced and understood only by the dalit-bahujans, not by brahmans who regard the manipulation and exploitation as systematic and not as part of their own individual consciousness. But the reality is that every 'upper' caste person takes part in that exploitation and manipulation and contributes towards the creation and perpetuation of such cultures in the Indian context.*
> (1996: 72)

Although Hinduism has a history of targeting other religions – Buddhism, Islam, Christianity, Sikhism – its main target has been its own co-religionists, the lowered castes and dalits, and adivasis. As the oppressed castes sought shelter in other religions, those religions incurred the wrath of brahmanism in different periods of history. In this sense, from its very inception, brahmanism has been promoting the worst kind of communal ideology. It has subverted genuine nationalism, democracy, secularism, economic progress and social justice. More than anything else, it was the brahmanic basis of the concept of nationhood, which by its language, mystique and eliticism led to the Partition in 1947, after having destroyed the possibility of a united democratic nation and a composite culture.

The recent ascent of the Hindu fascist forces represented by the Rashtriya Swayamsevak Sangh (RSS) and its political arm the Bharatiya Janata Party (BJP) represents the triumph of neo-brahmanism against the egalitarian aspirations of the lowered castes and classes. It is in part an upper caste backlash against growing popular assertions for equity and justice. As education – and concomitant socio-political consciousness – spreads to the dalit-subaltern masses and their demands for a share in political power and economic resources increase, the brahmanical forces have brought the politics of religious symbolism to the national centre-stage, polarising Hindus on the one side and Muslims, Christians, etc. on the other. Its real purpose, however, is to keep the people disunited so that they cannot confront the ruling classes on the issues of mass poverty, illiteracy, malnutrition, and unemployment. Seen in this context, the Ram temple conflict that was created as a reaction to the recommendation of affirmative action for the other backward classes, and the eventual demolition of Babri mosque in Ayodhya on 6 December 1992 was, more than an assault on the Muslim community, 'the declaration of war against dalits, adivasis, women, the bahujan samaj, the toiling castes and classes who have always been held as inferior by varnashrama dharma' (Omvedt 1995: viii).

The sinister intentions of the Hindu right were never in doubt but how did they succeed so spectacularly? The stage for their ascent to power was set by the Congress brand of hegemonic politics, which while boasting of its secular credentials shares the common elitist fraud and farce with the RSS-BJP:

Over the past fifty years, ordinary citizens' modest hopes for lives of dignity, security and relief from abject poverty have been systematically snuffed out. Every 'democratic' institution in this country has shown itself to be unaccountable, inaccessible to the ordinary citizens, and either unwilling, or incapable of acting, in the interests of genuine social justice. Every strategy for real social change – land reform, education, public health, the equitable distribution of national resources, the implementation of positive discrimination – has been cleverly, cunningly and consistently scuttled and rendered ineffectual by those castes and that class of people who have a stranglehold on the political process. . . . And the fascists didn't create it. But they have seized upon it, upturned it and forged from it a hideous, bogus sense of pride. They have mobilised human beings using the lowest common denominator – religion. (Arundhati Roy 2003: 42)

The Hindutva of the RSS-BJP is predominantly hegemonistic, it is more social than political, and the so-called Hindu backlash against the past humiliations supposedly heaped on it by Islam and Christianity is a shrewd tactic to arrest the democratic upsurge of the hitherto excluded and marginalised majority. Earlier, the Hindu brahmanic forces treated the toiling majority as the *mlecchas*. Now, dalit-subalterns are being co-opted into Hindu politics as tools against religious minorities. In retrospect, it appears that the dominant classes would not have succeeded in their sinister design to subvert the aspirations of the deprived majority had the Gandhis and Nehrus not batted for the former.

Gandhi and Nehru portrayed the caste system as bloodless, with not a trace of a 'lynched dalit corpse, or a single raped and bloodied dalit woman' (Baxi 2000: 66). Their nationalist discourse was innocent of any mention of the injustice or cruelty of the caste order. It is indeed amazing how dexterously they swept away the 'red tooth and claw' of brahmanic Hinduism and the caste-feudalism which perpetrated the most barbaric customs and practices against the lowered castes. While Gandhi used vague religious idioms and Nehru resorted to socialist and secular rhetoric, both of them, contrary to the popular myth, valorised the caste system. Their genius lay in the fact that they used an anti-colonial ideology to put on a great nationalist show, full of democratic sound and fury, while actually promoting the brahmanical supremacy that informed their selective reading of Indian civilisation and culture. Except their opposition to the Hindu-Muslim antagonism, which too was envisaged on the notion of unity of elites from the two communities, their socio-cultural construction of the past and the nationalism animated by that bore a startling similarity to the Hindu nationalism envisioned by the brahmanical chauvinists of earlier and contemporary eras.

Nehru (1996: 59) compared India to a palimpsest 'on which layer upon layer of thought and reverie had been inscribed, and yet no succeeding layer had completely hidden or erased what had been written previously'. Perhaps more than India, the comparison fits the popular images of Gandhi and Nehru themselves. The two, though different in outlook and belief – one austere, religious and anti-modernist, and the other flamboyant, secular and modernist – share all the 'progressive-secular' glories of India's freedom movement. Many things to many people, they have been deified or mythified as the founding fathers of nationalism, secularism, and democracy in India. To accept this textbook glorification, however, one has to read even their own writings selectively and perforce overlook the existence of the Phules, Periyars and Ambedkars, the freedom fighters from the other spectrum of society. Otherwise, what united Gandhi and Nehru, despite their deep differences on basic issues and what lay behind their carefully-crafted images would become apparent – their common belief in brahmanic caste culture which was to them the life-blood of Indian culture, the fulcrum of the wonderful unity in diversity, the very basis of Indian nationalism.

Unlike Nehru, Gandhi was not a great intellectual or ideologue: he was a faith-intoxicated man, a self-declared 'sanatani Hindu' who tenaciously believed in all aspects of Hinduism. His winning formula of defending, and then glorifying, caste-bound Hinduism, which made him 'God on earth' (Radhakrishnan) and 'more than God' (Krishnamachari) in the eyes of the elite intelligentsia was simple: he never spoke of Hinduism as it was but what it might be. Anyone who wants to protect Hinduism, has, necessarily, to justify caste since 'caste is the sheet-anchor of Hindu ship which might otherwise have dashed itself to pieces on the rocks of sterner and more solid faiths' (Nichols 1946: 68). No one knew this better than the 'sanatani Hindu' who throughout his life defended the un-defendable caste order by resorting to all kinds of devious logic, tortuous explanations, and select examples to prove that varna and caste have nothing to do with each other. Offering within the sanatana dharma a language for change and redress, Gandhi had the staggering ability to 'emotionalise' all issues. He expeditiously shifted – without changing – his definitions of caste, freedom, and nationalism, all of which were embedded in his trademark brahmanical obscurantism. Always speaking from the high moral ground in the name of the poor and the unfortunate, and constantly invoking truth and non-violence, he never lost his zeal to perform miracles – in the manner of a Mahatma – liberating the oppressed with the consent of the oppressor and raising the poor with the money of the rich. This is enough for his hagiographers to project him as a redeemer of the poor and an enemy of the prince. It is never unravelled how, through his constant evocation of *Varnashrama*, *Ram-rajya* and Trusteeship Gandhi supported the ascriptive caste order and the whole matrix of oppressive socio-economic concepts associated with it. Lest the real meaning behind his delicate equivocation on caste-feudalism be lost on some naive followers, he often came out to clarify his position. M. N. Roy, in his *Gandhism;*

Nationalism; Socialism gives an account of an interview in which Gandhi declared his determination to defend the princes and landlords by all means should ever any attempt be made to confiscate their property. This was a position he reiterated in different ways from time to time.

As Gandhi himself was emotional about all issues, so too his own personality, life-philosophy and public activities have been approached in a subjective and devotional manner by intellectuals after him. They ignore the practical side, the objective reality of Gandhi's upper-caste bias, the unmistakable orientation of his politics, and have gleaned from him some uniquely Eastern ideas of redeeming holiness. The endless wordsmithery of B. R. Nanda and Ashis Nandy and Richard Attenborough's cinematic biography are the classic examples of the mythification. Gandhi has been mythified as the poor's messiah, notwithstanding the fact that the main beneficiaries of his movement were the traditionally dominant classes, especially his brahman-bania associates and future professional politicians and captains of industry who reaped tremendous benefits at the cost of a people-oriented development after Independence. The unbridled admiration and gratitude the privilegentsia reserve for Gandhi is quite understandable. Following their lead, scholar-historians of almost all hues have fine-tuned what is called Gandhiana into an – albeit scholarly – deification of Gandhi.

Gandhi chroniclers never tire of recounting his historic role in mobilising the masses, without acknowledging that Gandhi's mass politics was oriented against the very masses – the poor, the deprived, the caste-oppressed – whom he used as foot-soldiers of the nationalist project. Gandhi never approved of the autonomous self-activity of the masses. They had to be 'unobtrusively' guided by the high caste notables. The caste elites projected Gandhi within the framework of brahmanic faith, tradition, and mythology as an *avatar* whose *darshan* was an ennobling end in itself. Shahid Amin concluded his research on Gandhi's visit to Gorakhpur in 1921, thus: 'To behold the Mahatma in person and become his devotees were the only roles assigned to them (the *sadharan janta* or ordinary people), while it was for the urban intelligentsia and full-time party activists to convert this groundswell of popular feeling into an organised movement' (1996: 4). The essential point is, 'even in the relationship between peasant devotees and their Mahatma there was room for political mediation by the economically better off and socially more powerful followers' (ibid.). In the *avatar* of half-saint and half-politician, Gandhi allowed himself to be manipulated and controlled by his 'trustees', the power elite. Paternalism was intrinsic to the Gandhian 'reconstruction' of Indian society.

Ambedkar, who had nothing but disdain for the politics of piety, and whose passionate struggle for the radical reconstruction of society brought him in confrontation with Gandhi on many occasions, contested Gandhi's ideas on caste, culture, and nation, arguing compellingly that his sanatani ideas were part of the Indian problem, not its solution. Critiquing Gandhian nationalism, he argued that political freedom without the deconstruction of the inegalitarian brahmanic ideology and practice, all talk of social democracy and economic justice was a farce. Ambedkar saw Gandhi as an orthodox moralist whose pacifism actually enhanced his upper casteist authoritarianism, and whose renunciations rid him of none of his desire to control and coerce the lowered classes.

In contrast Nehru was a self-conscious intellectual, a diehard secularist and an indefatigable propagator of scientific temper. A keen student of scientific history, he wrote *The Discovery of India* in the dying days of the British rule, to present a systematic nationalist history of India. In this much-celebrated work, Nehru uses the terms 'assimilation', 'synthesis', and 'unity in diversity' again and again to cover up flaws, failures, and fraud in the caste system. He endows India with the 'mysterious ability to conquer her conquerors, achieve synthesis, and maintain unity in diversity' (Narayanan 1975: 8). The recurrent themes of the inspired fiction of Nehru's discovery – the assertion of a national unity from very ancient time, India's genius for seeking a synthesis in apparent contradictions and the amazing staying power of the Indian civilisation – are unambiguously envisaged in the brahmanic myth of the golden past. In fact, Nehru attributes the national synthesis to brahmanism and caste system throughout his narrative. Attractively attired in his elegant prose, his book comes dangerously close to the hegemonic ideological matrix of brahmanical chauvinists (see also Aloysius 156-62).

Stuffed with acknowledged as well as free borrowings from

'European authorities' and local luminaries like Radhakrishnan, Nehru's imagined India rests on the thesis – the same brahmanic thesis of earlier Hindu nationalists from Dayananda and Vivekananda to Tilak and Savarkar – that the nation and nationalism in 'Bharatvarsha' or 'Aryavarta' is ancient. Its genesis he traces, like his predecessors, in the remote past when the Sanskrit-speaking Aryans came into India from the north-west, conquered (without an invasion?) the natives – the Dravidians to whom they considered themselves 'vastly superior' and the 'backward aboriginal tribes, nomads or forest-dwellers' (1996: 84) – and concocted a wonderful social synthesis through the varna/caste ideology, thus laying the foundation of the civilising current of Indian history. The indigenous backward people, Nehru maintains, were included 'at the bottom of the social scale' as shudras in Aryan society, that is, the 'nation', according to their natural disposition and inclination:

At a time when it was customary for the conquerors to exterminate or enslave the conquered races, caste enabled a more peaceful solution which fitted in with the growing specialisation of functions. Life was graded and out of the mass of agriculturists evolved the Vaishyas, the agriculturists, artisans, and merchants; the Kshatriyas, or rulers or warriors; and the Brahmins, priests and thinkers who were supposed to guide policy and preserve and maintain the ideals of the nation. Below these three were the shudras or labourers and unskilled workers, other than the agriculturists. Among the indigenous tribes many were gradually assimilated and given a place at the bottom of the social scale, that is among the shudras. This process of assimilation was a continuous one. These castes must have been in a fluid condition; rigidity came in much later. (Nehru 1996: 85)

Despite occasional protestations (caste 'brought about degradation in its train afterwards', ibid.: 84) and claims to the contrary (caste as 'a device to keep the Aryan conquerors apart from and above the conquered peoples', ibid.: 246), Nehru celebrates the 'cohesiveness and stability of the social organisation' (ibid.: 247). The institution of caste, he argues, evolved as an answer to the 'national' challenge of organising the harmonious co-existence of different races. It proved to be a unique and lasting solution to contestation and conflict between various groups. It has stood through the ages, and its power and cohesiveness, he stresses, derives from its functions. Brahmans, he holds, were 'honoured and respected by all' because of their high intelligence which they used to 'determine values and the preservation of ethical standards' and 'their (impressive) record of public service and personal sacrifice for the public good' (ibid.: 86-7). The brahmans were the brain behind the *dharma* – 'a conception of obligations, of the discharge of one's duties to oneself and to others', which 'stands out in marked contrast, with the modern assertion of rights, rights of individuals, of groups, of nations' (ibid.: 87). While attempting to prove that this brahmanic dharma went on to become the national religion and culture, Nehru cites the Vedas from which

flow out the rivers of Indian thought and philosophy, of Indian life and culture and literature, ever widening and increasing in volume, and sometimes flooding the land with their rich deposits. During this enormous span of years they changed their courses sometimes, and even appeared to shrivel up, yet they preserved their essential identity. (ibid.: 80-1)

The Vedic ideals and world-view of the Indo-Aryan race became enshrined, Nehru asserts, in all aspects of national life, religious and social, despite the 'successive waves of invasion and conquest by Persians, Greeks, Scythians, Mohammedans, and remained practically unchecked and unmodified from without down to the era of British occupation' (ibid.: 88). Thus the continuity 'between the most modern and the most ancient phases of Hindu thought' (ibid.).

Interestingly, the exalted theories of India's genius to 'create unity out of diversity' (Joad), 'the wonderful assimilative power of Hinduism' (Vincent Smith) and the unparalleled intellectual glories of the Vedic-brahmanic tradition (Max Müller) which keep Nehru enthralled through his narrative, were all discovered for him and other nationalist ideologues by European scholars. No wonder the basic formulations of the nationalist historiography bears an unmistakable resemblance to the colonial imagination of the Indian past. Nehru's history, too, though more liberal and sophisticated than the earlier histories, was erected on the architecture of European scholarship and Orientalism, which championed the Aryan theory, the associated linguistic symbiosis between Sanskrit and European languages and the spiritual myth about India. The race theory had resulted in stereotypes of the arrival of Aryans in India, the composition of the Vedas, the subjugation of the indigenous dasa-shudras, first through necessary violence and then through more peaceful instrument of caste, etc. According to this theory, the higher one's caste, the more Aryan (i.e. of 'European' descent) one was. In some basic ways these formulations served the vested interests of both alien and native ruling classes. The common Aryan ancestry could make the Hindu elite feel equal to the colonial masters and buttress their superiority over the lowered castes.

Apart from laying the strong foundation of colonialism which was based on convergence of interests of foreign and local elites, the latter being the main collaborators, the Indo-European thesis fired the imagination of many Europeans who saw themselves as distant cousins of the high caste Indians. For example, Max Müller, who was primarily responsible for popularisation of the word *arya* and East-West affinity, asserted that the same blood ran in the veins of English soldiers as in the veins of the dark Bengalis. It was clearly this feeling of kinship which inspired many European romantics to take upon themselves the task of recovering spiritual India with the help of Sanskrit pandits, their Indian brothers. Max Müller, Schopenhauer and Nietzsche would derive immense vicarious pleasure in discovering the spiritual-intellectual accomplishments of their common ancestors. Many of those, especially the German romantics, who were unhappy with the modernity-induced plebeianisation of Europe, and who later became the inspirational icons for Nazi Germany (see the Appendix to Chapter 4), sought salvation in the bosom of their Aryan homeland, its caste ideology, and its priestly philosophy. Hence the exaltation of the Veda-Upanishad, and the competitive zeal to outdo each other in discovering the splendour of the brahmanic literature. In spite of the critical writings of the utilitarians and evangelists, who had been to India and had seen the reality for themselves, the spiritual myth about India, thanks to these die-hard racist romantics, had survived in Europe. The myth was built into the concept of the mysterious, spiritual East as drastically different from the rationalistic, materialist West.

In a variety of ways, the Aryan theory and East-West dichotomy were useful for the elites of both societies. On the one hand, they provided legitimacy to colonial rule (spirituality-intoxicated Indians were not supposed to take care of the material side of life). On the other, the notion of the social superiority of Hindu elite – certified by the 'European authorities' – legitimised the brahman and allied castes as natural leaders of Indian society. Both swore by the caste system which had supposedly created a harmonious and stable society where everyone was given a hereditary job based on his natural tendencies and aptitudes! The degeneration, and here too there was broad agreement, began with the dilution of caste and establishment of Muslim rule. With so much crucial consensus, the colonial historiography had to be twisted only a little – to ward off and take care of colonial racism – and it was ready to be employed in the service of nationalist reconstruction.

The lure of the Orientalist exotica was too great for even a 'progressive radical' like Nehru to resist. The truth is, patriotic pedagogy in India was almost entirely derived from colonial historiography, especially its construction of the Aryan origins of Indian civilisation and culture. Over a period of time, it was finetuned in brahmanic national idioms by Dayananda, K. C. Sen, Bankim, R. C. Dutta, Tilak, Vivekananda, Ranade, Lajpat Rai, B. C. Pal, Aurobindo, Gandhi, Savarkar and S. P. Mukherjee. Nehru was among this national pantheon though his narrative was gentler and subtler than that of the others. The following roster of European statements faithfully quoted by Nehru in his *Discovery* within a space of a few pages may give us some idea of how closely his construction of history was embedded in the Western reading of the Indian past:

'*India . . . infinitely absorbent like the ocean*', Dodwell, p. 73.

'*. . . the wonderful assimilative power of Hinduism . . .*', Vincent Smith, p. 74.

'*. . . Vedic literature goes back to 2000 BC or even 2,500 BC . . .*', Winternitz, pp. 76-7.

'*. . . India here (in the Vedic verses) set out on a quest which she has never ceased to follow*', Dr. Macnicol, p. 79.

'*The importance of Indian literature . . . uninterrupted development . . .*', Macdonnell, p. 88.

'. . . *cultural growth . . . unbroken continuity . . . extending over more than three thousand years*', Max Müller, p. 88.

'. . . *the country most richly endowed with all the wealth, power and beauty . . . I must point to India*', Max Müller, p. 88.

'. . . *Where all the dreams of living men have found a home from the earliest days . . . it is India*', Romain Rolland, p. 89.

'. . . *no important form of Hindu thought, heterodox Buddhism included, which is not rooted in Upanishads*', Bloomsfield, p. 92.

'. . . *Upanishads . . . the solace of my life . . . the solace of my death*', Schopenhauer, p. 93.

'. . . *Vedant philosophy . . . human speculation . . . reached its very acme*', Max Müller, p. 93.

'. . . *The Bhagvad Gita and the Upanishad contain such godlike fusion of wisdom . . .*', G. W. Russell, p. 93.

'. . . *The Mahabharata . . . the idea of a single centralised India . . .*', Margaret Noble, p. 107.

'. . . *The Gita . . . the only true philosophical song . . . in any known tongue . . .*', William von Humboldt, pp. 108-9.

Paraphrasing these western scholars, Nehru even argues in an attractive manner that the caste order and brahmanical philosophy lie at the core of Indian genius for seeking and establishing national unity. In 'discovering' these and similar gems, his emphasis all along is to attribute to brahmanism the shaping of India's unity in diversity. Brahmanism, according to Nehru, is at the heart of Indian unity and nationalism, and has saved the nation throughout its long and turbulent history:

> . . . *in the ages since the Aryans had come down to what they called Aryavarta or Bharatvarsha, the problem that faced India was to produce a synthesis between this new race and culture and the old race and civilisation of the land. To that the mind of India devoted itself and it produced an enduring solution built on the strong foundation of a joint Indo-Aryan culture. Other foreign elements came and were absorbed. They made little difference. . . .[after periodic invasion] The reaction was essentially a nationalist one. . . . That mixture of religion and philosophy, history and*

tradition, custom and social structure, which in its wide fold included almost every aspect of the life of India, and which might be called brahmanism or (to use a later word) Hinduism, became the symbol of nationalism. It was indeed a national religion, with its appeal to all those deep instincts, racial and cultural, which form the basis everywhere of nationalism today.
(ibid.: 138)

Nehru adds here that Buddhism, though native to India, became a world religion, and as it developed and spread it became irrelevant in the national arena. 'Thus it was natural for the old brahmanic faith to become the symbol again and again of nationalist revivals' (ibid.: 138).

Such blatantly brahmanical formulations held up as the collective aspirations of all Indians and flaunted as cultural nationalism were championed by a person who was arguably the most liberal, progressive, and secular face of the Indian nationalism. It did not occur to Nehru while declaring the Vedic-brahmanic faith as the basis of unity and nationalism that such categories become meaningful only when they are, first and foremost, good and right in the human perspective. How can a tradition and heritage erected on an anti-egalitarian social philosophy be labelled as wholesome and national?

Moreover, in their enthusiasm to build up the brahmanical monolith of Indian culture and heritage, the upper caste nationalists ignored the humane and egalitarian shramanic tradition represented by Buddhism and various heterodoxies and the contribution of Islam and other faiths, thus underplaying the fact that Indian society consisted of diverse castes, classes, and communities. Since in their eyes the varna order ensured in the past a tension-free social existence, any decline in the brahmanical order signified a dark age. This was, of course, in keeping with the old brahmanic fear of erosion of caste-and-order expressed in the all-too-familiar dreaded term 'kali age'. For purposes of rhetoric though, for the progressive nationalists like Nehru, Buddhism, egalitarian heterodoxies and legacies of Buddha, Ashoka, Kabir and Nanak could 'safely be assimilated to a loudly proclaimed eclecticism by juggling around with the laws of logic'.

This nationalism, however, enabled the traditionally dominant castes, strategically placed with different levers of power in their hands, to project their selfish ideals and interests as national ideals and interests. The intellectual elite of invested interests co-opted other exploiting sections, and together they came forward to speak in the name of the nation as its sole representative. This also gave them a handle to crush dissent from below as 'anti-national' with accusations of lack of faith in the 'nation' itself (Aloysius 1997). Thus, the old brahmanic religion of power and privilege was effectively supplanted by the new nationalist politics of hegemony. As the ancient faith was sacred and supreme, so became the new religion of nationalism.

Despite a variety of formulations of the past, the common denominator and trajectory in all of them, as Aloysius contends, was clear and sharp: a preference for the Aryan races, their ideologies of hierarchy, 'their constant historical role in developing the identity of the nation', and the necessity hence of 'shaping the nationalist future by salvaging as much of these ideals as possible from multifarious modern attacks' (1997: 162).

It is precisely this neo-brahmanism in the name of nationalism that was challenged and exposed by leaders of the subaltern strata who saw themselves as heirs to the other traditions, the traditions of resistance, equity, and dignity. These leaders, whom Aloysius views as 'political nationalists', argued that the brahmanical socio-religious system was more sinister than the worst colonialism and, therefore, its annihilation must constitute an integral part of nation-building. Jotiba Phule, the first man to champion this subversive ideology, declared war on brahmanical colonialism. He attacked the whole ideological matrix of brahmanism since smashing the ideological defences of the ruling elite, he reasoned, was crucial to the struggle of human liberation.

The agenda of the non-elites, like that of the egalitarian heterodoxies to which they consciously attached themselves, was doing away with caste and social barriers, restoring confidence and dignity among the caste-oppressed and establishing a new order based on non-brahmanic values. Their vision of Indian history and culture was, thus, radically different. In a paradigm shift from the elitist approach, they tried to understand the past by the present and vice-versa. Their understanding of history, in other words, was animated by contemporary social and personal experiences. Kancha Ilaiah has made a pertinent point in this regard, stressing that 'personal experience brings out reality in a striking way'.

Instead of depending on Western methods, Phule, Ambedkar and Periyar spoke and wrote on the day-to-day experiences of the dalit-bahujan castes. I would argue that this is only possible and indeed the most authentic way in which the deconstruction and construction of history can take place.
(Ilaiah 1996: xii)

Thus, while struggling to reclaim their citizenship and to ensure their right to enter public places, the right to wear shoes and carry umbrellas, the right of their women (in the south) to cover their breasts; the right of access to religious places and educational centres; the right to give up agricultural bondage and the freedom to choose an occupation, the dalit-bahujan leaders approached history in search of the roots of contemporary reality and discovered India in a way that tore apart the basic formulations of elite ideology. Contending that mere survival was not enough, they pointed out that even this survival of India – or for that matter of any other society – was not due to obnoxious concepts like caste or race but the undying spirit of mankind.

While talking of the nation and nationalism Phule, Ambedkar, and Periyar stressed the caste-class structures of society, and hammered home the point that a society divided by social oppression could not constitute a genuine nation; those claiming to represent the nation were actually its destroyers since they not only rationalised or masked glaring inequalities of the past and present, but actually sought to maintain them as basis for their power (Omvedt 1994). They brought out the social conflicts and horror of the past and many of them presented the Aryan races as oppressive aliens and destroyers of peace-loving indigenous people. They despised the discriminatory ideals and injunctions of brahmanical literature as the weaponry of a power-hungry scheming people whose aim was to enslave the minds of toiling men and women through a fake religion based on an equally false philosophy. They attacked brahmanism as a pseudo-religion that created caste ideology to exploit the productive majority. They rejected Hinduism itself by arguing that it was symbiotically bonded with brahmanical tyranny, superstition, and irrationality. They felt that the new India required an equalitarian and rationalistic religion that could not be provided by reconstructed Hinduism. The search for an alternate religion as a moral foundation of an alternate culture was a common concern of these radicals (ibid.: 12). Phule formulated the *sarvajanik satyadharma* (the universal religion of truth); Iyothee Thass and Ambedkar returned to their 'old religion', Buddhism, and fashioned a neo-Buddhism out of it; many in the south found solace in a radicalised version of Shaivism; Narayana Guru formulated 'one religion, one caste, one god' while his more radical follower Ayyappan – in the manner of the atheist Periyar – proclaimed 'no religion, no caste, no god for mankind'. Some preferred to convert to more egalitarian religions like Christianity and Islam while subalterns in the north sought to create independent religions out of the teachings of their cultural icons such as Kabir and Ravidas.

In short, the non-elite thinker-activists of the nineteenth and twentieth century had turned to their own traditions of dignity and resistance, recognising the power of culture in the politics of transformation. Phule, Iyothee Thass, Periyar, Acchutanand, and above all, Ambedkar not only spent a considerable part of their intellectual energies on the task of recovering and developing the non-brahmanic tradition, but also strived to link it to their contemporary struggle for a casteless, democratic society. They were, even in an academic sense, the pioneering knowledge bankers; the tireless documenters of past and present atrocities against the lowered castes and women. They used this knowledge to expose the hollowness of the elitist version of history and also to confront the narrow, selfish basis of elite-led national project. They asked the self-styled nationalists to change their regressive mindset before claiming to represent the nation. Could Hinduism's vicious, vindictive, violent content vanish merely by labelling it 'cultural nationalism'? they asked. Challenging the patriotic pretensions of the 'progressive' elite who were presenting the deeply problematic past as the site of national glory, Phule wrote as early as 1873 in *Gulamgiri*: 'If the ancestors of these progressive and liberal men had really understood the meaning of patriotism, they would not have written essays in their books in which their own countrymen, the shudras, were regarded as lower than animals' (see O'Hanlon

1985: 203). Phule, Iyothee, Periyar, Acchutanand, Ambedkar and other social radicals asked the same question in different ways: was it patriotic to suppress one's own countrymen, the toiling majority, while one might be eloquent in contesting the colonial rule?

The socio-cultural struggle that Phule and Ambedkar started, however, was never completed. It remains a challenge to all who are on the side of justice and equity, who are part of the ongoing struggle for the abolition of caste, for the equality of women, and for the economic emancipation of the poor and underprivileged. Conventionally, the creation of history and ideological structure has been the fiefdom of the elite. Elite-oriented cultural constructs and historical structures become part of the architecture under which the common people are systematically crushed.

In India, the brahmanical vice-like grip on history and culture has been more entrenched because here the subordinate majority were for centuries denied access to education under shastric injunctions. *Na shudray mati dadyat* – 'do not impart education to the toiling people' – is a common refrain in the Dharmashastras. Under such a repressive system, the brahman elite stifled all cultural expression and creativity from below. Those who tried to overcome the system were brutally suppressed. The dominant class devised and operated a multi-pronged system of discrimination which was internalised through constant teaching of the values of social hierarchy. Eklavya lost his thumb and Shambuk his life for their breach of caste rules. The brahman teacher Dronacharya tricked the tribal boy to cut off his own thumb so that Arjuna, the Pandav prince, could become the best archer of his time. However, Dronacharya is revered in the 'great tradition' as the exemplar of a teacher – a national award for sports coaches has been instituted in the name of this perfidious teacher. The Prince of Ayodhya, who beheaded the meditating Shambuk because he was striving for spiritual excellence in violation of his shudrahood, has become the greatest cultural hero of the Hindu fascist forces. In high caste narrative, the Shambuk-slayer, who also exiled Sita on a mere suspicion of infidelity is presented as the protector of the weak and the undefended because he unfailingly upheld the patriarchal norms and varna order! Centuries of story-telling by the oppressor has added validity to the oppressive power and culture. The whole history and culture has been fictionalised in such a way that the toiling castes appear to be willing collaborators of the caste culture. The brahmans have always tried to co-opt and coerce non-brahmans into accepting the brahmanical ideologies, and thus become a willing tool and participator in their own oppression.

It is extremely difficult even for the educated people with a mind of their own not to succumb to the constant repetition of cultural constructs and images from distorted and falsified history that constantly reinforce the dominant ideology. Visionary leaders that they were, Phule and Ambedkar had keenly felt it, stressing the need to construct new paradigms of history. This could not be done without knowledge and education. Knowledge is the weapon of the fight against brahmanic myth-history. What they meant by knowledge was not mere literacy but 'the power to see through hegemonic ideology', which Phule, as Uma Chakravarti (1998, 2002) correctly says, termed *tritiya ratna*, 'the third eye', in his eponymous 1855 play. The spread of education, they never failed to emphasise, is absolutely necessary for the emergence of critical consciousness.

Without education, it is not possible to achieve the solidarity of the oppressed against their common tormentors. So long as people are uneducated – and disunited – they will be prey for manipulation and domination. Opposing the brahmanical culture and tradition does not count much unless it is accompanied by an attempt to build a counter-culture based on an inclusive and egalitarian ideology. Egalitarianism, contrary to what the pandits of the extreme right and left would like us to believe, is neither alien to India nor the gift of the West. Common people everywhere have a tradition of aspiring to build an egalitarian world. In India, this tradition is to be found in the heterodoxies of various inclinations, and particularly in the great civilising and humanising work of the Buddha and Ashoka, Tirumular and Basava, Kabir and Nanak. This creative and anti-hierarchical legacy was carried forward in modern India by, more than anybody else, Phule, Iyothee Thass, Narayana Guru, Ambedkar and Periyar.

In some micro studies, the rational-liberal and democratic orientation of this tradition is recognised, but it is seldom integrated with macro-level theoretical studies on Indian culture and society.

Introduction

This book is a small attempt in that direction. The effort here is to debrahmanise India's social history by revisiting some of the major sites of people's resistance and creativity. Our objective is to bring out the beauty and resilience of this long-suppressed tradition, and not to present a balance-sheet of its strengths and weaknesses. Those who are keen to find its weaknesses and failures can do so easily – often in exaggerated, grossly distorted forms – in the dominant historiography. This book is meant for those who are – or want to be – part of the ongoing struggle of human emancipation.

Chapter 1 traces the roots of Vedic-brahmanism, the institution of caste and a counter-tradition of egalitarianism represented by a differentiated heterodoxy termed as shramanism. It is argued here that at the heart of brahmanic theology, which is often paraded in the garb of high spirituality, lies the validation of power and violence. This fraud and facade of the 'chosen few' were always challenged by the shramanic heterodoxy, the roots of which could be traced to the early Vedic times. The antagonism between the two never came to an end. Looked at this way, this contest between the brahmanic and shramanic forces has been the defining feature of Indian society, at least since the time of the Buddha, the first major challenger to caste and brahmanism

Chapter 2 tries to debrahmanise the Buddha and Buddhism which represented the most potent – and perhaps the only successful – contestation of brahmanism. Contrary to the elitist-brahmanic reconstruction of the past, it was Buddhism and its advocacy of social justice, rational inquiry, peaceful co-existence, economic development and dynamic creativity that made India a great secular power and a civilised country in the thousand years of its overwhelming influence. It was the decline and eventual extinction of Buddhism along with the rise of autocratic brahmanism and caste-feudalism, that, more than anything else, sealed the fate of India, driving it into the long night of insularity, stagnation and extreme social fragmentation which lay its defences open for conquest. It was also the period when resurgent brahmanism indulged in wholesale fabrication to recast Indian culture in the brahmanical mould.

Chapter 3 delineates the roots of the heterodox, shramanic, Buddhist traditions, and the subversive orientation of the medieval subaltern saint-poets mostly within but some also without the Bhakti movement, a spectacular and pan-Indian site of lowered caste creativity and resistance. While their contemporary brahman adversaries saw their unseemly bhakti or preaching as socially subversive, modern elitist research highlights their religious fervour, alienating them from their actual social position in order to project them as metaphysical or mystical entities who were unaffected by the material conditions of their existence. However, seen in the historical context and the socio-religious sensibilities of the time, their basic vision and agenda was human rights, human dignity and human liberation against the ritualism and ascriptive ideology. The threat from below was so palpable that the proponents of varna-dharma and *saguna* devotionalism such as Tulsidas intruded the movement in order to sabotage it from within, while the more orthodox and reactionary elements tried to crush it with feudal-kingly support.

Chapter 4 is the exploration of the extraordinary nexus that existed between the British colonisation and the indigenous intelligentsia, feudal and propertied classes, and the subsequent rise of Vedic-brahmanic patriotism. Colonialism, like the earlier feudal-autocratic dispensations, found in brahmanism and caste a very potent instrument for keeping the masses submissive and divided. Under colonial patronage and the archaeology of knowledge derived from Orientalism, the moribund brahmanism gained a new lease of life by the discovery of the 'wonder that was India' and in due course went on to nationalise itself into octopus-like Hinduism. The reformism that Rammohun Roy pioneered became inseparable from brahmanical revivalism. Later, combining piecemeal radicalism with revivalism, Dayananda and Vivekananda were to attack, periodically and in patches, some odious aspects of the caste culture, but at the same time to defend 'their' original brahmanism and classical caste divisions. This reformism contained the potential of being co-opted into visceral communal politics, later represented by the likes of RSS and Hindu Mahasabha, which estranged the Muslim leadership which soon built its own communal and separatist agenda.

Chapter 5 focuses on the life and struggle of the nineteenth century social revolutionary Phule. Here we have delineated in historical perspective Phule's understanding of the cultural power of brahmanism, his pioneering exposition of the nexus between knowledge and power (he predated Foucault and Said by a century), his deconstruction of the dominant myth-history and construction of a subversive vision of India's past and present, his distinctive brand of socio-cultural radicalism based on unity among all the oppressed, his amazingly gendered view on women's oppression, his tireless effort and emphasis on mass education as an essential prerequisite for a new democratic culture, and his superb – and the earliest – diagnosis of Hindu nationalism as the obscurantist, self-strengthening movement of entrenched interests. It is indeed a measure of the ruthlessness of the dominant ideology that a cultural colossus such as Phule fails to find significant mention in the grand narrative of modernity and nationalism.

Chapter 6 comprises an unorthodox account of the dynamics, dimension and diversity of the post-Phule struggle of the subordinated classes in the subcontinent at a time when the privileged patriots were organising themselves first to demand a bigger share in the colonial dispensation and then to launch a movement for total transfer of power. Though the high caste nationalists now had to backtrack from their earlier crude valorisation of the caste system, they recognised only one oppressive relationship, that is, between the British and Indians. The oppressed classes, on the other hand, wanted social change. Actually, the colonial period saw two nationalisms, two movements: one for freedom from colonial rule without any change in power relations within Indian society, and the other, popularly known as anti-caste movements, which not only fought against hurt, humiliations, and oppression of the deprived masses, but actually struggled, as Omvedt (1994), Aloysius (1997) and several others have argued, for the actualisation of the concepts of citizenship and democracy.

The last chapter further probes the brahmanic-shramanic dichotomy which culminated in the confrontation between Gandhi and Ambedkar. Given the positions they chose to occupy in the body politic, Gandhi with his unshakeable faith in varnashrama dharma and trusteeship stood for upper caste political dominance, while Ambedkar wanted nothing less than the annihilation of caste and brahmanism. It was Gandhi's and Congress' intransigence and double standards on the principles and practice of equality and justice that compelled Ambedkar to stand apart from the hegemonic national movement. By contextualising their respective systems of ideas, especially on caste, culture, nation and democracy, we dispel many Gandhian myths. The epilogue critically surveys post-Independence structures of power that continue to discriminate against the lower strata of society in several visible and covert ways, despite constitutional laws to the contrary.

1

Historical Roots of Brahmanic Dominance and Shramanic Resistance

> Dominant human groups have long defined themselves as superior by distinguishing themselves from groups they are subordinating. Thus whites define blacks in part by differing melanin content of the skin; men are distinguished from women by primary and secondary sex characteristics. These empirical distinctions are then used to make it appear that it is the distinction themselves, not their social consequences, that are responsible for the social dominance of one group over the other.
>
> JEFFREY MASSON AND SUSAN MCCARTHY
> *When Elephants Weep: The Emotional Lives of Animals*,
> 1996: 40-1

We cannot understand the socio-religious worldview, caste ideology, ever-changing forms with unchanging hegemonic aspirations, or myths of brahmanism unless we clear the cobwebs of fiction and misunderstanding that have been woven around the Veda and Vedic religion. The Vedas (from the root *vid*, 'know') are claimed as the primary scriptures of the Aryan-brahmans, venerated as *apaurusheya* (not of human origin), eternal, and infallible. The Vedas were revealed, it is believed, to certain inspired *rishis* (sages) of old, and are therefore referred to as *shruti* (heard, implying revelation). It is claimed the Vedas existed in their divine form from the beginning of time. The Vedas, as we know, consist of four collections (*samhitas*) – *Rig*, *Sama*, *Yajur* and *Atharva* – of hymns, sacrificial formulas and detached verses, of which the *Rigveda* is the oldest and most sacred. Strictly the term Veda stands for the parts known as the *Mantras* and

Brahmanas. The appendages to the *Brahmanas* are known as *Aranyakas* (forest books), and the concluding portions of the *Aranyakas* are called the *Upanishads*. The Aranyakas, connected with mysticism and symbolism, form a transition to the philosophical texts of Upanishads (Walker 1983). The four Vedas and the Brahmanas together are known as *shruti*, while the Aranyakas and the Upanishads, along with the philosophy contained in them, are called *Vedanta* (the end part of the Vedas).

Actually, the Vedas are the creation of several generations of those Indo-Europeans who came into India from Central Asia in several waves starting from about 1400 BC. According to a recent work remarkable for synthesising data from a variety of sources – archaeology, linguistics and literature, the history of technology, geomorphology, and astronomy – the original Rigvedic hymns were composed in *c.* 1700 BC in Afghanistan before the Rigvedic Aryans arrived in the Ganga-Yamuna doab (Kochhar 2000). '. . . The composition of the *Rigveda* was taken up in south Afghanistan a few centuries after the demise of the mature Harappan phase. The later parts of the *Rigveda* as well as the later Vedic texts were however composed in India. Under the circumstances, some correspondence between the later Vedic texts and the later Harappan cultural phases is to be expected. There is however no shred of evidence to show that the Mehrgarhians, early-phase Harappans, and mature-phase Harappans had any cultural trait in common with the Rigvedic and Avestan people' (ibid.: 225). The new studies based on every possible source clearly show the remarkable and extremely close ties of language, culture, mythology and rituals between Rigvedic and Avestan Aryans as both formed part of one group – the Indo-Iranians – of Indo-Europeans (who got divided into the European and the Indo-Iranian), moving around the second millennium BC from their original home in the steppes north of the Black and Caspian Seas, southwards into the territories now called Europe and Central Asia respectively.

Parts of the Vedas composed in India bear out the fact that the Vedic people fought many battles with the indigenous inhabitants whom they called *dasa* and *dasyu,* and succeeded in subjugating them due to their use of horses and possibly some better arms. Gradually, the original invaders settled down amongst the native people, but antagonisms persisted, a fact amply attested by innumerable verses in the *Rigveda*. In all likelihood, the Aryans devised the system of caste in purely secular terms – primarily to retain their racial purity and impose their authority over the 'low-born' natives – but in the later Vedic period (i.e. after 900 BC), their descendants attributed the genesis of caste to divine will so that it acquired a halo of religious sanctity. Most historians are categorical that the *Purushasukta* in the tenth book of the *Rigveda*, which gives the religio-mythical explanation for the origin of caste, is the latest addition and interpolation. Originally, the Vedas consisted only of a few hundred verses but increasingly it got inflated, due to constant additions and interpolations, into a massive hotch-potch of history, legend, religious beliefs and ceremonies of the early Aryans. This because the verses were handed down the priestly tradition by word of mouth for centuries before they were finally written down. Thus there are innumerable interpolations which the brahmans interjected into it from time to time according to the exigencies of secular necessities and socio-religious imperatives.

Amidst the bewildering maze of rituals, sacrifices, nature-worship, and stray depictions of contemporary material life, it is difficult to decipher the basic Vedic ideology and worldview. In Kochhar's opinion, 'There is no uniformity in the quality and subject matter of the hymns. To take an extreme example, there are a few late passages in the *Rigveda* (1.126.6-7; 10.61.5-8) which nineteenth century British prudery would print only in Latin translation' (2000: 19). The task is made more difficult by pandits and Sanskritists who tend to make the Veda more and more esoteric in order to present it as the ultimate knowledge. Besides large-scale revisions and redactions, the language of the Vedas is obscure and ambiguous, and hence open to contradictory interpretations. The *Rigvedic* language is much older than Sanskrit which was the name given to the language on its regulation by the famed grammarian Panini. The Vedic text is so full of allusions and passing references for which no contexts are available, that a determined Sanskritist can read anything into it. This was often the case with brahmanical interpretations. Importantly, Kochhar has also pointed to the inherent limitations of the nineteenth-century Vedic scholarship: in absence of any archaeological data or guidelines from the field and the laboratory, Vedic scholars had to depend on intuition and surmise.

VIOLENCE AND DOMINATION UNDERPIN VEDIC IDEOLOGY

There are very few dispassionate studies which have tried to grapple with the Vedic conundrum. Most studies of the Vedic texts, both by Indian and foreign pandits, continue to perpetuate the myth that Vedic ideology comprises sublime and humane values within the cultural context of a complex cosmology. However, many studies have pointed out, with concrete examples and incisive analysis, that self-aggrandisement and dominance stand out as dominant Vedic themes in both religious sphere of ritual as well as in the secular domain. Morality, they argue, finds no place in the system of sacrifice, which regulates the relation of man to the divinities. Hidden in the unknowable mystery of nature, sacrifice is a mechanical act that is brought out by the magic art of the priest, who performs it for a fee. Sylvain Levi, one such scholar, has described the Vedic-priestly ideology thus:

It is difficult to imagine anything more brutal and more material than the theology of the Brahmanas. Notions which usage afterwards gradually refined, and clothed with a garb of morality, take us aback by their savage realism. (cited in Rhys Davids 1981: 240)

Violence (*himsa*, 'the desire to inflict injury') and domination in the social realm is indeed the leitmotif which runs throughout the Vedas. In fact, violence and power exercised over another were not only glorified on their own terms, but were represented as an 'integral part' of the natural order of things. The Vedic materialism and brutality is starkly manifest in the leitmotif of 'food' and eaters' that frequently punctuates the Vedic verses. As the *Shatapatha Brahmana* puts it, 'The eater of food and food indeed are everything here.' According to Doniger and Smith (1991), this was not merely a culinary metaphor but was meant as a depiction of the natural and social world organised into a hierarchically ordered food chain. In fact, the nutritional chain exactly described the order of the species. At the top of Vedic 'natural' order were the heavenly deities feeding on sacrificial oblations that were clearly represented as a substitute for the human sacrifices, next in the line on the menu. People consume animals, the next life-form; animals eat plants, who, in turn, consume 'rain' or 'the waters' from which all food is generated.

Eating and killing were regarded as two sides of the same coin. But eating was also frankly envisioned as the perpetual re-enactment of the defeat and subjugation of one's rival. . . . Eating was the triumphant overcoming of the natural and social enemy, of those one hates and is hated by. . . . Consumption was, in sum, the ultimate victory of the consumer over the consumed, of the victor over the vanquished, and of the self over the rival. (Doniger and Smith 1991: XXV-VI)

The Vedic natural and social order is defined and guided by the principle in which the strong consumes the weak. Like nature, society too is neatly divided into classes according to eater and eaten – the lower orders are food and fodder for the higher orders. The supposedly 'immutable', 'natural' and 'eternal' hierarchical distinctions between the higher and the lower orders, which provides the basis of caste ideology, are drawn on this Vedic principle. It is for this logic that Prajapati, the Lord of All Creatures, is portrayed in the *Katha Upanishad* as manifest on earth in the form of a series of mouths: 'The priest is one of your mouths. With that mouth you eat rulers. . . . The king is one of your mouths. With that mouth you eat the commoners' (ibid.: XXVI). In this hierarchical division, the brahman or priest eats the next most important being, the kshatriya or warrior/ruler, who in his turn eats vaishyas and shudras. Thus the higher orders live, feed, and thrive on the lower. The image of the lower orders as 'food' for their superiors is not just symbolic but the quintessential Vedic vision of social, political and economic relations within the society:

The Veda depicts a life where I gain only at your loss, my prosperity entails your ruin, my continued existence depends on your death, my eating requires that you become food. It is an order of things seemingly most advantageous to the one with the greatest physical strength and military might – the biggest fish, the top dog. The rank order of eaters and food in the natural world is straightforward: the physically more powerful eat the physically less powerful. And the principle supposedly holds when it comes to the social world. (ibid.: XXVII)

The basis of brahman supremacy over all others was established through control over the all-important sacrifice. The Vedic brahmans contended that it was from a cosmic and primordial sacrifice that the universe was created, and it was because of the repeated sacrifices that the universe continued. The logic was quite clear: by presiding over sacrifice the brahman plays the role of mediator between the divine deities above and the men below, and, thus, keeps the world going. So anyone who is desirous of well-being must turn to the brahman who will offer sacrifices on his behalf.

The Vedic celebration of power and violence is religiously retained in the later-day Vedic-brahmanism. This is manifest in the famous metaphor of the *matsyanyaya*, 'the law of the fishes', whereby the bigger fish (the strong) devours the small (the weak), and, the obsessive and constant glorification of *danda,* the force of punishment, as the king's main instrument to rule over the masses, in the *Mahabharata* and other brahmanical literature, especially the law books. The brahmans were in a minority, and despite their affinity with violence, they knew quite well that they could not subjugate, physically, the multitude. Therefore they devised the hegemonic caste ideology and constantly endeavoured to institutionalise it, socially and religiously, to maintain their 'peaceful' domination over the majority. If they could not conquer and consume others physically, they could enslave them mentally and psychologically, by breaking their confidence in themselves by constantly underlining their worthlessness and base birth under the cloak of religion.

Caste Indoctrination

This the brahman supremacists achieved through developing the simpler Vedic cosmology of nature and society into a complex and subtle Upanishadic metaphysics which came to the popularly known as Vedanta. As Meera Nanda (2002) has explained, the non-dualistic ontology of Vedanta (hence also known as Advaita, 'non-duality') does not separate matter or physical nature from the spirit or the moral realm. It discounts any separation between the subject – mind or consciousness, and the object – nature or the physical world. Its holism introduces a supernatural element – according to it, nature and human societies are mere reflections (or illusions, as the leading exponents of Advaita like Shankara would say) of the supreme spirit, Brahman. In this cosmos human society is modelled on the order of nature. Caste, gender inequality, and untouchability are, therefore, inextricably linked to the natural order. Thus, as Nanda says, the much-celebrated holism in brahmanical metaphysics or cosmology lies at the very heart of caste and gender hierarchy in India:

This imposes the claims of the natural and the sacred order on human subjectivity, ethics and morality: transgressions against the social codes simultaneously become transgressions against the natural and sacred order. Nowhere is the naturalisation (and sacralisation) of social order more evident than in the institution of caste. The caste hierarchies. . . are supposed to mirror the order of nature. Whether one is born a female or a male, a dalit or a brahman, is not an accident at all, but the working out of the natural laws of karma and rebirth that regulate the embodiment of Spirit. Castes, genders, animals, plants and inanimate objects are simply different forms of the same spirit, arranged in a chain of being, depending upon their karma or moral deeds. In this non-dualistic, inter-connected world, objects of nature take on moral significance (e.g. diseases are goddesses, animals and plants are auspicious for human life and purposes) while human morals have consequences for the natural order (e.g. women's sins can bring about death of her husband). (ibid.: 55)

Beginning with the Upanishads, Atma-Brahma-*chaturvarna-karma-punarjanma* and *moksha* became links in a chain and the entire chain became an unbreakable whole. Not for nothing, have the champions of Vedanta supported caste order, and the champions of caste order have invariably valorised Vedanta (Sardesai 1994: 209). But how was the idea of natural inequality and hierarchy in human affairs established at the popular level? To institutionalise the ideology of human hierarchy or caste and inject it into the lifeblood of Indian civilisation and people's psyche – at conscious, subconscious, and unconscious levels – new rituals and sacrifices were invented; mantras, *dakshinas* (gifts) and *prayashchita* (penances) were multiplied; fictions of gods were created and passed off as history; and, above all, mass ignorance was consciously encouraged and consolidated. Brahmanas were piled upon Brahmanas, Upanishads upon Upanishads, Aranyakas over Aranyakas, Smritis over Smritis, and then endless interpretations and commentaries upon them, commentaries and chopping inconvenient facts and adding new verses and passages dictated by the exigencies of time. In short, false knowledge and a pseudo-religion were promoted in place of real learning and humanist thinking.

Caste is an institutionalised hegemonic system in which a minority is enabled to live off the labour of the producing majority. This hegemony is sustained through the brahmanical socio-religious structure, which is, to use Gramsci's expression, 'a permanently organised force'. Caste ideology has been made 'an interiorised force' or an 'external law taken into psyche' so that 'culture becomes nature and individual learns to affirm and to reproduce the reality principle from within himself through his instinct'. Each person is born into a caste and is thereby either superior or inferior to someone else. The brahman is by birth endowed with all the great qualities, but the shudra is by birth unfit to come to the level of humanity.

The caste order was given religious and spiritual sanctity – mere mortals could not challenge it. In the words of Haq (1997: 17), while a brahman may fall from his superhuamn status, the shudra is subhuman all the way. The subhuman shudra cannot become man – in fact, he does not want to become man as he has killed the man in himself. He has the mind but he does not think, he has a will to act but he chooses not to act. The shudra is passivity/servility personified, he does not act but is acted upon. This is so because, as Manu says, 'slavery is inborn in the shudra'. He is supposed to submit to the same brahmans and gods who oppress him and bring to him all the miseries and sorrows of the world.

According to the *Purusha-sukta* or the Creation Hymn, in the *Rigveda*, the brahmans come from the mouth of the Purush, the Divine Man, the kshatriyas from his arms, the vaishyas from his thighs and the shudra from his feet.[1] This mythical theory was made the basis of the four-fold division of society, known popularly as the *chaturvarnya*. Etymologically, the word 'varna' means colour, and initially, to a great extent, caste had the implications of colour. Supposedly, the first two varnas or castes, especially the Aryan-brahmans, were fairer than the non-Aryans and Dravidians, the dark-skinned original inhabitants, who were branded and stigmatised as shudras. This is why the top two castes are known as *savarna* (literally, with colour) and the rest are despised as *avarna* (without colour). Varna meant a graded inequality in which brahmans were the controllers of society and custodians of religion and religious rites, and of intellectual pursuits in general; kshatriyas were warriors and rulers; vaishyas were the producers of wealth as cattle-rearers, agriculturists, and much later, as traders; and, shudras (some of them were later relegated as ati-shudra and branded as 'untouchables') were the servants of all the three higher classes, especially of the brahmans and kshatriyas.

The shudra was given the name *padaja* – 'born from the feet' – implying thereby that God created the shudra to be the eternal slave. Initially, the lot of the vaishyas, the producing class, was slightly better than the shudras, though later these two were often clubbed together as *paap-yoni* – those born of sin. The vaishyas were often bracketed with the shudras, for serving the brahmans and kshatriyas. The later Vedic period, during which various Arayankas and Brahmanas were composed, witnessed the systematic segregation of all productive communities – peasants, artisans and labourers – as shudras, who were *krishnayonih* (black people), *dasyun vishah* (descendants of Dasyus) and *tvacham krishname* (black skinned). This legitimised the Aryan-brahmans' colonisation and conquest of the indigenous people. Treated like social invalids, shudras were to be supported, to be fed, to be clothed with the remnants and castaways of food and clothes of the higher orders. They were not to hear the Vedas or wear the sacred thread. They were kept out of all *yajnas* and *anusthanas*.

We can assume that the shudras, who were superior in number and physical strength than the higher orders, resented their humiliation and subordination. They could have attempted to join hands with the *Vratyas* and other non-Aryans to destroy the brahmanical order. But the sources of the ancient period would not reveal this. All we know is, the shudra failed to subdue their opponents, most probably due to the divide-and-rule policy very effectively employed against them by the scheming priestly class. The brahmanical order, both at material and ideological levels, gradually consolidated its position, and eventually emerged as the dominant social philosophy after a prolonged process of conflict, hierarchisation and exploitation. In retrospect, it appears that, besides other factors, the shudras had to pay a heavy price for their inability to develop a powerful language like Sanskrit which the brahmans used with deadly effect to demean, destroy, and divide the shudras.

On the one hand, thousands of words were invented to uphold brahmanical supremacy and glorify the brahmans: *brahmajnani, vedagya, acharya, upadhyaya, devavani, shastragya, pandit, manushyadeva, bhudeva*, etc. On the other hand scores of words were coined to abuse the shudras: *danav, daitya, rakshas, pishacha, chandala, mleccha, kshudra, nikrishta, dwijadasa*, etc. The *Manusmriti* (II.31) sternly instructs the shudras to adopt names which should breed disgust, repulsion, and hatred. Most brahmanical works, especially the Dharmashastras, prescribe the respectful vocative terms which the shudras must use to address brahmans; and in reverse, they also mention the derogatory terms in which the brahmans was to address the shudras. Manu says, 'Speech is the weapon of the brahman, and with it he can slay his enemies' (XI.33).

Not surprisingly, the writers of the Smritis or Dharmashastras envisioned their religion in terms of strict adherence to endogamy, hereditary occupation and the rules of purity-pollution. The shudras were supposed to be treated, on religious ground, as two-footed beasts and bonded labourers. Entitled only to work and produce, they were debarred from acquiring education, collecting wealth and carrying weapons. Echoing the Dharamshastras, the *Shanti Parvan* in the *Mahabharata* stipulates that the shudra can have no absolute property because his wealth can be appropriated by his master at will.

Despised as ritually impure, a section of shudras, known variously as ati-shudras or antyaja, came to be regarded as a source of pollution, which gave birth to the practice of untouchability. Not only goldsmiths, blacksmiths, washermen, carpenters, physicians, but also singers, dancers and actors were considered untouchables (*Manusmriti*: IV.210-15). In course of time, the difference between the labouring class (shudras) and the agricultural class (vaishyas) got blurred because of the brahmanical contempt for physical work of any kind. Thus, the caste system was organised in favour of the two upper varnas – brahmans and kshatriyas – who lived off the labour and fruits of the two productive varnas.

Brahmanical Pseudo-Religion as Engine of Oppression

In Vedic lore the word *brahma(n)* denotes the sacred word – hymn, prayer, formulation of truth – and the title brahman is accorded to all persons of a particular caste who supposedly possess the qualities suggested by the word brahma(n). Says the *Shatapatha Brahmana*, 'Verily there are two kinds of gods: the gods themselves who are absolutely gods, and the priests who have studied Vedic lore' (see Walker 1983, vol. 1: 167). On the practical level, however, it meant nothing if not according *brahma* power to the brahmans. It is significant that the pre-eminent god of the post-Vedic brahmans was called Brahma, and the brahmans were regarded as the Brahma's sons, and, therefore, described as brahmans. In the *Brahamanas* there was the tendency to identify the brahman caste as symbolising the Brahma power (Varma 1974: 60). All this was a deliberate ploy to make the Brahma and the brahmans appear to be kith and kin. How the Brahma and the brahmans were made to resemble each other is revealed by expressions like *Brahma-hatya* and *Brahma-bhoj* which means 'killing of the Brahma' and 'feast in honour of the Brahma', respectively, but is commonly understood only as murder of a brahman and community meal for brahmans (Dhani 1984: 152). Another such word is *Brahmadeya*, widely used for land grant to a brahman. The body and the property of a brahman was made inviolable in the Dharmashastras (see *Manusmriti*: XI.72-82).

To top it all, a complex, labyrinthine metaphysical connotation was developed around the word 'Brahmana'. Brahmana was the name given to the 'Supreme Spirit' or impersonal monotheistic entity which subsumed all beings and all deities, the individual soul as well as the divine one. The Upanishads taught that the man who knows the Brahma becomes the Brahma and has complete sway over whatsoever he desires (Varma op. cit.: 62). The obvious intention was to present the brahmans as both gods and human beings endowed with exceptional abilities. This becomes apparent from epithets like *Bhudevata* (the Lord of the earth) and *Jagatguru* (the master of the universe) which they coined to assert their superiority over the rest (see Dhani op. cit.: 152-4; Walker ibid., vol. 1: 172-3).

According to the Upanishadic thinkers, only self – Atman – was worth seeing, hearing, thinking about and meditating on. To them, other beings and other things have no purpose other than being exploited for the self, they exist only for the sake of the self. This religion – if it can be called religion – was inspired by the impetus to dominate and control the rest of the population. To this end, they devised the caste system as the key instrument to institutionalise their domination, and accordingly they developed their religion revolving round caste as a cloak to legitimise their hegemony. There is little doubt that their caste ideology and religious system were made for each other. Not surprisingly, they came up with a religious philosophy that supported and glorified caste.

The caste ideology was founded on the twin religious doctrines of *karma* and *dharma*. The doctrine of karma expounded that one's present caste status was the consequence of deeds done in previous existences; thus, birth in a high caste was a reward, birth in a low caste a punishment. This implied that a person born in a high caste was intrinsically superior in intellect, ability and morality to a low-caste person. The karma theory reconciled the lowly person to his degraded condition. The related concept of dharma was to reinforce one's caste-duty. It is to be noted that dharma is now generally used to embody the religion of the highest moral order; it is often used as a suffix after the word 'Hindu' to show the humane, compassionate face of Hinduism. But it was not used in the same sense by the brahmanical masters who coined it.

Etymologically and originally, the word dharma means that which holds or sustains (society). The pertinent question is: what is to be held and sustained? The answer is categorical: the socio-religious structure (centred around caste). The Dharmashastras graphically describe the duties of the four classes, and prescribe unswerving adherence to one's caste-duty in all circumstances; any action contrary to one's prescribed caste-duty is declared *adharma* (prohibited action). The doctrine of karma and dharma ingeniously explained away all the social differentiation between brahman and shudra, king and commoner, exploiter and the exploited. The social and economic deprivation of the masses was presented as a necessary evil and given a religious gloss.

In order to institutionalise caste and establish the concepts of karma, dharma and *punarjanma* (the theory of rebirth), the priestly intelligentsia authored a large number of Smritis or Dharmashastras in post-Upanishadic times, roughly from 300 BC to AD 600. The Dharmashastras were claimed to be based on the Vedas, implying thereby that they too, like the Vedas, are infallible, inviolable and beyond the realm of any questioning and reasoning. *Manusmriti* is the best known of all such Dharmashastras which were basically law-codes presented as religious injunctions, and as such were part and parcel of the brahmanical scriptures, as the very word denotes.

The *Manusmriti* is traditionally hailed by the priestly class as the most important work after the Vedas. A famous – and apparently interjected – Vedic verse declares, 'All that Manu said is medicine, curer of all diseases.' This is an obvious instance of interpolation as the *Manusmriti* was written many centuries after the last Veda was composed. However, it shows the eagerness of its brahman authors to push back the date of its compilation in order to give it the aura of the 'Vedic sacredness'. It was claimed that whatever has been prescribed by Manu in his *Manusmriti* to be the duty of anyone is in perfect congruence with the Vedas, the embodiment of divine knowledge. What it implied was clear: thère was nothing to look – and think – beyond the *Manusmriti* as it was to illuminate the entire dharma, the nature of good and bad karma as also the unalterable duties of all the four varnas (*Manusmriti*: I.107, see Doniger and Smith, eds., 1991).

Caste, according to Manu, is the creation of God, and the brahmans, who are at the pinnacle of caste hierarchy, are the living embodiments of God on earth. In his own words, 'A brahman is a great god whether he is learned or imbecile' (IX.317), and the brahmans should be respected in every way, even if they indulge in crime (IX.319). Manu never tires of instructing peasants, workers and even kings to religiously serve the interests of the godly brahmans. He stresses that the greatest religion for shudras and women – who are born in sin – is to play the role of willing victims and slaves, ever ready to be manipulated and exploited without a murmur of protest, so that in the next life they may get a lift up the caste ladder.

Manu says that shudras are not entitled to education, to amass wealth, or bear arms. A brahman can take away any possession from a shudra, since nothing at all can belong to him as his own (VIII. 417). Women, similarly, are debarred from property and other natural rights. Manu places all women, irrespective of caste, in the category of the lowly shudra and expects them to surrender body and soul to men. The supreme duty of the king is to enforce this social arrangement under the guidance of his brahmans. His divinely-ordained duty is to sustain and strengthen the varna-dharma. However, Manu makes it clear that no matter how mighty a king be, he is inferior to even a brahman child. As he says, 'A ten-year-old brahman and a hundred-year-old ruler should be regarded as father and son, and of the two of them the brahman child is the father' (II.135).

The text is crammed with all kinds of abuse and savage injunctions against shudras and women.[2] Its not-so-hidden agenda is to establish a permanent brahmanical order through social hegemony, political domination and economic control. No doubt, the *Manusmriti*, carrying forward the varna spirit of the earlier works such as *Gautama Dharmasutra* and *Apastambh Dharmasutra* at its devastating best, is a trailblazing work as its broad social philosophy is followed by other influential law-books such as *Yajnavalkya Smriti*.

If we closely read the sacerdotal literature and situate the texts in socio-historical perspective, it becomes clear that they were written with the primary aim of establishing and maintaining the brahmanical hegemony. As written by various authors at different times, according to the exigencies of changed socio-economic and cultural geography, there are obvious external differences in them but in their core and essence all these works were produced to uphold and maintain the brahmanical self-interest. If we contextualise them, their exquisitely-sounding *shlokas*, *suktis* and *subhasitaanis* appear lovely and lofty only for the brahmans and allied upper castes. In the brahmanical religion and literature, there is absolutely no place for broader social utility or individual justice and freedom which are the heart and soul of any true religion.

The authors of the Vedic-brahmanic religion knew, as we shall discuss later, that there were other social ideals and paradigms in existence, which were advocated and adopted by their critics and opponents. Perhaps that is why they kept parroting that there was no greater sin than to question the infallibility of the Vedas. Having declared that 'one who speaks ill of the Vedas is an atheist' (*nastiko vedanindakah*), they claimed that other philosophical and religious thoughts were devoid of any intrinsic merit as they invariably led to disastrous consequences. The message was loud and clear for the people that anyone following a different path other than Vedic-brahmanism would come to grief sooner than later (*Manusmriti*: XII.95; *Bhagvad Gita*: III.35).

All circumstantial evidence points to the conclusion that the brahmanical texts we have cited were authored by men who were mortally afraid of the antagonistic multitude. They presented their philosophies in an obscure and ambiguous way so as to hide their real intentions. They were afraid of the common people, and had to contend with the subversive heterodoxies of many shades that were out to expose them. They couched their social views in religious terms in such a bewildering and self-contradictory manner that it was difficult to expose their intellectual vacuity. They kept their metaphysics sufficiently vague and open to multiple interpretations by referring to contradictory sources and authorities, one after the other. They composed their tracts in Sanskrit, a language that was understood only by the gods above and themselves, calling it the *devabhasa*, 'the language of the gods'. Commoners, shudras and women were debarred from learning it.

Yet the brahmanical leadership had to compromise on most issues with the masses. They had to, for instance, adopt the indigenous, black-skinned deities as their *ishtadevas*. Three of the most prominent brahmanic gods – Shiva, Rama and Krishna – are *shyam-varni* (black-skinned). And Shiva, as is well-known, has two divine consorts, the first one is Kali (of black colour), while the priests have to procure him a second one, Gauri (of white skin) to placate the God of Destruction. In other words, in the Gupta period brahmans appropriated several non-brahman beliefs, superstitions, deities, and sacred places, and ingeniously oriented them to buttress the caste culture. This, in brief, is the background to the Puranic religion.

CASTE, KARMAYOGA AND SWADHARMA IN THE GITA

The *Bhagvad Gita*, the finest philosophical efflorescence of brahmanic Hinduism and its most popular and oft-quoted scripture, centres on the caste philosophy through its specious glorification of *karmayoga* and *swadharma*. Like the 'wondrous' shruti-smriti, the *Gita* is 'honoured oftener than read, and understood far less than it is recited' (Kosambi 1992: 209). A far cry from extravagant claims that it is the infallible moral code for the guidance of human society, an objective and dispassionate study of the *Gita* shows it is not the sublime guide it is made out to be. This is not however to deny that this philosophical interlude in the epic *Mahabharata* by some unknown hands holds some lofty ideals about human nature. Its prescriptions for success in mental discipline are quite remarkable. However, the fact remains that these gems of wisdom are dazzling only in their splendid isolation, for, if one tries to delve beneath its surface and read between the lines, the *Gita* abides by the same brahmanical – and caste – mantra for salvation. Its much-glorified concepts of *swadharma* (one's dharma) and *nishkama karma* (dispassionate activity) are embedded in the idea of unwavering performance of duty of the caste to which one belongs by birth.

The word for duty used in the text is karma, which literally means action. The discerning reader can see that karma is used in the *Gita* to mean duty as laid down in the system of caste. The 'natural' duty of the brahman is acquiring religious and intellectual perfection (XVIII.42), while the kshatriya is obliged to rule the masses (XVIII.43); agriculture, tending to cattle and trade are duties of the vaishya (XVIII.44). However, it is on the 'natural' slavery of the shudra that the *Gita*, like other brahamanic texts, lays the maximum and most merciless emphasis: 'Service is the natural duty of the shudra' (XVIII.44).

Notwithstanding its linguistic subtleties and sophistication, this collection of 700 odd verses, presented in the form of a dialogue between Krishna and Arjuna, was, in all probability, written in response to the growing defiance of caste rules by the lowered castes and women, which is usually termed in the Puranic literature as the dreaded *Kaliyuga,* a decadent era marked by indiscriminate mingling among castes in terms of marriage and profession. In the very beginning of the dialogue (I.41), Arjuna says, *strishu dushtashu jaayate varnasamkara,* 'women's wickedness is responsible for intermixture of castes'. That is why the anonymous authors of the *Gita* keep drumming their central message that nothing is nobler than observance of one's caste duties, and nothing more heinous than the breach (III.35; XVIII.45; XVIII.47).

The *Gita* is an interpolation in the epic and clearly belongs to a much later period. Most scholars have fixed the date of its composition around the fourth century AD and, quite naturally, it draws heavily on the earlier orthodox Yoga and Vedanta philosophies as well as the heterodox Buddhist teachings. Some of its finest teachings (remain steadfast as 'a lamp in a windless place' even in trying circumstances, for instance) have in fact the imprint of the Buddha's constant stress on careful cultivation of the mind. Kosambi has even contended, and not without justification, that the *Gita* summarises a great deal of Buddhism quite efficiently in the mouth of Krishna (1992: 208). The *Gita*'s famous injunction of conquering desire – the deadliest foe of man – is quintessentially Buddhist teaching. However, while the Buddha insisted on surrendering one's desire for the need or comfort of others – for the greater welfare of mankind – which elevates one to a higher consciousness, and makes a man truly spiritual, Krishna is not bothered by such ethical concerns since this world, as he keeps parroting, is an illusion created by God. 'Neither yoga, nor knowledge, nor kindness, nor austerity, nor renunciation captivates Me so much as devotion to Me', he says. One's social action or inaction does not matter much in his scheme. As such, the *Gita*'s spirituality is dubious and its precepts can help – and have indeed helped – only to subvert human progress and nourish social evils

Like other brahmanical works, the *Gita*'s overriding concern, too, is to extol the varna-jati ideology, though here it is couched in delicate equivocation and splendid Sanskrit. Here the divine singer of the song is indeed magnanimous and prepared to grant salvation to even those 'born from the very womb of sin – women, vaishyas and shudras', provided these 'sinners' repose their faith in this divinity. In a ground-breaking appraisal of the *Gita*, Kosambi writes:

That the song divine is sung for the upper classes by the brahmins, and only through them for others, is clear. We hear from the mouth of Krishna himself (9.32): 'For those who take refuge in Me, be they even of the sinful breeds such as women, vaishyas and shudras . . .' That is, all women and all men of the working and producing classes are defiled by their very birth, though they may in after-life be freed by their faith in the god who degrades them so casually in this one. Not only that, the god himself had created such differences (4.13): 'The four-caste (-class) division has been created by Me'; this is proclaimed in the list of great achievements. (2000: 15)

The *Gita*'s gospel is essentially the ideology of caste-feudalism camouflaged as devotional or bhakti spirituality. From beginning to end, it extols the virtues of sticking to one's birth-based social position in the name of religion and divinity. Krishna does not invoke the concept of justice in his gospel for the sake of which wars are generally justified. Instead, he prepares the reluctant Arjuna for war by appealing to his caste duty and to the fear of loss of social face. Arjuna is born in a kshatriya caste whose duty, Krishna stresses, is to battle without being troubled about its consequences. Donning the role of the supreme God, he exhorts Arjuna to find and kill his enemies without scruples since creatures are destined to perish. Krishna the Lord has himself already slain them all, and Arjuna will be only the apparent cause of their death.

The karmayoga as espoused in the *Gita* is the principle of faithful and joyous performance of one's caste duty. It is specifically stated that '*swadharma* – one's duty or the duty of one's own caste – even performed imperfectly, is better than *paradharma*, another's duty or the duty appropriate to another caste, even if well performed. Another's duty brings disasters, one's own duty brings salvation (III.35). It further adds: There is no greater crime than abdicating one's birth-based occupation and marrying outside one's caste because 'mixture of castes leads to naught but hell' (I.42) and 'destroys all family and caste values' (I.43). Even the famous doctrine of the *nishkama-karma* expressed in the dictum *Karmany eva'dhikaraste ma phaleshu kadachan* (II.47) – 'your business is only with the work, not the fruit' – is loaded with implication for the disenfranchisement of toiling castes.

The *Gita* attempts to transform the discredited idea of ritual sacrifice into one of self-sacrifice, the dedication of all one's acts to God as a form of penance. At the worldly and social level, for all practical purposes, it reinforces the doctrine of slavery and servitude. It induces one to obey the dictates of God through his priestly-feudal representatives on earth. Its emphasis on action without any expectations of change is hardly an encouragement for a positive attitude to work. Further undermining the dynamic need for action, Krishna propounds the doctrine of *avatara* – the idea that gods are born in many forms many times – to reassure the devotee. 'For whenever dharma, or morality, declines and wrong increases, then I create myself. I am born again and again to protect virtue and to destroy evil' (IV.7).

The dharma Krishna speaks of is little more than righteousness in terms of caste ideology. Here, the notions of good and evil, morality and immorality, are embedded in the brahmanical ascription. The *Gita*'s precepts may appear an excellent moral recipe for the privileged few, but there is little doubt that its overall social philosophy is ranged against the producing and labouring classes. The elitist glorification of the *Gita* was chiefly due to this and the feudal doctrine of bhakti that extols unflinching loyalty to God and acquiescence in the established order. It is not just chance that the final scripting of the *Gita* by the brahman authors and the emergence of Indian feudalism in the Gupta period were almost simultaneous. The karma ideology and the theory of avatara taught social conservatism in the name of the religious self-surrender. It is significant that the *Gita*'s appearance coincides with the resurgent, militant brahmanism and decline and eclipse of Buddhism. While the pre-*Gita* period, with a strong Buddhist presence in the land, was marked by a vigorous social, cultural and economic life when the Indian civilisation flowered, the post-*Gita* period saw a stagnant and decadent society characterised by a closed economy, insular outlook, excessive caste conservatism, and growing tentacles of feudalism.

Innumerable devotees-cum-commentators of the *Gita*, right from Shankara, Ramanuja, Gyaneshwar, Madhav, Vallabh and Nimbaraka to Tilak, Aurobindo, Gandhi, Rajagopalachari and Radhakrishnan have read the poem out of context to project their own notions and concepts into the *Gita* verses. By taking advantage of the ideological contradictions and verbal jugglery that pervade the text, they have tried to defend the indefensible, and in doing so they have made the text amazingly mystifying and inexplicable. In fact, to interpret and reinterpret, unravel and illuminate the supposed layers and layers of *rahasya*, mysterious secrets of spiritual life, supposedly hidden in the *Gita* verses, has for centuries been a favourite pastime of the upper-class intellectuals. Shankara wrote the *Brahma Sutra* in the ninth century and Gyaneshwar his *Gyaneshwari* in the thirteenth century to illumine its hidden meanings. Many lesser luminaries followed suit, delved into the *Gita* and discovered their own pearls of wisdom from its depths.

Bal Gangadhar Tilak, however, was not satisfied with the standard commentaries of his illustrious predecessors, and, therefore, tried to dispel the darkness of ignorance with his own fertile imagination by authoring the *Gita-Rahasya*. For Tilak, the *Gita* mirrored karma-yoga, ceaseless action without desire for results. He ventured to suggest that the holy text taught *shatham prati shaathyam*, which means paying the villain in his own coin. (In a speech in 1897, Tilak claimed, as part of his anti-British rhetoric, that the *Gita* sanctioned the killing of enemies for 'unselfish' and 'benevolent' reasons. Later, Nathuram Godse, who knew the entire *Gita* by heart, also gave a similar interpretation of the sacred text to justify his assassination of Gandhi.)

Close on Tilak's heels, Gandhi claimed to penetrate the heart of the matter through his own treatise on the *Gita*, which supposedly anchored his principles of truth and non-violence. The Gandhian Vinoba Bhave, smitten by Krishna's divine gospel, recorded his own *Gita-Pravachan* while C. Rajagopalachari paid homage through his book *Bhagawat Gita* and Aurobindo even left the struggle for independence to delve into the elusive truth encapsulated in the mystical verses. In his *Essays on the Gita* about this celestial treasure-house of timeless wisdom, Aurobindo fancies that its influence is not merely philosophical or academic but immediate and living, and that its ideas are actually at work as a powerful shaping factor in the revival and renewal of the Indian nation and culture. (Having pontificated so he permanently retired to Pondicherry to concentrate on his spiritual sublimity, cutting himself completely off from the national life.) Radhakrishnan, who saw nothing but spiritual grandeur and splendour in the brahmanical wonder that was India, followed suit and came up with his own impassioned *Gita*-glorification in his own hagiographical style.

All these commentaries – from Shankara's to Radhakrishnan's – have very little critical substance. All of them are full of preconceived ideas and reveal little more than their own cherished views. Modern and 'nationalist' interpreters not only discovered a 'dynamic doctrine for action' in the *Gita*, but claimed that the Krishna's gospel was of 'universal' validity for India. After pronouncing that the *Gita* was the holiest scripture for 'the Hindu people', they went on to extend the claim to include the entire Indian population. 'The *Gita* has thus become the scripture of the new age. The main foundation on which its social doctrines, and even its political action depends. . . . No one can understand the developments which are taking place in India who has no appreciation of this fundamental fact' (K. M. Panikkar, cited in Lannoy 1999: 313).

In recent times the ideology of the *Gita* has strengthened the orthodoxy and preserved the sanctity of the 'sacred' brahmanical past; it has decidedly obscured the social situations and historical circumstances under which the *Gita* was composed. In an incisive study of the *Gita* and its devotees, Premnath Bazaz (2002) comes to this conclusion:

Since its appearance, the Gita has been repeatedly invoked to fight against the forces of revolution. If Shankaracharya sought its assistance in the ninth century AD to deal a death blow to declining Buddhism, Mahatma Gandhi utilised its teachings to annihilate the rising tide of secular democracy. This is true even though Shankara was dubbed as a crypto-Buddhist and Gandhi acclaimed as the champion of democratic freedom.

It is claimed that this holy text is the life-blood of Indian civilisation, and that every Indian believes in its ennobling message of selfless service. As Bazaz argues, these gentlemen do not tell the world why Indians lagged behind socially and civilisationally, deteriorated intellectually and morally, lost freedom and suffered so much and far so long after they had decided to abide by the *Gita* principles. The argument that the Indians accepted the *Gita* as their scripture but failed to live up to its ideals does not hold much water. When one argues that the *Gita* has been the most adored and popular scripture and its teachings are etched in the heart and mind of every Indian, it is absurd to contend that the sufferings of the people have not been caused by the acceptance of such scriptures (ibid.).

Actually, the secret of the timeless and mesmerising appeal of the *Gita* for the cultural supremacists is its unique ambiguity. Replete with contradiction, tautology, and rhetoric, the *Gita* slides into vague philosophical concepts. In fact, ambivalence and prevarication are its characteristic hallmark. Vedic polytheism is accepted in some places, in other places ridiculed and rejected. The idea of a supreme God or monotheism is affirmed categorically (IV.6) only to be rubbished in the next verse by the idea of avatar (God's incarnation) in human body (IV.7). Similarly, Krishna at one place disapproves the path of renunciation, while at another place recommends it as a method to realise the Supreme Spirit or Brahmana, and at third place he advocates *bhakti-marg* – the path of devotion to God – as the best path. Situating the gospel in social context, Kosambi has deconstructed the *Gita* mystique in these words:

Practically anything can be read into the Gita *by a determined person, without denying the validity of a class system. The* Gita *furnished the one scriptural source which could be used without violence to accepted brahmin methodology, to draw inspiration and justification for social actions in some way disagreeable to a branch of the ruling class upon whose mercy the brahmins depended at the moment.* . . . (2000: 15)

The utility of the *Gita* to the Indian elite, according to Kosambi, derives from its peculiar fundamental defect, its dexterity in seeming to reconcile the irreconcilable. Krishna never tires of underlining the great virtue of *ahimsa*, non-violence, yet the entire argument is an incentive to war. It is not possible to kill or be killed, the god tells Arjuna and then opens his 'innumerable voracious mouths' that have swallowed up all the warriors of both sides; Arjuna's killing of his kins is, thus, a mere formality as the demoniac god himself had already killed all of them (ibid.: 17).

Above all, Krishna himself as depicted in the *Mahabharata* is singularly ill-suited to preach morality. During the war he comes across as a ruthless politician revelling in the violation of the prevailing codes of fair play. A believer in the dictum 'the end justifies the means', he resorts to the crudest of means and dishes out the unfairest of advice at every critical turn of the war to defeat the enemy. The elimination of Bhishma and Dronacharya, Karna and Duryodhana – which had a crucial bearing on the outcome of the war – are all ensured through utterly unethical means. Bhishma was disarmed by the duplicity of placing Shikhandi before him. Yuddhishthira the Dharmaraj (the very embodiment of dharma) deceives Drona without batting an eyelid, saying Ashwathama, his son, has died, muttering sotto voce that it was actually an elephant. Near the end of the war, at Krishna's instance, Duryodhana was literally hit below the belt by Bhima. Karna, the greatest warrior on the Kaurva side who had the potential to defeat Arjuna and the Pandavas, was eliminated in a blatant contravention of the rules of war when he was unarmed and engaged in pulling the wheels of his chariot out of the mud. Earlier, Krishna's use of a crucial nugget of information about Karna's personal life – that he was the first born of Kunti – to wean away the greatest archer from the Kauravas traumatised Karna enough to force him to promise Kunti he would spare Yuddhishthira, Bhima, Nakula, and Sahadeva. Jayadratha, the killer of Abhimanyu, was ensnared by the 'divine' illusion of sunset – assured that the sun had set Jayadratha come out of his hiding and was killed by Arjuna, who had promised to kill him before the sun set for the day.

All this was done with Krishna's overt and covert approval. The list of Krishna's unethical deeds for the Pandavas, represented in the epic as role models of justice, righteousness, and religiosity, is staggering. Later, Krishna explains away all the outrageous acts with the argument that had he not resorted to such tactics, the victory would never have been won. The *Mahabharata* is replete with instances of immorality and injustices committed by its heroes. Drona asking for the tribal boy Eklavya's thumb as his *guru-dakshina* without remorse, is the most horrendous example of how outstanding talent in the subaltern strata was crushed by brahman gurus. This villainous guru is still worshipped in 'establishment India' as a model of inspirational teacher. As Kosambi comments sharply, it is perhaps in the same spirit and tradition that an outstanding modern devotee of the *Gita* and Gandhian non-violence, C. Rajagopalachari, extolled the virtues of non-violence as a method to gain power, but to be scrapped when power has been captured. 'When in the driver's seat', Rajaji said, 'one must use the whip' (cited in Kosambi 2000: 19).

Above all, the *Gita* is categorical in condemning the worldly life as 'transient and joyless' (IX.33). Its basic postulate is pessimistic and hence dismissive of wordly affairs. The *Gita*'s despondent view of life is not surprising as the brahmanical cosmogony is quite insipid. According to its mythology, creation began with *Satyayuga*, a golden age, when everything was perfect, men attained excellence in all respects and dharma existed as a four-footed being. Then degeneration set in: the next *yuga*, the *Treta*, was not so glorious as it had only three feet to support it. In the third *yuga*, the *Dwapar*, there was further decline as dharma was reduced to subsist only on two feet. Dharma was almost destroyed and crippled in *Kaliyuga*, the present era, as it is left with only one foot to hop about in this dark age, the period of crisis, chaos, and catastrophe.

The *Gita* with its slippery equivocation, astounding inconsistency and consistent insistence on caste, remains a perennial source of inspirational quotations that allows its dedicated readers to justify almost any action while shrugging off the consequences. After all, nothing is unjust and unethical in a world which is an illusion created by God. 'This slippery opportunism characterises the whole book. Naturally, it is not surprising to find so many *Gita* lovers imbued therewith. Once it is admitted that material reality is gross illusion, the rest follows quite simply; the world of 'doublethink' is the only one that matters' (Kosambi 2000: 17).

Albert Schweitzer has made another pertinent point:

Hinduism in the Bhagavadgita does not yet take the actual step of demanding ethical deeds. Love to God is for it an end in itself. Hinduism does not make love to God find expression in love to mankind. Because it fails to reach the idea of active love, the ethic of the Bhagavadgita is like a smoky fire from which no flames flare upward. One must ever bear in mind, that in the Bhagavadgita there is no question of love. (cited in Varma 1974: 328)

DANDANITI CENTRAL TO BRAHMANICAL POLITY AND STATE

Dharma as expounded in the brahmanical literature was essentially the varna-dharma and jati-dharma, and following this varna-and-jati dharma meant living up to one's ascriptive social responsibility and the trivialised individual morality based on it. All facts and fiction, legends and myths, fables and fantasies, stories and superstitions, were rendered in such a way as to preserve and strengthen the caste-bound social arrangements and institutions. The prime priestly precepts – upholding varna-dharma, patriarchal family values and rights of private property for the first two varnas at the cost of the last two – were to be made effective by the political elite led by a kshatriya king. For maintaining varna-dharma and containing social antagonism and conflicts, the king's power and glory was greatly enhanced by constant priestly propagation of the divinity of kingship and caste-feudal ideology (Sharma 83: 68ff).

In other words, brahmans and kshatriyas together formed the ruling alliance. Since both the brahmans and kshatriyas were parasites living off taxes, tribute and labour supplied by the producing masses, there were occasional fights for a share of the gains, but these conflicts were made up in the face of the opposition from below. The need for priestly-feudal bond is repeatedly emphasised in the brahmanical texts because, as the *Shanti Parvan* in the *Mahabharata* and the *Manusmriti* (IX.322) make clear, 'the brahmans cannot prosper without the support of the kshatriyas and the kshatriyas cannot prosper without the support of the brahmans' (Sharma 1983: 31; 1991: 248). Quite clearly, the nexus between the intellectual and political elite was crucial for institutionalising domination over the producing and labouring people. But there was no doubt who was in the driver's seat. The brahman elite manipulated and controlled the kings and feudal lords like puppets. The king was duty-bound, on religious ground, to bow to the brahman and act according to his instruction. In the *Mahabharata*, for instance, Bhishma preaches:

The highest duty of a crowned king is to worship brahmans; they should be protected . . . respected, bowed to and revered as if they were one's parents. If brahmans are contended, the whole country prospers; if they are discontended and angry, everything goes to destruction. They can make a god not-a-god, and not-god, a god. One whom they praise, prospers; and one whom they reproach becomes miserable. (cited in Dharma Theertha 1992: 90-1)

'Hindu' polity and state in ancient India were founded on the religious-philosophical outlook of brahmanism which, by believing in the divine creation of the social cosmos, supported the caste hierarchy and the concomitant concept of the domination of a few over the many. The brahmanical thesis of the divine origins of the social order made any rational and humanist political thought impossible. It was not possible even to raise the historical question of socio-political origins in the Upanishads and Dharmashastras.

The system of caste served despotic rulers in their conquest and exploitation. Caste is an effective system to keep people weak, submissive, and divided. For this reason, caste as an institution and ideology has been unfailingly patronised by almost all ruling groups down the ages. As Dharma Theertha has observed:

The scheme of castes and priest-craft was wide enough to afford scope for numerous exploiting groups, so that despotic monarchs, adventurous kings wishing to become emperors, usurpers to thrones desirous of priestly support, new invaders such as the Scythians, the Chinese, the Turks, the Greeks, the Rajputs, the Muhammadans and the modern Europeans, and Indian princes aspiring to Kshatriyahood and relying on Brahman help, all have patronised it in turns when it served them in their conquest or exploitation. (ibid.: 7)

The real or acquired status of kshatriyahood was made mandatory for according priestly legitimacy on kings and aspiring rulers. Kshatriyahood was always put on sale in India: anyone (including those from the lowered castes or casteless tribals or foreign groups) could buy it – and they did – from the brahman for a price and promise to rule according to the varna-dharma and jati-dharma. Kosambi has demystified the *hiranya garbha* (golden womb), the ceremony for symbolic rebirth into caste society, by which the tribal chiefs and aspiring rulers acquired kshatriya status, agreed to maintain the caste order, and converted the rest of the tribe into a subject peasantry:

A large vessel of gold was prepared into which the chieftain would be inserted doubled up, like the foetus in a womb. The brahmin ritual for pregnancy and childbirth was then chanted by the hired priests. The man emerged from the 'womb of gold' as if reborn, having also acquired a new caste, or even a caste for the first time; this was not the caste of the rest of the tribe when they were absorbed into society, but one of the classical four castes, usually kshatriya, with the gotra of the brahmin priest. . . . The brahmin priests received the golden vessel as part of their fee, which made everyone happy. . . . *All this amounted to keeping down a newly created set of vaishyas and shudras by brahmin precept and kshatriya arms.*

(1992: 171)

In this tradition kings are given power and divinity, making the *danda* – the role of coercion and punishment – central to the state. In the brahmanical polity, *dandaniti*, rule by force, is the chief principle of state management. Manu and other law-givers proclaim loudly that the whole world is governed by the *danda* – Agni burns through fire, Surya sends forth his beams through fear, through fear Vayu blows. According to *Manusmriti*, the *danda* is the king and the man, he is the inflicter and he is chastiser. The *danda* alone chastises all the subjects. Justice is the *danda* (VII.17-18).

Other brahmanical authorities vie with Manu to eulogise the role of *danda*. Among the precepts of the *Mahabharata* there is one which states, 'Right leans on might (*danda*) as a creeper on a tree. As smoke follows the wind, so might follows might' (see Walker 1983, vol. I: 267). The drone of *danda*-devotees goes on and on: *Danda* moves the universe, piercing, cutting, wounding, maiming, afflicting, causing panic in the hearts of all; it is *danda* and *danda* alone, irresistible and terror-striking, that makes the earth prosper, that brings about morality and makes virtue possible (ibid.). The following paean to the *danda* in the *Mahabharata*, addressed to the king, which celebrates the crudest form of what is called social Darwinism, is particularly striking for its sinister implications:

All the limits established in the world, O King, are marked by danda. . . . *No man will sacrifice if he is not afraid, nor will he give gifts or hold to his promise.* . . . *I see no being which lives in the world without violence. Creatures exist at one another's expense; the stronger consume the weaker. The mongoose eats mice, just as the cat eats the mongoose; the dog devours the cat, O King, and wild beasts eat the dog. Man eats them all – see dharma for what it is! Everything that moves and is still is food for life.* (quoted in Doniger and Smith 1991: XXXI)

The *Mahabharata* eulogises the *Dandaniti*, the policy of *danda*, so much that it interchangeably uses *Dandaniti* with *Rajadharma*, the policy of the state:

When Dandaniti becomes lifeless, the triple Veda sinks, all the Dharmas howsoever developed, completely perish. When traditional Rajadharma is departed from, all the bases of the divisions of the Ashramas are shattered. In Rajadharma are realised all the forms of renunciation, in Rajadharma is revealed all knowledge. In Rajadharma are centred all the worlds. (see Varma 1974: 102)

In the *Arthashastra*, the much-acclaimed treatise on statecraft, Kautilya is concerned with the preservation of varna-dharma through *danda* in the same way as are other brahman writers of previous and successive ages. He minces no words in declaring that '*Danda* and *danda* alone protects this world and the next' (*Arthashastra* III.1). His *danda* is employed to uphold the 'brahmanical social organisation which rests for its validity on the Vedas'. He is concerned with the strategies of winning war but hardly ever with social welfare; he is interested in taxing irrigation without bothering to build dams. In brahmanical texts kings are never urged to provide support to the poor, as in the Buddhist tradition, as it is protection of varna-dharma and jati-dharma that is more important. The decay of dharma that characterises the *Kaliyuga*, a chaotic era of all-round decadence and perversion, is not moral decadence, lack of commitment for fellow human beings or neglect of social welfare, but the mixing of the varnas and upsetting of the social order structured in favour of the two higher varnas.

Kautilya, who is hailed as the 'architect of Hindu secular statecraft', requires every varna to perform its functions, and declares that the person who observes his duty attains heaven and infinite bliss. The world is destroyed, he warns, on account of violation of caste duty leading to the confusion of castes. He tersely instructs the king that he should never allow the people to deviate from their caste duty (Sharma 1991: 253ff). This 'statesman' accords – and justifies – the privileged position and highest honour to brahmans in keeping with other brahmanical texts that allow three important privileges to the priestly class: exemption from physical torture and capital punishment even for the most heinous of crimes; various privileges from the state; and, the right to demand honour and gifts from everyone. The *Arthashastra* says that brahmans are *bhudeva*, deities on the earth: *ye deva devalokesu cha brahmanaha*, 'brahmans occupy the same position among human beings as gods occupy in heaven' (ibid.: 255).

The challenge to the brahmanical power from the lower orders, reflected among other things in the establishment of powerful shudra dynasties like the Nandas and the Mauryas, was considerable in the Kautilya's time, which explains in a way Kautilya's friendly overtures and conciliatory posturing towards the Mauryas. However, his unbridled glorification of the brahmans and the Vedic religion leaves no doubt where his loyalty lies. In contrast to the favours extended to the brahmans, he exhibits a naked antagonism towards non-brahmanical faiths and sects. Vrishalas and Pashandas, who were shramanic ascetics including some Buddhist monks, were marked out by him for harassment and discriminatory treatment (ibid.: 261). There are several instances all culled from the *Arthashastra* which show his intolerance towards Vrishalas, Pashandas, Sakyas, Ajivikas, the lower orders and the sects who were opposed to the brahmanical system of life.

Kautilya also comes across as a champion of untouchability. He recommends separate living quarters for supporters of heretical sects and those who followed 'unclean' occupations. 'The Pashandas and Chandalas were required to live on the border burial grounds' (ibid.). A. B. Keith has made a sharp observation in this regard: 'It is a very misplaced patriotism which asks us to admire the *Arthashastra* as representing the fine flower of Indian political thought. It would, indeed be melancholy if this were the best that India could show against the *Republic* of Plato or the *Politics* of Aristotle' (cited in Rangarajan 1992: 35-6).

SHRAMANIC COUNTER-TRADITION OF RESISTANCE AND EQUITY

The historical roots of the anti-caste movement can be traced in the shramanic tradition – a tradition of resistance and equity propounded by shramans,[3] a long line of differentiated heterodoxy, who were non-Vedic and antagonistic to the brahmanical religion and politics (Chakravarti 1996; Thapar 2001). The shramans rejected the scriptural and brahmanic authority, *karmakanda*, and varnashrama-dharma. Most importantly, they stood against the brahmanical scheme of disenfranchising masses from their human and property rights.

Even before the emergence of the two most renowned shraman teachers, the Buddha and Mahavir, in the sixth century BC, Kautsa, Brihaspati and several others had challenged the claims of the religious or spiritual power of the Vedic hymns. They had challenged the brahmans to produce their Brahma in flesh and blood. They were, perhaps, the earliest proponents of Lokayata. The Lokayatikas or Charkvakas were materialists, contemptuously dubbed the Vedic rituals and ceremonies as the outright and outrageous fraud indulged in by priests to eke out a livelihood (Chattopadhyaya 1992, 2001; Sardesai 1994). They declared that the mantra-chanting priests were rogues out to cheat and fleece the people whose productive occupations, they emphasised, were dignified, whereas those who smeared their bodies with ashes and lost themselves in Vedic humbug were good-for-nothing parasitic idiots.

Etymologically, Lokayata means prevalent in the world. The name suggests that its ideas were fairly well-known to the people as it was part of the folk culture. Unfortunately, there is very little information about the original formulators of this school and their authentic ideas and world-outlook. In all probability, Lokayatika ideas were distorted and destroyed by their brahmanical opponents. D. P. Chattopadhyaya, in his pioneering work on the subject, contends that Lokayatikas were pro-people and proto-materialist and sharply critical of the brahmanical way of life. Elsewhere he has quoted verses and aphorisms culled from the writings of some brahmanical idealists themselves. Even in rough and free translation, Lokayatika's biting satire and contempt for the brahmanical order are unmistakable:

Heaven and liberation are mere empty talk. There is no soul that is imagined to go to the other world. The actions prescribed for the caste-society (varnashrama) do not really yield their alleged results.

If (as claimed by the priests) the animal killed in the Jyotistoma sacrifice attains heaven straightway, why does not the sacrificer kill his own father (and thus ensure heaven for him)?

The authors of the three Vedas are just cheats and cunning thieves. All the learned formulas – the meaningless spells jarvari-turvari – like the wife taking the horse's phallus (i.e. a part of the Ashvamedha sacrifice), are nothing but the inventions of cheats for the purpose of obtaining their sacrificial fees. (see Chattopadhyaya 2001: 214-15)

Sardesai, in his *Progress and Conservatism in Ancient India* (1994), has correctly stressed that the driving principle of the Lokayata was more social than philosophical. Their views are not only directed against the caste order and brahman domination, they are also brutally polemical. Sardesai (1994: 219-20) cites many Lokayata aphorisms from a Marathi work by Sadashiv Athavle, which give fairly comprehensive information about the Lokayata ideology:

The body, the face and all limbs (of all people) being similar, how can there be any distinctions of varna and caste? Such distinctions are unscientific and cannot be defended.

Agriculture, cattle-breeding, trade, state service, etc. are occupations of the wise. They should be followed. But those who smear their bodies with ashes and perform Agnihotra and other religious rites are devoid of intelligence and manhood. Hence, men should pursue sciences and arts which are of practical utility and based on practical knowledge.

Real bondage lies in servitude. Real Moksha lies in freedom.
There is no such thing as Moksha. Death is the end of life.
There is no rebirth. There is no other-world.
Dharma is the conspiracy of the crafty. Fools fall victim to it.
Those who composed the three Vedas were hypocrites, crafty people and devils.

The rejection of the divine sanctity of the Vedas and, thus, the very basis of brahmanic hegemony reveals a deep resentment among the non-Aryans, Asuras, and Dasa-Dasyus who were being persecuted by the Aryan-brahmans under the cloak of religion. There are numerous examples in the Upanishads, Puranas and epics of defiant characters who contested Vedic ritualism and beliefs. The *Chandogya Upanishad* speaks maliciously of the *Asura*-views which were ranged against the brahmanical worldview. In Valmiki's *Ramayana*, there is a reference to Jabali who denounces the rituals and condemns the cult of sacrifice as an invention of interested, sinister, and fraudulent individuals. As late as in the ninth century, Shankara has mentioned the anti-Vedic Kavsheya in his commentary on the *Brahma Sutra*. Such critics of the brahmanical religion must have enjoyed wide support among the masses or else they would have been eliminated by their opponents who preached and practised *Vaidiki himsa himsa na bhavati*, 'the Vedic violence is no violence'. It is not without significance that the Aranyakas, Brahmanas, Smritis are crammed with stringent injunctions against the challengers of the Vedic religion. The threat from the masses who were not willing to fall in the brahmanical line, must have been very serious.

The institutionalised subjugation and enslavement of the producing and labouring people into lowered castes, and the latter's struggle to liberate themselves from the oppressive order, are the social context of India's history, culture and philosophy. Therefore, what is 'glorious' tradition for India's elite is a nightmare for the oppressed masses. One's triumph and supremacy is the other's travails and tragedy, for the simple reason that the historical-cultural glories of the oppressor and the oppressed cannot be one and the same. There is little doubt that almost all religious and secular literature in Sanskrit, sources of the Indian past, are the brahmanical propaganda which tells only one side of the story. There is no valid reason not to believe that the brahmanical sources do not give us the actual facts of life of India; they give and are meant to give what the brahmans thought the facts to be.

When the Sanskrit literature, whether the dharmashastras, the epics, or any other, refers to varna or caste, the attempt is not to realistically describe the society but to prescribe for it. The references represent projections; the Brahmanic texts are an attempt to delineate an ideal model and impose it on the society. They are a manifesto for a particular form of social inequality.

(Omvedt 2003: 133)

Brahman records, to take an example, completely ignore the great Mauryan monarch Ashoka except for referring to him in some texts as a Buddhist and shudra. Besides maintaining a conspiracy of silence against their opponents, there are far too many evidences which suggest that the Sanskrit texts were frequently subjected to interpolations, tendentious redactions, and plain fabrication. As Dharma Theertha has pointed out (1992: 115-16),

There is hardly any Sanskrit composition which has not been tampered with, altered or added to by them. There is no famous rishi or teacher in whose

name they have not concocted scriptures. There is no sacred book into which fiction and legend and imaginary history have not been interpolated. . . . Veracity as to facts was never a feature of brahman authors, so much so that historical unreliability has become a universal literary characteristic of the Sanskrit language. The best critic would be unable to separate. . . . where facts end and fiction begins. This is even more the case in regard to the so-called sacred literature.

The wholesale forgeries in Sanskrit texts largely remained undetected before the modern age because only brahmans could read and interpret them for others. The Sanskrit texts were generally held to be too sacred to be put to human reasoning. It is only in recent times that some Western and Indian scholars, with their secular approach and expert knowledge of the subject, have been able to unearth the forgeries committed by the brahman scribes, commentators, and thinkers. 'The full story of forged texts in Hinduism has yet to be written' (see Walker 1983, vol. 1: 362-5). Besides pointing out the interpolation of the *Purusha-sukta* in the *Rigveda*, Max Müller has shown how the brahmans 'mangled, mistranslated and misapplied' the original word *agre* to read *agneh* in order to provide Rigvedic support for the burning of widows (Walker ibid.). K. M. Panikkar, in his *Hinduism and the Modern World,* has referred to the fabrication of a Shankara text by the brahmans of Malabar to sanction the custom of unapproachability. Scholars like R. S. Sharma (1991) have pointed out rampant distortions in the epics to suit the brahmanical viewpoint. Didactic digressions on the superiority of the priestly class in the *Shanti Parvan* in the *Mahabharata* are too obvious. In the brahmanised *Ramayana,* the author has made Rama use the word thief (*chora*) for the Buddha (Varma 1974: 297). While spurious records and fictitious dynastic pedigrees for brahmanised rulers abound in the sacerdotal texts, especially the Puranas, 'the Mauryas are described in these texts as *sudra-prayastvadharmikah,* 'mainly shudras and unrighteous' (Thapar 1999: 12).

While elite historians of various inclinations still cling to the Sanskrit sources to reconstruct the Indian past, and, as a result, most history books still dish out little more than the brahmanical perspective, some new studies using more credible sources – archaeology, the history of technology, and alternative linguistic-literary materials – are shattering the old stereotypes and shedding light on the real instead of the ideal. It is no longer possible to hide the historical reality under the weight of received wisdom.

To put it another way, in stark contrast to the elitist historiography based on Sanskrit sources, the history of India since the Vedic period has largely been a history of endless conflict, confrontation, and clashes between the traditions of autocratic brahmanism and egalitarian shramanism. The need, therefore, to reconstruct a real history in place of the brahmanic fiction and mythology that goes in the name of 'ancient India' is crucial.

In the ancient period the brahmanical social order did not go unchallenged. The political economy and social organisation structured in favour of the first two varnas were never endorsed by the victims of the system. The lowered castes strove to throw off the yoke of inhuman, oppressive order. That is why all the brahmanical texts, especially the Dharmashastras, are full of exhortations to maintain the varna-dharma, repeating ad nauseum that the vaishyas and shudras should never be allowed to deviate from the functions allotted to them, otherwise chaos – terrible and unmanageable – would descend on the world. *Sama* (manipulation), *dama* (coercion), *danda* (punishment), *bheda* (discrimination), *niti* (morality), *aniti* (immorality) – everything was legitimised in the naked quest of power and often invoked to be employed to keep the lowered castes and classes in order and discipline. The intellectual and political elites always advocated and adopted the strongest measures to quell eruptions of protest and rebellion from below.

No matter how savagely the ruling classes dealt with the resistance movements, social crisis in one from or other kept erupting at regular intervals upsetting the applecart of the varna order. One such major crisis occurred during the third century AD described in the Puranas as *Kaliyuga* (the age of anarchy) characterised by large-scale *varna-samkara* (literally, intermingling of blood between castes). As R. S. Sharma (1983, 1990a) has argued, *varna-samkara* did not merely mean the intermixture of blood between four varnas – heralding the horrible *Kaliyuga* that invariably invites the wrath of Gods resulting in unspeakable catastrophes. It also meant the lower orders refusing to carry out their caste duties.

Emphasis on the importance of coercive mechanism (danda) in the Shanti Parva and the description of anarchy (arajaka) in the epics possibly belong to the same age and point to the same crisis. The Kali age is characterised by varna-samkara, i.e. intermixture of varnas or social orders, which implies that vaishyas and shudras, i.e. peasants, artisans and labourers, either refused to stick to the producing functions assigned to them or else the vaishya peasants declined to pay taxes and the shudras refused to make their labour available. (Sharma 1983: 31)

Since the masses, especially the shudras and the ati-shudras, never reconciled to the brahmanical religion and social order, and kept registering their protest in one form or another, they are usually referred to, in the brahmanical literature, as hostile, violent, boastful, short-tempered, greedy, ungrateful, utterly undependable and unfit for any responsible work. Sharma writes in *Shudras in Ancient India* (1990a), there are at least nine verses in the *Mahabharata*'s *Shanti Parvan* stressing the necessity of combination and harmony between the brahmans and kshatriyas which clearly indicated some combined opposition on part of the two lower orders. He cites one revealing passage, in which it is bitterly complained that at one stage the shudras and vaishyas, acting most wilfully, began to unite with the wives of brahmans (ibid.: 280). This is a striking instance of vengeance of the victims – shudras, vaishyas and women – against their oppressors.

Like the *Manusmriti*, the *Shanti Parvan* defines a vrishala (i.e. a shudra) as one who defies *dharma* (ibid.: 281). The *Anushasan Parvan* portrays the shudras as 'destroyers of the king' (ibid.). The rebellious attitude of the shudra can also be inferred from a passage of the *Narada Smriti* which declares that, if a king does not exercise coercive force, all castes will abandon their respective caste obligations, but the shudras will surpass all the rest. Yajnavalkya repeats the provision of Kautilya that the shudra who pierces the eyes of others, pretends to be a brahman, and acts against the king must be heavily fined. A passage from a manuscript of the *Shanti Parvan* ordains that dasas and mlecchas should be dealt with by the same agencies, and that force should be used against the chandalas and mlecchas (ibid.).

All these are clear suggestions of tension and antagonism

between the upper and lower classes in the ancient Indian society. This explains why the king is repeatedly enjoined in the brahmanical texts to uphold the 'divinely ordained' caste system, more specifically to keep the vaishyas and shudras in their place by forcing them to fulfill their obligations. As R. S. Sharma has shown, terms such as *Kaliyuga, varna-samkara* and *arajaka* (anarchy) are invariably described in the brahmanical literature as conditions in which what collapses is the caste order when the authority of the first two varnas is eroded and caste rules are flouted on a massive scale.

Popular Heterodoxies Debunk Elite Historiography

All these instances of social antipathy and conflicts are culled from the brahmanical literature. When one takes into account the non-brahmanical sources, especially the Jain and Buddhist Pali texts to reconstruct the past, one comes across two distinct traditions and ideologies in ancient Indian society. The antagonism between brahmans and non-brahmans ran so deep that the former, despite their preposterous claims to be worthy of worship by the latter, had not attracted much love. A popular ancient saying, still current, is 'if you meet a snake and a brahman, first kill the brahman.' Such revulsion against the priestly class was perhaps due to charlatanesque nature of their socio-religious claims. Positioning themselves as gods on earth, the brahman law-makers, for example, ruled that to accuse a brahman of a crime was sinful even if the brahman was guilty.

Another ancient saying, still current in north India, mocks the superiority claimed by the priestly class: *anna manna swaha, panditji bauraha* (chanting mantras are useless and those who do that have gone raving mad). The villagers in the north still use a genial though highly sarcastic word – Babaji – to address the priest. Its subtle connotation is one who is fatuous and empty-headed. A more explicit term to mock the 'foolish priest' is *ponga pandit*. It may be noted that a great deal of shudra/subaltern subversive expressions lie undiscovered in the maze of folk and oral traditions. In fact, hardly any of them have been recorded in writing, especially in the hegemonic Sanskrit language.

To rewrite Indian history as a genuine social science demands rigorous and imaginative use of existing materials from popular culture and heterodox sources and writings. R. S. Sharma, who has rigorously studied the entire spectrum of early Indian social history, suggests that 'on the whole the social structure from the 6th century BC to the 5th century AD in mid India may be called vaishya-shudra based society in the sense that vaishyas were peasants and shudras were artisans, slaves and hired labourers' (2001: 17). Later, the difference between vaishyas and shudras was blurred and both worked mainly as cultivators. Shudras, however, have invariably been portrayed as serving the three higher classes in the dominant historiography on the basis of ancient Sanskrit texts. More than description of the reality, this was brahmanic prescription. Hsuan Tsang, the Chinese pilgrim who visited India during AD 629-45 when Harsha was the most important ruler of the north India, has categorically contradicted this shastric stereotype. In his vivid account of the time, he calls the shudras agriculturists.

Similarly, most elite historians mask or ignore the fact that Buddhism was conquered through a violent process (see Chapter 2). The Buddhists were targeted by the resurgent brahmanical forces in the post-Mauryan India. Buddhism and brahmanism were locked in a deadly combat for many centuries before the former was finally driven out from the land of its birth. One such incident is narrated by Hsuan Tsang himself when he narrowly survived an assassination bid on his life by the brahmans. The brahmans were incensed because the Chinese pilgrim was able to convert the Shaivaite Harshavardhan to Buddhism. Subsequently, Harsha became a great patron of Buddhism and convened a grand religious conference at Kannauj, his capital, which was attended by kings of twenty countries, including the Kamrupa ruler Bhaskarvarman. Hsuan Tsang, who initiated the discussion, eloquently spoke of the virtues of Buddhism and challenged his audience to refute his arguments. 'But none came forward for five days and then his theological rivals conspired to take the pilgrim's life. On this Harsha threatened to behead anybody causing the least hurt to Hsuan Tsang. Suddenly the great tower caught fire and there was an attempt to assassinate Harsha. Harsha then arrested 500 brahmanas and banished them and some of them were also executed' (Sharma 1990b: 173). So much for the gradual and peaceful absorption of Buddhism by brahmanical Hinduism!

The violent brahmanic attack on Buddhism is corroborated by many historical instances. One such case involves the Shaivite king Shashank of Gauda, a contemporary of Harsha. Shashank cut off the Bodhi tree at Bodh Gaya where the Buddha got his enlightenment. He removed the Buddha image from the shrine near the Bodhi tree and replaced it with a *Shiva-linga*, obviously in a naked display of hostility towards the Buddhists. On the other hand, the Palas in Bengal, who were staunch supporters of Vajrayana, a contemporary form of Buddhism, declared war on brahmanism. The Palas and Vajrayanis declared that what was righteous to the followers of the shruti-smriti would be unrighteous and irrelevant to them and what was unrighteous to the smriti-worshippers would be righteous to them. It was a sequel to this endless hostility between the two that Kapalikas, Aughars and many others started living a life which was against all canons of the caste codes. 'The leaders of this great movement of the underdog were the famous Siddhas who were either low-caste thinkers or broken brahmans. All restraints were defied, all bonds with the codes snapped and men revelled in cultivating the forbidden' (Upadhyaya 1989: 89). Throwing all material and sexual prohibitions to the winds, they led a care-free life believing that the best way to conquer temptation is to yield to it. Culturally speaking, this movement was a total rejection of the ascriptive institutionalised brahmanism. With a liberal and unorthodox faith, it prepared the ground for the egalitarian Bhakti and Sufi movements which engulfed India in succeeding centuries.

Similarly, the philosophies of India are not neatly divided between the idealistic and the materialistic systems, as emphasised by many Marxist scholars, but between the shraman or *nastika/ varna-virodhi* (anti-transcendalistic/non-Vedic/anti-casteist) and the brahman or *astika/varnavadi* (transcendalistic/Vedic/casteist). It may be noted that *nastikata* in Indian tradition initially did not mean thorough-going atheism – more often than not the term was used to denote opposition to the polytheistic superstitions and caste ideology that informed the basic aspects of Vedic-brahmanism. The original meaning of the term nastika (in opposition to astika) is 'someone who denies the authority of the Vedas'. As Dhani (1984) has argued, the casteist basis of the Vedic-Aryan philosophy and its exponents' preoccupation with their self-interest suggests that an astika – 'one who abides by the Vedas' – had also to be one who believed in his own self-interest, served best through his group's interest. The group interest could be served best by the secret knowledge embodied in scriptures which was in the custody of the brahman policy-makers or those who 'knew'. Anyone who questioned their authority or philosophy of caste and rituals was condemned as a nastika, an atheist or non-conformist, a sort of out-caste. The phrase coined for this was *nastiko veda-nindakah* (Dhani 1984: 135).

Seen from the socio-historical perspective, the philosophies of *Lokayata*, Buddhism, and Jainism belong to the nastika or shramanic stream while Vedanta, Nyaya and Vaisheshika schools of philosophy are astika or brahmanic. All shramanic systems, though differentially articulated, had their monastic order called *gana* (tribe) or *sangha* (organisation) which were casteless. Advocates of the shramanic world-view like the Buddhists, Jains, and Ajivikas, who explored areas of belief and practice different from the Vedas and Dharmashastras, were sharply opposed to the caste system and *karmakanda*.

The hostility between the shramanic and brahmanic systems was so acute that it was likened by the second century BC grammarian Patanjali to the enemity between the mongoose and the snake. He uses the example of shraman-brahman to illustrate an antagonistic compound – *samahaar dvanda* – and remarks that the opposition of the two was eternal – *yesham cha virodhah shashvatika* (Chakravarti 1996: 41; Thapar 2001: 58). The two opposite systems were so important before and during the Buddha's time that the period as a whole has been characterised by Barua, in his *Pre-Buddhist Indian Philosophy*, as the 'Age of the Shramanas and the Brahmanas' (Chakravarti 1996: 41). The Buddhist and the Jain texts, the inscriptions of Ashoka, the description of India by Megasthenes and the account of the Chinese pilgrim Hsuan Tsang, covering a period of a thousand years, all refer to two main religious categories – the brahmans and the shramans (Thapar 2001: 58).

The opposition between the brahmans and shramans, the latter typified by the Buddhist-Jain monks, is a constant feature of the literature of the two systems. Brahmanical literature has several instances of derogatory statements about the Buddhists and Jains as worthless heretics. On the other hand, the Buddhist-Jain texts, especially the Buddhist Pali texts, refer to brahmans as liars and exploiters whose vices include pride, deceit, greed, and even crimes such as matricide and patricide, beside milder negative traits such as gluttony.

'This indigenous view of the dichotomous religions of India is referred to even at the beginning of the second millennium AD by Alberuni who writes of the Brahmans and the Shamaniyya' (Thapar 2001: 58). The shramans often preached a system of universal ethics which embraced all without the distinction of caste and communities. 'This differed from the tendency to segment religious practice by caste which was characteristic of brahmanism' (ibid.). Denying any privileged position to the priestly class and rejecting the notion of any ascriptive qualifications for salvation, the shramanic ethic was egalitarian and universalist, though its lay followers, duped by the incessant brahmanical propaganda, later fell victim to the caste system.

To sum up, a scientific and credible history of ancient India cannot be reconstructed without the context of social stratification, political economy and cultural establishment. The contents and purpose of brahmanical and non-brahmanical intellectual articulation cannot be appreciated in a decontexualised fashion. The social and religious ideas generated by the elite were symbiotically related to its self-interests. Similarly, the thinking and ideology of the lower orders was inextricably linked to their survival: this prompted them to reject, sometimes totally and at other partially, the basic assumptions and formulations of the brahmanic culture.

2

Buddhist India: Against Caste and Brahmanism

> When the whole country was basking in the sunshine of great ideals of brotherhood, when the king [such as Ashoka] and the commoner were co-operating . . . [and] producing glorious blossoms in the fields of science, literature, arts and architecture, when the people of India liberated from their bondage were carrying joyful tidings of emancipation into distant lands and filling the world with the fragrance of the Buddha's teachings, alas! in the land of that Buddha, the brahman priests were studiously engaged in polishing the chains of imperialism and replenishing the armoury of aggression and exploitation with Manu Sastras, Sukra Nitis, Puranas, idolatrous temples, Kali worship and other literature and institutions of wily priestcraft.
>
> SWAMI DHARMA THEERTHA
> *History of Hindu Imperialism*, 1992: 96

A parallel movement ranged against the Vedic-brahmanic tradition of domination and discrimination can be traced from the time of the Buddha and Mahavir in the sixth century BC. The Vedic-brahmanic religion and philosophy was basically envisioned to establish a permanent sytem of brahmanic rule where the shudras, or the masses, would be kept in perpetual ignorance and subjugation. Both at the levels of ideology and praxis, caste was the primary instrument to achieve this nefarious objective. Its propounders insisted that those who did not approve of the caste system should not be allowed to live in the mainstream since they can do something which might upset the applecart of varna. The dissenters, the brahman demanded, must go away on their own or else should be sent forcefully to the forest *(aranya)* to gain self-realisation *(atmabodh)* through self-mortification *(tapashcharya)* and give up their life there.

All this was done under the cloak of religion and scriptures to offset the ever-lurking danger of a backlash from the caste-oppressed. However, the victims of institutionalised discrimination kept attempting to break free. Many of them followed the caste regimentation more in breach than in honour. On the other hand, the perpetrators of the caste hierarchy kept devising new and more effective ways – the most striking among these measures was the policy of divide and rule implicit in the graded hierarchy of caste – to deal with opposition from the lower orders.

It must be pointed out here that it was various ways of resistance from below that explain whatever social mobility took place in ancient – and modern – India, and not the in-built dynamism in the caste system itself as fondly held by the apologists for the brahmanical order. Significantly, the heterodoxies of many kinds, particularly the shramanic leaders representing a socially inclusive ideology, came up not only with doctrines which bypassed the Vedic gods and beliefs, but some of them also raised the banner of *chattaro vanna samasama honti* (all the four castes are equal) against inegalitarian and hierarchical principles. However, the brahmanical propagandists kept alive, in theory as well as practice, their shastric injunctions such as *shudranamepa janmatah* (a shudra is a shudra by birth), *shudram tu karyeta dasyam* (shudras would have to do slavery), *na shudray mati dadyat* (shudras should not be given any knowledge), etc.

The sixth century BC was a period of momentous changes in the Gangetic valley, not only in the material life and social organisation – in the wake of the Iron Age and what has been labelled as the second urban revolution when old tribal institutions were giving way – but in the realm of ideas and world-view as well. On the one hand, the Vedic-Upanishadic teachers were trying to establish their supremacy through floating fanciful, highly speculative socio-religious doctrines, and on the other, a range of non-conformists and *nastikas*, literally the 'deniers', were coming up with ideologies – mostly materialist and at least much less speculative – challenging the infallibility of the Vedas, the existence of Brahma and, above all, the claims of the brahmanic priesthood to higher knowledge and superior status through divine intervention. This milieu threw up a personality whose religion – Buddhism – spread in many parts of the world even before the Christian era.

Gautam Buddha's call to develop understanding and compassion for suffering humanity and his historic challenge to caste and brahmanical unhumanitarianism, along with his opposition to the socio-religious structure that supported Vedic sacrifice and superstition, the discriminatory deities and rituals, the caste theory and the Upanishadic gobbledygook, was one of the many heterodox shramanic ideologies being articulated in different voices of the time. Outstanding among them were six independent teachers – Ajita Keshkambal, Prakuddha Katyayana, Puran Kassapa, Sanjaya Belathaputta, Niggantha Natputta, and Makkali Gosala. Popularly recognised as *saman (shraman)* or *paribbajaka* (Sanskrit, *parivrajaka*), these religious strivers and mendicants – which these two terms respectively mean – gave voice to opinions, in sharp contrast to the brahmanical portrayal of a harmonious, though grossly unequal society, which revealed how contentious and cacophonous the society actually was.

These thinkers had a wide variety of philosophical visions but there was no difference of opinion among them on the point that all people were equally subject to the same laws, material or otherwise. On this common matrix, these strivers admitted everyone, irrespective of caste, to their ranks. By ruling that anyone could become a striver, they could make a dent in the brahman's pretensions to pre-eminence. These thinkers carried forward the well-established tradition of the earlier sceptics, materialists, and free thinkers, who were implacably opposed to the Vedic-Upanishadic theology and way of life. As Carrithers (1992: 121) has correctly underlined, it was from this intellectually fecund community that Buddhism and Jainism arose.

Anti-Vedic atheistic ideas were also present in Virochana's philosophy as mentioned in the *Chandogya Upanishad* and revealingly labelled there as the *Asuropanishad*. The Lokayata philosophy propagating thoroughgoing materialism, as its very name suggests, was popular. The eponymous *Brihasapatisutra*, also known as *Lokayatasutra,* which expounded the classic matter-over-mind materialist thinking, existed in some form till the second century BC as can be judged from Patanjali's reference to it. Later, the Lokayata materialism became synonymous with Charavaka, who was supposedly a disciple of Brihasapati.

Jainism and Buddhism in the sixth century BC represented the most powerful challenge to the Vedic-brahmanism. The Jain ideas were already shaped by Parshva in the preceding century, emphasising non-violence, eschewing the property of others, advocating no possessions of one's own, and adherence to truthfulness. Vardhamana Mahavir, the celebrated founder of Jainism and famous contemporary of the Buddha, added, among other things, self-mortification and absolute sexual abstinence to the list of Jain tenets propounded by Parshva. Essentially atheistic, Jainism emphasised that purification of the self could be achieved through asceticism, non-violence, truthfulness, and celibacy. The excessive stress on non-violence and self-mortification, however, proved a dampener and could not win a mass following for this religion.

More importantly, Jainism failed to present a viable and coherent socio-religious alternative to the Vedic-brahmanism. Its lukewarm criticism of caste and its philosophy of individual salvation through extreme austerities was unable to enthuse the common man, and thus it failed to capture the mass imagination of the contemporary society. To counter the Vedic religion, the Upanishadic absolutistic metaphysics and the brahmanical social order, 'a more balanced and effective philosophy was needed – a philosophy which grasped the contemporary consciousness of the masses, could appeal to the average human psyche, and also give an impetus to social development. Buddhism was a product of these socio-economic and ideological conditions' (Ilaiah 2000: 43).

Buddha's Humanitarian Synthesis of Mind and Matter

The most outstanding figure that emerged in the sixth century BC from an impressive array of heterodox shramanic teachers was none other than Gautam Siddhartha (563-483 BC). His life story is fairly well-known. Born at Lumbini, Kapilvastu, situated in the foothills of the Himalayas, in the territory of the Sakya republic headed by his father, he took his leave of family life at the age of twenty-nine, attained Buddhahood, the 'Enlightenment', at Bodh Gaya at the age of thirty-five, and died in Kusinara at the age of eighty. For fifty years he traversed the kingdoms of Magadha and Kosala (corresponding to south Bihar and eastern Uttar Pradesh of today), as well as the adjoining republics and principalities, conversing, teaching, and converting people to his religion. Besides generating awareness about love, non-violence and truth among the masses, he raised and trained a dedicated band of bhikkhus (brothers) and bhikkhunis (sisters) to carry forward his humanitarian mission. In a sharp break from brahmanical exclusivism, he recruited disciples from all castes and classes, both men and women. The Buddha and his mission are recounted in great detail in the historical records and Pali canon.[1]

The Buddha produced a cultural-ideological synthesis by combining various strands of shramanic thinking with the dialectics and social reality of the time. He rejected both the mindless asceticism (by asserting that complete self-mastery is not an end in itself but a means to higher individual and social goals) and the absolutist Vedic-Upanishadic theology along with its tyrannical social construct (by declaring that there is a *dhamma*, which according to Mrs. Rhys Davids' analysis he originally used for universal 'standard' or 'norm', which holds good for all mankind). He repudiated both the anarchic individualism of the ascetics who had broken away from all social bonds in their unbridled individualistic pursuit of perfection, and the Vedic-brahmanic regimentation of the different strata of people in hereditary ways of life. Charting a different course, he founded a religion, though not in the orthodox sense, and built a sangha or organisation, which could only be entered on abandoning brahmanic values, and which offered conducive conditions for both individual satisfaction and social development.

Some scholars who define religion narrowly in terms of belief in God, ritualism, or a set of sacred dogmas have branded early Buddhism as a system of morality or ethics rather than a religion. But religion, as we know, is basically about our understanding of what life is about. In this sense Buddhism, from the beginning, was a full-fledged religion. No doubt it was utterly unorthodox. Apart from its empiricistic and anti-metaphysical orientation, Buddhism was primarily concerned with universal values and the morality by which it urged men to live. In other words, Buddhism was a way of life – but it must be added, its way of life was in sharp contrast to the casteist and ascriptive (Hindu) way of life. The Buddha's morality was not derived from absolutist speculations and the divinity of caste, the theories of heaven and hell, or the individual soul and the cosmic one. While the popular beliefs in heaven and hell were for the Buddha nothing but pleasurable and painful feelings one experiences in this life, he regarded the belief in an immortal soul as pernicious because 'it was a theory harmful to the religious life in that it tends to generate selfishness and egoism' (Kalupahana 1976: 41).

Unlike the self-proclaimed avatars or messengers of God, the Buddha did not claim to be an enlightened know-all, capable of answering all questions. He admitted on several occasions that he did not have answers to all questions. He even took a categorical position against the personality cult being built around him by some of his followers. There is no evidence that he himself ever accepted the title 'Buddha'. Nor did he give false hope to any spiritual aspirant. He repeatedly advised his disciples to be their own path-finders: 'I never undertake to secure salvation for anybody under any circumstances whatsoever; understand the dhamma and you will cross the ocean'. His classic phrase, *atta dipa bhavata attasaran* – 'be a lamp unto yourself, be a refuge of yourself' (frequently cited in the Buddhist corpus; for instance, the Mahaparinibbana-sutta of the Digha Nikaya) – leaves no doubt whatsoever that he did not want anyone to take his teachings on trust, but to test them in the light of personal experience. He did not want his followers to stop thinking, as does Krishna in the Gita exhorting everyone that everything of any importance has already been revealed by him and the only need was to follow the path faithfully. Instead, the Buddha did not wish his religion to be encumbered with the dead wood of the past, and enjoined his followers to be alive to changing reality and change for the better with changing times.

The Buddha's objective temper and humility are diametrically different from the intellectual conceits and arrogance displayed by the teacher-sages of the Vedic-Upanishadic tradition. In a well-known philosophical debate between the leading Upanishadic master Yajnavalkya and the extraordinarily brilliant Gargi, recorded in the Brihadaranyaka Upanishad, the latter asks many searching questions, which enrage the great sage who threatens her with dire consequences: 'Shut up woman, or your head will break into pieces', implying 'do not transgress limits or you may go raving mad' (see Chakravarti 2002: 117).

Whatever the Buddha was, he was not a prisoner of received wisdom or dogma. Logical and lucid, systematic yet unabsolutist, he was a rationalist thinker, an empirical theoretician who discounted all metaphysical propositions as 'meaningless strings of words, sentences which conform to the rules of grammar but are lacking in meaning, even though they are capable of arousing strong emotional responses in the people'. Kalupahana's acclaimed study of Buddhist philosophy (1976), based on the most authentic Pali Nikayas, demonstrates the empiricistic attitude of early Buddhism which rejects transcendental reality and metaphysical speculations because they cannot be experienced through the senses or extrasensory perception. Nowhere is this more clearly stated than in the *Sabba-sutta* of the *Samyutta Nikaya* where the Buddha says:

. . . What, monks, is 'everything? Eye and material form, ear and sound, nose and odour, tongue and taste, body and tangible objects, mind and mental objects. They are called 'everything'. Monks, he who would say: 'I will reject this everything and proclaim another everything,' he may certainly have a theroy (of his own). But when questioned, he would not be able to answer and would, moreover, be subject to vexation. Why? Because it would not be within the range of experience (avisaya). (cited in Kalupahana 1976: 158)

A genuine free-thinker, the Buddha encouraged all to think independently for themselves. This makes Buddhism, in the words of Edwin Arnold, 'the proudest assertion ever made of human freedom'. His 'dogma', if any, was a strong disapproval of any dogmas and authorities. Talking to the people of the Kalama clan, the Buddha famously said:

Do not believe in hearsay; do not believe in what is handed down through generations; do not believe in anything because it is accepted by many; do not believe because some revered sage or elder makes a statement; do not believe in truths to which you have become attached by habit; do not believe merely on the authority of your traditional teachings. Have deliberation and analyse, and when the result accords with reason and conduces to the good of one and all, accept it and live up to it. (The Anguttara Nikaya, I, 188, see Woodward and Hare 1932)

Never dull or argumentative, the Buddha took an objective and compassionate view of life. His intellectual detachment was combined with a sense of social commitment. He begins from an axiom, a very general formulation of truth concerning suffering. His world-view evolves from this basic and very visible truth of universal suffering. The experience of suffering due to inevitable decay and disintegration is so widespread that it actually forms the connecting link between all sentient beings – human beings, animals, birds – who otherwise have very little in common. This idea of suffering is not conceived in a negative or pessimistic light, but as an empirical reality. Far from suggesting cynicism and resignation, it is the fundamental thesis of a world-embracing and a life-affirming philosophy, because there does not exist any other experience that is as pervasive and universal (Govinda 1961: 48). Here, it is the foundation of a universal brotherhood which is exquisitely visualised in its principle of universal love and friendship, expressed by the Pali term *metta* (Sanskrit, *maitri*). It celebrates and reinforces the idea of fellow-feeling and compassion among all living creatures. In a moving and sublime exhortation (the *Metta-sutta* in the *Sutta Nipata*, see Max Müller, ed., *SBE*, vol. X, part II), the Buddha has defined *metta* as such:

> *Mata yatha niyam puttam ayausa ekaputtamanurakhe*
> *Evam pi sabbabhutesu manasam bhavayet aprinamam.*

> (As a mother, even at the risk of her own life, loves and protects her child, so let a man cultivate love without measure toward all living beings.)

There are several such passages in the Buddhist Pali literature which extol the idea that one should recognise oneself in the pain of others. The opening verse of the 10th Chapter of the *Dhammapada* says: 'All beings are afraid of pain, all beings are afraid of death. Recognising oneself in others, one should neither kill nor cause to kill.' Based on universal values such as *ahimsa* (non-violence), *prajna* (rational, holistic and humanist application of knowledge), *karuna* (compassion) and, *samata* (equality), the Buddhist quest of individual accomplishment is not divorced from social responsibility. These complement and invigorate each other. In the Buddha's teachings, as much emphasis is given to community awakening and community organisation as to the awakening of the individual. He suggests that happiness and selfishness are not compatible, that unless one comes out of one's own selfish, egoistic self, one has very little chance of attaining inner peace and equanimity. As the Buddha says in his discourses and dialogues:

The cause of all disturbance is lack of compassion. It corrupts the body, speech and mind; it harms the family no less than strangers. If those who strive for virtue will only remember compassion, only good can result.
(tr. Edwards 2001: 8)

The Buddha's philosophy and practice stand in direct opposition to any ideology and structure that privileges a few at the cost of the multitude. He repudiated the intolerance and authoritarianism of brahmanism by stressing that his religion was not for a select few but for the whole of humanity. Embedded in the concept of universal *metta*, his dhamma was committed to the welfare of the entire community of sentient beings. Unconditional love for all beings is the Buddhist therapy to heal worldly wounds. Such a love becomes the basis of its compassion. By becoming compassionate, the Buddha says, one can become a healing force in this world of misery. It was under the influence of such ennobling teaching that the King Ashoka later set up hospitals for not only fellow human beings but also animals and birds. The Buddha's own life was a living embodiment of the gospel of *metta*.

Buddhist Dialectics an Anti-Thesis of Upanishadic Absolutism

Steering clear of Vedic sacrificial culture and metaphysical scholasticism of the Upanishads, the Buddha enunciated Four Essential Truths, beginning with the self-evident presence of suffering. The first truth is that there is *dukkha*, sorrow and suffering in life. The second, that all this is caused by man's unbalanced life and selfish desire (later, and it is extremely important, he blamed oppressive socio-economic conditions as well for man's misery, see the *Digha Nikaya* 3.58 ff; Kosambi 1992: 113). The third, that there is emancipation from all the miseries, for which the Pali term is *nibbana* (nirvana in Sanskrit). When he spoke of *nibbana*, he was referring to exhilarating freedom – accompanied by due vision and equanimity – that a man experiences after getting rid of his individualistic self-indulgence and uncontrolled mind. The fourth truth is the way to reach that end – which he visualised in *Atthangika Magga* or Eightfold Path that leads to this emancipation. The core of *Atthangika Magga* is to be found in *majjhima patipada* or the middle path that rejects the two extremes of Upanishadic idealism and mindless materialism, hedonistic indulgence and asceticism bordering on self-mortification. Anyone can find the middle path through following the *Atthangika Magga* consisting of Right View, Right Thought, Right Speech, Right Action, Right Living, Right Endeavour, Right Mindfulness, and Right Concentration, which leads to *nibbana* – to knowledge, to calmness, to awakening.

The Buddha explained the beauty of the middle path through the metaphor of the *sarangi*. If the strings of the musical instrument are too loose or too tight, will there be the mellifluous melody? In the Buddhist scheme of things, awareness and compassion are the means, and wholesome, healthy transformation – individual as well as social – is the end. Individual happiness, the Buddha was categorical, cannot be achieved in isolation and extremity. Individual and society are interdependent, and hence, to be happy, one must create happiness around oneself. In this sense, the Buddha's 'middle path' is imbued with radical potential – once its essence is absorbed and its spirit unleashed, it would bring about a transformation in the mind and heart of the individual and society. The transformation it would usher in shall be peaceful, wholesome, avoiding the two extremes of mindless materialism and obsessive spirituality. By laying emphasis on the middle path, the Buddha implied that extremes are absurdities, a sickness. An obsessed man is a danger to himself, and to the society at large. So, he insisted on avoiding extremes and instead recommended treading cautiously in the middle, which alone would bring balance, symmetry, and beauty in life.

Emphasising that an unanalysed life is not worth living, the Buddha often insists on bringing awareness to one's life. He says that like kaleidoscopic images in a dream, man is delusioned by fleeting emotions of all kinds. So long as the dream lasts, the image appears to be real, but on self-awakening it vanishes. Awakening requires self-examination, discipline and insight sufficient to transform oneself at the very core, so that one is no longer blinded by false beliefs and delusive images. For this he himself does *vipassana* (literally 'to look within'), a simple and effective meditation, and recommends the same to others. Meditation – aimed at stilling the mind and bringing about insight – begins with the Buddha. It is his gift to humanity. Anyone who does *vipassana*, looks within and without, strives for one's own and others' welfare, aspires to be like the Buddha, is a Boddhisattva. Perhaps the term Boddhisattva was originally used in this sense, though later its connotation became mired in superstitious belief in the Buddha's incarnations.

Through meditation and rigorous thinking, the Buddha developed a method to understand the dynamics of life and world. He was the first to propound dialectics, the art or science of discovering and testing truths by discussion and logical argument. His dialectics led him to enunciate the law of causality and ceaseless change which forms the central core of Buddhist philosophy. In his very first discourse at Sarnath, famous in history as the *Dhammacakka-ppavattana*, or Setting in Motion the Wheel of the Law, the Buddha said:

Let us put aside such unprofitable and unsolvable questions (avayaktani) as the questions of beginning and end. I will teach you dhamma. That being thus this comes to be. From the coming to be of that, this arises. That being absent, this does not happen. From the cessation of that this ceases. This is the dhamma. Whoever accepts dhamma, accepts the law of paticca samuppada (dependent origination). (The *Majjhima Nikaya*, also see Rhys Davids, *Dialogues of the Buddha* II: 45)

According to the Buddha, *paticca samuppada*, the law of causation or dependent origin, is the truth about the world. In fact, he maintained that whoever understood it, understood the essence of his dhamma. All natural and social phenomena are to be understood in accordance with this theory, not in terms of a Creator or transcendental reality. As Kalupahana has explained, the world for the Buddha is not only a set of objects found in space and time, related or unrelated, but includes feelings and dispositions, likes and dislikes. The world consists not only of mountains and rivers, trees and stones, but also of men and animals with behavioural patterns. Causality explains the pattern according to which all these things function. A man's dispositions, likes and dislikes, influence his judgement about good and bad, truth and falsehood, which are relative rather than absolute (Kalupahana 1976: 63-4).

Paticca samuppada is the corner-stone of the Buddhist dialectic. It exemplifies that everything is relative, constantly changing, mutating, evolving, decaying and disintegrating. It implies *anicca*, the idea of impermanence, and holds that nothing exists by itself, that everything is relative. Everything is the effect of some cause; cause and effect are interrelated as one thing flows from the other. Buddhism, not surprisingly, also explains the processes of bondage and freedom, unhappiness and happiness, both at the individual and social levels, in terms of causation.

The Buddha developed this philosophy of evolutionary change along with his thesis of *anattavada* (*anatmavada* in Sanskrit), 'the theory of no-soul'. He postulated that what is called the soul is in reality a physical and mental aggregate of five *anicca khanda* or 'impermanent conditions', namely (a) *rupa*, form or the physical body, (b) *vedana*, feelings, (c) *sanna*, idea or understanding, (d) *sankhara* (*sankara*), will, and (e) *vinnana* (vijnana) or pure consciousness. All these elements go into the making of human personality or what is called the soul. The Buddha, thereby, implied that the soul was only a name for the constituent elements of experience and was the result produced by a simultaneous manifestation of these elements.

Some scholars refuse to grant Buddhism its philosophical distinctiveness, even as they loudly proclaim Hinduism's 'tolerance'. Radhakrishnan says, 'It was Buddha's mission to accept the ideology of the Upanishads at its best and make it available for the daily needs of mankind. Historical Buddhism means the spread of the Upanishad doctrine among the peoples. . . . Such democratic upheavals are common features of Hindu society' (1962, vol. I); and he himself contradicts this statement in another place, '. . . the religion of Buddha is an aristocratic one. It is full of subtleties that only the learned could understand, and Buddha had always in view the Samanas and the Brahmanas . . .' (ibid). In the brahmanical stereotype, Buddhism is foreshadowed by the Vedic-brahmanic worldview, especially the Upanishadic ideology. Some scholars have gratuitously declared 'The Buddha was born a Hindu. He lived a Hindu and died a Hindu' (Rhys Davids, see Bhattacharyya 1993: 37). Radhakrishnan makes a similar statement: 'Early Buddhism is not an absolutely original doctrine. It is no freak in the evolution of Indian thought' (1962, vol. I: 360).

The underlying assumptions behind such uncritical statements are three – (a) that the Buddha accepted the traditional Hindu doctrines of transcendental reality, karma and rebirth, (b) that the Buddha set out to 'reform' brahmanic Hinduism and, (c) that all Upanishads are pre-Buddha. All these assumptions and the thesis based on them are preposterous, to say the least. First, the Buddha did not accept anything unexamined, without personally verifying it. Acceptance of the theories of transcendental reality expressed in the Upanishadic terms *Atman/Brahmana* because they were enunciated by the elders is simply untenable for a person like the Buddha. Then, there is absolutely nothing in the life of the Buddha to indicate that his aim was to cure the ailing brahmanism. The main thrust of his ideology and struggle was in opposition to the keynote of the brahmanical system. By taking a stand against Vedic sacrifice and Upanishadic *Atman* and *Brahmana*, and rejecting the whole idea of caste as false, he left no doubt whatever that his priority lay well beyond the Vedic-brahmanism.

The Buddha coined the word dhamma for a religion of principles. It was subsequently semantically imitated by the brahman priests as dharma but to mean a religion which was founded on certain (sacrificial) rites and (caste) rules.[2] Contrarily, the core and foundation of the Buddha's dhamma is morality which is humanist, universal, and transparent. All else is subservient to morality in this religion. Here, one is free – in fact, duty-bound – to reject any scriptures if their injunctions clash with the requirements of morality. On the other hand, in the case of brahmanism, the Vedas are *apaurusheya* – not of human origin – and hence revered as infallible and inviolate. The Buddha had to reject the Vedas – which he did quietly, without fuss – because they not only glorified a whole lot of discriminatory, violent and immoral 'gods' who tortured and killed their enemies and envisioned Brahma as a lord of the universe who created the four classes of men, but also enjoined the performance of rituals involving animal – and in some cases even human – sacrifice. As Ambedkar has argued in *The Buddha and His Dhamma*, the Vedic religion is chiefly concerned with the relation between man and God, while Buddhism, for which morality is *dhamma*, is centred around the relation between man and man. The Vedic-brahmanism, he stresses, is not founded on morality; whatever morality it has acquired over the centuries is not an integral part of it, but a separate force which is sustained by social necessities and not by its basic religious injunctions. With Buddhism the exact opposite is the case.

In determining whether an action is good or bad, the Buddhist criterion is whether or not that action leads to happy or healthy consequences, physical and mental. If an action involves only one's self, then it is one's own happiness that becomes the criterion; if it concerns others, it is the happiness of others; if it involves both, it is the happiness of both. The Buddha's classic definition of good and bad is to be found in the *Ambalatthika-Rahulovada-sutta* of the *Majjhima-Nikaya*:

Whatever action, bodily, verbal, or mental, leads to suffering [byabadha, literally, illness] *for oneself, for others or for both, that action is bad* (akusalam). *Whatever action, bodily, verbal or mental, does not lead to suffering for oneself, for others or for both, that action is good* (kusalam).
(see Kalupahana 1976: 62)

Kusala, which conveys the idea of 'wholesome' and 'healthy', is truth (*dhamma* or *sacca*), and *akusala*, 'unwholesome' or 'unhealthy', is untruth (*a-dhamma* or *musa*). A morality that requires man to love his fellow beings and prompts him to safeguard the social interest, especially of the weak and the vulnerable, does not require supernatural intervention or divine sanction. 'It is not to please God that man has to be moral. It is for his own good that man has to love man', says Ambedkar (*The Buddha and His Dhamma*, BAWS vol. 11: 323). If there is liberty for some but not for all, and equality for a few but not for the majority, the only remedy, according to Ambedkar, lies in 'making fraternity universally effective'. This was the morality that the Buddha interchangeably used for dhamma.

It is to be noted that the Upanishadic philosophy was not yet crystallised as most Upanishads, contrary to what is popularly believed, were composed after the Buddha's time. Dharmanand Kosambi, a major scholar of Pali and Sanskrit, contends that not only all Upanishads but a major portion of the Aranyakas and Brahmanas as well were written after the Buddha's time. He cites the lists of lineage given in the *Shatapatha Brahmana* and the *Brihadaranyaka Upanishad* which mention 35 generations after the Buddha who continued compiling these works. Historian H. C. Raychaudhury calculates 30 years for each generation but Kosambi brings it down to 25 years to be more realistic. This shows that these writings extended up to 875 (35 x 25) years after the Buddha's death in 480 BC. In other words, the last Upanishads were composed as late as the Gupta period, i.e. the fourth and fifth centuries AD. Shankara's famous commentaries on Upanishads were written in the ninth century AD. Even an *Allopanishad* was concocted by the opportunistic Sanskritists during Akbar's regime (see Kosambi's *Bhagwan Buddha: Jeevan aur Darshan*, pp. 25-6; for more detailed discussion of the subject, see his *Hindi Sanskriti Aani Ahinsa* in Marathi).

Even assuming that the Buddha was familiar with the essential Upanishadic formulations, his original thinking was in sharp opposition to the Vedic-Upanishadic teachings. Through a maze of theological, theosophical and metaphysical conceptions, the Upanishads tried to discover some unchanging, eternal reality behind all the changing and temporary phenomena of the world. The quest for the Absolute led the Upanishadic seers to the concept of an eternal soul and its eternal Creator. The Buddhist philosophy, characterised by the *paticca samuppada*, *anatta*, and *anicca*, remains, contrary to the beliefs of most scholars, the antithesis of Upanishadic teaching. The Upanishadic philosophy is absolutist. It stresses that the soul is eternal, unchangeable, and non-material. It can be used to defend the caste system and enslavement of many by a few as absolutist and divinely-ordained because not even a blade of grass moves without God's consent. Buddhism aimed at shattering this eternal, static, and socially obnoxious philosophy which supported exploitation. That is why Buddhism was called *anatmavada* as against the Upanishadic *atmavada*.

In fact, the Vedic-Upanishadic fixation to divine will make

any materialistic socio-political investigation impossible. The Buddha changed all that by bringing psychological-scientific factors into the realm of natural, as well as social and political formation. Buddhism says that changeability is one of the basic principles of nature. Life in this world is dynamic, ever-changing, involving growth, maturity, and then decay and disintegration, and, therefore, defined as that which finally disintegrates – *lujjati ti loko*. The *paticca samuppada* propounds the dialectics of growth and change that characterise the world. The Buddha says in the *Dhammapada* that everything that lives also dies. Everything has a cause; when the cause disappears the effect also disappears. That is why this theory is also known as the theory of impermanence. Where there is a beginning, there is an end. Where there is unity, there is also separation. Where there is life, there is death.

The concept of causation and changeability brings out the dynamic character of existence and conceives the individual as well as society from the standpoint of life and growth. The social message emanating from the Buddhist philosophy is not hard to find. The Buddha's prime purpose was to heal the festering wounds of society. His mission was to build a well-off society in an all-round way and create a situation where new forms of creativity and compassion could blossom. Buddhism unleashes a dynamic process which is capable of bringing forth new ideas to meet new challenges, and developing revisions and ideology to move forward. It does not intend to make people passive or inactive. The Buddha constantly stresses that bhikkhus must serve the people whole-heartedly, dedicate their life to the development of compassionate and constructive dhamma, and be ready to make every personal sacrifice. He wanted people to develop the *bodhi hradaya*, the awakened heart, the compassionate heart. Such awakened individuals, he believed, would change the world and make it a better place than it has been. This is a message not of despair and resignation; but of hope and rejuvenation. Buddhism strongly believes in the power of social action.

The brahmanic cliche against Buddhism for being a world-renouncing, pessimistic religion is baseless. A pessimist would hold that life is full of sorrows, there is endless suffering in this world, and there is no way out. In Buddhism, the truth of suffering is only half the truth as it propounds that there is suffering in the world, but there is a way out. The Buddha takes up universality of the suffering only as the starting point of his thinking, after that he proceeds to its anti-thesis – the truth of happiness, the truth of the cessation of suffering. He urges people to avoid what produces suffering and to do what produces happiness. The more we free ourselves from greed, hatred and ignorance, the greater will be our happiness.

For the Buddha, *nibbana* is the joyful experience of liberation from life-constricting fetters. What he means by *nibbana* is not cessation of activity but acquiring mastery over the self by which one can get rid of lust, selfishness, stupidity, temptations, attachments and the resultant suffering and sorrow. It is not an invocation to the extinction of individuality, it is a plea to obliterate the untrammelled ego. It is a plea to give up activity of the wrong type, not activity of the right type. Man has to remake himself, has to evolve into a transformed individual, a compassionate individual. Buddhism says nothing in the world is complete in itself, everything is interdependent, and hence, to be free and happy, one must create freedom and happiness for others. *Nibbana* is not other-worldly and absolute; it is to be achieved in this very world, in differing degrees, step by step, and this is all that is expected of a person living in a society.

The highest priority was to grapple with the real problems faced by people at large. The Buddha regarded *avyakrit* – abstract or hypothetical – questions as examples of futile intellectual jugglery. He not only stood by reason, but also argued that only that reason is valid which is tested on the anvil of practice. This implies that reason divorced from practice degenerates into abstract absurdities. While the Upanishads strove to collect all the logic and metaphysics to prove that the core and essence of the man is the *Brahmana* or *Atman* and the supreme aim of man is to discover it and merge his unreal individual self with the real cosmic self, the Buddha changed the logic by asserting that heightened consciousness or personal perfection can be attained by doing good to people in distress. He constantly warned his followers against getting trapped in abstruse metaphysical hair-splitting discussions, and instead set out to discover the cause and cure of sorrow and suffering.

Searing Indictment of Caste

As manifest in his constant emphasis on *prajna* combined with *karuna* and *samata*, the Buddha wanted to evolve a new human character and personality for *bahujana hitaya, bahujana sukhaya* (good of the many, happiness of the many). The term *bahujana* (literally, the majority of people) was his coinage for the commonality, who despite their innate goodness and service to the society were kept deprived and marginalised. The eloquent phrase, *bahujana hitaya*, leaves no doubt that the Buddha's ambition was to reconstruct the world where the few are not more precious or privileged than the multitude. He was opposed to the idea that people of 'lower' classes have to be sacrificed, that not everyone can be treated equally, if stability and prosperity are to be maintained. Instead he insisted that individual happiness can best be based on the promotion of happiness of all. Happiness, the Buddha sternly warns, could not be built on the miseries of others:

Don't try to build your happiness on the unhappiness of others. You will be enmeshed in a net of hatred. (Dhammapada, XXI, 2; tr. Easwaran 1986)

Since his commitment was to the social ideal which does not allow the few to dominate the many, the Buddha's opposition to any ascriptive ideology like caste or brahmanism was absolute. Kancha Ilaiah comments that since brahmanism was constructing a religious structure and process that would make the common people serve brahmanical interests by supporting *brahman hitaya, brahman sukhaya*, the Buddha reframed the whole spiritual and material process to embody a new worldview: *bahujana hitaya, bahujana sukhaya*. By negating brahmanism he shifted the emphasis from hierarchy to the masses (Ilaiah 2000: 209-10). The Buddha's own words to describe those who refuse to conform to this ideal are worth quoting: *mogham sa ratthapindam bhunjati*, 'useless consumers of society's wealth' (see Sankrityayan 1990: 1).

The Buddha attacked, relentlessly and powerfully, in his discourses and conversations, the caste system, social inequality, and brahmanical supremacy. His attitude to the injustices of the caste system and the barrenness of the brahmanical rituals have been the main factors and significant reasons in his appeal to the people

(Chattopadhyaya 1992: 466-7). It is precisely for this reason that he became a rallying point for the oppressed, the underprivileged, the lowered castes and women. From its very inception, for multiple reasons, Buddhism was uniquely placed to become 'the biggest socio-religious movement in Indian history' (ibid.).

The Buddha was the first man in history to visualise that there was a single species 'man', and that mankind was a biological unity. In the *Vasettha-sutta* of the *Sutta Nipata*, in his answer to the question as to what makes a man a brahman, the Buddha reminds his questioner of the fact that whereas in the case of plants (large or small), insects, quadrupeds, serpents, fish and birds, there are many species and marks by which they can be distinguished, in the case of man there are no such species, and no such marks. He draws the conclusion that distinctions made between different men are only matters of prejudice and custom; that it is wisdom and goodness that make the only real distinction; and that it is only the ignorant who had, for so long, maintained that it was birth that made a man superior or inferior.

The Buddha maintained that social hierarchies and divisions based on occupation developed at a certain stage in social evolution, and that the existing social structure and hereditary duties were not divinely designed but conceived and nurtured by a particular class. He pointed out that basically there were two interchangeable categories of people – masters and servants. A rich person could buy the services of the poor and the latter had to serve the former in lieu of wages. Discarding the notions of *jativada* and *gottavada* – casteism and clanism – which he perceived to be superfluous divisions that hindered social and spiritual progress, the Buddha asserted that all the four castes/classes are equal and pure – *chatuvai suddhi* and *chattaro vanna samasama* (the *Assalayana-sutta* and the *Madhura-sutta* of the *Majjhima Nikaya*).

On tour in villages, towns and cities, the Buddha had to face repeated allegations from brahmans: that he moved about and preached that all the four varnas were equally pure or that they all had the potential to become virtuous. On several occasions, he and his followers even had to face abuse and harassment on this count.[3] The *Digha Nikaya* mentions the interesting story of Lohitya, a brahman of Salvatika village under Kosala, who argued with the

Buddha that a self-realised person like him should not share his wisdom with the commoners as it would unnecessarily confuse simple people faithfully following the traditional ways. The Buddha countered by suggesting that if a wise man had a winning idea which could do good to humanity, he owed it to himself and society to teach it to all, even if it went against the grain of established beliefs.

The Buddha was not a social revolutionary and crusader against caste in the modern mould, but his social and political philosophy clearly stood against caste and brahmanism. This was eloquently expressed in the *Vasala sutta* of the *Sutta Nipata* (verse no. 135):

Not by birth does one become an outcaste,
Not by birth one becomes a brahman,
By deeds one becomes an outcaste,
By deeds one becomes a brahman.

The Buddhist Pali texts, it is important to understand, used *brahman* as a term of reverence and not in a caste sense. Uma Chakravarti's incisive study of early Buddhism makes this clear:

The Buddhists, as is usual with them, use the vocabulary of the brahmanas which they infuse with their own meaning. Chandala is used by the Buddhists to express a moral value and not to indicate low birth. In a hard-hitting attack on the brahmanas Buddha turns the table on them. He applies the term brahmana chandala for a brahmana who leads an immoral and depraved existence but claims at the same time that he can remain undefiled and pure, like the fire which burns unclean things but remains pure in spite of it. (1996: 107)

It is to be noted that during his time the caste system and social hierarchies were in the formative phase and not yet crystallised. While the brahmans had started asserting identity of individuals and professional groups based an ascribed varna status, the society at large had not yet accepted birth-based status group. Chakravarti's study of the period establishes that the brahmanical varna stratification was more a theoretical concept than put into actual practice. In contrast to the brahmanical texts, the term varna (Pali *vanna*) appears in the Buddhist texts only in the abstract – here no one is ever described as belonging to any particular varna by birth.

Chakravarti verifies that only two of the social groups, the khattiyas and brahmans, of the brahmanical scheme are verifiable as existing categories in the Buddhist texts. The categories *vessa* and *sudda*, she stresses, occur only in passages where there is a theoretical discussion about caste.

In the brahmanical texts the vessa *is associated with agriculture, cattle-keeping, and trade, and the* sudda *with service. But nowhere in the Buddhist texts are people or groups occupied with agriculture, cattle-keeping or trade, referred to as vessas, or those associated with service referred to as suddas. Instead the Buddhist texts associated agriculture with the* gahapati, *the cattle keeper is described as a* gopaka, *and the term* vanijja *is used for the trader. . . . Similarly while there are no suddas there are innumerable references to dasas and kammakaras who are associated not with service of the higher vannas but with providing labour for their masters who are almost invariably gahapatis. . . . The significant factor in Buddhist society for purposes of identification, particularly for the service groups, were the occupational divisions among people. The function actually performed by a person provided the basic identity of individuals.* (ibid.: 106-7)

Though the society of the Buddha's time was not yet a fully developed caste society, his opposition to the emergent forces of caste and brahmanism, which he perceived as dangerous and destructive, was uncompromising and total. The Buddha emphasised time and again, employing beautiful and telling metaphors to drive home the point, that caste had no place in his religious order:

As the great streams, O disciples, however many they be, the Ganga, Yamuna, Aciravati, Sarabhu, Mahi, when they reach the great ocean, lose their old name and their old descent, and bear the only name, 'the great ocean', so also my disciples (of all castes and social categories) when they, in accordance with the law and doctrine which the order has preached, forsake their home and go into homelessness, lose their own name and their old paternity, and bear only one designation, shraamans *(ascetics). . . .* (the Udana, V, 5; also the Vinaya Pitaka, II, 9; see Oldenberg 1927: 152)

It was the basic egalitarian character of Buddhism that earned it brahmanical contempt and antipathy. The brahmanical antagonism against Buddha and his people ran deep and it was nowhere more candidly expressed than in the Buddha's well-known dialogue with Vasettha, a brahman who had come to him with the intention of becoming a Buddhist. In the *Agganna-sutta* of the *Digha Nikaya*, Vasettha reveals that the exceptional brahmans like him who embrace Buddhism are held in great contempt by their brahman relatives. The Buddha asks him to explain in 'what terms the brahmans blame and revile you'. Vasettha replies as follows:

Sir, the brahmans say this: 'The brahman is the highest caste, the others are low; only the brahmans are fair-complexioned and well-born, the non-brahmans are dark and low-born. Brahmans are own sons of Brahma, born of his mouth, offspring of Brahma, created by Brahma, heirs of Brahma. But you have forsaken the best social rank, and have gone over to the low-born . . . the shaven beggars, the menials, those black-skinned and footborn Buddhists, the offscouring of your kinsman's heels. . . .' (see Rhys Davids, *Dialogues* III: 78)

The Buddha laughs off the brahmanic claim of racial superiority, and makes this famous retort: 'Surely, Vasettha, the brahmans . . . forget their own heritage? For the women of the brahman are seen to have periods, to be pregnant, to give birth and to suckle babies, and yet those very brahmans born out of vaginas, say that they are born out of the mouth of Brahma.' Resorting to this rather combative style, very untypical of the Buddha, he goes on to assert that no one is inferior or superior by birth; there are good people and bad people in all ranks – 'khattiya, brahman, vessa, sudda'. . . . 'Now seeing, Vasettha, that both bad and good qualities, blamed and praised respectively by the wise, are distributed among each of the four classes, the wise do not admit those claims which the brahmans put forward' (ibid.: 78-9).

This conversation and the Buddha's arguments that followed thereafter in the *Agganna-sutta* need some elaboration as they are resonant with deeper significance. There is more here than meets the eye. The Buddha was also known as Sakyamuni – the sage of the Sakyas – and his followers, the Buddhist monks, were often described as Sakyaputras – the sons of the Sakyas – as Gautam came from the Sakyas, a distinct ethnic group, who though living in the outskirts of the Vedic civilisation regarded themselves as kshatriyas. However, as Vasettha's description clearly brings out, the brahmans dismiss the Buddha, his people and his followers as being in effect the despised shudras, the lowest rank of menials. As Carrithers has pointed out, brahman contempt of the Buddha and his people smack of what we would today call racial prejudice. With biased stereotypes, the brahmans manage to heap scorn on the Buddha, his people and his followers all at once (Carrithers 1992: 128). They saw the world as neatly divided into different species: a brahman is not just a priest by vocation, but inherently endowed with purity of birth, physical beauty, personal purity, virtue and wisdom. Likewise, calling someone a shudra not only brings out the image of a manual worker but someone condemned to misery and slavery. It is a view which has the divisiveness and simplicity of apartheid, where there are no individuals, only the whites (brahmans) and the blacks (shudras).

It is this mentality that the Buddha opposed. Viewing the dialogue with Vasettha in proper perspective, his reply, involving some basic knowledge of biology against the brahman's theological knowledge (where he is born of Brahma's mouth) is, to use Carrither's words, not only 'extraordinarily apt' but also 'effective'. It appears that stung by the brahmanical abuse and insult, the Buddha, for a change, drops his equanimity.

There are critics who have pointed out that the Buddha did not oppose the caste ideology, he merely tried to replace the superiority of the brahmans by the khattiyas, since he himself was a khattiya. This argument does not hold much water as he has accorded the top rank to the khattiyas not without a profound irony. He emphasises that the khattiyas are the best only for those who believe in lineage; this is not *his* criterion of judging an individual. This may be a ploy he employs at times to put the arrogant brahman firmly in his place. At one level, in a rhetorical flourish, he may be suggesting that even on the basis of birth you (the brahman) are not the best. However, after taking a pot-shot at the imperious brahman, he makes it quite clear that the supreme individuals are those people – irrespective of their caste and lineage – who represent the finer qualities of wisdom and compassion. While stressing the search for truth the Buddha tells Vasettha that he and others like him who have left their past identities of family, caste, and clan now can say they are 'strivers, sons of the Sakyas'. And the seasoned followers of the Buddha can say with pride 'we are true sons of the Buddha, born of his mouth, born of the truth, made by the truth, heirs of the truth'. Thus the Buddha turns the entire brahmanical structure upside down and then presents an alternative vision of a casteless society. He is also the one to put the casteless principle into practice; he gathers his followers from all castes and calls them sons of the Sakyas, making no distinction between them on the basis of background.

Devastating remarks about the pretensions of brahmans are scattered through many parts of the Pali canonical literature. The early Buddhist texts refer to disputations of the Buddha with Ambattha and other brahmans on superiority being based on birth and hereditary status. Asserting that an individual's assessment should take into account only his worth, the Buddha said:

In the supreme perfection in wisdom and righteousness, Ambattha, there is no reference to the question either of birth, or of lineage or of the pride which says: 'You are held as worthy as I', or 'You are not held as worthy as I'. . . . For whosoever, Ambattha, are in bondage to the notions of birth or of lineage, or to the pride of social position, or of connection by marriage, they are far from the best wisdom and righteousness. It is only by having got rid of all such bondage that one can realise for himself that supreme perfection in wisdom and in conduct. (Rhys Davids, *Dialogues* I: 123)

Despite relentless pressure from brahmanical quarters, the Buddha remained steadfast in his commitment to the social and religious welfare of all, without distinction of birth, caste or (later even) gender. He supported the 'lower' castes, the weak and the despised in two ways – first and ideologically, by taking a position against caste; and second, at the practical level, by admitting persons of all castes and creeds including the untouchables and women in his sangha. *Theragatha* and *Therigatha*, the Pali texts which form part of *Khuddaka Nikaya*, mention many persons of the 'lowest' castes (including a scavenger) occupying important places in the Buddhist order. Upali, accepted as the chief authority after the Buddha himself, was formerly a barber. There was a separate order of sisters, with their own organisation. Punna and Punnika were earlier slave girls, while Sunita was a Pukkusa, one of the 'low' tribes. Nanda was formerly a cowherd and Dhania a potter. The two Panthakas were actually outcastes as they were born of the union of a slave with a woman of high caste. Sati, Kapa, Sumangalamata, and Subha were all born of parents belonging to 'low' castes.

The Buddha also received into his order women like Ambapali, the royal courtesan of Vaishali, his foster-mother Mahaprajapati Gautami, as well as the 'low' caste girl Prakriti, vagabonds like the unnamed man of Rajgriha, and robbers like Angulimala. He did not observe any distinction as to caste or gender – after having overcome his earlier prejudice/reluctance to recruit women – in admitting persons to his organisation or preaching his dhamma.

On the basis of such evidence, Rhys Davids concludes: 'As regards his own order, over which alone he had complete control, he ignores completely and absolutely all advantages or disabilities arising from birth, occupation and social status, and sweeps away all barriers and disabilities arising from the arbitrary rules of mere ceremonial or social impurity' (Rhys Davids, *Dialogues* I: 102). Had the Buddha's views won the day, the evolution of social grades and distinctions would have gone differently and the caste system would never have been built up in India (ibid.: 107).

PARADIGM OF HUMAN LIBERATION

Early Buddhism championed humanist and egalitarian values. The Buddha was not living in today's world and there is no point in judging his precepts and practices by the modern democratic principles. However, the social dimension of early Buddhism that emerges from the historical records was definitely radical for that time and era. Its social vision threw new light on social relations. As the Buddha says, the world is in a perpetual process of coming into existence and passing away, so be ever-vigilant to know what is dying out and what is coming into existence. His last words to his disciples were *vayadhamma sankhara, appamadena vattetha* – 'worldly objects are transitory; be on your guard' (the *Mahaparinibbana-sutta*). It was an exhortation to reject the outdated and accept the new. Applied to both individual and social levels, it was a ringing call for transformation and wholesome change. Without this, individual and social progress was not possible.

Seventh century Buddhist logician Dharmakirti has given a devastating expression to the quintessential Buddhist opposition to the brahmanic teachings in his masterpiece, *Pramanavarttika*:

> *Vedapramanyam kasyachit kartivadah*
> *snane dharmechha jativadavalepah,*
> *Santaparambhah papahanaya cheti*
> *dhvastaprajnanam panchalingani jadye.*
>
> The unquestioned authority of the Vedas;
> the belief in a world-creator;
> the quest for purification through ritual bathings;
> the arrogant division into castes;
> the practice of mortification to atone for sin;
> – these five are the marks of the crass stupidity of witless men. (cited in Jaini 2001: 47)

Worth, and not birth was the Buddhist criterion to judge an individual. In Buddhism, *nibbana* – freedom from pain and misery – is not the monopoly of the chosen few but can be attained by all, irrespective of caste or gender, provided the right type of means are employed. By acquiring character, compassion, and wisdom, every individual can secure his salvation. The Buddha also talks about *kamma* (*karma* in Sanskrit) but his concept of *kamma* is that what one has sown in this life, one must reap here and now. One cannot escape the consequences of one's actions by indulging in religious rites and performance. Buddhism does not believe in divine intervention or pre-destination. Only by one's own efforts and will-power can one achieve liberation. Even the Buddha had to pass through a travail of spirit to attain enlightenment. His personal name was Gautam Siddhartha, the Buddhahood was an attainment which he acquired after waging an epic struggle to overcome his weaknesses. The state of joyous liberation he achieved has been and can be reached by others too. There is, however, not one magic formula or one illuminated path that can guarantee everyone's freedom; therefore, the Buddha wanted his followers to be a light unto themselves – *atta-dipo bhava*.

Speaking in the people's language, and employing the simplest of words to convey his ideas to the common man, Gautam Buddha attacked brahmanical obscurantism and declared all rituals irrelevant and unnecessary for a good life. His discourses, delivered in plain style, often took the form of Socratic questioning and parables in which he spurned metaphysical mysticism and abstract speculation, and constantly reminded his listeners not to fall in the word-trap, stressing that the meaning was important, not the word – *arthah pratisaranama na vyanjanam*. Aware of the mischief of brahmanical intellectualism and verbal jugglery, of the immense pretensions of the clever, he often cautioned his followers against the trap of theorising. In other words, his creative ideas were addressed to the whole of society, especially to the weak and the underprivileged, who were more susceptible to the designs of the brahmanical elite.

Seen in the modern perspective, the Buddhist attitude towards women, however, was not very progressive. Conditioned by the patriarchal spirit of the time, the Buddha's views on women were problematic and ambivalent. He saw them as weak and inferior. Ananda, his favourite disciple, who had a more enlightened view on women, had to persuade him to allow women to join the sangha. However, the Buddha's positive response to women's demand to be admitted in the sangha was commendable, and in keeping with the liberal and more inclusive culture that Buddhism was creating against brahmanism. Transcending the contemporary anti-women ideology, the Buddha finally accepted the woman's right to develop her personality, acquire knowledge, and attain salvation. Though women were not accorded equality with men within the sangha, their arrival on the hitherto prohibited area was a welcome step. Freed of the bonds of family and household drudgery, the restless women tried to make most of the new life.

As Mrs. Rhys Davids underlines in her Introduction to *Psalms of the Early Buddhists*, it is difficult to imagine today the emancipative experience many women felt after joining the sangha. The bereaved mother, the childless widow were emancipated from grief and agony; the wife of rich man from the emptiness of an idle life of luxury; the poor man's wife from the oppressive poverty; the young girl from the humiliation of being handed over to the highest bidder; the thoughtful woman from the ban imposed on her intellectual development by convention and tradition. Escape, deliverance, freedom from suffering – mental, moral, domestic, social – from some situation that has become intolerable, are poignantly expressed in many songs of the *Therigatha* (Mrs. Rhys Davids 1980: xxiv). The percentages of bhikkhunis' hymns in which the goal achieved is envisaged as emancipation, is considerably higher than the corresponding proportion in the hymns by the bhikkhus (ibid.). We see in the songs their celebration of the newly-found freedom. Sumangalamata joyously exclaims:

> O Woman well set free! How free I am,
> How wonderfully free from kitchen drudgery,
> Free from the harsh grip of hunger,
> And from empty cooking pots,
> Free too of that unscrupulous man,
> The weaver of sunshades.
> Calm now and serene I am,
> All lust and hatred purged.
> To the shades of the spreading trees I go
> And contemplate my happiness. (see Ilaiah 2000: 189)

While Kisagotami lovingly portrays the Buddha as a kind and noble friend (*kalyan-mitta*), some women intimately relate themselves to their mentor, and claim spiritual fatherhood in him. Uttama exults:

> Buddha's daughter I,
> Born of his mouth, his blessed word, I stand!
> (Mrs. Rhys Davids 1980: 37)

And so does Sundari:

> Thou art Buddha! thou art Master! and thine,
> Thy daughter am I, issue of thy mouth. (ibid.: 141)

In the context of women's subjugation of the period, the Buddha's gesture of sympathy and understanding gave the unhappy, harassed women a new hope and confidence. With the change came the positive energies and understanding to lead a new and promising life. Vasitthi's verse beautifully expresses it:

> Now all my sorrows are hewn down, cast out,
> Uprooted, brought to utter end,
> In that I now can grasp and understand
> The base on which my miseries were built. (ibid.: 80)

The Buddhist recognition of dignity and equality of human beings has won the hearts of generations of people, especially from the subordinated communities. As the Buddha symbolises the possibilities of an egalitarian alternative to the discriminatory brahmanism, he has a lasting appeal to the subjugated segments of Indian society. Buddhism was able to fire the imagination of Ambedkar in the twentieth century, inspiring him to author his classic *The Buddha and His Dhamma,* and embrace this religion with millions of marginalised dalits. Ambedkar turned the Buddha's historic resistance against brahmanism into his own socio-ideological quest for a civil religion of equality, liberty and fraternity. But even before Ambedkar many leaders from subaltern strata had recognised in Buddhism an antithesis to discriminatory brahmanism. One such leader was Iyothee Thass (1845-1914) of Tamil Nadu who had identified the emancipatory potential of Buddhism (see also Chapter 6). It was in fact Iyothee Thass who, by founding the South Indian Buddhist Association with several branches both within and outside India as early as 1910, had pioneered the movement of Buddhist regeneration in India (Aloysius 1998).

The engaged Buddhists do not see the Buddha as a beatific mystic eternally meditating under a banyan tree, but as a compassionate hero intensely engaged with the sufferings of the marginalised. Daya Pawar's elegant poem, *Buddha,* brings it out beautifully:

> *I never see you in*
> *Jeta's garden*
> *sitting with eyes closed*
> *in meditation, in the lotus position,*
> *or*
> *in the caves of Ajanta and Ellora*
> *with stone lips sewn shut*
> *sleeping the last sleep of your life.*
> *I see you*
> *walking, talking,*
> *breathing softly, healingly,*
> *on the sorrow of the poor, the weak,*
> *going from hut to hut*
> *in the life-destroying darkness,*

> *torch in hand,*
> *giving the sorrow*
> *that drains the blood*
> *like a contagious disease*
> *a new meaning.* (tr. Zelliot and Karve, see Joshi 1986: 159)

A similar sentiment is expressed in Bhagwan Sawai's poem entitled *Tathagata* where Buddha is artistically resurrected as the friend and redeemer of the underdog:

> . . .
> *Tathagata*
> *I've come to you*
> *my sorrows interred in my bones*
> *bringing my darkness within the radius of your light*
> *Take me within your fold, away from this darkness*
> *Out there, I've worn myself out, slogging in their carnival*
> *losing my self-identity*
> . . .
> *Tathagata*
> *Ask no questions, questions are alien to me,*
> *I do not know myself*
> *Out there, there was nothing but darkness and rocky muteness*
> *So transmigrate into me from that picture*
> *in flesh and blood, into my effusive being.*
> . . .
> *Tathagata*
> *I do not want you in your yogic postures as in the pictures*
> *before whom I could place my offerings of flowers and prayers*
> *Pardon the slaves of fetishism*
> *Who created idols in your name and festivals.*
> (tr. Radha Iyer, in Dangle 1992)

The new Buddhist movement that Ambedkar spearheaded has indeed provided an alternative to the oppressed to escape from subjugation and humiliation. In every society, religion has been a major source of power and culture and also a supplier of a value system that promotes social integration. Despite modernist prophets of 'doom', religion has neither vanished nor lost its significance in social life around the world. Ambedkar's decision to embrace Buddhism was animated by this reality. Ambedkar argues, as did sociologist Durkheim in *The Elementary Forms of the Religious Life*, that as religion embodies 'sacred morality' it serves the function of social integration in society. Without it, there would be anarchy. The other option, dictatorship, is also dangerous. In anarchy and dictatorship, liberty is lost. A free and democratic society, therefore, needs a new, egalitarian and rationalistic religion. Such a religion Ambedkar found in Buddha's dhamma. While embracing Buddhism, he emphasised that 'religion is necessary for people in distress. The poor man lives on hope. The source of life is hope. If this hope is destroyed, then how will life go on?' That Ambedkar was not wrong in his 'hope' is borne out by this eye-witness account of the famous Buddhist conversion that he led in 1956 at Nagpur:

All of them, even the poorest, came clad in the spotless white shirts and saris that had been prescribed for the occasion by their beloved leader. Some families had had to sell trinkets in order to buy their new clothes and meet the expenses of the journey, but they had made the sacrifice gladly, and set out for Nagpur with songs on their lips and the hope of a new life in their hearts. . . . Some stayed with relations in the Mahar ghettoes, while others were accommodated in school buildings that had been taken over for the purpose. Many simply camped on any patch of waste ground they could find. . . . By the end of the week 4,00,000 men, women, and children had poured into Nagpur, with the result that the population had nearly doubled and the white-clad Untouchables had virtually taken over the city. The Caste Hindus, who were accustomed to think of the Untouchables as dirty and undisciplined, gazed with astonishment at the spectacle of tens upon tens of thousands of clean, decently dressed, well behaved and well organised people in whom they had difficulty in recognising their former slaves and serfs. (Sangharakshita 1986: 129-30)

The emancipatory, exhilarating experience the dalits felt after embracing Buddhism is corroborated by many of them. One such description is given by writer-critic Shankarrao Kharat:

I have accepted the Buddhist Dhamma. I am a Buddhist now. I am not a Mahar nor an untouchable nor even a Hindu. I have become a human being. . . . I am equal with all. I am not low born or inferior. . . . With the acceptance of Buddhism my untouchability has been erased. *The chains of untouchability which shackled my feet have now been shattered. Now I am a human being like all other... I am now free. I have become a free citizen of Independent India.* (cited in Shah 2001)

Alternative Vision of Social and Political Institutions

The Buddha was not merely a spiritual leader but also one of the earliest and most outstanding political philosophers. His theories of the state and kingship, too, were morally inspired and socially committed. His ideal society had no place for inequality or poverty. In his opinion the role of state and power was crucial to the creation of a better social environment. It was the duty of those wielding power to ensure justice and a means of subsistence to everyone. His views on this, culled from the *Samyutta Nikaya,* are forthright: 'It is possible really to rule as a king in righteousness, without killing or causing to be killed, without practising oppression or permitting oppression to be practised, without suffering pain or inflicting on another.'

As is well known, the Buddha himself came from the Sakya clan which had a republican polity; his father was at one time the elected head or one of the heads of the state. Born and brought up in a democratic milieu, it was not unusual for the Buddha to become a champion of republicanism. The structure of the Buddhist organisation founded by him was based on the republican principles. It gave opportunity to all the members to express their views freely.

It is not without significance that kings in general are treated with contempt in the early Buddhist literature. The power-obsessed kings here invoke the image of cruelty and stupidity and are put into a list of disasters – floods, fire, famine, and other such calamities – to be avoided at all cost. This is understandable, both in historical circumstances of the time when monarchies were swallowing up the smaller republics, and in the universal perspective of how kings exercise brute power. Early Buddhism envisioned a kind of state in which the ruler was chosen by people and worked at their behest. As the *Aganna-sutta* of *Digha Nikaya* attests, Buddhism advocated the theory of *Mahasammata*, the Great Agreed On or the Great Elect. This was a polity based on agreement between the people and the person whom they elected as king (see Rhys Davids, *Dialogues* III: 77-94).

Since the 'Great Elect' received his authority from the people there was the assumption that political authority lay in the people. It were the people who fixed for him a portion of their produce in lieu of his services. The king, elected to serve the state, was supposed to remain in office as long as he satisfied people's needs; and, in return he was entitled to collect taxes. Here, the king's power was in direct proportion to his social responsibility. There was even a provision to dislodge the king who did not deliver the goods. This is reinforced by a Buddhist sutta that tells how disaster strikes a kingdom in which the ruler fails to provide succour to the poor. Such a king was not allowed to be in office. A scintillating commentary on the theory of 'Great Elect' was made by one Aryadeva, a Buddhist ideologue, in these words:

What superciliousness is thine, (O King!) thou who are a (mere) servant of the multitude and who receivest the sixth part (of the produce) as thine wages. (see Varma 1974: 195)

The Buddha underscored the connection between economic welfare and social morality. Crime could not be suppressed merely through force and punishment, he emphasised, pointing out that poverty was a major cause of immorality and crime. Charity and donations to anti-social elements in order to lure them away from crime would only exacerbate evil action. His recommendation, therefore, was to improve economic condition of people by supplying seed and food to agriculturists and furnishing necessary capital to traders. He also suggested that the state servants should be paid adequately to stop corruption. He thought that only a holistic and integrated approach would generate a conducive atmosphere for development of the state and its citizens. His suggestion that the surplus accumulated should be spent in public welfare such as digging wells, water ponds and planting groves along the trade routes is a remarkably modern view of political economy.

In his study of the Buddha as a political philosopher and system-builder, Ilaiah has shown how he had created the sangha system as an organisational and institutional alternative (based on dhamma) to the brahmanical social structure and authoritarian monarchial state. While for the brahmanical law-makers the maintenance of varna-dharma and adherence to caste rules were the cornerstone of justice, the Buddhist justice system was based on the principles of equality and individual freedom. Its notion of justice was a broadly secular concept which struck at the root of the hierarchical division of society. Admission to the sangha was based on the criterion of character. Likewise, the laws and norms pertaining to the maintenance of discipline and harmony within the sangha was anchored in equalitarian values – one person one vote, and one vote one value. Leading by example, the Buddha himself functioned as one among equals. Every issue within the sangha was decided either by consensus or majority opinion. The administration of monasteries – management, maintenance, recording of important items, accounting of money and grain collected as alms, and commodities produced collectively – bore democratic functioning. Property of the sangha was owned collectively. The Buddha had no quarrel with the division of labour as production needs special expertise in each field, but he was opposed to the breaking up of society into immobile social groups, just as he was against the degrading of productive labour (Ilaiah 2000: 218-20).

The Buddha was the first major proponent of peaceful co-existence among states. He prevented a war between the Sakyas and Kolias. He also tried, though unsuccessfully, to prevent the war between the king of Kosala and the Sakyas. Later, King Ashoka, inspired by Buddhist pacifism, adopted this doctrine of peace. Under the Buddhist influence, the monarch of the mightiest military strength of his time preferred *dhammaghosha* (affirmation of righteousness) over *bherighosha* (proclamation of war).

Buddhist Ascendancy and India's Past Greatness

It is not generally acknowledged that by striking a fine balance between the pursuit of individual growth and the wider objective of liberating humanity from suffering, it was the Buddha and Buddhism that made India a great cultural force in the ancient world. India's achievements in republican statecraft, in the arts and literature, and in cultural contacts with the world could be traced to the liberating power of the grand movement started by the Buddha. It was Buddhism that taught mankind the respect for animal life and the importance of *ahimsa* (non-injury) to others. It was the Buddhists who built the earliest hospitals for men as well as for animals. It was under the Buddhist influence that most Indians learnt to privilege mercy over mindless and wasteful sacrifice.

In the third century BC, Ashoka's missionaries, carrying the Buddhist message, fanned out in different directions. His son Mahendra and daughter Sanghamitra went to Sri Lanka. Other Buddhist monks in later centuries travelled to Greece in the west, to Tibet in the north, and to China and Japan in the east, where Buddhism took firm roots. The history of the propagation and diffusion of Buddhism is a record of kindness and selfless service. It spread, quietly and gently, around the world on the strength of its universal message, without ever using force or coercive method. Over the centuries Buddhism took the shape of a global movement. (The accompanying chronological illustration explains it.)

THE SPREAD OF BUDDHISM

c. 563-483 BC	Life of the Buddha.
c. 370	The Vaishali Council registers divisions following rival interpretation of Buddhism.
c. 255	King Ashoka converts to Buddhism.
c. 240	Sri Lanka embraces Buddhism.
c. 150	Menander, the Greek king, promotes Buddhism in northwest India and Afghanistan.
c. AD 65	Buddhist missionaries arrive – and get a toehold – in China.
c. 120	Buddhist Council in Kashmir standardises major texts of Mahayana school.
c. 120-62	Kanishka, the Kushana king, patronises Buddhism in Gandhara, Punjab and Sind.
c. 200	Buddhism enters Indonesia.
c. 400	Buddhism arrives in Korea.
c. 400-10	Fa Hsien visits India at the behest of the Chinese emperor, to collect authentic Buddhist texts.
c. 400-500	Buddhism reaches Burma.
c. 540	Buddhism arrives in Japan.

c. 640-5	Hsuan Tsang in India; King Harshavardhan accepts Buddhism.
c. 850	Buddhism penetrates China.
c. 1300	Buddhism adopted in Thailand.
c. 1890	Faint beginning of Buddhist revival in India with establishment of the Mahabodhi Society and South Indian Buddhist Association.
c. 1900	Buddhism reaches America and Europe.
1956	The Ambedkar-led mass conversion in India.

Buddhism developed a precise system of logical inquiry and injected a scientific and rational outlook in Indian intellectual life. Leading ideologues of Vedic-brahmanism borrowed many threads from Buddhist teaching, used them to strengthen their own defences, and then in their characteristic vein disclaimed indebtedness, and instead tried to write off Buddhism as a mere offshoot of the Vedic-Upanishadic tradition. Blunt through it might seem to suggest, it was Buddhism which taught the basic lessons in humanity to the brahmanical teachers. Actually, many Buddhist ethical verses in Pali were rendered into Sanskrit and interpolated in the Vedic-Upanishadic tradition to show off its humanist face. Such borrowed and isolated verses or maxims are often cited by the modern votaries of this problematic tradition to take on their critics. One famous example they never fail to quote is 'may all beings be well and happy . . .' :

Sarvepi sukhina santu, / sarve santu niramaya
sarve bhadrani pashchantu, / ma kashchit dukhbha bhavata.

As Angar Ee (1994: 53) claims, the above lines in Sanskrit are the verbatim imitation of the original Buddhist verse in Pali:

Sabbe satta sukhi hontu, / sabbe hontuch khemino,
sabbe bhadrani paschantu, / ma kacchi dukha magame.

It is also to be noted that whatever reforms took place in brahmanical Hinduism, which played a crucial role in ensuring its survival, was largely a result of the intellectual and moral stimulus provided by Buddhism. 'The so-called high Hindu ethics and personal morality is very largely a Buddhist achievement; a lasting reform and refinement inherited by later forms of brahmanism' (S. C. Sarkar, cited in Walker 1983, vol. I: 186).

The Buddhist ascendancy from the 4th century BC to the 6th century AD (when ancient India was at its creative best), was not the mythologised Hindu India, it was the Buddhist India. During the millennium Buddhism remained the major determinant of Indian civilisation, though in conflict throughout with the hegemonic brahmanism which it opposed (Omvedt 2003: 125). The early republican states and many political and administrative systems are traceable to Buddhist influence. Three of India's great kings in the ancient period – Ashoka, Kanishka and Harshavardhan – were Buddhists. The first systematic historical records in India were kept by Buddhists. India's two earliest and greatest universities at Taxila and Nalanda, were Buddhist centres of learning. In the realm of language and literature, practically every Indian language, begins with Buddhist works (Walker, op. cit.). The Brahmi script which Ashoka used in his inscriptions and from which the Devanagari of Sanskrit derives, the emergence of the Prakrit languages as a vehicle of powerful regional cultures, and the impressive communication system across the length and breath of the subcontinent, all owe their indebtedness in one or other way to the Buddhist movement.

Even the first known major poems in the classical Sanskrit were written by a Buddhist, Ashvaghosha. Similarly, the first Sanskrit drama was authored by Ashvaghosha. The art of fable (in the *Jataka* stories) is Buddhist in origin. Likewise, Buddhist architecture flourished centuries before the earliest known brahmanical temples, and many Buddhist features were incorporated into Hindu temples from Buddhist models. The earliest sculpture seen at Bharhut, Sanchi, Bodh Gaya, Amaravati, and other places is Buddhist. The most famous of the early paintings in the history of Indian art are the Buddhist frescoes at Ajanta.

The Mauryan King Ashoka (269-232 BC) may have been a product of the Buddhist ideology. He represents one of the few rulers in history for whom absolute power did not spell absolute corruption. Beginning as an emperor of conventional ruthlessness, he underwent a profound change of heart under the Buddhist influence after his blood-soaked victory in the Kalinga war in which several hundred thousand people were killed, maimed, and rendered homeless.

By pursuing a policy of peace and development-oriented pragmatism, Ashoka not only succeeded in knitting together most of the Indian subcontinent, a tremendous feat by any standards, especially in that period, but his reign also witnessed remarkable progress in economic and commercial activities, besides cultural and artistic efflorescence.

Indian art and architecture, not the least valuable part of Indian culture, may be said to begin from Asoka in spite of Indus Valley construction. The ruins of the Asokan palace at Patna were still impressive to Chinese pilgrims in AD *400, seemingly the work of genii and supernatural agencies. Asoka spent a great deal on much more important public works that would give no profit to the state. Hospitals were founded all over the empire for men and beasts, with free medical attendance at state expense. Shady groves, wells with steps leading down to the water, fruit orchards and resting-places were systematically laid out on all major trade routes. . . . These new constructions, which must have been an absolute godsend for the traders, especially because of the doctors and veterinaries available at many of the stations, were located not only in Asoka's domains but also beyond his frontiers. This agrees precisely with the duties of the benevolent chakravartin emperor which are mentioned in the Buddhist discourse.* (Kosambi 1992: 160-1)

Kosambi goes on to comment that such public welfare is not visualised in Kautilya's *Arthashastra*, the founding text of brahmanical statecraft. Ashokan structure of administration in the use of uniformity of civil and criminal laws along with the renouncement of violence and abjuration of war was a repudiation of imperialist policies advocated by Kautilya who considered upholding of discriminatory varna-dharma and conquest of neighbouring territories and peoples as the duty of a king. Obsessed with the authoritarian state, Kautilya wrote on espionage and violence. He was only interested in raising – and maximising – taxes and winning wars and not in social welfare. Unfortunately, it is Kautilyan vision of state characterised by *danda-niti*, the rule by force and coercion, that has caught the imagination of elite historians and 'nationalists' who do not consider the polity of Buddha and Ashoka Indian enough to be admired and emulated.

Above all, Ashoka's sterling contribution to Indian civilisation is his magnanimous policy of *dhamma* which held together a vast and heterogeneous empire. His *dhamma* – founded on the broader principles of social responsibility, uniform laws, tolerance, and non-violence – was deeply influenced by his personal faith in Buddhism. Yet Ashoka was not concerned with making Buddhism the state religion. His spirited quest for a just and egalitarian order made him set aside discriminatory ritualism and brahmanical privilege, but he never attacked brahmans and their freedom to teach in any way. Though himself a Buddhist, he adopted a policy of impartiality to all communities and religious sects. He asked the people to respect both shramans and brahmans. His broad-minded outlook and ability to comprehend the requirements of ruling diverse groups of people with understanding and compassion placed him in a league of his own. He was an outstanding example of what the Buddha called *chakkavatti dhammiko dhammaraja*, the righteous ruler.

Declaring that *savve munisse praja mama* (all people are my children), he laid stress on general observances such as consideration towards slaves, servants, aged people, and even to animals. The famous Ashokan inscriptions were not just an exercise in moral exhortations, they often consisted of reports upon the results so far achieved. Even allowing for official exaggeration, these results have been remarkable. Not only his officials acted with forbearance, but the people at large positively responded to the king's public-spirited measures. Rock Edict 5 reports that people are increasingly abstaining from the sacrificial slaughter of living creatures, and behaving properly with their relatives and elders. The king and the commoner were cooperating, and there was something approaching what may be called public order and decency. As an inscription proclaims, 'Now by reason of the practice of piety by his Majesty the King, the reverberation of the war-drums have become the reverberation of dhamma.' All in all, Ashoka's *dhamma* was aimed, in Romila Thapar's words, at building up an attitude of mind in which social responsibility and personal behaviour were of key importance; it was a plea for the recognition of the dignity of man and for a humanistic spirit in the activities of society (1984: 85).

Counter-Revolution and Brahmanical Revivalism

Apparently, Ashoka and his successors were not interested in giving the brahmans the preferential treatment or immunities that they had long been used to. Ashoka introduced the policy of uniformity in civil law (*vyavahara-samata*) and also in criminal law (*danda-samata*) for all sections of society. The officials (*rajukas*) were instructed to implement this policy (4th Pillar Edict). He also prohibited the killing of animals and birds and discouraged superfluous rituals performed by women (Inscription no. 6). All this was the result of the anti-sacrifice attitude of Buddhism which Ashoka and his successors had adopted. Then there was the neglect of Sanskrit, the exclusive language of brahmanic priestcraft. Such a policy hit the economic interests of the brahmans who depended on donations and gifts given to them in various rites and sacrifices. Under the Mauryan policy, the socio-cultural superiority of brahmans and the credibility of the sacerdotal literature that upheld it was being eroded. Take, for example, the question of genealogy and ancestry. These ideas were not of any concern to the Mauryas, and they never claimed a kshatriya status or even to belonging to a family of high status – a necessary brahmanic requirement for kingly position. No wonder the brahmanic texts describe the Mauryas as the *shudra-prayastv-adharmikah*, 'mainly shudras and unrighteous' (Thapar 1999: 12).

Led by Pushyamitra Shunga, the brahman commander of the last Mauryan king Brihadratha, brahmans hatched a conspiracy. Pushyamitra beheaded his master during a military parade in 185 BC. That the regicide – a rare example of military coup in the ancient India – was the brahmanical backlash against the egalitarian Buddhism is borne out by the fact that soon after his accession, Pushyamitra, who was a disciple of the famed grammarian Patanjali, revived Vedic sacrifices and performed the Rajasuya Yajna. Pushyamitra began the persecution of the Buddhists and the vandalisation of their monasteries and shrines. After burning scores of monasteries in and around Pataliputra he went to Sakala (Sialkot in West Punjab) and offered a reward of 100 *dinars* or gold pieces for the head of every Buddhist monk (Burnouf, *l'Introduction a l'Historie on Buddhisme Indien*, see Ambedkar, *BAWS*, vol. 3: 269; also Sastri and Srinivasachari 1980: 139). That he unleashed a reign of terror against the Buddhist monks and adherents is corroborated by many sources including the Tibetan and Chinese records. Works such as *Divyavadana,* and account of Tibetan historian Taranath, describe him as a ruthless persecutor of Buddhists and Buddhism. He destroyed and burnt all the viharas from Pataliputra to Sakala. As H. P. Shastri says, 'The condition of the Buddhists under the imperial sway of the Sungas, orthodox and bigoted, can be more easily imagined than described. From Chinese authorities it is known that many Buddhists still do not pronounce the name of Pushyamitra without a curse' (cited in Amdedkar, ibid.).

Rejecting the traditional trajectory of Indian history, Ambedkar in his incomplete book *The Revolution and Counter-Revolution in Ancient India* has made the conflict between Buddhism and Brahmanism the corner-stone of restructuring the past. Ambedkar has termed this regicide the beginning of a brahmanic counter-revolution marked by virulent orthodoxy. (The historian Jayaswal too, in his *Manu and Yajnavalkya,* has termed the brahmanical reaction the 'orthodox counter-revolution', see Datta 1983: 165.) The objective of the brahmanical forces was to destroy Buddhism, which was still powerful and popular among the masses, and to replace it with brahmanism and its discriminatory principles of social and political organisation. Ambedkar has underlined the fact that the process of the decline of Buddhism in India was a violent one, and not a process of gradual adjustment and absorption into Hinduism as is routinely portrayed by the elite historians. Ambedkar has fixed a date for the beginning of Smriti literature or Dharmashastras, which was to provide the framework of the varna-jati system, the laws relating to *anuloma* (husband's caste higher than wife's) and *pratiloma* (wife's caste higher than husband's) marriages, the systematic degradation of the vaishyas and shudras and the institutionalised subjugation of women. He cites various sources to prove that ascribing the *Manusmriti,* the most notorious brahmanical law-book, to the divinity and legendary name of Manu was an 'utter fraud':

The author of Naradasmriti writing in about the 4th century AD *knew the name of the author of Manusmriti and gives out the secret. Manu is the assumed name of Sumati Bhargava who is the real author of Manusmriti. . . . According to scholars whose authority cannot be questioned Sumati Bhargava must have composed the Code which he deliberately called Manusmriti between 170 BC and 150 BC. Now if one bears in mind the fact that the Brahmanic Revolution by Pushyamitra took place in 185 BC there remains no doubt that the code known as Manusmriti was promulgated by Pushyamitra as embodying the principles of Brahmanic Revolution against the Buddhist state of the Mauryas.* (BAWS, vol. 3: 270-1)

Ambedkar quotes some verses from the *Manusmriti* to show the author's naked antagonism to the Buddhists and Buddhism. This was fully supported by the brahmanical regime of Pushyamitra. He further argues that the brahmans exploited their monopoly over religious literature to reassert their social and political domination, and to crush Buddhism once and for all. Other brahman or brahmanised kings of the time followed Pushyamitra's lead by persecuting the Buddhist followers and destroying their monasteries and educational institutions. Ambedkar sees a striking parallel between the Muslim invasions of Hindu India and the brahmanic invasions of Buddhist India. The Muslim invaders of various stock – Arabs, Turks, Mongols and Afghans – fought for supremacy among themselves but were united in their common mission to destroy idolatry. Likewise, the brahmanic invaders of Buddhist India, the Shungas, the Kanvas and the Andhras fought among themselves for supremacy but had one common goal, to destroy Buddhism. The brahmanic invasions of Buddhism, in Ambedkar's view, were the more damaging. The Muslim invaders, he argues, destroyed only the outward symbols of Hinduism – the temples and *maths*, etc.; they did not cause any subversion of the principles and doctrines which governed the spiritual life of the people. The effect of the brahmanic invasions, however, was to thoroughly destroy the Buddhist principles that had been accepted and followed by the masses as the way of life (ibid.: 273-4). Armed with *shastra* (weapons) and shastras (scriptures), the resurgent brahmanism annihilated and drove out Buddhism as a living religion and occupied its place. Buddhism was 'smothered in the embrace of [brahmanic] Hindu inclusiveness long before the Muslims destroyed the monasteries' (Lannoy 1999: 336).

In his analysis of the destruction of Buddhism, Ambedkar,

significantly, has mentioned a 'subversion' theory. He did not substantiate it as he could not complete the book but the tone and tenor of his reconstruction of the past leaves no doubt that subversion involved the insidious role of the brahman-Buddhists. According to an eminent historian, 'From the very beginning the Order contained brahmins who might have [outwardly] renounced caste but retained their intellectual traditions. The current brahmin ideology (not ritual or cults) was often taken for granted, just as the brahmins had given up beef-eating and accepted non-killing (*ahimsa*) as their main ideal. The higher philosophies of both Buddhist and brahmin began to converge in essence. Neither admitted the material world as real' (Kosambi 1992: 179). In other words, they continued to be brahmans as well as shramans and probably observed their caste exclusivism as well. They produced dubious doctrines akin to the doctrines and metaphysics of brahmanism which culminated in the Mahayana school which increasingly became dominant and very nearly succeeded in destroying the basic epistemology and spirit of early Buddhism. The Buddha had not said that things did not exist. His theory of causation or impermanence stated that things were constantly coming into being and going out of existence. The Mahayanists interpreted this to mean that since everything is momentary, therefore, nothing exists. Along with this exposition of *shoonyavada*, the theory of void, the Mahayanists transformed the Buddha himself into a god and introduced his several incarnations, along with innumerable deities and even hobgoblins into Buddhism which provided scope for ritualism and priestcraft.

Speculation regarding the nature of the Bodhisattva, or the Buddha after death, a question which the Buddha himself had considered metaphysical and left unanswered, became the dominant theme of Mahayana. The Buddha's original concepts of *kamma* and *nibbana* too were substantially distorted. Buddhism was turned into a cobweb of metaphysical speculation and superstition, very much like Vedic-brahmanism. The early Buddhism had successfully contested the Upanishadic idealism and relegated it to the margin, of the social and psychological make-up of the time. It was the Mahayanists who revived the Upanishadic idealism in the form of *shoonyavada*, which said that the world was a void. Out of this void emerged all kinds of superstitions and obscurantist ideas which gradually elbowed out rationality and the materialist outlook of early Buddhism. In a move of far-reaching consequences, the brahman-Buddhists also gave up the people's language Pali and adopted Sanskrit. Nehru observes,

Probably it was due to the Brahmins, who later joined it, that it developed more along philosophical and metaphysical lines. . . . It may have been due also chiefly to the Brahmin Buddhists that the Mahayana form developed. . . . Mahayana doctrine spread rapidly but it lost in quality and distinctiveness what it gained in extent. The monasteries became rich, centres of vested interests, and their discipline became lax. (1996: 175-9).

The magical, transcendental assertions of the Mahayana form of Buddhism and, to a lesser degree, the Hinayana's obsession with individual *nibbana*, was, in many ways, a travesty of the profound humanism and social radicalism of early Buddhism. The apologists for the brahmanical system found it convenient to quote contradictory examples from various forms of deformed Buddhism – such as the phenomena of Mahayani deification of the Buddha, and Tantraism and Lamaism of the later periods – to prove that there was no fundamental difference between brahmanism and Buddhism. The high priests of the Vedic tradition, in their desperation to eliminate Buddhism, even tried to co-opt the Buddha in the brahmanical mould by depicting him as the ninth avatar of Vishnu, even though, quite significantly, they did not set up his statues in their temples, or construct new viharas and stupas.

Various unsavoury developments in the later-day Buddhism gave the brahmanical authors a handle to use against the radicalism and searching philosophy of early Buddhism. In fact, the brahmanical ideologues like Shankara found the distorted notions of Buddhism attractive enough to appropriate and promote. They not only used Mahayana nihilism to kill the scientific spirit of early Buddhism but also established their *mayavada* (the theory of illusion) on the bedrock of *shoonyavada*. It is in this sense that Shankara, who coined the famous maxim *brahma satyam jagat mitthya* (This world is illusion; the Brahma, or the world beyond, is the only reality), is known as a crypto-Buddhist. This 'crypto-Buddhist', whose real ambition was to establish brahmanic dominance, described Buddhism as *sarvavainashika*, the destroyer of all, and declared that the Buddha was an 'enemy of people'. A sworn campaigner against Buddhism, Shankara is said to have founded his Sringeri-math on the site of a Buddhist monastery.

Ambedkar argues that the history of India before the Muslim invasions is a history of mortal conflict between brahmanism and Buddhism. Reiterating that the brahmanical counter-attack led by Pushyamitra Shunga was engineered by the brahman elite to overthrow Buddhism, Ambedkar does a post-mortem of the *Manusmriti*, which he terms as the veritable manifesto of triumphant brahmanism, and spells out its many damaging and lasting effects on Indian society (*BAWS*, vol. 3: 275).

A dispassionate dissection of the brahmanical literature and other sources between the first century BC and the third century AD, indeed bears out the revival of militant brahmanism. The revival had three characteristic features – hostility to all languages not Sanskrit; an intolerance towards all religions not the sanatani Vedic-brahmanism; and a prejudice against all castes not brahman (Walker 1983, vol. 1: 172). 'To the revival is due the sanskritisation of Indian thought and the brahmanisation of Indian social codes by the scribes' (ibid.: 363). The hallmark of the revival, and its only raison d'être, was the glorification, even the deification, of the brahman caste. The manifesto of the counter-movement was the *Manusmriti*, the first systematic treatment of brahmanical law. From now on brahmans declared themselves to be supermen, claiming respect, reverence, and worship even from kings and gods.

With the rise of aggressive brahmanism, political and administrative developments after the Mauryan period tended to feudalise the state apparatus. The most striking development, R. S. Sharma stresses in his well-known study of Indian feudalism, was the practice of land grants made to brahmans (*brahmadeya*) which was sanctified by the injunctions in the Dharmashastras, Puranas and epics. The *Mahabharata* devotes an entire section to praising such gifts of land (1980: 1-2). The practice became quite frequent and subsequently, particularly from the Gupta period, the grantees were given administrative rights as well. 'Thus the widespread practice of making land grants . . . paved the way for the rise of brahmana feudatories, who performed administrative functions not under the authority of the royal officers but almost independently' (ibid.: 4).

FORGERIES TO RE-CAST INDIAN CULTURE
IN THE BRAHMANICAL MOULD

It was in this period of triumphant brahmanism that the Vedas, smritis, epics and other religio-secular works were thoroughly revaluated and tampered with. It was a time for the wholesale recasting of Indian life and culture into the brahmanical mould. To this period belong the sanskritisation of the *Mahabharata, Ramayana,* and other bodies of literature (Walker, 1983, vol. I: 362-5). In order to buttress the brahmanical edifice, brahman authors suppressed facts, changed names, confused places and periods, and intermingled fact with fiction. This period witnessed wholesale counterfeiting of the Vedas and other scriptures, the accumulation of false data, and the creation of fictitious dynastic pedigrees. So inextricably is fact interwoven with fancy in Indian historical annals that the shramanic traditions, especially what many historians have rechristened 'Buddhist India', was completely suppressed, or at the best, grossly misrepresented in some fleeting references. Ashoka, who advocated equal 'reverence and liberality to shramans and brahmans', is depicted as a hated Buddhist and a despised shudra. 'The brahman records completely ignore him until the time when, ten or twelve centuries afterwards, all danger from his influence had passed definitely away.' Ashoka, whose name seems to have been expunged from Indian history, had to be discovered by James Prinsep in the nineteenth century on the basis of his rock edicts and other Indian and foreign records, especially the Ceylon chronicles.

Kosambi has drawn attention to the fact that the brahman never bothered to record and publish the caste laws he defended. The basis for a common law on the principles of equality was lost. Justice and jurisprudence were reduced to a farce. 'Crime and sin stand hopelessly confused, while juristic principles are drowned in an amazing mass of religious fable which offers ridiculous justification for any stupid observance.' The use of Sanskrit as the language of the rituals, and royal genealogies concocted for the ruling chiefs and aspiring kings for a price (including the promise to defend the caste order) helped create a pan-India brahman elite. These pandits, however, never showed any interest in a study and analysis of various guilds and city records that existed through the ages, nor did they bother to develop social morality:

Indian culture lost the contributions that these numerous groups (tribal, clan, jati caste, guild, and perhaps civic) could have made. The civilising and socialising work of the Buddha and of Asoka was never continued. The tightening of caste bonds and of caste exclusiveness threw away the possibility of finding some common denominator of justice and equity for all men regardless of class, profession, caste, and creed. As a concomitant, almost all Indian history is also obliterated. (Kosambi 1992: 173)

The genesis of Sanskrit literature is traceable to this period. Up to then, there had been no literary work in Sanskrit. Sanskrit was revered as the sacred language of the gods in which there was no place for 'profane' worldly literature. It was a contrived, inflexible and incommunicable language, jealously guarded by the self-strengthening orthodoxy who used it as a vehicle of sacerdotal gobbledygook. Pali and Prakrit, with their many regional varieties, were the spoken and written languages in the north, while Dravidian languages were the means of communication in the south of the Vindhyas.

The *Mahabharata* and the *Ramayana* were long current in the Prakrits before they were rendered in Sanskrit. According to Keith, they were re-written in Sanskrit, involving translations and elaborations of Prakrit originals, in the early years before and after the beginning of the Christian era. Tinkering with the texts of the *Mahabharata* is evident from scientific scrutiny. As Walker has pointed out, the conversion of the original heroic adventures into a sort of brahmanical bible was not always cleverly done, for in the Sanskrit redactions the priestly interest overshadows the heroic, and the legends related are often distorted to suit the brahmanical viewpoint. Sidhanta has written in *The Heroic Age of India* that everything is viewed from the angle of the priest, and instead of a straightforward narrative, there are many didactic digressions on the sanctity of the brahmans. Pargiter is equally categorical: 'The brahmanical versions are a farrago of absurdities and impossibilities, utterly distorting all the incidents' (see Walker 1983).

The Sanskritised *Ramayana*, too, carries the indelible imprint of major priestly editing. Regarding this epic, it is generally agreed that 'the pronounced brahmanical tone did not characterise the original work, but was given to it at the time of the revival, when much additional material was also introduced'. In the brahmanised text, to cite one example, Rama is represented as saying that those who accept the teachings of Buddha should be punished. The brahman author has even made Rama use the word thief – *chora* – for the Buddha in the *Ayodhyakanda* (Varma 1974: 297). The reference to the Buddha clearly indicates that the *Ramayana* was recast in the post-Buddha period and represents the reassertion of resurgent brahmanism against the Buddha's anti-Vedic teachings.

Not only the epics, but a great deal of secular literature in Sanskrit – poetry, the beast fable and the fairy tale – are translations and elaborations from Prakrit originals. The *Katha-sarita-sagar*, the best-known Sanskrit collection of stories, is said to have been based on an earlier work composed in Prakrit (Walker 1983, vol. 1: 364; see also Kosambi 1992: 203-4).

Benjamin Walker says that the story of forged texts in brahmanical literature has yet to be written. He points out that the period of the brahmanical revival was the age that fixed the criterion for every subsequent interpretation of Hindu life and culture. According to him, it was at this time when the ancient Indian traditions as they existed in the regional languages were taken over, adapted to the priestly bias, and hammered into the new mould of Sanskrit. The earlier tomes were rendered into Sanskrit for the deification of brahmans and the damnation of all others, especially shudras and ati-shudras. The indigenous writings were first sanskritised and then the whole of Sanskrit literature was brahmanised. Local and original names were altered to fit the Sanskrit alphabet; native sentiments were put through the mill of Sanskrit syntax, and a great deal of indigenous material irretrievably lost. This wholesale change and substitution, Walker says, was nothing short of calamity:

Interpretations of pre-Sanskrit and what might be called 'un-Sanskrit' life were further distorted by wilful tendentiousness that shaped into orthodox from the mythology, history and even the geography of ancient India. Its corruptions crept into the regional languages by its insistence on its own sanctity and stilted rules. And in most instances it debased what it influenced. The noble early poetry of Tamil, characterised by simplicity and realism, never recovered its freshness after contact with Sanskrit, and Tamil literature was thereafter subjected to the artificialities of the northern tongue. Practically every vernacular literature has suffered in like manner as long as it lay under the shadow of Sanskrit influence. (Walker 1983, vol. 1: 364).

That Sanskrit monopolised the intellectual and cultural space after this period of brahmanical revival is also attested by an analysis of inscriptions. The brahmanical revival climaxed during the Gupta period (i.e. fourth to sixth centuries AD), after which Sanskrit symbolising the brahmanical hegemony gradually elbowed out Prakrit. Prior to the Gupta age, more than 95 per cent of inscriptions were written in Prakrit and concerned non-brahmanical shramanic sects, mainly Buddhist and Jain, and only five per cent in Sanskrit concerned brahmanism. 'The position is almost entirely reversed in favour of Sanskrit and brahmanism in the post-Gupta period. The power of the priesthood must have been tremendous, almost tyrannical, to have achieved the phenomenal reversal. The number and nature of spurious inscriptions after the seventh century AD confirm the continuance of this tendency' (ibid.).

3

Medieval Mukti Movements of the Subaltern Saint-Poets

We'll set fire to divisions of caste,
We'll debate philosophical questions in the market place,
We'll have dealings with despised households,
We'll go around in different paths.

PAMBATTI SITTAR
the medieval Tamil poet, cited in Kailasapathy,
in Schomer et al., eds., *The Sants*, 1987: 391

Simmering tension between the liberal-humanist shramanic school and the conservative-exclusivist brahmanic tradition has been the defining feature of India's social history, reflected throughout the ages in many obvious and also many subtle ways. A series of medieval socio-religious movements, broadly – though not quite appropriately – termed the Bhakti movement, which peaked in the fifteenth and sixteenth centuries in the north with the emergence of a remarkable line of subaltern saint-poets (Kabir, Ravidas, Dadu, and Nanak, among many others) after traversing a long, uneven journey from about 500 AD, are another classic site of the brahman-shraman tussle. Starting in the deep south in the sixth century, gradually spreading northward through Karnataka and Maharashtra, and engulfing north India and Bengal from the fifteenth century onward, these movements from below are a watershed in Indian history not only in religious-literary terms but also in broader socio-cultural contexts. They represent a cultural revolt and scintillating examples of toiling caste creativity. Though brahmans occasionally climbed on the Bhakti bandwagon, the radicalism of the movement was shaped and spearheaded by artisans, cultivators, and labourers who composed poems and hymns of unsurpassable beauty in the people's languages. It is these compositions that laid the foundations of most regional languages. The lowly origins of its popular heroes is a striking feature of the Bhakti movement which was also animated by the lively presence of many outstanding and powerful women.

Although the exponents of the movements that stretched unevenly over centuries in different parts of the country differed widely depending on varying circumstances of time, place, changed socio-political atmosphere and individual religio-cultural sensibilities, opposition to caste hierarchy, brahmanic ascription and religious externalia was a common thread that bonded them together in a cohesive whole. Their egalitarian syncretism encompassed in its bosom various strands of multi-cultural diversity of India, including liberal elements of folk Hinduism and Islamic egalitarian thinking, especially of the Sufi variety.

In this sense, their movement, contrary to the traditional trajectories of dominant historiography, represented a sort of resurrection of the earlier shramanic heterodoxies. In this context it is significant to underline that their God was not the transcendental brahmanic God; their God had an existence within their own being in the form of individual and social conscience. Look within to realise God and decide what is right and wrong for you and others was their common refrain. Conceived and envisioned in the mould of desirable social transformation, in direct contrast to the brahmanical tradition, this God was revered not for maintaining the hierarchical order but to change it all by gracing everyone, irrespective of caste and creed, who led a virtuous life. As such, the Bhakti (devotion) movement should be appropriately renamed, as Aloysius suggested to this writer, Mukti (liberation) movement.

The top leaders who shared striking similarity on this count included outcaste brahman Basava, the leather-worker Haralayya, and the proto-feminist Akka Mahadevi (Karnataka); the tailor Namdev, the village servant Chokhamela, the grocer Tukaram, the vegetable-grower Savata Mali (Maharashtra); the weaver Kabir, the cobbler Ravidas, the cotton comber Dadu Dayal, the rebellious princess Mira, the khatri Nanak, the potter Gora, the barber Sena (the north). Though the multi-faceted, monotheistic, sometimes even agnostic Tamil Sittars or Siddhas like Tirumular, Sivavakkiyar and Pambatti Sittar who sang subversive songs did not belong to the established Bhakti stream, they shared their anti-caste radicalism with Kabir, Ravidas, and Tuka.

The general backdrop of the movement was the chaos in the wake of the Muslim invasions, the worsening economic conditions, and poverty made worse by the brahmanical tightening of socio-religious restrictions. There was an excessive multiplication of gods and goddesses, an unprecedented proliferation of castes by an unending process of permutation and combination involving all kinds of commensal and connubial prohibitions, a growing insistence on purity-pollution rules, and an increasing feudalisation of land and land-relations.

Such explosive situations provoked popular protests and radical revaluations of prevalent values. The ferment thus generated, especially among the downtrodden communities, threw up many culture heroes, popularly recognised as saint-poets who came up with their unique ideology which involved belief in one God, a passionate advocacy of social justice, and a reposing faith in people as the means and measure of all things, material as well as religious.

Of late, the dalit-subaltern radicals and those engaged in the ongoing work of recovery of the Indian past are increasingly stressing a close relationship between Buddhism and various streams of Bhakti movement. Bhakti, some of them have argued, was profoundly influenced by the ethos of Buddhism, and the difference between the two was more in appearance than in reality. They categorise both as protest movements against brahmanism. The Bhakti stalwarts insisted that true religion is important to both individual and society as it does not merely concern an individualistic search for moral edification or spiritual progress but also determines the relations between people. It is important that in their use of religious idioms they shaped the terms of the debate in a secular context. In other words, though religious in style, the cut and thrust of the debate they generated was social and political. Equally significant, most of them took recourse to free-thinking and rationalism embellished with an exquisite humane touch, instead of shastric parroting, to drive home their point.

Imbued with humanism and social radicalism, the Bhakti leaders across India laid stress on spirituality and universal brotherhood as they tried to create a broad-minded and compassionate religion that had been lost in external formalism and caste dogmatism. Their emphasis on spiritual equality was emblematic of their vision of social justice and deep sympathy for the common people. In this sense, they were pioneers of the paths that attracted many among the masses to some form of Hinduism. Importantly, their religion was not only anchored in ethical principles in social relationships but also pervaded with a healthy respect for material life. For them, religion was the inspiration of human endeavour and social justice, and had nothing to do with the escapism of a world-renouncing recluse.

In a true saintly fashion, without making unnecessary noise, these cultural leaders relegated the brahmanical deities with their discriminatory rites and rituals to the background, replacing them with a *nirguna, nirakara* (qualityless, formless, all-pervading) God as the ultimate symbol of universal love, compassion and justice. Their God stood on the side of the oppressed, the weak, and the defenceless. In fact, these saint-poets laid greater emphasis on the devotee than on God. Ultimately, God, or religion for that matter, they argued, was for the devotee. Kabir and Tukaram, two of the most charismatic leaders of the movement, would say that there was no duality between God and devotee because both of them, by entering into a holy alliance, had become one.

SOCIAL RESISTANCE IN RELIGIOUS IDIOM

The saint-poets, who came from society's underclass, in many ways clothed their rebellion against injustice and oppression in an obedience to God. Their devotion was to a God who 'stirred up rebellion' in the hearts of devotees. This God exhorted and inspired his devotees to free him from the idolatrous – and ignominious – fetters of the pseudo-religion founded and jealously guarded by the unscrupulous pandits and maulvis. In this concord, the deity and the devotee were determined to rescue religion and society from the clutches of corrupt elements. Striving for a true religion was not an end in itself but a means to bolster humanist values and ethos for a better social order. This becomes clear from the way these saint-poets brought into play the monotheistic radicalism to script a social revolution without open rebellion.

More important, these saint-poets did not advocate detachment from normal worldly life as a prerequisite for salvation. They were practical and advocated normal family life in society. They themselves set examples by leading productive and balanced lives. Most of them were married, and did some job to earn their living – Kabir did weaving and Ravidas worked with leather. Unlike the brahmanical gurus, they recognised the dignity of labour, connected it with social service and laid emphasis on the spiritual value of every kind of labour. Guru Nanak, for example, exhorted the religiously-inclined to seek God 'in the fields, in the weaver's shop, and in the happy home' instead of the temple and the mosque. They strongly disapproved renunciation, asceticism, and celibacy as the means of enlightenment. For instance, Kabir calls the religious aspirant maintaining celibacy a *hijara* (eunuch) and pokes fun at the yogi who in his quest of heaven tonsures his head, takes a vow of celibacy, and shuns worldly life:

> *If shaving your head*
> *Spelled spiritual success,*
>   *heaven would be filled with sheep.*
> *And brother, if holding back your seed*
> *Earned you a place in paradise,*
>   *eunuchs would be the first to arrive.*
>   (tr. Hawley and Juergensmeyer 1988: 50)

Kabir targeted the 'sacred' language, saying, 'Sanskrit is like *koop-jal* (well-water), a stagnant pool of water, and bhasha, or the people's language, like *behta nir* (water of the brook)'. This was, by and large, the stand taken by almost all saint-poets in every part of the country. The result was Sanskrit lost its dominance. Even many brahman authors, including Gyaneshwar and Tulsi, were forced to write in local languages. This led to an extraordinary efflorescence in regional languages of thoughts that were spontaneous and imbued with people's sentiments.

Caste was the main target of these leaders. It was to them what the Church, the symbol of organised and 'degenerated' Christianity, was to the eighteenth century French philosopher Voltaire. Those who attacked caste as wrong, inhuman, and futile announced their 'arrival' on the scene. In a dramatic development, the cultural-religious leadership shifted from the brahman priests well-versed in *karmakanda* and Sanskrit scripture to those who composed verses in vernaculars and interacted with the masses in their own idiom. Energised by fresh leadership and new ideas, Bhakti became a campaign for socio-cultural change. Writing in 1900, M. G. Ranade saw it as a popular protest movement of historic importance:

. . . like the Protestant Reformation in Europe in the sixteenth century, there was a Religious, Social and Literary Revival and Reformation in India. This . . . was not Brahmanical in its orthodoxy, it was heterodox in its spirit of protest against forms and ceremonies and class distinctions based on birth, and ethical in its preference of a pure heart, and of the law of love, to all other acquired merits and good works. This was the work of the people, of the masses, and not of the classes. At its head were Saints and Prophets, Poets and Philosophers, who sprang chiefly from the lower orders of society – tailors, carpenters, potters, gardeners, shop-keepers, barbers, and even mahars. (cited in Zelliot 1996: 8-9)

The large-hearted and practically excommunicated 'occasional brahmans' who joined the movement – a Ramananda here and a Gyaneshwar there – had been influenced by the humanism of the subaltern saint-poets and not the other way round as is made out by the dominant historiography. A case in point is Ramananda, who is credited to have brought the Bhakti to the people of all castes and creed in the north. According to this thesis, widely accepted in academic discourse, Ramananda was the guru of all important saint-poets of the north including Ravidas (the leather worker), Sadhana (the butcher), Dhana (the Jat), Sena (the barber), Pipa (the Rajput) and also Kabir (the weaver) who supposedly 'tricked' Ramananda to accept him as his disciple.¹ It was this outstanding line of saint-poets who spearheaded the Bhakti movement in the north, and, thus, Ramananda – by virtue of being their mentor – was accorded the status of the father-figure of the movement in the north India. Undoubtedly, this was a later concoction, designed to bring all the radical saint-poets into the traditional brahmanical fold. If those saint-poets could be seen as followers of a shastric brahman, then their subversive words would only be those of (mild and harmless) reformers within the Vedic-brahmanic tradition. This could also be – and was – presented as an example of brahmanical broadmindedness that amounted to draining those saint-poets of any revolutionary potential and, then, presenting them, with little bit of doctoring their texts, as self-contradictory mystics.

The brahmanical supposition is untenable, first of all, on chronological grounds. These saint-poets appeared in different times and it was not possible for Ramananda to have had all the disciples attributed to him. Second, there is hardly any mention of Ramananda in the available utterances of his so-called 'disciples'. By all accounts, those saint-poets were independent figures whose socio-religious awareness was shaped by their own observation and experiences. According to David Lorenzen, there is hardly any similarity and relationship between Ramananda and Kabir. After all, why would a champion dissenter like Kabir, who had nothing but contempt for the brahmanical culture and religion, 'trick' a brahman into accepting him as a disciple? It is not hard to see that the brahmanical scholarship concocted Kabir's connection with Ramananda in order to blunt his attack on brahmanism (see also Dharmveer 1997). This case is nothing if not a classic case of brahmanic appropriation of shramanic intellectual property.

A recent and rigorously researched Marathi book *Sahitya Setu* by the linguist-scholar Shridhar Kulkarni has convincingly proved that it was not Ramananda but the great Maharashtrian saint-poet Namdev who played the pioneering role of 'bridge-builder' between the north and the south. It may be noted that Namdev, in his later years, had become an itinerant saint and had finally settled in Punjab, composing his poems and spreading the *nirguna* devotionalism among the locals. As many as 61 poems out of Namdev's 300 odds poems have found a niche in the *Guru Granth Sahib*, and all major saint-poets from the north including Kabir, Nanak, Ravidas, and Dadu Dayal have praised Namdev. Kulkarni's book, while outlining Namdev's crucial role in the cultural regeneration in the north, also expounds the theory that it was the Maharashtrian saint-poets, particularly Namdev, who first realised the potential of Hindi as a possible common language.

True, the long-drawn cultural movements consisted of several streams and regional variations but there was a uniformity in the fundamental tenets. The leaders of the movement in all regions were close in spirit to the heterodox traditions – the Buddhist, the Jain, the Sahajyani offshoot of Buddhism, the Tantrik and the Nathpanthi. Tantrik and Nathpanthi ideas were expounded by non-conformist ascetics called Siddhas who were generally non-brahmans and mostly drawn from the lower orders of society. The Bhakti leaders' contempt for Sanskritic tradition and scriptural authority was rooted in this medieval shramanic tradition, chiefly represented by the Sahajiya Buddhists and Nath-Yogis who were popular in Bihar and eastern India. From the early medieval period, perhaps as early as the eighth or ninth century, the Siddhas and Yogis had been communicating their ideas in the common tongue, *bhasha*, in some form of western Apabhransha or old Bengali. Whatever their religious and cultural orientation, there was no question about their thoroughgoing social radicalism. Anyone, irrespective of caste, creed, or sex, could be initiated into the Tantrik and Nathpanthi orders. There are instances of women from the category of 'untouchables' being accepted as gurus. Their use of forbidden food and drink and advocacy of free sex as a means to attain awareness could be interpreted as an open revolt against the excessive do's and dont's preached by the pandits.

The Nath-Siddhas' unconventional beliefs and practices, however, were reason for the brahmans to brand them as immoral. It is significant that most brahmanised feudal lords and kings viewed the Siddhas with suspicion and hostility and tried to crush them as far as possible. Although the Tantriks and Nathpanthis enjoyed great popularity among the masses, they had often to bear the brunt of priestly-feudal wrath. The esoteric nature of their practice and the secretive manner in which they communicated their ideals and conducted their activities can be understood as a device to escape social and political persecution. Faced with increasing witch-hunting, the Nathpanthis, under Gorakhnath's charismatic leadership, adopted a high moral tone and tried with some success to avoid brahmanical attack. It is a measure of their organisational success that they were able to set up their centres not only in different parts of the north and western India but also in the deep south. It were these socio-religious forces that provided a conducive atmosphere for the Bhakti movement to take root in all parts of the country.

On a broader historical canvas, the movement may be interpreted as a spontaneous, unstructured mass opposition to the dangerous ascendancy of the priestly-feudal alliance in the wake of the systematic liquidation of Buddhism. The spectre of Vedic-brahmanic hegemony, kept in check for a long stretch of time by the Buddhist movement, was haunting the caste-oppressed. Bhakti was the sub-conscious attempt of the lowered caste people to meet the challenge of the resurgent and aggressive brahmanism which was reflected in writings and activities of Kumaril Bhatta and Adi Shankara who pulled out all the stops to revive the varnashrama-dharma and other ascriptive tenets of Vedic-brahmanism. As Satish Chandra says, reactionary revivalism was manifested most clearly in the persecution of Buddhists and Jains, with almost all Buddhist shrines being forcefully converted into Hindu temples. By all indications, this revivalism was carried out in a systematic manner by the caste-feudal leadership:

It was also reflected in the Hinduisation of many tribes and the consequent growth of many new jatis or sub-castes, which had to be fitted into the existing structure by putting forward the theory of varnasankar, i.e. the growth of mixed castes. The rise of image worship, often accompanied by gross superstitions, and the elaboration of a religion of works (karma) were other features of the religious ideas of the period. This socio-religious order was supported and buttressed by the Rajput-Brahman alliance. Thus, any effort to disturb the established social order viz., the varna system and the religion of works, would not only have to face the opposition and hostility of the entrenched brahman class, but also invited repression at the hands of political authority. (Satish Chandra 2001: 118)

This may explain why, despite its early stirrings, as reflected in the social ideology of the heterodox sects, radical bhakti in north India could not broaden its base or become a movement here in the initial stage. The movement emerged in the south where brahmans were in lesser number and concordance between them and the feudal lords was still being forged. The kshatriya caste hardly existed in the south, the two main social categories being shudras and brahmans. The movement did not take roots in the north until the arrival of Islam which somewhat slackened the vice-like grip of brahman-kshatriya combine over the masses.

KABIR AND MONOTHEISTIC RADICALISM IN THE NORTH

As in the south and the Deccan, in the north too, the movement transcended its religious confines and established itself as a powerful platform for a new socio-cultural dispensation. Many factors were responsible for this unique development. First, the prestige and power of the brahmans was on the wane, following the defeat of their feudal lords and consequent establishment of the Delhi Sultanate. Second, at about the same time, the movements of the Nathpanthis and Siddhas openly challenging the caste system and supremacy of the brahmans, had gained popularity among the masses. And the third factor was the coalescence of the Bhakti thought with Sufi philosophy – their give and take, action and reaction upon each other. Undoubtedly, Sufi ideas, basically liberal and emancipatory, influenced Bhakti doctrine in great measure: some typical Muslim concepts, especially the tenets of equality and brotherhood, echoed and invigorated the social vision of the leaders of the movement. It is to be noted, however, that the mysticism of the Sufis was not encouraged by the Bhakti saints who generally denounced detachment from worldly life as escapism.

Kabir, who led the movement in the north, lived in the second half of the fifteenth century. Said to be a foundling, he was adopted by a Muslim weaver and was brought up in the same profession, thus earning his living by weaving. In earlier times, weavers, or julahas, the creators of the fabled Indian textiles, were organised into guilds. They enjoyed a respectable position in society and many of them, especially in the eastern region, were Buddhists. But after their absorption in the orthodox caste system, their systematic degradation as a 'low caste' began. In Kabir's time, his community was treated contemptuously by the elite. The proud julahas, however, never reconciled to their social humiliation, and when the opportunity came they revolted against the priestly-feudal order of Hindu society by embracing Islam in the age of the Delhi Sultanate. But the entry into the religion of the ruling Muslims did not solve their problems as their social position remained by and large the same. Snubbed by the feudal-aristocratic Muslim ruling class, their need for social dignity and religio-cultural recognition remained a distant dream.

For Kabir, who was born and brought up in such a family and social milieu, the brahmanical shibboleths of high-born and low-born and the oppressive nature of caste was not merely a subject of animated discussion, but a question of life and death. His trenchant critique and life-long crusade against the discriminatory system should be understood in this context. Though illiterate, Kabir had the rare critical faculty and the exceptional ability to articulate his iconoclastic ideas of life and religion. It is significant that he consciously put to use his experiences, observation, and intellect as ultimate in forming his life-philosophy and world-view in an age dominated by orthodoxies of all kinds. It is on account of this scientific temper coupled with the rare courage of conviction that he dared to reject with supreme confidence the solutions offered by tradition and shastra. In a magnificent poem, addressed to his implacable orthodox adversaries, he proclaims that his criteria for assessing reality is *aakhin ki dekhi* (his own observation), while the shifty-eyed pandit, he points out, takes recourse to *kaagad ki lekhi* (writing on paper) to pull wool over people's eyes.

> *How can ours – yours and mine mind meet!*
> *I say what I have seen.*
> *You say what you have read.*
> *I want to disentangle the complexity of truth.*
> *And you keep it under wraps to*
> *Further complicate the matter!* (see Dwivedi 1999: 247)

Kabir defied orthodoxy and ridiculed the claim to a divine origin of caste. He mocked the umpteen pretensions of Muslim clerics, and rejected pilgrimage, idolatry, sacrifice, and other such practices with a brilliance unprecedented in history. Hess says his 'constant effort was to strip away disguises, force confrontation, expose lies, promote honesty at every level. His socio-satirical poems, his psychological probes . . . his crazy and paradoxical and mystical poems, do not inhabit separate categories. They are unified by a principle of radical honesty that sweeps through marketplace, temple, body and mind, that will no more allow you to delude yourself than to cheat others' (1986: 21).

In the fragmented and insular medieval society dominated by caste, ethnicity, and religious identity, Kabir's advocacy of the unity and equality of all was nothing less than revolutionary. He tried to demolish the barriers that separated man from man. He either dismissed the Hindu and Muslim ideas of God and religion or else equated them, saying that Ram and Allah are identical. Kabir's God is 'neither in the temple nor in the mosque'; He is *ghat-ghat mein*, 'in every heart'. For him, God is not an object, nor the sort of reality that one can speak of and conceptualise, certainly not the sort one can see and worship. He found the sacrifices that priests made to the gods and goddesses hideous, and he thought it was utter nonsense to picture God in a succession of animal and human incarnations 'whose form could then be worshipped and adored and whose stories could spawn an industry of religious texts, complete with their brahman interpreters' (Hawley and Juergensmeyer 1988: 43).

Kabir is an exponent of the *nirguna* (literally, formless) school of religion. The *nirguna* bhakti does not need religious institutions, structures, or priests to be mediators between God and individuals. 'The religion he knows, if religion it is, is of a totally different order from the admonitions and assurances that put bread and butter on the tables of qazis and pandits.' Kabir is forthright in asserting that various rituals and practices and texual authority are evolved by the privileged classes to control and rule the masses:

Veda and Koran are traps laid
for poor souls to tumble in. (Hess and Singh 1986: 52)

Emphasis on religious externals perpetuates animosity between adherents of different religions. From this point of view, Islam is not very different from Hinduism, despite its advocacy of a theology which is very close to the *nirguna* spirit. Hence, Kabir loathes both the hypocritical mullas and the unscrupulous brahmans and pours scorn over them. Kabir is always combative and pugnacious, unwilling to let the opponent off the hook. In poem after poem he makes a mockery of their injunctions, admonitions and pious assurances to the people. All this he does to undermine the prestige and authority of the priestly class in the eyes of the common man. For him, this was the necessary first step from the point of view of liberating the people from the priestly-feudal thrall. His insatiable hunger for the truth, regardless of the cost, often brought him in confrontation with the priestly classes of both the communities.

The brahman was almost always at the receiving end of Kabir's caustic comments. For him, the brahman was 'the craftiest, the most unkind, the most status-conscious and vanity-ridden man on earth'. In Kabir's eyes, it was the brahman, more than anyone else, who was in need of basic education and character training in humanity and kindness. To Kabir, even his bhakti was a pretence, since that bhakti had no compassion and love for the other creations of God. One major agenda of Kabir's life, therefore, was to make the brahman aware of his ignorance, his greed, his dishonesty and his utter callousness towards fellow beings, especially the untouchables. He did this using that most potent weapon he was so marvellous at wielding – ridicule.

Tearing into the claims of a birth-based elite, he challengingly asked: '*Re baman tu bamani jaya, aan baant se kahi na aaya*'.[2] Elsewhere he is equally pugnacious in rubbishing the high status claimed by the brahman: 'Do you have milk in your veins while we have blood? (if not) how are you a brahman and we shudras?' Kabir saw refractions of the divine in all human beings who were quintessentially no different from one another. He had nothing but contempt for those who didn't see this essential unity of mankind:

> It's a heavy confusion.
> Veda, Koran, holiness, hell, woman, man,
> a clay pot shot with air and sperm . . .
> When the pot falls apart, what do you call it?
> Numskull! You've missed the point.

> It's all one skin and bone, one piss and shit,
> one blood, one meat.
> From one drop, a universe
> Who's Brahman? Who's Shudra? (ibid.: 67)

Kabir revels in puncturing the brahman's pretension to enlightenment. He shows up the pandit who projects himself as the repository of all knowledge, as 'a rank ignoramus, a pompous fool lacking insight into reality'. He expresses contempt for the babble of the pandit and compares his holy books to 'a cell made of paper' in which to imprison fools. The pandits were to him 'lovers of lust and delusion' who had the temerity to 'laugh at the (real) lovers of God'. He scoffed at their claim to intellectual superiority – 'the pandits' pedantries are lies' – and sarcastically asked: 'Read, read, pandit, make yourself clever/Does that bring freedom?' The *Kaliyuga* was to him, 'the age of phoney brahmans', and Veda and Puranas 'a blindman's mirrors'. The pandit, he says, is a 'buffoon' who searches the sky but can't find out how to quell his pride. The pandit's meaningless rituals and prayers, ignorance and pride have made him a laughing stock; no one could be lower than such a pandit:

> The pandit got lost/in Vedic details
> but missed the mystery/of his own self.
> Worship, prayers,/six sacred activities,
> four ages teaching Gayatri,
> I ask you: who's got liberty?
> You splash yourself/if you touch somebody,
> but tell me who/could be lower than you.
> Proud of your quality,/great with authority,
> such pride never brought anyone good . . . (ibid.: 85)

Some people erroneously see Kabir as an eclectic reformer of Hinduism and Islam. Some have even tried to portray him in the brahmanical mould. Attempts have been made to create an image of Kabir that complies with the shastric-puranic tradition. He has also been branded as an 'individualistic' and a 'mystic' and denied recognition even as a social critic and reformer. Kabir's real path and ideology, however, leave no room for mystification and ambiguity. It is not difficult to see his thoroughgoing radicalism, and his impatience with ascriptive values and norms. In no uncertain terms, Kabir declares his independence from both Islam and Hinduism, relentlessly attacking the dogmas and follies of both the institutionalised religions. He tries to ignite a similar autonomy and fearlessness in those who aspire to be his followers. In a well-known couplet he announces:

> *I've burned my own house down,*
> *the torch is in my hand.*
> *Now I'll burn down the house of anyone*
> *who wants to follow me.* (ibid.: 5)

Kabir trod an untrodden path, singing *Apanee raah tu chale Kabira* – 'Go your own way, Kabir'. His own way was not hamstrung by the rules of the establishment, its religion, custom, caste, or scripture. It was a way made luminous by his worldly perception and inner experience. Despite persistent threat to his life, he never desisted from telling what he saw around him. What he saw around him – the sectarian zealots killing each other in the name of their religions – deeply troubled him; he could not reconcile himself to this 'mad' world:

> *Saints, I see the world is mad.*
> *If I tell the truth they rush to beat me,*
> *If I lie they trust me.*
> *I've seen the pious Hindus, rule-followers,*
> *early morning bath-takers –*
> *killing souls, they worship rocks.*
> *They know nothing.*
> *I've seen plenty of Muslim teachers, holy men*
> *reading their holy books*
> *and teaching their pupils techniques.*
> *They know just as much.*
> *The Hindu says Ram is the Beloved,*
> *the Turk says Rahim.*
> *Then they kill each other*
> *They buzz their mantras from house to house*
> *puffed with pride.* (ibid.: 42)

Pioneer of a new culture, Kabir's stress was on a restructuring of society on egalitarian lines and not a mere co-existence of different castes and communities. Much before Phule and Ambedkar, he stood and fought for total annihilation of the caste order. Joining a non-caste group was one of the ways to escape the suffocating sufferings within the caste boundary, as many sects and organisations had done in the past. That was the raison d'être why the followers of Kabir founded an independent religious community, the Kabir-panthis. It received enthusiastic response from the artisans and cultivators, the worst sufferers of the existing socio-religious system.

Kabir has an enduring appeal for the subordinated people as a living symbol of the anti-establishment.[3] A full-blooded critic of the status quo, he wanted nothing less than a complete overhaul of the diseased system. He waged a relentless struggle for the liberation of society from dogmatic fetters of every kind in favour of an alternative culture which accords dignity to everyone, including the last man in the street. Compromise and half-way solutions were not his way. His fight against the forces of retrogression and oppression was total and relentless.

Ravidas was another Bhakti stalwart in the north who came from the lower rungs of society. He himself indicates the wider family in which he felt he belonged by mentioning several of his illustrious predecessors. The names he gives are that of Namdev, Trilochan and Kabir (Hawley and Juergensmeyer 1988: 12). While the first two hailed from western India, Kabir lived in Benaras, Ravidas's home city. 'In mentioning these three as recipients of divine grace along with himself, Ravidas underscored his sense of solidarity with a tradition of bhakti that flowed with particular animation in the lower ranks of society' (ibid.).

Like his kindred souls, Ravidas's spirituality is tinged with humanitarian ethos and egalitarian values. His conception of God – as 'deliverer of the poor', 'uplifter of the lowly', and 'purifier of the defiled' – reflects his concern for the weak and the marginalised. He raises crucial questions about the hierarchical social order and speaks of an ideal society 'where none are third or second – all are one', and where the people 'do this or that, they walk where they wish'. In his moving and mellifluous words:

Tohi mohi, mohi tohi antar kaisa
(Between you and me, me and you
How can there be a difference?)

His disdain for the brahman and allied castes who proudly uphold the shastras and discriminatory socio-religious order based on them often comes to the fore. He chastises all those who denigrate people belonging to castes and communities other than their own. He stresses that even the lowest of the low can rise to great heights by acquiring noble qualities – in fact, he considers such a self-realised person superior than the priests, heroes and kings:

> *A family that has a true follower of the Lord*
> *Is neither high caste nor low caste, lordly or poor.*
> *The world will know it by its fragrance.*
> *Priests or merchants, labourers or warriors,*
> *halfbreeds, outcastes, and those who tend cremation fires –*
> *their hearts are all the same.*
> *He who becomes pure through love of the Lord*
> *exalts himself and his family as well.*
> *Thanks be to his village, thanks to his home,*
> *thanks to that pure family, each and every one,*
> *For he's drunk with the essence of the liquid of life*
> *and he pours away all the poisons.*
> *No one equals someone so pure and devoted –*
> *not priests, not heroes, not parasolled kings.*
> *As the lotus leaf floats above the water, Ravidas says,*
> *so he flowers above the world of his birth.*
>   (tr. Hawley and Juergensmeyer 1988: 25)

It was Ravidas who gave the call of *jaat-paat puchhe nahi koi, hari ka bhaje so hari ka hoi* (don't ask about caste, whoever is a devotee of God belongs to Him). With this understanding, he kept engaged in his leather-work and repeatedly referred to his humble birth, underscoring the dignity of an occupation and caste that had come to be regarded as disgraceful. He scoffs at the pretensions of the deluded high-born and defies conventional wisdom by arguing that despite his supposedly 'low' occupation he too is as important as the 'well-born', many of whom come to him to pay their homage:

> Oh well-born of Benaras, I too am born well known:
> my labour is with leather. But my heart can boast the Lord. . . .
> I, born among those who carry carrion
> in daily rounds around Benaras, am now
> the lowly one to whom the mighty Brahmans come
> And lowly bow . . . (ibid.)

Ravidas mocks at the ideas of untouchability and pollution in a beautiful poem *With What Can I Worship?* The poet pictures an innocent young girl asking questions about the offerings to be made to the deity. Here Ravidas teases those obsessed with purity that everything is tainted, but does real worship need such items in the first place?

> Mother, she asks, with what can I worship?
> All the pure is impure. Can I offer milk?
> The calf has dirtied it in sucking its mother's teat.
> Water, the fish have muddied; flowers, the bees –
> No other flowers could be offered than these.
> The sandalwood tree, where the snake has coiled, is spoiled.
> The same act formed both nectar and poison.
> Everything's tainted – candles, incense, rice –
> But still I can worship with my body and my mind
> and I have the guru's grace to find the formless Lord.
> Rituals and offerings – I can't do any of these.
> What, says Ravidas, will you do with me? (ibid. : 26)

Another outstanding saint-poet was Kabir's Rajasthani follower, Dadu Dayal (d. 1603). It is significant that Dadu calls his path the path of *nipakh* or non-sectarianism. This was a bid to rise above the disputations of various religious communities and establish harmony among the masses. Declaring that he did not want to be considered either a Hindu or a Muslim, he summarily dismissed all revealed scriptures, valuing only personal devotion to the nirguna God and to humankind. In many of his poems which possess great beauty and force, Dadu asserts that all human beings have the same spirit and essence; and that differences based on colour, caste, or race are meaningless. He deplores the fact that the world is divided among antagonistic sects and communities as very few dare to defy the sectarian traditions.

Writing towards the end of the seventeenth century, Dharmdas, Darya Saheb and Yari Saheb of Bihar also underlined the same sentiments, emphasising the fundamental unity of man and irrationality of the birth-based caste. Dharmdas celebrated castelessness, stressing its necessity for social harmony. Darya Saheb said, 'All human beings suffer from hunger or thirst, or feel pain or pleasure in the same way'. The forms of rituals and various modes of beliefs, he stressed, cannot make a difference to the status of human beings. Similarly, Yari Saheb insisted that 'Gold is the same everywhere whether it is, in melted form or an ornament. Who can say which is higher and which is lower?' (Chandra 1978: 141)

Towering above these figures is the charismatic personality of Guru Nanak (1469-1546), who founded a new faith, Sikhism. One of the stars of the Bhakti movement, Nanak drew the attention of the people in the simple and interactive language of the Punjab to the true relationship between God and man, and man and man. Traditional brahmanism looked down upon the Punjab as a fallen land and out of bounds for the varnashrama-dharma: ethnically and culturally the region saw the mixture of many ethnic identities and cultures. Nanak's arrival on the scene further invigorated the assimilative trend and gave a fillip to the process. Nanak unleashed the spirit and forces that brought about a major change in the religious, social, and political outlook of the Punjabi people.

The founder of Sikhism campaigned for a universal religion based on the principle of equity, and attacked divisive caste and meaningless rites and rituals. Proclaiming 'I am neither a Hindu nor a Muslim, I am a man', he laid emphasis on the importance of true knowledge and wisdom manifested in love and compassion for fellow human beings as a true means of attaining spiritual qualities. Religion, he stressed, consists not in strings of words but in high thinking and noble behaviour. And only those who look on all men as equal – and treat them humanely – are truly religious. As Grewal contends, 'He shows no appreciation for the ruling classes, whether Hindu or Muslim. He displays no sympathy for the religious elite. He identifies himself with the ruled, the common people. What moves him deeply is their misery, ignorance and helplessness. . . . That they should not be denied the means of liberation was, for Guru Nanak, the supreme purpose of human life. His message, therefore, was meant for all. The universality of his message is the obverse of his idea of equality' (1999: 19-20). Guru Nanak's was a vision which inevitably clashed with all ascriptive and sectarian ideology. Not surprisingly, he discarded the brahmanical scriptures, incarnations, and idolatry, and despised the selfish priests who sold superstition and false hope to the gullible masses.

Nanak's socio-religious vision differed with the Vedic-brahmanism in a fundamental way as the path shown by him was based on humanitarian concern, in which the theological aspect was not divorced from the sociological one. In his eyes, truth is not only an abstract notion of the Supreme Reality but also a practical principle of social conduct. Guru Nanak – and the Gurus who succeeded him – believed that the world we live in is true because it is God's creation. If the Creator is true, so is his creation. The material world is not illusion or 'maya' but a living reality. The Gurus emphasised that we cannot shirk our family and social responsibility by branding the world as illusion. We all are responsible for our life and we are endowed with abilities to take control of life through thoughtful action and necessary discipline. Nanak always laid emphasis on virtuous living by saying, 'Truth is higher, but higher still is truthful living.' The basic thrust of his teaching is the development of the personality towards pure, truthful, and socially fruitful action. The steps he prescribes to his followers to achieve the goal of self-actualisation are simple: participation in productive activities and proper human conduct. Condemning beggary and living on alms, he forbade his followers to going to any parasitical gurus. He wanted them to earn their living the hard way, for 'those alone know the right path who earn their bread by the sweat of their brow and share it with others.' The personality so conditioned, he insisted, must wage a ceaseless struggle, not only with one's selfish ego, but also in the external world of human relation.

The *Adi Granth*, which contains the teachings of Nanak and constitutes the central core of Sikh theology, incorporates several poems from the nirguna saints. It was an unmistakable way, as some have argued, of relegating the traditional religious elite to the margin. It is indeed remarkable that the social ideas and activities of Guru Nanak bore a striking similarity to that of Kabir and Ravidas, whom he held in the highest esteem. Nanak challenged caste distinctions, both by precept and example. To give a sense of confidence and dignity to the poor, he would prefer to eat with persons of lower classes. A case in point is a well-known incident that has become a part of the folk memory. At Sayyidpur he stayed and dined with Lalo, a carpenter, and declined the feast of Malik Bhago, a high caste landlord, on the ground that the latter had accumulated his wealth by exploiting other people while the former earned his bread by the sweat of his brow. Nanak also established a radical practice by insisting that those who follow him must be willing to eat in a common kitchen – *langar* – where everyone could take a meal irrespective of his caste or gender. In a rare frisson of compassion for those held in contempt for their lowly origin, he expresses his feeling that the devotees of God from lower castes 'may wear shoes made from my skin'.

It is not hard to see that the rise of the Sikh community as an extremely hardworking and prosperous people in a country teeming with poverty-stricken masses is largely the result of egalitarianism and the dignity of labour enshrined in the ideology of Nanak and his successors. At the instance of the last Guru, Gobind Singh, every male Sikh bears – and shares – the surname Singh, as does every female Kaur. In doing so, the Guru's obvious objective was to make the traditional caste identities unimportant. In this and other respects the Sikh Gurus were harbingers of modern ideas which have greatly contributed in making Indian culture more humane and democratic.

Many Bhakti leaders, particularly Kabir and Nanak, transcended sectarian differences and consciously incorporated the bright elements of all faiths, including Islam, in their teachings. They protested against the low position given to women, and encouraged them to join their menfolk in various activities. When the followers of Kabir, Ravidas, and Nanak gathered together, women were included in the gathering.

Mirabai, the Rajasthani Rajput princess, the author of some of the finest hymns in Hindi, broke out of her golden-gilded prison to become a disciple of Ravidas. A high-caste princess taking a guru from among the 'untouchables' represents a rebellion against the casteism and patriarchy of the medieval society. According to Parita

Mukta, Mira after leaving her princely home found a new community among the marginalised castes and communities of Rajasthan and adjacent regions. Mira, she contends, forged a new bond with the despised and toiling people. In her new life, companionship made up for material deprivation. Mira made a radical reversal in which manual labour, even the skinning of animals and dyeing of skin, became revalued. All this is exquisitely – and unambiguously – expressed in her own words:

> *Mira found a guru in Rohidas.*
> *She bowed at his feet, and asked his blessings.*
> > *Refrain: Mira's Mohan, come to the Mertni's desh.*
> *I have nothing to do with caste or other divisions.*
> *Let the world do what it will,*
> *I offer you my body, mind and soul.*
> > *Mira's Mohan, come to the Mertni's desh.*
> *I skin animals and dye the skins.*
> *My work is to dye.*
> *This dyeing is dear to me, this dyeing is dear to me,*
> *Dye my soul in it. . . .* (Mukta 1997: 112)

Mira's radicalism is unmistakable. Her abandonment of her feudal husband, her acceptance of the 'untouchable' Ravidas as her guru, her audacity of joining the company of saints, her love affair with the despised communities, all paint the picture of a sublimely rebellious character. Her 'outrageous' behaviour and subversive activities were nothing short of a stinging insult to the 'Rajput honour'. There are stories about her insulted husband, the Rana, how he tried everything he could to 'reform' his wayward wife, to bring her back. When he failed to win her over, he sent her poison. Mira disappears, or dies, under uncertain circumstances. Many contend, and so does Parita Mukta, that Mira, in all likelihood, was eliminated in revenge on the orders of her outraged husband.

SIDDHA REBELLION IN TAMIL NADU

The poetry of the sixth century Tamil saint Tirumular who sang 'Caste is one and God is one' and who equated Love with God – instead of defining God as Love – marked the beginning of the *siddha marga* in the deep south. This movement reached its high-water mark between the fourteenth and eighteenth centuries. The Siddhas or Sittars, who hailed from subaltern groups and sang subversive songs, cast aside the dreary externalia of religion, and embraced brotherhood, love and compassion, extolling these human expressions as the intrinsic worth of religion. In this sense, apart from Tirumular, they carried forward the legacy of two other Tamil cultural icons, Tiruvalluvar (c. AD 300-400), the 'low' caste author of poetical classic *Kural,* and Nandnar, the eighth century untouchable saint who struggled against brahmanical tyranny to enter the socio-religious domain.

Combining spiritual excellence with social regeneration, the Siddhas transcended artificial barriers and prejudices. Imbibing the fundamental strain of universalism of their Tamil predecessors, one of whom sang 'Every village is the village of my birth and everyone is my kith and kin', they set a new benchmark in humanism. With a unique blending of knowledge and compassion, similar to the Buddhist spirit and very akin to the Siddha approach in the north, the Tamil Siddhas sought yogic and spiritual experience for a blissful individual and social consciousness. As believers in the unity of mankind, they were 'implacable opponents of the caste system and the gradations of orthodoxy and respectability that it gave rise to' (Kailasapathy 1987). The radical anti-hierarchical and anti-brahmanical thrust of their poetry is so similar to the poems of nirguna radicals like Kabir that they often appear to be carbon copies of one another. Regarded as heretical like Kabir, they too were hated and hounded by reactionary forces, who branded them as religious *panchamas,* or outcastes as they 'challenged the very foundations of medieval Hinduism: the authority of the shastras, the validity of rituals and the basis of the caste system were often questioned by the Siddhas' (ibid.: 389). For their non-conformist views and lifestyle, they were considered dangerous, and hence persistently persecuted by the establishment.

In fact, it were the unorthodox Siddhas, and not those Shaivaite Nayanars and Vaishnavaite Alvars, who carried the torch of humanist radicalism in Tamil Nadu. The Nayanars and Alvars, though more flexible and liberal than the arch orthodoxy, confined themselves to religious and philosophical concerns within the precincts of Vedic-brahmanic ideology. Traversing the Dravidian land with Sanskrit scriptures in tow, they built the brahmanical temple cult with the associated settlements and tenants, and, thus, played a crucial role in subduing the Dravidian culture and literature; they drove out Buddhism and Jainism which had had a very strong presence in the region for centuries. In a major way, they helped in the processes of Aryanisation/Sanskritisation of the Dravidian culture. Working as 'peaceful' cultural ambassadors, the so-called Sanskritist apostles of the medieval harmony and synthesis helped the brahmanic-feudal combine in socio-cultural subjugation of the Tamil land, which was quite a violent process:

Tamil literature makes it painfully clear that the foundations of the medieval synthesis were soaked in blood from battles that established the temple-centred, devotional Brahmanical religious ceremonial practice at the centre of the agrarian order. . . . The Sanskritic and temple-centred character of Tamil verse during medieval times distinguishes it sharply from earlier epochs and nourishes a popular belief in Tamil Nadu today that medieval South India succumbed to an invasion of Brahmans from the north.
(Ludden, cited in Omvedt 1994: 41-2)

Historians relate the origin of caste, slavery, and the segregation of people as untouchables to the process of Aryanisation of south India which reached its peak during the period of Imperial Cholas. Chola rule brought about, among other things, basic changes in land relations. Large sections of original inhabitants like Paraiyars and Pallars were unsettled from their land due to large-scale distribution of land as gifts to brahmans — known as the *brahmadeya* and *agrahara* grant — by the Pallava and Chola kings during the seventh to eleventh centuries. The brahmans, who were until then mostly priests and advisers to their feudal lords, now also became landlords. This greatly facilitated their socio-cultural agenda embedded in the ascriptive hierarchy. In his *Slavery in the Tamil Country: A Historical Overview*, S. Manickam observes, 'It is difficult to say when the institution of slavery originated in the south. Perhaps the conquest of southern India by the Aryans and the consequent fusion between them and the inhabitants of the land could have been the possible cause of the birth of Caste System and the institution of slavery which is closely allied with the former' (quoted in *Frontline*, 25 April 2003). Oppression and isolation of those pushed down to the bottom of social hierarchy grew in intensity in pace with the Aryanisation process. And with it grew a tradition of protest and resistance against the discriminatory system.

The Tamil Siddhas' resemblance to the Tantrik and Nath-panthi movement in the north are unmistakable, although there is no authentic study yet on this subject. It is also surprising that the various streams of Tamil Siddhas invariably count Gorakhnath as one of their illustrious elders (Kailasapathy 1987: 387). Critical research on the Tamil Siddhas is hampered by an acute absence of reliable editions of Siddha literature, and this is not fortuitous. Since the Siddhas' views frequently clashed with those of the Vedic-brahmanic thinking, the latter school has tried its best to obscure and distort the Siddhas' works. Not surprisingly, the official brahmanical Shaivism has purposefully excluded Siddha views from its vast canonical corpus and social philosophy. As a scholar points out, their poems have been left to the common man to preserve as best as he can.

Whatever little materials we have clearly suggest Siddhas' complete detachment from the brahmanical norms and cultural patterns. All of them manifest a protest, expressed often in very strong terms, against the forced formalities of life and religion. Antithetic attitude to religious practices and beliefs of the ruling classes is the common thread that bonds them together.

It is not difficult to see that Siddha ideology was shaped by their social position – most of them came from families of shepherds, temple-drummers, potters, fishermen, hunters, etc. In fact, there are stories among the Siddhas that some of them came from other culture traditions as well, Chinese and Arabic. This belief is founded on the evidences of co-operative connection with these people in the fields of medicine, alchemy and astronomy (ibid.: 406). There is also the popular belief that the first major Tamil Siddha, Tirumular, came from Kashmir. These stories may or may not be true, but they definitely point to certain inter-mingling of the Siddhas and Muslim saints. It is important that two Muslims Sufis – Pir Muhammed and Mastan Sahib – are included in the list of Siddhas. All this must have widened their cultural horizon and contributed to their liberal and egalitarian outlook. Irrespective of the fact that their egalitarianism was ideology-driven or otherwise, they were clearly ranged against the caste distinctions practised by the higher castes – brahmans, vellalas (affluent peasants) and vanigas (merchants). There was no place for any discrimination with regard to caste in the Siddhas' fraternity.

The most powerful voice in the entire array of Siddhas is that of Sivavakkiyar. Like Kabir, he is merciless in attacking and ridiculing the priestly orthodoxy. Sivavakkiyar's poems brilliantly bring out the humanist and anti-brahmanical sentiments which are so characteristic of the Siddhas:

> The chanting of the four Vedas
> The meticulous study of the sacred scripts,
> The smearing of the holy ashes,
> And the muttering of prayers,
> Will not lead you to the Lord!
> Let your heart melt within you.
> And if you can be true to yourself
> Then you will join the limitless light
> And lead an endless life.
> You dumb fools performing the rituals
> With care and in leisureliness.
> Do gods ever become stone?
> What can I do but laugh?
> Of what use are temples,
> And of what use are sacred tanks?
> Slavishly you gather to worship
> In temples and tanks! (ibid.: 390)

Sivavakkiyar employs simple similes to convey his ideas. He cites commonplace, domestic instances to drive home his point. This is what he does in the following verse while trashing the theory of eternal soul and transmigration:

> Milk does not return to the udder,
> Likewise butter can never become butter-milk;
> The sound of the conch does not exist once it is broken;
> The blown flower, the fallen fruit do not go back to the tree;
> The dead are never born again, never! (ibid.: 401)

In their intense monotheism and strong condemnation of idolatry, the Siddhas, like the *nirguna* stalwarts in other parts of the country, consistently exposed and criticised the powers of orthodoxy:

> When once I knew the Lord,
> What were to me the host
> of pagan deities,
> Some fixed in temple shrines,
> Or carried in the crowd;
> Some made of unbaked clay,
> And some burnt hard with fire?
> With all the lying tales
> That fill the sacred books,
> They've vanished from my mind.
> But yet I have a shrine –
> The mind within my breast.
> An image too is there –
> The soul that came from God.
> I offer ash and flowers –
> The praises of my heart;
> And all the God-made world
> Is frankincense and myrrh
> And thus where'er I go
> I ever worship God. (Jordens 1985: 278-9)

The poems of Pambatti Sittar, 'the Snake-Charmer Siddha', are modelled on the songs of the professional snake-charmers. He too is trenchant in his denunciation of brahmanical ideology:

> The four Vedas, six kinds of Shastras,
> The many Tantras and Puranas,
> The Agamas which speak of the arts,
> And various kinds of other books
> Are of no use; just in vain.
> So dance snake, dance!
> In a statue of stone whanged with a chisel
> D'ya think there's understanding?
> D'ya think the idiots of the world
> Have any understanding?

> *Will a flaw in a pan go away*
> *If you rub it with tamarind?*
> *Ignorance won't go away from the idiots*
> *So dance snake, dance!* (Kailasapathy 1987: 390-1)

Pambatti Sittar's poems are extremely popular in Tamil Nadu to this day. Tamilians sing his songs as the folk poems of snake-charmers. These extraordinary poems of the ordinary people give us an unusual insight into their psyche. These poems are a testimony to the fact how dearly they hold their own egalitarian culture against the looming threat of Vedic-brahmanism. Pambatti's verse, cited above, ends on a note where he talks of 'setting fire to divisions of caste' and 'taking philosophical questions to the market place'. This leaves no doubt about the real intentions of the Siddhas.

It is not hard to see why the Siddhas' songs are still on the people's lips. Their poems reflect a warm and positive attitude to the world and life. They faced the drab and dreariness of everyday life with a kind of philosophical stoicism that was reassuring to the common man. As peoples' philosophers, they radiated an attitude that was humanistic and life-affirming. They played their parts as singers, magicians, healers, physicians – all rolled into one – and tried to mitigate people's miseries, keeping alive the earlier tradition of the great shramans who gave out their all for the good and the happiness of the multitude. Siddha love of humanity is manifest in every word and act. Tirumular's oft-quoted line – 'May world be as happy as I am' – brings out the majestic concern for all human beings.

The Siddha language has often been described as rough, rugged, and paradoxical. And strange as it may sound, their language bears close resemblance to Kabir's *sadhukkari* (mixed language), rough rhetoric and *ulat baansian* (upside down language). On the one hand, as outcastes and wandering recluses rebelling against all forms of establishment including the literary, which was particularly oppressive in Tamil, the Siddhas had a strong preference for the people's language, the colloquial. And, on the other, because of their multiple yearnings and unresolved doubts including their passion for spiritual accomplishments (that had to be attempted at individual basis) and their desire for social awakening and transformation (that demanded popular participation), they had to invent a language that can best be appreciated in context. Divorced from that context, their idioms and diction appear to be highly esoteric and contradictory, which give their cultural adversaries an excuse to label them (like Kabir again!) as mystics. Whatever the reality, the Tamil Siddhas, like Kabir, were not interested in nurturing mysticism. They were highly committed individuals whose agenda was nothing less than bringing a complete turn-around in personal and social affairs. If we read them in the social context, their seemingly difficult language becomes lucid and luminous. All the Siddhas abhorred Sanskritised Tamil and their poems brimming with popular epigrams, witticisms, earthy adages, and wisecracks carry the colloquial expression and vocabulary of the common people. Their fluid vocabulary does not accept a division between the sacred and the profane, the refined and the coarse. Interestingly, like Tagore who was profoundly influenced by Kabir, Subramania Bharathi (1882-1921), the towering Tamil poet of the twentieth century, was highly impressed by Siddha ideology and poetry. He consciously employed Siddha folk meters and colloquialism in his poetry and went on to declare in his autobiography, 'There were many Siddhas before me, I too am one in their line.'

Virashaiva Socialism in Karnataka

A remarkable episode in the medieval socio-religious history of south India is the rise of Virashaiva movement in Karnataka. Virashaivas or 'heroic followers of Shiva' – also known as Lingayatas – too, like the other offshoots of the Bhakti movement, are characterised by the combination of egalitarianism and spiritual excellence. The movement arose in the twelfth and thirteenth centuries under the dynamic leadership of Basava. A brahman by birth, Basava had refused to undergo the *upanayan* (sacred thread) ceremony that entitles a high caste male to become *dwija*, the twice-born. Having thus declassed/decaste himself, he gained the confidence of the masses, and led a movement against brahman domination. The movement targeted those rituals and practices that sanctified inequalities and exploitation. Adopting a multi-pronged strategy aimed at a cultural transformation, Basava, who later rose to become the prime minister of the Kalachuri king of Kalyan, gave the movement a cohesive shape and radical orientation.

The movement was remarkable in the sense that it not merely endeavoured to reform the established order but strove, through competition and confrontation, to transform the power structure of time-honoured traditions. It was a spirited quest for equal access of the unprivileged classes to political power and economic share, and, at the same time, for limiting the arbitrary powers wielded by the brahmans (Bali 1978: 67-100). Embarking on a revolutionary journey, it took the shape of a mass movement as men and women cutting across castes, high and low, joined the experimental community of Lingayatas. They created their own sacred literature in the form of *vachanas*, short lyrical exhortations and devotional hymns. Over two hundred writers who composed these vachanas used the colloquial idiom of Kannada, shorn of all Sanskrit pedantry, and advocated ideas extraordinarily liberal for the time, several of which betray shramanic influences. Their literature rejected almost completely the caste system. Their anti-casteism was supported by emphasising the spiritual value of every kind of labour, connected with a strong emphasis on social service.

The egalitarian ideals of the Virashaivas implied a new morality in which the people were required to break with their problematic past and give up all caste pride together with the vices of their background. Everyone had to accept converts from the lower strata as equals. Basava advocated and encouraged full commensality and connubium within the community. One such incident, a sparkling cameo in India's social history, showcases Virashaiva's boundless passion for what is today called social engineering. It involves the violation of that most 'sacred' law laid down by the Dharmashastras – a marriage of a brahman girl with an 'untouchable' boy. Crossing this last frontier, Madhuvayya (or Madhuvaras), a patrician brahman who (like Basava) was a minister in the court of Bijjala at Kalyan, gave his daughter in marriage to the son of Haralayya, the lowest of the low in caste hierarchy who did leatherwork to earn his living. This kind of marriage was considered to be the worst form of *pratiloma*, highly unnatural, and hence strongly objectionable. An *anuloma* relation involving a higher caste man and a 'lower' caste woman was somewhat forgivable, but a *pratiloma* relation was the stuff of utter opprobrium in brahman eyes.

Outraged by this marriage, the reactionaries, led by King Bijjala, started a vicious witch-hunt against the Virashaivas. According to the contemporary records, both fathers together with the bridegroom were arrested, blinded, chained to the leg of an elephant, and then dragged to death along the streets of the town. Large-scale persecutions followed, forcing the Virashaivas to flee the town and take shelter in distant and safer places (Schouten 1995: 48-50). Many contemporary and later works in Kannada celebrate the martyrdom of Madhuvayya and Haralayya. Haralayya went on to become an iconic figure in the history of the Virashaivas – many regard him as the forerunner of the dalit fight for emancipation in the recent times.

Basava himself set an example by renouncing his high caste status and office. Declaring himself as the relative of the lowest devotees in the community, he proudly described his new family ties in a number of fascinating vachanas. One such is unmistakable testimony to his radicalism.

> *The boy of the servant in Cannayya's house*
> *and the girl of the maid in Kakkayya's house –*
> *they both went to the field to gather dung*
> *and then they made love.*
> *A child was born to them – that was me.*
> *So say the Lord of the Meeting Rivers be my witness!*
> (Schouten 1995: 51)

In another popular vachana Basava exhorts people to rise above all differences, underlining the close connection between social values and spirituality. Basava sublimely discards his background, his family and caste, and hopes to be admitted into the new circle of people who share the same spiritual and social values:

> *O Lord, let them not say:*
> *to whom belongs he, to whom, to whom?*
> *Let them say: he is ours, yes ours, ours!*
> *O Lord of the Meeting Rivers,*
> *let them say: a son of your house!* (ibid.: 25)

In several vachanas, Basava insists that he owes the bond with God to the 'low-born' devotees in the Virashaiva community and not to his brahman family. In a vachana he dissociates himself from his aristocratic-brahman background and sketches a family portrait which includes only devotees from the most humble background. He even uses his close relationship with the 'low' caste devotees as an argument which must compel God to show his mercy:

> Our Cannayya, the untouchable, is my father,
> and our Kakkayya, the tanner, is my uncle;
> See, Cikkayya is our grandfather,
> and our Bommayya, the lute-player, is my elder brother.
> So why do you not know me,
> O Lord of the Meeting Rivers? (ibid.: 52)

The 'untouchable' Madar Cannayya, idolised by Basava in the above vachana as his father, was a major Virashaiva saint-poet. He castigates caste in one of his vachanas by presenting a remarkable line-up of celebrated cultural personalities from the despised castes:

> Sankhya was a sweeper;/Agastya, a huntsman;
> Durvasa, a cobbler;/Dadhichi, a locksmith;
> Kasyapa, a blacksmith;/Romaja, a coppersmith;
> Kaundilya, a barber;
> So, why should you then,
> In ignorance of this,
> Insist on caste? (Ray et al. 2000: 480-1)

Many saints entreat their fellow beings to give up their caste identity and loyalty. In a long poem, Allama pinpoints the 'six errors' one must overcome in order to become a truly religions person. The first major barrier, he says, is *jati* that hinders people to realise their real worth. The second fallacy is the varnashramadharma that gives sanctity to four caste categories and four stages of life. The other errors, according to Allama, are the pride in one's own background (*kula*), lineage, name and native land (Schouten 1995: 54-5). In other words, one simply cannot become a Virashaiva without forsaking one's belief in distinctions based on caste.

Siddharama, for instance, asserts that caste is anathema to a Virashaiva:

> *What does it mean to belong to the system of the four castes?*
> *Look, he is a Virashaiva who transcends the four castes.* (ibid.: 54)

Comparing innumerable vachanas like the ones quoted above with the egalitarian Buddhist texts, Schouten points out that Basava appeared to be deeply familiar with – and influenced by – the teachings of the Buddha. This, he says, was not improbable as Buddhism was very strong in several regions in Karnataka:

> *... In 1095, only about ten years before Basava's birth, a large Buddhist monastery was founded in Dambal (in the present Dharwar district). Dambal later became one of the most important religious centres of Virashaivism. ... The strong resistance against the caste system, as it occurred in the Buddhist tradition, was still preserved in the last strongholds of Buddhism in northern Karnataka when Basava tried to find an alternative for the strict Brahmana values of his family. It is an obvious suggestion that he also acquainted himself with the Buddhist tradition. In that tradition, he would certainly have been fascinated by the egalitarian philosophy that rejected discrimination on the basis of caste.* (Schouten 1995: 61)

A sparkling feature of Virashaivism is the strong presence of women who played a significant role in the movement. There were many influential female ascetics in early Virashaivism. There are instances of women who joined their husbands in the radical movement on an equal footing. The movement severely criticised the brahmanical legitimation of female subordination and tried to build a new vision on the man-woman relationship. It was characteristic of Virashaivism that there was place in it for the most unconventional of women like Akka Mahadevi and Muktayakka. The foremost woman among vachanakaras, Mahadevi was mainly interested in her individual redemption, but her spiritual insight has social implications. The following poem is an exquisite and typical example of this:

> *Those who have become equal by love,*
> *Should they heed background or pretensions?*
> *Those who have gone mad,*

> do they know shame or restraint?
> Those who are loved by the Lovely Lord of the Jasmines,
> Could they have loyalty to the world? (ibid.: 30)

Akka Mahadevi appears to imply here that traditional distinctions are of no value to those who experience the divine love. Background or pretensions do not matter to the true devotees, made equal for love. The word *kula* includes all factors which are determined by birth, such as family, gender, and caste. In her own ardent style, Akka says that those besotted with divine love are like insane people who do not care for the established rules and cherished values.

The Lingayatas adopted a pragmatic approach to realise their ideals and came up with alternative rituals, ceremonies, taboos and other religio-cultural symbols. The movement not only rejected the core values and social institutions associated with the brahmans, it also developed an institutional framework for an egalitarian order:

In its desire for 'human relationships', it felt it was necessary to break down interpersonal barriers and conventional norms that prevented interpersonal contact on issues like interdining and intercaste marriage, i.e. it discarded the notions of purity and pollution between brahmans and non-brahmans. It revealed the realities hidden by rituals, practices, conventions of brahmans, in order to be liberated from the oppression of brahman domination.
(Bali 1978: 69)

The movement laid special emphasis on the dignity of labour and connected it with social progress and spiritual uplift. All people were required to work to earn their living irrespective of their status. Social mobilisation was taken up vigorously, and people were recruited to the community through the institution of *math*. All in all, the Virashaiva movement was a 'social upheaval by and for the poor, the low-caste and the outcaste against the rich and the privileged . . . ' (Ramanujan, cited in Bali, ibid.).

The aims and achievements of the Virashaiva movement were ahead of other such movements. And despite its later decline and disintegration as the movement fell victim to rigidity and social hierarchy in its own ranks against which they once fought so heroically, the Lingayatas today form the single largest ethnic group in Karnataka. Though the movement later lost its initial zeal and fervour for social change and gradually faded away, its legacy of struggle against brahmanical domination still continues. In fact, it was the community of Lingayatas that provided the core structure for the backward classes movement in the Madras Presidency in the twentieth century.

VARAKARI MOVEMENT IN MAHARASHTRA

Maharashtra was another region where the Bhakti movement made its powerful presence felt. From the thirteenth to the seventeenth century, there flourished an essentially heterodox resurgence, known popularly as the Varakari movement which contributed a great deal to the transformation of Maharashtrian society and culture. Here too, the saint-poets from the lower spectrum of society struggled for religious equality and demanded social justice based on the humanitarian principle. Though they employed some traditional religious symbols and acts, rather than launching a direct attack on or hostility with the privileged and the powerful, there is little doubt that their concern for the poor and the caste-oppressed implied a strong disapproval of the vested interests of the power groups (Sardar 1978: 102). Since socio-economic control was often exerted through the medium of religion and culture, the Bhakti leaders' emphasis on equality in that sphere was both appropriate and effective as a means of expressing dissent and protest. By doing so, they not only opened the gates of knowledge, religion, and culture for the hitherto excluded castes, but also explored and utilised the potential of social change that such opportunities entailed. Since they struggled to make available all knowledge, even the most sacred one, to everyone, through people's own language – a distinct hallmark of the Bhakti movement everywhere – they also made a historic contribution in the growth of Marathi language and literature.

The religious upheaval in Maharashtra had strong social undercurrents which carried the seeds of the popular non-brahman movement that submerged the region in the nineteenth and twentieth centuries. M. G. Ranade was forthright in calling the Bhakti movement 'unbrahmanical' and a basically 'heterodox' protest movement 'of the masses, and not of the classes'. The 'occasional brahmans' like Gyaneshwar and Eknath who joined the movement were notable exceptions who were shunned and snubbed by their caste members. For instance, when Gyaneshwar, his brother and sister, who were children of a brahman ascetic, returned to the living of a householder, they were greeted with the choicest abuse. Earlier, their parents, who had scandalised the community by re-entering into the householder's stage, had to expiate their 'sins' by giving up their lives – they were forced to drown themselves in a river. Similarly, Eknath, who dared to feed the 'untouchables' at a community dinner, had to undergo a purificatory rite. What is surprising is the fact that despite being despised and humiliated by caste bigots, Gyaneshwar and Eknath easily caved in before the reactionaries.

Ghurye has concurred with the view that the occasional brahman saints '. . . cannot be regarded as being wholly in a direct line of this movement. They still laid much emphasis on the philosophical aspect of religion' (2000: 103). The fact is, many of these liberal brahmans were deeply impressed by the ideals of the 'low-born' Bhakti leaders. This made them give up some of their caste prejudice, but come as they did from the highest echelon of the caste hierarchy, they found it difficult to present a forthright critique of the discriminatory system, not to speak of joining the battle against caste. Their emphasis on problematic shastric tradition, which Ghurye euphemistically calls 'philosophical aspect of religion', was due to their inability to come out of their caste cocoons. Ghurye, however, is candid in admitting that, 'Almost everywhere the Brahmans figured as opponents of the new movements which appeared to them to upset the good old Brahmanic way of salvation through proper rites and ceremonies and to undermine the system of caste' (ibid.: 104).

The task of reform and transformation in Maharashtra, as elsewhere, was left to the shudra saint-teachers who ingeniously wielded different religious idioms to challenge the power structure based on the caste ideology. At that time, religion was used by the elite to maintain a hold on the people in terms of material benefits and free services, especially through institutionalised caste beliefs and practices. Like their associates in other regions, the prime target of the Bhakti leaders in Maharashtra was this pseudo-religion and its untenable dogmas that had become the tool of the rich and the powerful to perpetuate the exploitative system.

The movement in Maharashtra produced three outstanding saint-poets: Namdev, a *shimpi* or tailor by profession, who flourished in the later half of the fourteenth century; his great contemporary Chokhamela who hailed from the 'untouchable' Mahar caste; and perhaps the greatest of them all, Tukaram (1608-50), who also came from a 'low' caste. They all belonged to the Varakari sect with its main deity Vitthal at Pandharpur. Contrary to historical reality, the Varakari school has been ingeniously appropriated in the orthodox Vaishnava cult and, then, conveniently linked to the Vedic-brahmanic tradition. In the orthodox version, the popular cult of Vitthal as a young cowherd boy merges into the cult of brahmanised Krishna. Nothing can be farther from the truth.

It is well-known that in the Varakari ethos it is not the deity that grants salvation, but devotion to the name of God – the invisible Supreme Reality. Unlike the brahmanical orthodoxy, it is this ardent devotion to the formless God which is the rallying point of all Bhakti saints in Maharashtras and elsewhere. But the elite chroniclers and historians, save some candid remarks by a Ranade here or a Ghurye there, have tried to present the Maharashtrian movement as basically conformist and conventional. They conveniently seek its roots in orthodox Vaishnavism and portray the Varakari luminaries as faithful followers of the Vedic-brahmanic tradition. Underlining the brahmanic appropriation of the Varakari leaders, Vaudeville writes:

In modern times, a renewed enthusiasm of the literate, and especially of the Brahman elite, for the Varakari poet-saints, has accentuated the tendency to view the medieval literary tradition of Maharashtra as essentially orthodox and Vaishnava. Furthermore, books were written from this point of view in both Marathi and Hindi, comparing the sants of Maharashtra with their counterparts in northern India and Karnataka. This has led to considerable confusion and to erroneous interpretations, particularly concerning the northern sants, who cannot be said to fit into an orthodox Vaishnava pattern at all. (1999: 246)

She views the Maharashtrian bhakti centering around the

Vitthal cult as 'nominal' Vaishnavism, and delineates its roots in Tantric form of Shaivinism inherited from the Nathpanthi tradition. In fact, the very icon of Vitthal was originally a Kannada deity, revered by the Lingayatas and Nathpanthis which bore a close similarity to the Shiva character which is suggested by the *Shiv-linga* as its headgear:

> *The mysterious apparition of Vitthala on the bank of the Bhima river at Pandharpur did not, however, result in the immediate conversion of the population to Vaishnavism. Shiva remained the supreme deity – as attested to by the most ancient temple in Pandharpur, the Pundalik temple, now half submerged in the river bed. To this day, it remains a Shiva temple, in the hands of low-caste Koli fishermen.* (ibid.: 251)

Besides, the earliest texts written in Marathi, the *Vivekadarpana* and the *Gorakha-Gita*, belong to the Nath tradition which traces Gorakhanath's spiritual heritage to Adinath or Shiva himself. There is evidence, Vaudeville says, suggesting the strong presence of Nathpanthis in the region. While the pandits of the Vedic tradition never mixed with the 'low' caste people, the Nathpanthis freely fraternised with them, gaining great popularity among the caste-oppressed.

Just as important, the formal or informal founder of the Varakari lineage was Namdev and not Gyaneshwar as established by the Sanskritist spin-doctors who trace the origin of saint tradition in Maharashtra (as well as the entire Bhakti movement) to the Vedic-brahmanic ideology. In one tradition Namdev is said to be the disciple of one Nagratha – a name that clearly suggests a connection with the Nathpanthi lineage. Besides, many others link Namdev with Visoba Khechara, whom the former is popularly believed to have accepted as his guru. The name Khechara – literally 'one moving in the air' – too refers to a Siddha, an accomplished master endowed with supernatural powers. His first name, Visoba, derived from *visne*, literally to rest or lie at ease, again points to the spontaneity and ease which was the hallmark of the Sahajiya Buddhism and its related tradition of Nath-yogis (ibid.: 252-3). Whatever the actual historical reality, in the brahmanised historiography Namdev is portrayed as an orthodox Vaishnava saint whose life and career revolved around the traditional bhakti. Any critical study of Namdev and other Varakaris, however, leaves no doubt that they all were extraordinary figures endowed with a capacity for original thinking and analysis.

It appears more likely that given the time-spirit of the age, the non-elite saint-poets found it difficult to express their socio-religious ideas independently, and many of them, especially in Maharashtra, expediently took recourse to the time-honoured shastric tradition by discovering radical meanings in the orthodox religion and scriptures. The Varakaris were hardly in a position to take on the power structure. However, there is little doubt that by opening the door of personal accomplishments to everyone, they wanted to create a ferment in society, so that a new culture could evolve where there would be no distinction between man and man on the basis of caste, creed, and gender. If we keep in mind the dominant role that religion played in that era – not only in social life and caste structure but also in the domains of knowledge, art, literature, philosophy, ethics, family life – we may better appreciate the dynamics of their religious politics which was not divorced from social and material liberation of their people.

Namdev, who set the social parameters of the movement in Maharashtra, for instance, asks in a forthright manner, that if milk given by cows of different colours is the same, how could the distinction between the supposedly 'high-born' and 'low-born' stand scrutiny. While discarding caste, the tailor Namdev sometimes weaves his professional pride into the texture of his exquisite devotional songs (see Vaudeville 1997: 332).

Deeply troubled by the ugly social reality, the devotee in Namdev entreats God to intervene and play a pro-active role in destroying the brahman-shudra duality. He poignantly asks God that when the brahmans insult a true devotee like himself (Namdev) shouting 'Shudra! Shudra!' and bash him up and throw him out of the temple, does it not amount to insulting God Himself?

> *When I entered the temple,*
> *they all went mad after me:*
> *Shouting 'Shudra! Shudra!' they beat me and threw me out:*
> *what shall I do, O my Father Vitthala?*

If you grant me salvation after death,
who will know about it?
When those Brahmans called me Dhedh,[4]
was it not a blow at your Honour?
You are known as the Merciful, the Compassionate One,
all-powerful is Your arm!
Then the temple itself turned round towards Nam
and turned its back on the Brahmans! (ibid.: 341)

Namdev pleads to God to do something about this gross injustice here and now! Presenting his case before the Almighty, he also appears to mock the theory of transmigration: 'If you grant me salvation after death, who will know about it?' So, he demands justice in this life in full public view so that it can serve as a lesson to the anti-social elements. He is even able to convince God to take 'action' against the culprits: the temple representing 'the Compassionate One' moves closer to the true devotee, Nam, and turns it back on the hypocritical priests! This poetic justice is achieved by the radical spirit of the Bhakti saints with which they envisioned God and religion. In their hands religion became a weapon to challenge the injustice and oppression of the power elites. Since the very injustice and oppression had its basis in brahmanical ideology it was imperative that the essential spirit of religion be used as a counter-weapon to subdue the perpetrators of social wrongs.

In his social activities and verses, Namdev discarded the traditional religion and its mechanical performances and rituals, emphasising that religion should better concern itself with the people's misery and helplessness. A man of the masses, he gave expression to the inner and worldly agonies of man in his poems that stress love, compassion, sensitivity, and other such sentiments. Later, he became itinerant, and finally settled in the Punjab where he played the role of a bridge-builder between the north and the south in the context of Bhakti radicalism. Significantly, it was probably Namdev who devised the medium of *kirtan* – congregational singing – outside the precincts of the temple complexes, the doors of which were closed to the lower classes. This policy that included and embraced everyone, especially the lowly people, in religious affairs was a bold step towards the democratisation of society. No wonder Namdev attracted a huge following among the masses, and became a symbol of inspiration for many talented poets from the lower orders in Maharashtra and northern India. Outstanding among his admirers were Janabai, Gora Kumbhara, Narhari Sonar, Joga Paramananda, Savata Mali, Banka Mahar and, above all, Chokhamela.

Chokhamela is a striking personality in the long lineage of Varakari saint-poets. Born in 'untouchable' Mahar caste, he was a contemporary and a close friend of Namdev. He is to the Maharashtrian dalits what Ravidas is to the dalits of north India. This gifted poet of rare human sensibility composed lyrical poems of exquisite beauty in Marathi known as *abhangas*. His poems, like other Bhakti verses, are devotional on the surface but subversive in their social content as they encapsulate strong dissent and protest against the culture of oppression. Suffused with ennobling ideals and moral values, they take up the cause of the poor with God. The harsh and inhuman circumstances in which the untouchables were forced to live made him take, at times, a radical posture and an attitude of defiance. The prevailing state of desolation and abjection among the untouchables made Chokhamela question God's sense of justice. In a state of utter anguish, he confronts his dear God thus:

Extremely bad food to one, very good to the other; one may not get food even after demanding and another gets pleasure and the grandeur of kingly title . . . is this your sense of justice? (Sardar 1978: 123)

Chokha can get exasperated with his God because in the Varakari tradition the Almighty entertains a very special love for the poor and the lowly. Vitthala's love for his devotees is not simply the expression of his own loving and merciful nature, it is a real and reciprocal love which makes the god as much dependent on his true devotees as they are on him. Namdev has testified that Vitthala entertained a special love for the poorest and lowliest of them all, Chokha the Mahar. 'It is characteristic that in the legends related to the encounters between Vitthala and Chokhamela, it is always the god who takes the initiative' (Vaudeville 1999: 226). When Chokha is abused and turned out at the temple gate by the brahmans, and even his devotion from outside is regarded as a source of pollution, the deity plays tricks on the sanctimonious brahmans:

making a mockery of their pretensions to 'purity', the god is delighted in the company of the 'polluting' Chokha. 'It is as though He actually resented being a prisoner in His own temple, bound by the endless pretentious rituals of the priests. It is as if God Himself were sowing the seeds of social rebellion in the hearts of the downtrodden' (ibid.)

However, the temper of Chokha is less rebellious than that of Kabir and Ravidas, who were more radical in their rejection of rituals and beliefs, including idol-worship. But Chokha's devotionalism, too, represents an attack on the unjust and inhuman caste order that denied the 'lowly born' even the right to offer prayers. Many scholars, however, greatly underscore Chokha's compliance with orthodox custom and his acceptance of his own station of life as a lowly Mahar. They point out that excepting the occasional, and often feeble, criticism of the concept of untouchability, his poems are by and large anchored in the traditional devotion and piety of the devotee. In support of their claim, they cite a few selected poems, probably distorted over time, which were published in the name of Chokha. Most such poems are spurious, because many bear the names of later saints. In reality, while the brahmans were using God to support an ascriptive social order which privileged them and demonised the majority, saint-poets like Chokha were doing their utmost to reclaim God on the side of justice and human dignity. An authentic voice does come through in some of his available poems, where Chokha leaves no room for ambiguity. On being hounded and persecuted by the temple brahmans, Chokha cries his heart out:

> O Vithu! Now run to my help! Hurry up!
> The Badves (priests) are beating me (saying):
> 'What crime have you committed?
> That garland of Vithoba, how has it come to your neck?'
> They abuse me, crying: 'The mahar has polluted God!'
> (Vaudeville 1999: 230-1)

On the question of purity and pollution, Chokha says, 'God alone is pure; no one else is pure, everyone is impure'. What Chokha really implies here is: either everyone is pure, or everyone impure, because in essence there is no difference between man and man.

Distressed by his despised place in society due to his 'low' caste, Chokha even accuses God in a poem of being 'cruel' while 'casting me away to be born'. In another *abhanga*, he narrates the suffering that he has to endure every day because of his caste:

> O God! Vile is my birth,
> How then could I serve You?
> People shout at me: 'Get away, get away!'
> How then could I meet You?
> If they happen to touch my hand
> They pour water on themselves!
> O my Govind! O my Gopal!
> Chokhamela cries for Your mercy! (ibid.: 230)

And then, unable to control his anger against the brahmans who have made life hell for people like him, an infuriated Chokha let out a torrent of curses:

> Cursed be their actions, cursed be their thinking,
> Cursed be their birth and their life!
> Cursed be their 'Knowledge of the Absolute' –
> tis all but vain talk –
> There is neither pity nor forgiveness nor peace in their hearts!
> Cursed be those postures and those hair knots of theirs –
> In vain did they put on an ascetic garb!
> Says Chokha, cursed be the birth of such people:
> In the end they'll endure the torments of hell! (ibid.: 232)

The Varakari tradition reached its pinnacle of glory and popularity with Tukaram in the seventeenth century. A legend in his own time, he is perhaps the brightest star in the Varakari firmament. Born in a grocer's family, he was persecuted by brahmans for the growing popularity of his rebellious social thinking. He is a poetic genius whose lyrical poems echo the heart-beat of the common man. He has the power to penetrate the heart of material and spiritual life from a simple and humanitarian point of view. He is truly a people's poet; his poetry is free from the pretentious pedantry of Sanskritist wordsmiths. A man of profound social conscience, it is the affection of the lowly and the poor that he sought in his devotion, a quality that has greatly endeared him to the marginalised people. His deep affinity with the poor, his outrage against injustice and caste oppression, and his powerful advocacy of equality and brotherhood make him an iconic figure for the suffering multitude. It is not surprising that people in villages still sing his songs.

Among Tuka's ardent admirers was Mahatma Phule, who considered him to be the pre-eminent saint of cultivators. The similarity between Tuka's and Phule's critique of brahman power, despite their different modes of articulation, is striking. There is little doubt that Phule and his friends found in Tuka a kindred spirit and a role model. Tuka's popular maxim, *satya asatyashi man kele gwahi* – 'to decide as to the nature of truth and untruth, one should go by one's own reflection and experience'. In a virtual denunciation of the sacerdotal literature, Tuka continued by deriding scripture-quoting pandits as 'beasts of burden'. The knowledge that is acquired, Tuka argued, by the dispassionate survey of the world is far superior to the one contained in the scriptures. No scholar of Sanskrit and not versed in any of the scriptures (which was any way beyond the reach of a shudra), Tukaram did not criticise the shastras outright. Yet he came down heavily on vainglorious pandits whose sole claim to greatness rested on their monopoly of the Sanskrit scriptures. Berating those 'highly educated idiots' for upholding the ideals of authority and status based on caste, Tukaram rejected the caste culture that surrounded him, and demanded a radical alteration in the ascriptive ethos advanced by the self-seeking orthodoxies. He categorically said:

> *Compassion means good feeling towards all living things,*
> *And also the destruction of the evil-doers.* (Nemade 1997: 49)

True religiosity, he asserted, is not represented by temple paraphernalia but by service to mankind:

> *The light is lit within;*
> *Tukaram says, I now remain only to serve others.* (ibid.: 46)

His definition of a man of God reiterates his deep sympathy with the society's underclass:

> *He is the true saint who embraces the oppressed and unfortunate;*
> *God is found with him.* (ibid.: 54)

The humanising and socialising work of the Varakari tradition was taken further by Tukaram, who relentlessly questioned and challenged brahman domination. His bold utterances against caste and widespread adherence to caste in the name of religion often attracted vituperative comments from his brahman adversaries. Tukaram responded by presenting the holier-than-thou pandit as a figure of ridicule, laughing at his 'Vedic parrotry', making a mockery of his hypocrisy, and taking pot-shots at his pathetic pride and pomposity:

> *Well done, O God, you made me a Kunbi,*
> *Otherwise I would have been doomed by hypocrisy.*
> . . .
> *Tuka says, you go on with your Vedic parrotry,*
> *Don't come in my way.*
>
> *Had I been learned, it would have brought calamities on me,*
> *I would have been subjected to pride and arrogance,*
> *I would have taken the path of hell* . . . (ibid.: 30)

While the Bhakti saints in other regions, especially in the north, had adopted a monotheistic radicalism eschewing all forms of idolatry, the Varakaris, including Tukaram, adopted a middle way by honouring their only God, Vitthala. However, all of them had similar socio-religious agenda and their common target was the entrenched brahman orthodoxy. For example, in response to the brahmanical humiliation and worthlessness heaped on the shudra masses, Tuka retorted, 'It is only we, the shudra devotees, that know the real meaning of the Vedas, others only carry the load of it.' In another *abhanga* he says sarcastically and bluntly, '. . . the learned brahmans will have to become servile to us' (ibid.: 36).

The injustice, misery and poverty that Tuka saw all around him exasperated him so much that he even threatened his God to do something about it or else:

> *I shall spoil your good name*
> *If you continue to be indifferent.* (ibid.: 44)

When Tukaram realised, to his agony, that God was not showing any interest in mitigating man's misery, he did not even hesitate to write:

To me God is dead,
Let him be for those who think that he is. (ibid.)

It was in such moments of sublime distress and disappointment that a seasoned devotee like Tuka cried out to God:

I am ashamed of calling myself your servant,
You are cruel and callous
You allow your children to cry with hunger. (ibid.)

Tuka with cymbals in his hands, singing his soul-stirring lyrics that celebrated social equity and unity based on it, became extremely popular. While his adversaries were scratching their heads debating such questions as 'Can a shudra's mind perceive knowledge? Can he be a spiritual leader?', people from far and near flocked to hear Tuka at his native place. Adding insult to the injured pride of the pandits were many brahmans, including women, who would attend Tukaram's group singing, defying the caste injunction. One such follower was Bahinabai, a poet in her own right, who invited the wrath of the conservative brahmans. All this is recorded in Bahinabai's autobiography which also confirms several stories regarding the brahmanic persecution of Tukaram (Nemade 1997: 28-33).

The brahmans held Tuka guilty of many offences including belittling the value of Sanskrit learning. Their earnings dwindling, one Mambaji, who nurtured a long-standing rancour against Tukaram, viciously targeted Bahinabai and her family. Bahinabai writes that Mambaji and others convinced the respected Pune brahmans of Tuka's culpability and launched a witch-hunt against the shudra poet. The Patil of Tuka's village was persuaded to file a suit and take exemplary action against the 'guilty'. Tuka was thrashed, his cow was beaten to death (a shudra's cow is not that holy for the pandits, after all!), he was ex-communicated, and his writings prohibited. According to legend, a collection of his songs was thrown into the river.

Why were the pandits intent on destroying Tuka's verses? The answer can be found in Tuka's own words:

We possess the wealth of words,
With weapons of words we will fight;
Words are the breath of our life,
We will distribute the wealth of words among the people. (ibid.: 59)

The humiliation of ostracism and isolation, and the ordeal of being deprived of his verses, that this genius of the seventeenth century had to undergo are not easily imaginable in this age. All that Tuka could say to defend his subversive verses was that he was ordered by God to compose his songs. With God on his side, he continued to compose verses. The end of his life is shrouded in mystery. After Tuka was forced to throw all his writings into the river in around 1645, he went into a prolonged silence and meditation, refusing even food. According to the legend, after thirteen days of continuous fasting, his papers floated up on the water. Strangely enough, this 'incident' is corroborated by several of his contemporaries. The news of the miracle spread far and wide and Tuka's followers celebrated it as their glorious triumph over the tormentors.

By all accounts, this miraculous incident appears to be a ruse to avert any popular protest against Tuka's persecution. It does not seem unlikely that the people had actually come forward to rescue their beloved saint-poet who was being tortured and humiliated by the brahman adversaries. All we have to interpret this incident is based on the brahmanical account since Tuka and his followers have not left any written document regarding the same. Popular resistance may have forced the pandits to lift the ban on Tuka's writings. The 'miracle' might have been invented as a compromise by the chroniclers to obfuscate and sugarcoat the bitter brahman-shudra antagonism which gave birth to this crisis in the first place.

Unlike Shankara, the Varakaris never denounced *sansar*, this wordly existence, as *maya* or illusion. As Tukaram says, 'That the world is *maya* is a half-truth, as it so appears to the human intellect' (Nemade 1997: 12). None of the Varakaris were enamoured of renunciation and asceticism. Tukaram said the begging-bowl was shameful (ibid.: 55). Leading Varakaris such as Gora Kumbhar, Narhari Sonar, Savata Mali, and Sona Nhavi led a normal family life and carried on their household duties. This balanced, life-affirming approach brought in a unique reconciliation of wordly and spiritual life, which was an outstanding feature of the movement. With the inculcation of human values and right kind of attitude, Tuka was confident that he would commit the whole world to happiness.

The Varakari tradition has made a tremendous contribution to Marathi language and literature. Its leaders played a pivotal role in generating progressive broad-mindedness and social consciousness among the people. Its democratic influence broke down caste distinctions and accorded respect to the long-suppressed shudras and women. It is a measure of the Varakari catholicity that it accommodated not only the lowered castes but also Muslims within its fold on an equal footing. Its ethos thus provided a counterpoise to the brahmanic domination and discrimination. In an initiative of far-reaching consequences, the Varakaris cast aside Sanskrit and adopted Marathi as the medium of literary and religious activity. Since their literature carried a direct appeal to the lowly people, they consciously broke the heavily Sanskritised tradition of Marathi literature by using colloquial idioms and commonly understood words. They successfully contested the prestige of Sanskrit by producing high quality literature in their mother-tongue. Making a mockery of the intellectual snobbery of the pandits who paraded the extraordinariness of Sanskrit by calling it *devabhasha*, they asked if Sanskrit was supposed to be the language of the gods, was Prakrit or Marathi the contribution of thieves and lowly elements?

However, the Maharashtrian saint-poets could not develop a consistent radical critique of brahmanism like their counterparts in the north and south because some of their fellow-travellers – Gyaneshwar and Eknath, for instance, who came from brahman families – found it difficult to disown their scriptures. On the one hand, they approved of equalitarian thinking and made some appropriate noises, but on the other, they strongly upheld the shastras and smritis that sanction all kinds of division between individuals on 'religious' grounds. Both Gyaneshwar and Eknath insisted that every person must follow his caste role prescribed in the 'holy scriptures'. Gyaneshwar went to the extent of suggesting that even if a brahman were to be hungry he should not eat the delicacies of a shudra. This author of *Gyaneshwari*, the popular Marathi rendition of the *Gita*, was even against speaking with the untouchables! Eknath, relatively more liberal, also insisted on the observance of caste restrictions concerning eating and drinking. They had no problem with the caste hierarchy as it had the authority of the Vedas. Gyaneshwar clearly advocated that anyone interested in making his life meaningful was duty-bound to accept the guidelines outlined in the shruti-smriti, and must discard the things that have been condemned by the shastras (Sardar 1978). Ramdas, brahman religious icon of the seventeenth century, was more forthright: 'Can we expect our *antyaja* (the lowly born) to be our guru because he is a pandit (i.e. learned)? asked Ramdas. No!

Social Dimension of Bhakti and the Brahman Backlash

The defining feature of the Bhakti movement was a radical religiosity suffused with the spirit of dissent and protest, intimately bound up with the campaign for a socio-cultural change. Its subaltern leaders wielded devotionalism as a cultural weapon against caste. In fact, the transformatory zeal was at the heart of the movement and devotionalism was an offshoot of this zeal. The common people found in religious idioms a means of working towards a just, humane and egalitarian order. The language of their protest in a vocabulary and idiom which the folk could understand was especially imperative in the absence of modern democratic ideas and institutions. This does not mean, as suggested in the elitist historiography, that their resistance was confined to the religious sphere. Their dissent extended to the social, political and economic spheres and also to cultural ideas and institutions. In other words, the devotionalism they employed was a decoy.

The orientation of the movement gave the much-maligned lowered castes a positive self-image as it rejected the innately inferior status to which they were relegated by the brahmanical Hinduism. Its ideology was essentially the ideology of a new society where the absolute value of the so-called low-born was not inferior to that of so-called high-born. Implicit in its vision was the recognition that the people who worked with their hands were as good (or better) as those – priests and feudal lords – who did not. Leaders of the movement realised that a society which does not accord respect to labour does so at its own peril. Kabir and Tukaram were categorical that begging was like death: a religious person should not beg from door to door. Demanding labour from everyone, they contended that though the world was afflicted by poverty, ignorance and sorrow, miseries could be overcome by work and a virtuous life. This was in direct contrast to the parasitism of the major figures of the priestly culture such as Tulsidas, who shunned physical work in the belief that chanting magic mantras alone was the panacea for all the ills besetting the individual and society.

Many flag-bearers of the institutionalised brahmanical religion joined the movement to contest and sabotage from within the ideals of the *nirguna* saint-poets who had 'challenged the tenets of feudalism in a feudal age'. It is significant that against the monotheistic radicalism of *nirguna* bhakti, poet-devotees belonging to priestly or upper classes – Chaitanya, Surdas, Vidyapati, Vallabhacharya and, above all, Tulsidas – professed *saguna* bhakti. While the first four were besotted with their flute-playing Krishna, his *lila* (playfulness) and dalliance with damsels, Tulsi made Rama – the paternalistic upholder of the varnashrama-dharma – his hero. They also celebrated love, harmony, and morality but within the hierarchical structure of varnashrama. Anusooya's teachings to Sita in Tulsi's *Ramacharitamanasa* leaves no doubt that greater than truth, compassion, and love was adherence to the socially imposed ascriptive duties. Against the attemped subversion of the brahmanical order by *nirguna* stalwarts such as Kabir, Ravidas, Dadu, and Nanak, the proponents of *saguna* school tried to establish the infallibility of the shastras, and prescribed adherence to the caste code of conduct as necessary for good life. Caste was essential for social stability. Salvation was to be sought within the confines of the varna dharma. The stark absence of any significant poet-thinker from the subaltern categories within the *saguna* devotionalism is not surprising.

The choice of *saguna* worship, ranged as it was against the *nirguna*, was crucial and pregnant with significance. *Saguna* bhakti implied worship of gods and their *avatars* whose mythology was the brain-child of the priestly class, and was authoritatively confined in the *itihas-purana* and Sanskritised versions of the *Ramayana* and

Mahabharata. The *nirguna* preference for an impersonal deity instead of *devas*, their *avatars* and *lilas* (which effectively explained away the social division of labour – disenfranchising shudras and women from education, power, and wealth) was, in all likelihood, deliberate and premeditated. Thus the tension between *saguna* and *nirguna* was profound, and assumes special significance in the socio-cultural context of medieval India. At the cultural-ideological level, it reflected the ongoing struggle between the caste elites and the subaltern masses. It is not for nothing that in the *Uttarakanda* of *Ramacharitamanasa*, Tulsi, arguably the greatest exponent of *saguna* school, beats his breast bemoaning the emergence of shudra religious preachers as the unmistakable sign of degradation in the *Kaliyuga*. Appalled at what the shudras taught, Tulsi wrote with a vengeance against shudra teachers. How aghast and indignant was Tulsi at the rise of religious teachers from the lower orders is borne out by these acerbic, sarcastic lines:

> *Je baradham teli kumhara/Swapach kirat kol kalwara*
> *Nari mui grihsampati nasi/Mur murai hohin sannyasi.*
> (People of the lowest castes according to the varna-dharma – oilmen, potters, dog-eaters, Kirats, Kols, distillers – shave their heads and turn religious mendicants when their wives die or they lose their household goods.)
> (Prasad, tr., 1990: 634)

Tulsi's *Manasa* is replete with slighting references to the lowered caste saint-poets like Kabir, Ravidas, and their followers. Caustically commenting on the contemporary reality, Tulsi laments his age as a decadent *Kaliyuga*, in which the shudras consider themselves as learned as brahmans, enter into disputations with them, and dare to give discourses on religion and society:

> *Sudra dwijanha upadesahin gyana*
> (Shudras instruct the brahmans in religious wisdom).
>
> *Badhin sudra dwijanha san ham tumh tei kachhu ghati*
> (Shudras dispute with brahmans, 'Are we inferior to you?')

And,

Te bipranh san aapu pujavahin/ubhay lok nij haath nasawahin
. . .
*Sudra karahin jap tap brata nana/Baithi barasan kahahin purana
Sab nar kalpit karhin achara/Jai na barani aniti apara.*
(They, the low-caste religious teachers, allow themselves to be worshipped by the brahmans and ruin themselves in this world and the next. . . . Shudras indulge in all sorts of prayers and penances and vows and expound the Puranas from an exalted seat. Everybody follows a course of conduct of his own imagination, and the endless perversions of morality are beyond all description.) (ibid.: 634-5)

Tulsi's Rama is not synonymous with God – the name Rama as a 'vocable without syntax or grammar', and therefore *nirguna* as Kabir and Nanak expounded – but an incarnation of God, born the son of a king to establish and maintain a kingdom of varna righteousness and brahmanical supremacy. The Sanskrit *Ramayana* of Valmiki, too, is full of caste chauvinism; this Tulsi further reworked to invigorate brahmanism and caste. The story of Shambuk, a shudra aspirant to spiritual power, narrated in the *Uttarakanda* of Tulsi's *Ramayana* is a blatant example of the brahmanical attempt to reinforce the caste ideology. As the story goes, Shambuk was practising religious austerities and that resulted in the death of a brahman's son! The bereaved father reported the tragic news to Rama, and Rama through meditation came to the conclusion that the brahman's son had died because Shambuk the shudra was practising meditation in violation of his caste duty. Rama tracked down and killed Shambuk. This resulted in the resurrection of the dead brahman.

This story leaves no doubt that the redactor had lost all sense of moral and social propriety in his eagerness to justify the self-interests of the priestly class. Such a mindless and barbarous act – committed by no less a person than Rama who is *Maryada Purushottam* (the embodiment of Man Supreme) – and its glorification is not surprising when education was monopolised by a particular caste which used it to gain hegemony over the masses. Not only this, Valmiki's Rama is even made to pronounce in the *Ayodhyakanda* that the Buddha was a thief and that those who accept his teachings and do not believe in the deities, should be punished. Rama is not only presented as an enemy of the shudras but also as a staunch defender of patriarchal order. He forces Sita to undergo a fire-ordeal to prove her chastity.

Above all, the symbiotic relationship between the apologists for brahmanism and devotees of Rama is the most arresting aspect of the *Ramayana* created by Tulsi. A caste champion like Tulsi could not have got a more popular story than the *Ramayana* and its legendary hero to propagate the varna ideology. Throwing all poetic sensibilities and intellectual honesty to the winds, Tulsi frequently uses abusive words and malicious contempt for the people belonging to lowered castes. Following in Manu's footsteps, he commands the shudras to worship a brahman even if he indulges in a most shameless behaviour. 'Though a brahman curse you, beat you or speak cruel words – he should be worshipped, so sing the saints', Tulsi put these words in Rama's mouth. He goes on to recommend shamelessly:

> *Pujiye bipra sil guna hina*
> *Sudra na gun-gyan pravina.*
> (A brahmin must be revered though he be devoid of amiability and virtue; not so a shudra, however distinguished for all virtue and learning.) (ibid.: 414)

Tulsi's diatribe against shudras, appears interestingly, to be a typical brahmanic rebuff to Ravidas' rational exhortation,

> *Brahman mat pujiye, jau howe gun-hin*
> *Pujahin charan chandala ke, jau-howe gun-pravin.*
> (Don't honour a brahman who is without merit; honour instead the feet of a chandala who is virtuous and talented.)

Tulsidas spews venom and hatred against women and shudras in an abusive language that has no parallel in decent literature. Lamenting the decadence of women in the Kali age, he writes, for example, in the *Uttarakanda*:

Women have no ornament except their tresses and have enormous appetite (are never satisfied). Though miserable for want of money, they are rich in attachment of various kinds. Though hankering after happiness, they have no regard for piety, stupid as they are. Though they are poor in wits, their minds are hardened and know no tenderness. (ibid.: 636)

As self-appointed guardian of the reactionary pandit community, Tulsi was, apparently, rattled by the unprecedented emergence of cultural leaders from below. They had started thinking for themselves. Tulsi's own town – Benaras – was reverberating with Kabir's and Ravidas' seditious teachings, openly mocking the fatuous brahman and his shruti-smritis. By announcing loud and clear *sadho, utthi jnan ki aandhi*, Kabir had triumphantly declared the storm (movement) of knowledge blowing across everywhere.

In hindsight, it appears that the presence of Muslim rule provided the right atmosphere to the movement in the sense that the new rulers were not very enthusiastic about supporting the Hindu elite as the earlier Hindu kings had done. Armed with a newfound confidence, the subaltern cultural leaders surged forward to challenge the established religious and social order. The brahmanic leadership retaliated, intruded the movement, and invoked the legendary king of Ayodhya. The Shambuk-slayer came to their rescue this time too to reassert their supremacy in society. A morally questionable work like the *Ramacharitamanasa* extolling the virtues of casteism was glorified, and transformed into a vehicle for the reimposition of caste culture and feudal values. No wonder, Tulsi was the last major poet of the bhakti cult in the north. His triumphant celebration of varna ideology marked the end of the movement. The people's movement that started off as a protest against oppression and injustice was ultimately appropriated by the caste champions who smothered its humanist spirit and subverted its egalitarian agenda.

4

Colonialism, and Birth of Vedic-Brahmanic Nationalism

> The national bourgeoisie of underdeveloped countries is not engaged in production, nor in invention, nor in building, nor labour; it is completely canalised into activities of the intermediary type. Its innermost vocation seems to be to keep in the running and to be part of the [colonial] racket.
>
> FRANTZ FANON
> *The Wretched of the Earth*, 1963: 150

The decadence of the political leadership of Indian society was thoroughly exposed when the East India Company gradually conquered and colonised this vast land, from the second half of the eighteenth century on the ruins of the Mughal empire. The feudal kings and nobles, with an exception of a Tipu here or there, were too self-indulgent, weak, or myopic to ward off the external attack. In fact, many of them schemed against each other, co-operated and collaborated with the British for selfish gains, and thus helped establish British supremacy. The backward, oppressed, impoverished, and caste-divided masses – conditioned for centuries to bear all sorts of injustices and inequalities – were in no position to react to the foreign conquest of their country.[1] The caste system had for centuries been the scourge of Indian society, responsible for social fragmentation, economic decline, cultural stagnation, and an insular outlook resulting in the neglect of science and technology – all factors combining to facilitate British conquest. Starting their winning streak from Plassey (1757) and Buxar (1764), the British in the course of a few decades established their Raj throughout India with crucial support from the ever-opportunistic aristocratic upper classes, Hindu and Muslim. It is axiomatic that no external power can establish an enduring domination over a conquered people except with the latter's tacit toleration or active support, and the colonial conquest of India was no exception to this.

The British lost no time in recognising and reciprocating friendly overtures from the Indian ruling classes. The rajas and nawabs who accepted British suzerainty were left untouched and brahmans and allied castes were rewarded with positions in the colonial dispensation, especially in the revenue administration, as born-again zamindars and rent-collectors. Striking a deal with the native elites, the British adopted a policy of no interference in social and religious matters. The British, however, for diverse reasons, resented the Muslims and preferred and promoted the Hindu elites, giving them the status of 'natural leaders' of the majority community. Historical evidence and new research suggest that within the colonial discourse 'India' meant 'Hindu'.[2] Moreover, the colonial construction of Hinduism was not pluralistic. It was textual, that too, confined within the brahmanical texts and scriptures. Steeped in their own scripture-based religion, the British equated the shastras with the Hindu religion, and erroneously assumed that the brahmanical scriptures had universal following among diverse Indian communities and tribes. For instance, in 1792, Jonathan Duncan, the British Resident at Benaras, recommended the 'Institution of a Hindoo College or Academy for the preservation and cultivation of the Laws, Literature and Religion of this nation at this centre of their faith, and the common resort of all their tribes' (see Kochhar 2000: 9).

The early colonial rulers and British discoverers of Hinduism in cahoots with the local elites, mainly male brahman Sanskritists, resurrected and presented Manu as the 'parent of Hindoo jurisprudence'. The *Manusmriti* was flaunted – and foisted on the Hindus – as a 'system of duties, religious and civil, and of law, in all its branches, which the Hindoos firmly believe to have been promulgated in the beginning of time by Manu . . . a system so comprehensive and so minutely exact, that it may be considered as the institutes of Hindoo law' (Jones, see L. Mani 1989: 111).

The British did not want to understand – and there was none to tell them – that the sacerdotal literature in Sanskrit represented only the brahmanical world-view. It appears that the denigration and subjugation of the masses under the brahmanical system appealed to the British colonialists as it was in keeping with their own colonial design and racist ideology. The colonialists, as Kosambi (2000: 45) stresses, 'wanted as far as possible to yield to brahmanism, as it was always a convenient tool for subjection of the natives'. Anyway, they could hardly afford to alienate the aristocratic-priestly classes whose active support was so vital for their survival in India. As we shall see later, the discovery of a common Indo-European heritage with the concomitant Aryan race theory, at the very beginning of colonial rule, provided the British with a powerful vehicle to reach out to the Hindu elite. Both shared a hegemonic ideology which provided the foreign and native elites with a common language in which they were able to discuss and agree on important aspects of socio-cultural order in the subcontinent. Thus the British were from the very beginning to perpetuate the oppressive native tradition and institutions, by giving these a new legitimacy and a fresh lease of life. The liberals in the British administration who wanted to tinker with inhuman laws and practices were allowed to do so in only a few cases.

ORIENTALISM, ARYAN RACE THEORY, AND NEO-HINDUISM

Warren Hastings (1732-1818), the Company's first Governor-General who laid the foundations of British administration in India, took the momentous decision to rule the subcontinent in accordance with its own traditions. He enjoined that in all suits regarding inheritance, marriage, caste and other social and religious matters, the laws of shastras with respect to Hindus and those of the Koran with respect to Muslims would be strictly adhered to. Hastings also made it clear that these laws would be expounded and interpreted by the brahmans and *maulvis* for their respective communities (Kejariwal 1988: 23). As traditional rules for Hindus, dictated by priestly whims and fancies, were vague, varied and often contradictory, the British decided to find out exactly what these traditions were. This called for collection and codification of information and knowledge about India's culture, religion, and social organisation. In this respect, in a significant move with far-reaching consequences, the British privileged the brahmanical tradition and treated the Dharmashastras, especially *Manusmriti*, as the 'Hindu social law' and made them the basis of their legal system.

The British ignored the existence of all other systems and traditions in Indian civilisation because the brahmanical framework better suited their interests. Reviving and privileging *Manusmriti* (which extols brahmans and treats shudras and women as sub-human creatures fit only for slavery and worse) over other alternative systems, both within Hinduism including the non-brahman and tribal practices as well as the systems of Buddhism and Jainism and those of Islam and Sikhism, was clear evidence of colonial patronage to the brahmanical tradition.

Nathaniel Halhed with assistance and guidance from a bunch of pandits, produced Manu's laws as *A Code of Gentoo Laws*, subtitled *Ordination of the Pundits* in 1776. The preface to the Code clearly states commerce with India and the 'advantages of a territorial establishment in Bengal could be maintained only by an adoption of such original institutes of the country as do not intimately clash with the laws and interests of the conquerors' (see Sharma 1983: 3). The codification, in a major way, also brought home the point that though Sanskrit was defunct it was not dead. Halhed also authored *Grammar of the Bengal Language* in 1778 and went on to translate several Sanskrit texts such as the *Bhagavat Purana* and *Shiva Purana* into English. Soon after, a systematic and institutional endeavour to discover Indian culture and religion was made with the establishment of the Asiatic Society of Bengal in 1784 under the leadership of William Jones (1746-94). Indological studies got further boost with the establishment of the Bombay Asiatic Society in 1804 and of the Asiatic Society of Great Britain in 1823.

Hastings' academic protèges – William Jones, Charles Wilkins, H. T. Colebrooke, and James Prinsep – learnt Sanskrit and many other things from the pandits, and engaged in research on India, mainly through the ancient Sanskrit texts. Wilkins published a Sanskrit grammar in 1779, and rendered the *Bhagvad Gita* into English in 1785. This was the first published translation of any major Sanskrit work into a European language. Jones, a gifted linguist and scholar, soon established himself as a renowned Sanskritist and translated the *Manusmriti* and Kalidasa's *Abhijnanshakuntalam* into English. These were subsequently rendered into several European languages. With the publication of his three essays 'On the Hindus', 'On the Gods of Greece, Italy and India', and 'On the Chronology of Hindus' in *Asiatic Researches* (the journal of the Asiatic Society), Jones came to be regarded as an authority on Indian religion. Most significantly, Jones essayed a seminal paper *On the Origin and Families of Nations*, based on the then state of research, which brought out several features underlining the striking similarity between Sanskrit, Latin, and Greek. Jones' work is considered the starting point of 'comparative philology' and the consequent debate on the Indo-European family of languages and the migration of peoples. Comparative philology having indicated a close relationship between Sanskrit and some European languages, there came into currency the 'Aryan theory of race', which the Orientalists in India and Europe used to assert an ethnic kinship between Europeans and the ancient Aryan people. It was assumed that the Indo-Aryans were the torchbearers of world civilisation. The upper castes in India wielded the theory to assert the antiquity of everything Indian.

The affinity between Sanskrit and European languages fired the imagination of several scholars in Europe who popularised the idea of a common Indo-European homeland and heritage. The upper caste Aryans in India came to be regarded as the lost brothers of the white Europeans. A distinction was drawn between the master race, the high caste Aryans, and their subjects – lower-caste non-Aryans and Dravidians. The high caste Indians were thrilled with the discovery as it gave them an identity with the colonial rulers. Proclaiming their blood relationship with the British rulers, Keshab Chandra Sen, for example, declared at a public lecture in Calcutta in 1877, '. . . in the advent of the English nation in India we see a reunion of parted cousins, the descendants of two different families of the ancient Aryan race . . .' (Thapar 1975: 12). The appeal of this theory was wide and enduring. When Gandhi was working as a lawyer in South Africa, he addressed an open letter (1894) to the members of the legislature protesting against the ill-treatment of the Indians and demanding equality on the grounds of race. Since the British and the Indians were from the same Aryan stock, he reasoned, how could the Britishers rule over their own blood brothers? It was unfair for one set of Aryans to rule over another set, he wrote and then went on to describe, quoting copiously from European scholars and administrators, the accomplishments of the brahmans in various fields (see Gandhi 1979: 176).

The interest of European scholars such as H. H. Wilson, C. Lassen, H. T. Colebrooke, Monier Williams, and above all, Friedrich Max Müller, in ancient Aryan culture and Sanskrit texts gave birth to the legend of 'the wonder that was India'. They spoke glowingly about the Aryan civilisation and went on to create a romantic image of India – an India of sublime spirituality, opulence, Vedic-Upanishadic splendour, and epic heroism. Not surprisingly, such glorification was well received by the upper castes. They found the Aryan connection flattering because it connected them, on the one hand, to the mighty British, and on the other, vindicated their superiority over the 'lowly' masses and alien Muslims. The Orientalists and their Indian mimics saw Indian civilisation as derivative from Aryan civilisation, and the caste system was applauded as a means by which people of diverse racial and cultural backgrounds were brought together and subjected to the 'civilising' influence of the Aryans. Such was the hold of the Aryan theory among the nationalists that a scholar like R. K. Mookerji could write as late as 1956: 'The history of India is mainly that of the Aryans of India. Its source is the *Rigveda* which is the earliest book not merely of Indians but of the entire Aryan race' (1956: 48).

In fact, the Indian elite received philological discoveries and Aryan race theory in a manner which can only be called racist. Nirad Chaudhuri says:

In ancient times what might be called Hindu nationalism retrospectively was based on their belief that they were 'Aryas', and as such not only different from other peoples and communities, but also superior. Anyone who is at all familiar with Sanskrit literature cannot be unaware of this, cannot remain ignorant of what the notion of being Arya meant to the Hindu of ancient times. (1974: 315-6)

Orientalists like Max Müller, Chaudhuri's 'Scholar Extraordinary', who never visited India, were however ignorant of this. Taking inspiration from the selective passages from the Vedic-

Upanshadic texts, Orientalists fantasized and invented an India that was the other-worldly country of philosophers, given to metaphysical speculation, and utter disdain for their mundane existence. In the words of Max Müller, the ancient Indians were not 'active, combative or acquisitive' but 'passive, meditative and reflective' (1892: 101). For Orientalists like him, the study of Sanskrit was an academic venture to retrieve a lost wing of the early European culture. In *India: What Can It Teach Us*, he wrote:

. . . we should not leave out of sight our nearest intellectual relatives, the Aryans of India, the framers of the most wonderful language of Sanskrit, the fellow workers in the construction of our most fundamental concepts, the fathers of the most natural of natural religions, the makers of the most transparent of mythologies, the inventors of the most subtle philosophy and the givers of the most elaborate laws. (1892: 15)

The India the Orientalists imagined was invariably mysterious, exotic, exalted, and, later even erotic, graced with all kinds of eclectic and esoteric holymen. The romantic Orientalists were said to be utterly unhappy with the changes taking place in their own society in the wake of modernisation and industrialisation. It is significant that many of them never visited India. Showing his solidarity with Aryan Indians, Max Müller even took the Sanskritic name Moksha Mula. And, it was not a case of unrequited romance. Vivekananda, the knight-errant of neo-Hinduism and an ardent admirer of the Moksha Mula, was so besotted with the scholar's championing of Indian spirituality, that he even came to revere Max Müller as the incarnation of Sayana![3]

A new scholarship from erstwhile colonies has established Orientalism as the dominant ideology with which the West ruled the East. Such scholarship, however, discards the role of indigenous elites who played a crucial and collusive role in constructing the hegemonic ideology. In his acclaimed study of Orientalism and the values and motives underpinning it, Edward Said writes:

Taking the late eighteenth century as a very roughly defined starting point Orientalism can be discussed and analysed as the corporate institution for dealing with the Orient – dealing with it by making statements about it, authorising views of it, describing it, by teaching it, setting it, ruling over it:

in short, Orientalism as a Western style for dominating, restructuring and having authority over the Orient. (1978: 3)

This hard-hitting critique may be true in the case of Islamic world where Orientalism had become confrontationist. But in the case of India Orientalism was seductive and collaborative as it took the form of Indo-Europeanism. In the Indian context Said's reading of Orientalism grossly overlooks the collusive role played by the native privileged groups. His theory does not take into account the complicity and culpability of native notables in India who played a very crucial role in the making of the Oriental stereotype of Indian culture and civilisation. The Aryan race theory, a key construct of Orientalism, for example, found tremendous support among the dominant classes in India for reasons given above.

Indology and Orientalism were a joint and mutually beneficial project of the foreign and indigenous elites. Max Müller, who researched at Oxford and popularised the term Aryan race, was funded by the East India Company (Kochhar 2000: 9). Let us see what Max Müller wrote about Rammohun Roy's visit to England in 1832:

For the sake of comparing notes, so to say, with his Aryan brothers, Rammohun Roy was the first who came from East to West . . . making us feel once more that ancient brotherhood which unites the whole Aryan race, inspiring us . . . and invigorating us for acts of nobler daring in the conquest of truth than any that are inscribed in the chronicles of our divided past.
(see Kochhar 2000: 9)

Robertson has shown in his study of Rammohun Roy that Colebrook and Wilson's view of Vedanta, which eventually became identical with the standard Orientalist discourse on Indian philosophy, was heavily based on Roy's writing on the subject (1999: 55-73). Similarly, the writings of Halhed, Holwell, Wilkins and Jones provided material for Priestley's comparison of the laws of Moses and Manu. The resurrection of Manu as the Hindu law-giver was a joint endeavour of Western and Indian pandits. As Sumit Sarkar has correctly argued, 'Colonial knowledge was not just a Western superimposition: such an interpretation gravely underestimates the extent and significance of inputs from relatively privileged Indian groups with autonomous interests and inclinations' (1997: 23).

In course of time some British Orientalists were compelled by colonial ideology to run down the theory of Aryan grandeur and heroism in the face of emerging Hindu nationalism. But it was the European Indologists who first constructed the myth of the splendour of the ancient Aryans, which was reechoed and relayed with gusto in the works of elite Indian scholars. In the Indian context, therefore, contrary to what Edward Said has said, Orientalism was not merely a West *versus* East conflict. Orientalism *vis-a-vis* India was oriented and favourably inclined towards the indigenous elites because in its framework, the Indian culture was to be studied in the linguistic and religious aspects of Aryan-brahmanism, detached from the reality of actual social evolution. The overall emphasis of the Orientalists was on courtly culture and brahmanic literature as against material reflection in mass cultural production. The native privileged groups had no problem either with the British Raj or with Orientalist discourse. In fact, alien rulers and local influential elites had worked closely together to construct Orientalism as well as colonialism in mutual self-interest. If the colonial dispensation in India had fattened the British, it also empowered and enriched their native hosts as never before.

In Orientalist scholarship there was no effort to corroborate the shastras with the non-brahmanical, Buddhist and shramanic texts, more empirical historical sources and archaeology. There was no effort to juxtapose the self-serving brahmanical texts with the vastly different social and cultural reality of India's past as encapsulated in alternative cultural and material sources. In other words, the Orientalist construction of the ancient India was semi-historical at best. It was the same Orientalist scholarship which was later made the basis of the discovery of India's past by the Indian elites in the name of nationalism.

It was in this process of imaginative construction of India's past that a new type of Hinduism, erected on the edifice of brahmanical texts and interpretations, and nurtured by colonial policies and polity, came into existence. The brahmans have always tried to monopolise knowledge; they have always controlled information, and have never hesitated to use and manipulate information to suit their interests. It was they who had provided selective information to the British on indigenous tradition and institutions, on an unprecedented scale, at an all-India level, particularly in Calcutta, Bombay and Madras. This gradually generated the consciousness and dynamics for a new religion 'the likes of which India had perhaps never known before' (Frykenberg 2001). The British rulers, who took policy decisions and presided over the executive, judicial and legislative functions of the colonial state, had become puppets in the hands of the native high caste officials, secretaries, munshis, and vakils, who worked with them every day and heavily influenced their decisions and policies:

The hosts handled most of the paper work. They had done this before, for previous rulers. Now they did this again and did this in such a way that the rulers themselves became instruments of local and indigenous influences. Local officials, either Brahmans or Non-Brahmans who were of 'high' varna and ritually 'clean' by local standards, exercised a crucial, if not determining, role. In course of time, these very ingredients of the state rulership, both European and Native, served to bring modern Hinduism into being.

(Frykenberg 2001: 89)

'Hindu' or 'majority community' were identities consciously created in the colonial period, in contrast to 'Muslim' or 'minority community'. The new Hinduism came about through the simultaneous interplay of various factors at work both within and outside the colonial power structure. Within the political structure of the colonial state, the process of the making of Hinduism was facilitated by the information put in by brahmans and allied upper castes. Outside it, reform movements emerged which, as we shall see later, were primarily aimed at the self-strengthening of the elite rather than upliftment of the entire society. It was a complex and prolonged process which was at once social and political, cultural and religious. What it led to, as a consequence, was, what Romila Thapar has brilliantly delineated and termed as 'syndicated Hinduism'. The new Hinduism was primarily brahmanic and Sanskritic, ornamented at times with invocations of shramanic humanism, and bits and pieces of Islamic egalitarianism and Christian catholicity to enhance its universal appeal and attraction. The new Hinduism flourished under the colonial regime because, as Frykenberg has compellingly argued, the British Raj was actually, for most intents and purposes, a de facto 'Hindu Raj'. Dissecting the anatomy of the Raj, he writes:

The Raj, as an imperial system of rule, was a genuinely indigenous rather than simply a foreign (or 'colonial') construct; that, hence, it was more Indian than British in inner logic, regardless of external interferences and violations of that logic by Britain (especially during the Crown period of this Raj); that, in terms of religious institutions, indigenous elites and local forces of all kinds were able to receive recognition and protection, as well as special concessions, from the State; and moreover, that they had been able to do this in direct proportion to their ability − whether by power of information control, numbers, noise, skill, or wealth − to influence local governments. (Frykenberg 2001: 90)

At the instance of brahman notables, shramanic religions like Buddhism, Jainism, Sikhism, and various streams of popular or folk Hinduism and egalitarian tribal culture opposed to ascriptive brahmanism were systematically marginalised, and the scripture-based Hinduism was accorded informal status as something of a national religion of India. From many Indian schools of philosophy − at least there were ten major schools including the Buddhist and Jain philosophies − only Shankara's Vedanta was picked out and promoted as the representative philosophy of India. Shankara's glorification of eternal caste system along with his recipe of *brahma satyam jagatmithya* (only Brahma is real; the world is an illusion), and his advocacy of *sahanam sarvadukhanam apratikarapurvakam* (all kinds of sorrow should be borne without the least resistance) in *Vivek Choodamani*, came handy to buttress the Oriental myth of India as a society wallowing in its timeless and unchanging ethos of sublime resignation to the divine dispensation. The *Bhagvad Gita*, with its sanatani teaching of *nishkama karma* (work without any desire of result), *avatarvad* (ideology of incarnation) and excessive trust in one's fate reinforced by the theory of *karma* and *punarjanma*, was projected as the holy book of the Hindus. The brahmanical religion and culture was not only proclaimed as highly assimilative and all-encompassing of Hinduism, but was also glorified as an amazing 'way of life'. This was not the handiwork of the European scholars alone; the Hindu elite played a very active part in this colonial construction. Hinduism as an undefined, richly ambiguous and open-ended way of life, after all, safeguarded the interests of the privileged castes because it concealed the all-important truth that if Hinduism was a way of life, it was a caste-feudal way of life. And, then, which culture or religion is not a way of life?

ROY, REFORMS, RENAISSANCE: FACTS AGAINST FICTION

The upper caste elite were the first to come in contact with the Western culture and English education, and made the most of the new opportunities offered by colonial rule. This interaction between the foreign and indigenous elites led to the making of the English-educated middle class – 'Indian in colour and blood, and British in taste, in attitudes, in intellect', to use Macaulay's much-maligned phraseology. The British needed this class to rule this gigantic subcontinent. It was created by the colonial rulers to play the role of intermediaries between them and the millions they ruled.

The more thoughtful among the native intermediaries, among them clerks, professionals, and absentee landlords, began thinking about their deplorable social situation and backwardness. Living in cities like Calcutta with modern English men and women, many of their social customs and practices, especially the enslavement of their women, appeared appalling to them and they began looking for ways and means of removing them. However, while taking stock of the Indian reality, they did not look beyond their caste and class interests. The poverty-stricken and caste-oppressed masses never figure in their thinking, except in the case of popular rhetoric to which they often resorted in order to win more and more concessions and benefits from the British. For them, Indian society was confined, for all practical purposes, to the traditionally powerful social groups. While the majority of the emergent middle class was still enamoured of the traditional ideas and institutions, the more enterprising among them took the initiative to yoke together brahmanical ideology and modern Western thinking. Such self-strengthening attempts at 'modernisation' were propelled by the need to acquire qualifications for various jobs under the colonial government as well as to retain their hegemony in the changing socio-economic scenario. This process of adjustment and 'reform from within' is usually hailed in historiography as the 'Indian renaissance' or the 'great national awakening'. Pioneered by the British-friendly landlord class, which had become extremely wealthy at the cost of peasants' pauperisation, the 'awakening' was basically an elite and exclusive affair and adjustive in nature.

Rammohun Roy (1772-1833), a 'Raja' and a 'Rai Bahadur' as well as the one-time dewan of the East India Company, was the first major architect of this modernisation. The rationalism and the spirit of inquiry that we find in the writings of Roy and other reformers of the time were largely generated by the paradigmatic thoughts brought in by their exposure to Western education, but they had also inherited a social situation and cultural milieu that was dominated by the brahmanical world-view. What Roy and his followers had actually done was to selectively assimilate some modern European thoughts with the ancient brahmanical ideas and institutions. In his incisive study of the Bengal renaissance, David Kopf has convincingly shown how the high caste reformers 'used the idea of the West as a means for modernising their own traditions . . . for pouring the new wine of modern functions into the old bottles of Indian culture' (1969: 205). This marked the beginning of the 'Neo-Hinduism' and its ingenious interpretation of the tradition. The modus operandi here was to connect modern Western ideas and values to the brahmanical past and then claim modern ideas and values as part of the Hindu tradition. This process of redefining and reinterpreting brahmanical tradition in the modern light resulted in the emergence of neo-Hinduism. Writing on this phenomenon Indologist P. Hacker explains:

More important than the fact that foreign elements have been added to the tradition, have been reinterpreted and provided with new meanings as a result of this encounter with the West. . . . The link which the Neo Hindus find to their tradition is one may say an afterthought, for they first adopt Western values and means of orientation and then attempt to find the foreign in the indigenous . . . afterwards they connect these values and claim them as part of Hindu tradition. (cited in Basu 2002: 50)

It is important that the model or concept of the ancient India projected by Roy was embedded in a utopian brahmanical order which supposedly created and nurtured a great civilisation. Roy was, of course, greatly helped in his imaginative creation of the past by the Oriental scholarship in the preceding years. The India of the past, he maintained, was an ideal society when men followed the 'doctrines of true religion', and enjoyed freedom under a just and competent government. The lot of women was no different; they had property rights and full independence in all respects. The government strictly followed the separation of powers – the brahmans were the legislators and kshatriyas were given executive power. The degeneration started, according to Roy, with the system of absolute kshatriya rule when the brahmans became 'nominal legislators' under the Rajputs and the real power, whether legislative or executive, came to be exercised by the latter. The Rajputs, he said, exercised 'tyranny and oppression for a thousand years', then the Musalmans 'from Ghuznee and Ghore invaded the country . . . and introduced their own tyrannical system of governance' (see Mukherjee 1993: 382).

Raja Rammohun Roy stressed the benefits of a lasting and deep bond between the class of zamindars that he represented and the colonial masters. To cement this marriage of convenience between the British and Indian elites, Roy even floated the idea that a permanent colony of Englishmen should be established in India (Mukherjee 1993: 375). Parading as 'the most obedient servant' of the British (he ended his every letter or petition to the colonial authorities with this appellation), Roy considered colonial rule as 'benevolent' and the 'providence of God'. Singing paeans to 'enlightened' English rule which ended, to use his own words, 'the rapacity and intolerance' of Muslim rule, he rhapsodised, 'Divine Providence at last, in its abundant mercy, stirred up the English Nation to break the Yoke of those tyrants (Muslims) and to receive the oppressed natives of Bengal under its protection' (see Biswas 1998: 209-10). Thus the essential ingredients of the ideology of the *bhadralok*, namely, the valorisation of brahmanic values, selective modernity, and a pro-British and anti-Muslim orientation, were all present in embryonic form in the intellectual make-up of the Father of Modern India.

The tiny middle-class intelligentsia that Roy led from the front was culturally rooted in the Sanskritic background. Since they could not transgress their shastric tradition, they showed amazing ingenuity in superimposing modern and progressive ideas on the quintessentially ascriptive and conservative brahmanical ideology. It can be argued that they donned the garb of modernisation because their own interests demanded it, and not because they deliberately set out, as is often argued by their admirers, to modernise Indian society. Hamstrung by the semi-slavery of their women, and the resultant all-round degeneration including an alarmingly dwindling population of the sub-caste from which Roy hailed, they realised that the vestiges of the past – the practice of sati, enforced widowhood, polygamy and purdah system – were obstacles to progress. It may be noted that all these regressive practices, which became the focus of attention of the early reformers, were mostly prevalent among the upper strata of society, especially brahmans. Women of lower strata enjoyed relatively more freedom of movement and a better status in the family, as they were beyond the pale of strict brahmanical patriarchy. In fact, widow-remarriage was quite common among the lowered castes who were not as obsessed with managing or controlling their women's sexuality as were the upper caste men, and also because most of them hardly owned any property, which was more often than not the main reason of wealthy upper castes' opposition to marriage of their widows. Also, unlike their upper caste counterparts, women of working classes did not lead a secluded life as in addition to their domestic chores they also had to work in the fields alongside men.

However commendable a step it was to champion the cause of the long-suffering women who were routinely bracketed with shudras in the brahmanical texts, the cause of the lowered castes, destroyed and dominated by prolonged caste-feudalism, was never taken up by the reformist leaders of the nineteenth century. Occasionally, the more sensitive among them voiced concern about the caste problem in abstract terms but it was never matched with a concrete plan or action to annihilate the caste monster. The issues around which the refrom movement revolved – abolition of sati, widow remarriage, polygyny (prevalent among kulin brahmans of Bengal), removal of the purdah system, and later the demand for more English schools and colleges along with better representation in the colonial administration and affairs of the state – were oriented to modernise a tiny and privileged section of Indian society. The movement was confined to the brahman and allied castes.

Regrettably, the methods and instruments which the reformers employed for reforms, 'modernisation' and the 'reordering' of society, were anchored in the brahmanical values of ancient India. Highly selective in their acceptance of liberal-democratic ideas from the West, the reformers' advocacy of change was not based on the ideals of humanism, rationalism, or utilitarianism – as the cornerstone of a new society – but those of the authority taken from the brahmanical scriptures and Dharmashastras (Sharma 1983: 4-5). The reformers never tried to win public opinion by proving to the people the inhumanity and absurdity of the social evils sanctified by the shastric tradition. Instead they presented the 'wonder that was India' and tried to persuade their castemen to progressive ideas by convincing them that the reforms were in consonance with the ancient texts. The tendency to misquote or misrepresent brahmanical scriptures in support of reforms and progressivism was carried forward by the future reformers and can well be summed up in the words of R. G. Bhandarkar:

In ancient times girls were married after they had attained maturity, now they must be married before; widow marriage was then in practice, now it has certainly gone out. . . . Interdining among the castes was not prohibited, now the numberless castes cannot have intercommunications of that nature.
(see Sharma 1983: 10)

Ironically, valorisation of the problematic past itself became the overwhelming concern of the reformers, and issues – for which the shastras were being ransacked – were given a quiet burial. Widely regarded as the first modern advocate of women's rights and whose historical fame is largely built around his campaign against the system of widow immolation, Roy did not base his case against sati because it was a despicable crime against women but because sati, as he speciously argued, had no scriptural sanction. Since he revered the *Manusmriti* as the founding text containing the 'whole sense of the Vedas', he insisted that no code be approved which contradicted it (Lata Mani 1989: 109). Not surprisingly, the arguments about shastric sanction gained precedence over the subject for which the past was being invoked:

Tradition was not the ground on which the status of women was being contested. Rather the reverse was true: women in fact became the site on which tradition was debated and reformulated. What was at stake was not women but tradition. (ibid.: 118)

As the socio-cultural awakening was taking place in this insular, past-obsessed environment, the revivalism of the supposed brahmanical glories of ancient India became integral to the reform ideology. Roy and his reformist friends had no problems in toeing the brahmanical ideology that for centuries had been the main source of the worst kinds of superstition and obscurantism that vindicated the horrendous exploitation of the masses and women of all classes on religious grounds.

It is one of the great ironies of modern Indian history that progressive reformers and their orthodox opponents were both ransacking the same brahmanical texts to support or oppose the reform agenda. The irony of the reformist situation became clear when Roy selectively quoted the 'sacred' texts in support of his campaign to ban sati. The conservative elements led by Raja Radhakant Deb (1784-1867) ransacked the same texts and cited more authentic instances to prove that sati did have the sanction of the shastras. As Sharma points out, 'In this particular case the enlightened opinion of William Bentinck was of more moment than the texts marshalled by Raja Rammohun Roy' (1983: 5).

It is also noteworthy that while condemning sati through shastric invocations, Roy was condemned to glorify austere widowhood – he in fact hunted up and published the texts praising ascetic and chaste widowhood in order to controvert the reactionaries who were supporting sati. Roy argued, 'Manu in plain terms enjoins a widow to *continue till death* forgiving all injuries, performing austere duties, avoiding every sensual pleasure, and cheerfully practising the incomparable rules of virtue which have been followed by such women as were devoted to only one husband' (see Lata Mani 1989: 103). This created a major problem for those later reformers who supported widow-remarriage and opposed polygamy. Such examples show how deeply flawed – and dangerous – was the reform-through-shastric-mandate.

The reactionaries opposing even limited reforms and the reform enthusiasts both swore by the same sacerdotal texts as their authority. Both sides delved into the shastras to dish out highly coloured examples to prove their points. Both sides tried to build their cases on the past precedents to resolve current controversies. In the middle of the nineteenth century, for instance, ancient texts, especially the *Manusmriti*, were selectively quoted in favour of the abolition of polygyny, which was prevalent among the kulins of Bengal. However, when challenged by the conservatives, the reformers could not prove a case for strict monogamous conjugality from any brahmanical scripture. Similarly, the campaign for widow remarriage under the leadership of Ishwarchandra Vidyasagar (1820-91) was based on the premise that the marriage of widows was permissible under the shastras. When questioned, Vidyasagar quoted from the text of Parashara illustrating that a woman can take a second husband under certain circumstances. Predictably, this was countered by orthodox pandits who contended that Parashara did not enjoy much authority in ancient times as his law-book was compiled only in about the eighth century (Sharma 1983: 7). The reactionaries turned the tables on Vidyasagar by quoting from Manu, the pre-eminent law-giver, who permitted only the remarriage of shudra widows who had remained virgins.[4]

Obviously, the shastras and scriptures which generally represent ancient brahmanical values provided more armoury to the conservatives than to the progressives who were taking too much liberty to conveniently interpret them to suit their reform agenda. To make matters worse, the reformers rarely invoked the liberal ideals of equality and reason. Instead they chose to indulge in futile shadow-boxing with the scripture-quoting-conservatives with chanting mantras of their own. In fact, in discovering great ideals and progressivism in the Veda-Upanishad and shastra-smriti, the progressives surpassed even the traditionalists, invigorating brahmanical ideology and in the long run helping the hands of conservative fundamentalism. Falling back on the obscurantist shastras meant, in actuality, the negation of a rational and humanist approach to social problems.

Movements for social reform spearheaded by organisations like the Brahmo Samaj in Bengal, and later by Prarthana Samaj in Maharashtra, Veda Samaj in Tamil Nadu, and the Arya Samaj in

Punjab and northern India were ideologically guided by, as their very names suggest, the vision of brahmanical values.

The Brahmo Samaj that Roy founded in 1828 initiated a controlled attack on what was considered essentially unbrahmanical dogma, superstition, and polytheism, through ingenious but unhistorical reinterpretations of selected scriptures. In his debate with Christian enthusiasts, Roy had made his position amply clear by insisting that what he was defending was 'the genuine Brahmanical religion, taught by the Vedas, as interpreted by the inspired Manu, not the popular system or worship adopted by the multitude' (cited in Singh 1987: 95). His avowed aim was to purge the ancient and 'sacred' brahmanical tradition of modern-day corruption. Roy and his acolytes, in their rhetorical flourishes, sometimes attacked degenerate caste practices as 'undemocratic', 'inhuman' and 'antinational' but at the same time maintained that the original caste system was a wonderful institution, a glorious division of labour. Roy was, indeed, the pioneer who showed how to adopt and adjust the brahmanical ideas and institutions to a changing situation without rupturing the sanatani fabric. A close examination of Roy's ideas leaves us in no doubt that brahmanism in its original form was for him a glorious ideology. So the problem was not to get rid of brahmanism but to fully and firmly re-establish its norms and values for the advancement of society. No wonder Roy himself saw his reform movement as an attempt to preserve its pristine glories: 'The ground which I took in all my controversies was not that of opposition to brahmanism but to a perversion of it' (cited in Mehrotra 1971: 2).

Moreover, Roy himself did not bother to practice the progressivism he preached. For all his defiance of the Hindu orthodoxy, he was particular to the end of not losing his caste in the eyes of his orthodox critics. To the very end, he avoided eating with anyone who belonged to any other religion or caste. Even in England he maintained this abstinence with his English friends, of whom he had many (Kriplani 1981: 54). He never ate any food that was forbidden by the shastras for a brahman. And, when he went abroad in 1830 he took his brahman cook along (*Rammohun Rachnavali* 1973, Introduction; cited in S. K. Biswas 1998: 207-8). So also Dwarkanath Tagore (1794-1846), a prominent Brahmo Samaji and chief financer of Roy's movement, continued idol-worship and all priestly paraphernalia in his home, against the basic Brahmo tenets.

Roy talked of individual freedom, but it was firmly based on his concept of a caste society where only the higher and educated castes mattered. The 'lower' castes, he maintained, were 'superstitious' and 'fettered with prejudices' while the higher classes were aware of 'true doctrines', and therefore, had acquired 'the dignity of human beings'. In Calcutta only his Brahmo Samajis, he thought, were able to acquire such dignity. He found this high-low division a natural and universal phenomenon. Such a society, he opined, was implicit in the Veda-Purana, which introduced a plurality of gods and goddesses for the ignorant masses with 'limited understanding'. For the enlightened few, there had been the Vedantic doctrine of monotheism. Leaving the 'unredeemable' masses to their fate, he concerned himself only with the patrician classes of India and England. He pleaded that Europeans be encouraged to settle in India, but wanted only 'persons of character and capital'. Similarly, he wanted to shut the doors against 'persons of lower classes' and include only rich merchants and zamindars – 'respectable and intelligible classes' – in the political system (Mukherjee 1993). He insisted that only 'natives of respectability' should be appointed as collectors 'in lieu of Europeans' (ibid.).

On top of Roy's religious agenda was his advocacy of monotheism and the worship of a formless Supreme Being. What, then, was radically new in this approach? In Roy's time, millions of followers of Islam, Christianity, and Sikhism in India and elsewhere believed in monotheism and there had been a long and strong tradition of *nirguna* even among a section of the lower strata of Hindus. Much before Roy, cultural icons like Kabir and Nanak had led far more radical and monotheistic movements. Actually, there was nothing novel or revolutionary in Roy's religious ideas, except for the fact that he based his idea of monotheism in the brahmanical tradition. Other than this 'discovery', which was no less inspired by the monotheistic doctrines of Christianity and Islam, Roy never supported anything that attempted to breach brahmanical scriptural authority. He did nothing that had no approval of the shastras.

More importantly, Roy's attempts at religious reform did not have any impact on the ground. The ineffectiveness of his highly coloured 'religious radicalism' is laid bare by none other than the prominent right-wing historian, R. C. Majumdar:

> ... *The illuminated gates of two thousand Durga Puja pandals in Calcutta whose loudspeakers and Dhak or trumpets proclaim in deafening noise, year after year, the failure of Rammohun to make the slightest impression from his point of view on 99.9 per cent of the vast Hindu samaj either in the 19th or 20th century.* (cited in Pankratz 2001: 374)

Elitist history textbooks greatly exaggerate Roy's role in the making of modern India. Instead of presenting an objective evaluation of Roy and his *bhadralok* movement, there is a hagiographical tendency to lionise him as 'the morning star of modern India', 'the inaugurator of a moral revolution', 'the prophet of a new age', the Renaissance figure who brilliantly led the emergent middle classes in the early nineteenth century. He is even hailed as the 'father' of modern India (but the historians who decorate him with such superlative adjectives do not elaborate who his 'children' are). The crucial questions of what social groups comprised the new middle classes, and what their aspirations and motives were in spearheading the reform movement are conveniently pushed aside.

Roy came from a Radi Kulina brahman family, which traditionally enjoyed high social status in the caste hierarchy of Bengal. This sub-caste produced many outstanding personalities including Roy, Vidyasagar, Surendranath Banerjee and Ranglal Banerjee. Some have argued that the social reforms were initiated not only to enhance the social and economic position of the emergent middle classes, but also to safeguard the interests of the Radi Kulina caste. Thus:

The strict laws of endogamy, prohibition of widow remarriage and polygamy left many Radi Kulina brahmana women childless, and consequently the caste was losing in number. A 17th century Bengali poet prophesised that if the strict laws of endogamy and pollution continued, the Kulins would soon disappear. It seems that the social reforms concerning sati, widow remarriage and polygamy aimed at increasing the birth rate. (Mukherjee 1993: 367)

Almost all members of Roy's Atmiya Sabha, which transformed into the Brahmo Samaj in 1828, belonged to Radi Kulina or Bhanga Kulina caste. On the other hand, the Dharma Sabha, the relatively orthodox organisation founded by Raja Radhakant Deb, was dominated by sanskritised and upwardly mobile castes such as kayasthas and subarnavaniks. Roy's outfit was committed to some measured reforms that had become a historical necessity for survival of his caste. Not compelled by such compulsions, the Dharma Sabha members could afford to take a more hardened approach towards the reform agenda centering around sati and widow-remarriage. However, it is significant that the Dharma Sabha adopted, for quite obvious reasons, a more liberal approach on the caste question than Roy and his Brahmo Samaj. As early as 1832, the Dharma Sabha called a special meeting on the shudra-brahman relationship (Mukherjee 1993: 365). The crucial issue to be debated was whether the shastras permitted a shudra, if devout and righteous, to claim respect from brahmans and whether brahmans were permitted to partake of such a shudra's *prasada*. The pandits gave the judgement that a brahman should always command respect from a shudra, and under no circumstances should a brahman eat a shudra's *prasada*. Predictably, this judgement was challenged by the kayasthas and subarnavaniks. Bhairava Chandra Dutt, a subarnavanik, wrote a pamphlet, *Shree Shree Vaishnava Bhakti Kaumudi*, to refute the pandits' claim and establish that a righteous shudra could – and should – command respect from brahmans.

Thus caste conflicts were often fused with cultural and class conflicts. The traditional ascriptive ideology and institutions, instead of dying out, were adapted to changed situation and actually strengthened in the process by both the Brahmo Samaj and the Dharam Sabha. It is a brahmanical construct to portray Roy's Brahmo Samajis as paragons of progressivism, and to consign the members of Dharam Sabha as arch-conservatives. In fact, there was a very thin line of difference between Raja Rammohun Roy and Raja Radhakant Deb. Like Roy, Deb too was a Sanskritist and champion of Western education. Both wanted to settle contemporary issues through *shastrartha*. Both supported modernisation in their own way while remaining glued to the problematic tradition. Both were Rajas – one real (the British had accorded the title to Radhakant Deb) and the other wannabe (the British denied the title of 'Raja' to Roy despite a strong recommendation from the titular Mughal ruler, Akbar Shah II; however, as a consolation he was decorated with the title Rai Bahadur).

The reformers and their orthodox opponents shared the brahmanical ideology despite their conflicting views on some issues. Besides being united in their unflinching support to the colonial rule (which had provided them unprecedented opportunities to rise in life), there were many influential people who had one foot in the Brahmo Samaj and the other in the Dharam Sabha. Dwarkanath Tagore and his younger cousin Prasanna Kumar, for example, were a kind of link between the 'progressive' Brahmo Samajis and 'conservative' Dharam Sabhais. Then Dwarkanath and Deb openly came together in 1837 to form the Landholders' Society, which was later rechristened the British India Association. Later, Dwarkanath's son Debendranath Tagore (1817-1905), who succeeded Roy as leader of the Brahmo Samaj, had no hesitation in becoming Secretary of the British India Association, whose President was Radhakant Deb. By 1845, Debendranath was also speaking the language of the conservatives and was also using his 'rationalist-intellectual' organisation, the Tattvabodhini Sabha (which was later merged into the Brahmo Samaj) to vindicate the 'great Vedic doctrine' (Simeon 1986). In this sense, he was the precursor of the Vedic-brahmanic obscurantism, paving the way for Dayananda's Vedic fundamentalism.

In the first half of the nineteenth century, some *bhadralok* intellectuals appeared to be impressed by the ideals of democracy and liberalism. However, at the practical level, almost all of them remained orthodox – 'social conservatism combined with an openness to western education'. Whatever little radicalism there was in the Brahmo movement was gradually replaced by social conservatism in the advancing years of the century. The brahmanic values and colonial loyalism, very much present in Roy's political thinking and social vision, crystallised into hardcore British allegiance and anti-Muslim sentiments after 1850. 1857 revealed their true colours when *bhadralok* intellectuals of many hues vied with each other to show their absolute loyalty to the British rule. The Calcutta newspaper *Hindoo Patriot* in its edition dated 11 June, 1857, advised the educated class to remain loyal because: 'in three more generations they will have the best part of the property of the country in their hands... they have a splendid future before them, but which can be realised only by the continued existence of British rule' (cited in Simeon, ibid.). The *Sambad Prabhakar* editor Ishwar Chandra Gupta (1810-59) denounced the rebellion as a Muslim conspiracy aimed at destroying *Ram-rajya* under the British:

This (English) rule is as blissful as the rule of Ram . . . we are all getting our fulfilment in all aspects of our life as children by a mother under the aegis of the ruler of the world, the Queen of England. . . . Let the goddess of British Raj remain steady and let us enjoy the heavenly bliss of independence forever. (ibid.)

In keeping with other apologists for the Vedic religion, Gupta in his *Bharat Bhumir Durdasa* linked the degraded status of India as 'the subject race' to the 'error and delusion' through which 'we ceased to venerate the Vedas' (Basu 2002: 18-19). It may be recalled that Ishwar Chandra Gupta and Bhudeb Mukhopadhyay, another social reactionary in brahmanical mould, were inspirations to Bankimchandra Chatterjee who further elaborated this brand of Hindu nationalism and patriotism in his creative and critical writings. It were these gentlemen along with their numerous successors who firmly laid the foundation of the communal brahmanical revivalism in India. The national revival became irretrievably entangled with the racial and religions revival. The restoration of the 'supreme Hindu culture' began to be used interchangeably with the national awakening. Nationalism became another name for the Sanatan Dharma, the orthodox Hindu religion of the past. Aurobindo's definition of nationalism leaves little doubt in this regard:

. . . Not a mere political programme. Nationalism is a religion that has come from God. . . . If you are going to be a nationalist, if you are going to assent to this religion of nationalism, you must do it in the religious spirit. . . . When it is said that India shall expand and extend itself, it is the Sanatan Dharma that shall expand and extend itself over the world. (see Thapar 1975: 12)

Dayananda's Valorisation of the Aryan Race and Vedic Culture

No discussion of the nineteenth century socio-cultural awakening would be complete without assessing the role of Dayananda Saraswati (1824-83) and the revivalist movement in the north that he spearheaded through the Arya Samaj founded by him in 1875. Dayananda's ideology was not very dissimilar from that of the early reformers of Bengal and elsewhere, except for the fact that he had a more fundamental vision of the past based on the myth of the Vedic golden age. A religious man of fervent imagination and boundless energy, Dayananda created, rather than recalled, that heavenly era in the Aryavarta, the land of the 'superhuman' race of Aryans, in which the first men were born; Sanskrit, the 'mother of all tongues and the language of gods', was spoken; and, not only did 'theoretical wisdom flourish but also the practical industrial sciences'. The Vedas were 'not only true, but they contained all truth, including the ideas of modern science'. Born in Bombay but nurtured in Punjab, the Arya Samaj subsequently spread its tentacles in many parts of north India. The Arya Samaji rhetoric of the glorious Aryan civilisation became part of the Hindu consciousness of the region. The movement brought in its wake a mythological awareness of the past permeated with 'an Aryan consciousness accompanied by its attendant baggage of associations such as virility, spirituality and highmindedness' (Chakravarti 1989: 54).

Dayananda published in 1875 his magnum opus *Satyartha Prakash* (The Light of Truth). He wrote it in Hindi on the suggestion of Keshab Chandra Sen to make it accessible to the masses, but in his characteristic style he linked his Hindi to Vedic Sanskrit and gave it a new name – the Aryabhasha. *Satyartha Prakash,* perhaps the most influential and controversial *granth* of Hindu revivalism, contains Dayananda's recipe for the regeneration of Hindu religion and society and, naturally, came to be regarded as somewhat of a manifesto of the Arya Samaj movement. Dayananda was a zealous reformer and for any reformer of the time it was necessary to come to grips with the caste question. He wholeheartedly supported the ideals of *varna-vyavastha* but criticised its wrong application which bred degenerate practices and corruption. What was required, therefore, was to weed out the degenerate elements that had crept into the perfect varna model of social organisation. It does not need reiteration here that his pontifications against deformed caste order and priestly corruption were largely negated by his own utopian valorisation of *chaturvarnya* and his clarion call to 'go back to the Vedas' as a panacea for all the contemporary malaises.

Dayananda's social vision and his views on caste were shaped by his faith in brahmanical ideology and metaphysics. Denouncing idolatrous and superstitious practices of contemporary Hinduism, he remained committed to orthodoxy in several basic ways – belief in the superiority of Vedic faith over all religions; allegiance to *sadadarshanam* (the six philosophical schools) and to various Hindu names for the one God; and faith in *karma* and transmigration of soul. He asserted in the *Satyartha Prakash* that there were three eternal existences – God, the soul and matter – and that the soul underwent transmigration according to the law of *karma*. He therefore fully accepted the theory of *karma* and *punarjnam*. This theory, as we have seen earlier, is the most reactionary metaphysical construct of brahmanical religion, which justifies the status quo, however oppressive and inhuman, on the ground that every being is born in a particular situation because of his or her actions in the previous births. Dayananda not only accepted all this, he even rattled off, like a veteran *karmakandi*, the list detailing what sins would lead to birth in what species (Talwar 2001: 48-55).

A willing prisoner of the *karma* doctrine, Dayananda did not deem it necessary to launch an attack on caste, nor did he expect any anti-caste action from his followers. This also explains why his views on shudras were self-contradictory, and his concern to uplift them was, at best, half-hearted. In the first edition of the *Satyartha Prakash*, for example, he advocates school education for shudra children but denies them the right to study the Vedas. In the second edition of the book, published in 1884 after his death, he allows worthy, righteous shudras to study the shastras but still prohibits them from reading the Mantra Samhita, the most sacred section of the Vedic literature. In a similar vein, he gives the provision that a shudra can study but is not entitled to the investiture ceremony – *yajnopavit* – which enables one to become *dwija* or to use the Samaj idiom, the pure Aryan (Talwar 2001: 38). He enjoined the wearing of the sacred thread by the 'twice-born' as one of the 'signs of learning that distinguish the literate twice-born castes from the illiterate shudras'. At another place he advises shudras to eschew disagreement, envy, and ego, and to earn their livelihood by serving the three higher varnas (ibid.: 36). Most significantly, he did not have anything to say about millions of outcastes and tribals who were traditionally beyond the pale of *chaturvarnya*.

Dayananda's social orthodoxy is also borne out by his campaign for *shuddhi* or 'purification' programme which became a major flashpoint of communal confrontation. His Vedic chauvinism emboldened him to adopt an attitude of unusual belligerence and confrontation towards 'inferior' and 'fake' religions such as Christianity, Islam, Jainism, and Sikhism. In the *Satyartha Prakash*, he pours scorn and venom on other faiths. The superiority of the Aryan religion was self-evident to him. Armed with this Aryan fundamentalism, he embarked on a programme of *shuddhi* which meant the reconversion of those people who had been supposedly polluted by converting into other religions like Islam or Christianity. The controversial programme generated heated debate and raised the communal temperature to a dangerous level. Even among Hindus it triggered discord between upper and lowered castes because *shuddhi* also belittled all other than pure Aryans as lesser human beings. Implicit in the *shuddhi* was the concept of *pavitra* (pure) and *apavitra* (impure), the cardinal principle which validates the caste system. This was evident from the fact that purified or reconverted persons were given the 'original' jati/varna to which they belonged before the conversion. This is significant because their jati/varna was not determined by their qualities and deeds, but by their ancestors' birth in a particular jati. This exposes the Arya Samaj's claim that the original varna-vyavastha was an ideal social system where one's position in the caste hierarchy was determined by one's worth and not birth.

A close and critical reading of the *Satyartha Parkash* exposes the ethical system of the Samaj as crude in the extreme. Dayananda supports many of the ideas of Manu in all their barbarity. An individual, for example, is encouraged to kill those whom he regards as monstrously evil men. The king is advised to have the adulterer burned alive on a red-hot iron bedstead, and the adulteress devoured alive by dogs, in the presence of many men and women. However, it is in his anxiety to control women's sexuality that Dayananda drops all veneer of decency. As Uma Chakravarti has pointed out, Dayananda's conceptualisation of womanhood is inextricably linked to the way he deals with the sexuality of women. 'What was central to Dayananda's thinking was his understanding of the role of women in the maintenance of race, and inter alia, concern about their sexuality. Motherhood for Dayananda was the sole rationale of a woman's existence but what was crucial in his concept of motherhood was its specific role in the procreation and rearing of a special breed of men. For example, the *Satyartha Prakash* lays down a variety of rules and regulations for ideal conception' (1989: 56). Driven by his concern for a healthy and pure stock of Aryans, Dayananda even advocates for the appointment of (shudra) wet nurse so that the (Aryan) mother can recuperate quickly to be ready to conceive again:

It is best therefore, for the mother not to suckle her child. Plasters should be applied to the breast that will soon dry up the milk. By following this system the woman becomes strong again in about two months. Till then the husband should have thorough control over his passions and thus preserve the reproductive element. Those that will follow this plan will have children of a superior order, enjoy long life, and continually gain in strength and energy so that their children will be of a high mental calibre, strong, energetic and devout. (ibid.)

It was this obsession with the management of female sexuality for a regenerated race of Aryans which also shaped Dayananda's ambivalent position on widow remarriage. Emphasising the importance of motherhood, he supported remarriage of both men and women if there were no children from earlier marriage. As a solution to the remarriage question and the problem of sexuality, he hit upon the idea of *niyoga*, the early Aryan practice of sexual relationship without marriage for the purpose of procreation. In support of *niyoga*, Dayananda ransacked various ancient texts and conveniently interpreted them to uphold the practice. There was no immorality in this practice, he declared, because the rationale for both marriage and *niyoga* was to beget healthy and strong children. At the same time, Dayananda was emphatic that a woman can *niyoga* only with a man of the same or higher varna, and not under any circumstances, with a man of lower varna (Talwar 2001: 44). As Uma Chakravarti comments, 'This was one form of the nationalist resolution of women's sexuality; to use her biological potential for child bearing in the service of the physical regeneration of what was seen as a now weakened Aryan race' (1989: 60).

Dayananda's recipe of reform-from-within was fraught with sinister consequences. By declaring the Vedas as infallible and an inexhaustible source of all knowledge past, present, and future, the Arya Samaj firmly laid the foundation of brahmanical revivalist politics. Throwing all reason and rationalism to the winds, Dayananda blithely declared that if one knew the correct way to interpret the Vedas, one would discover all modern chemistry, engineering, and even military and non-military sciences in the holy book. Later, Vivekananda and Gandhi would defend the Hindu scriptures which routinely denigrate shudras and women on the same obscurantist line, arguing that before criticising the 'holy Hindu books' one must learn how to interpret them.

However, Dayananda was not unique in arguing that 'truth, wherever it is found, it is of the Veda'. Other gladiators of Hindu nationalism revered the Vedas in the same vein. Vivekananda, for example, believed that basic principles of all sciences are to be discovered in the Vedas. He even discovered Darwin in the holy book: 'The idea of evolution was to be found in the Vedas long before the Christian era; but until Darwin said it was true, it was regarded as a mere Hindu superstition' (*The Complete Works*, vol. VIII: 25). Aurobindo Ghose (1872-1950) went many steps ahead and declared that Dayananda actually underevaluated, far from overestimating, the depth and range of the Vedic wisdom:

There is then nothing fantastical in Dayananda's idea that the Veda contains truths of science as well as truths of religion. I will even add my own conviction that the Veda contains other truths of a science which the modern world does not at all possess, and in that sense, Dayananda has rather understated than overstated the depth and range of the Vedic wisdom.

(cited in Arvind Sharma 2001: 398)

Underlining the importance of Dayananda's Veda-centric movement in the creation of a national consciousness, the militant nationalist ideologue B. C. Pal (1858-1932) has pointed out that prior to the Arya Samaj, Hinduism suffered from the acute lack of a universal scripture that other religions like Christianity and Islam have in the Bible and Koran. He praises Dayananda for taking inspiration from the evangelical Christianity and Islam in order to create and foster a similar militancy in Hinduism (Biswas 1998: 218). It was indeed Dayananda, Pal gushes, who showed to the Hindus that there could not be a purer religion or a purer social order than the one envisioned in the Vedas. In Pal's opinion, the Vedic order is indeed superior even to 'the social idealism inspired by the dogma of Liberty, Equality and Fraternity of the French illumination'. He reiterates that it was this Vedic religious revival 'to which we owe so largely the birth of our present national consciousness' (ibid.: 220). He was not wrong.

Self-Strengthening Modernisation of Brahmanical Tradition

The Sanskritic reformers and nationalists overlooked the damage done to Indian society by entrenched brahmanical tradition. The Hindu elites who had revered the sacerdotal literature in the name of patriotism papered over the malignant social contents and sinister implications of those texts for the commoners. What were the reformers/nationalists trying to prove by selectively picking out and focusing light on the favourable passages from the 'sacred' texts? And, more importantly, were the reformers not aware of a more humane and wholesome tradition, the shramanic tradition of dissent and resistance represented by the early Buddhists, Jains, the subaltern saint-poets and liberals of the folk Hinduism? Why were they so passionate about adjusting the ancient brahmanical ideas and institutions to the changing socio-cultural conditions? Why were they so enthusiastic to link, quite unhistorically and illogically, their relatively progressive thinking and modern ideas to the obscurantist texts?

The answer lies in the fact that all of them were literati, champion scholars of Sanskrit, and hailed from the same brahmanical background. Rammohun Roy was a superb Sanskritist, and so were other stalwarts of the reform movements – Ishwarchandra Vidyasagar,

Debendranath Tagore, Dayananda Saraswati, and R. G. Bhandarkar. They were all brahman scholar-reformers speaking in colourful and different voices but unanimous in a commitment to the brahmanical culture and values. Their interpretations of the quintessentially conservative texts for social reform, in retrospect, appear to be fundamentally and fatally flawed. Of course, they succeeded to some extent in convincing the colonial masters and moulding the upper caste Hindu opinion (which goes in the name of Indian opinion) in favour of their caste-centred, self-strengthening reform agenda. But by remaining indifferent to the plight of the majority, they were only furthering the marginalisation of the masses.

In fact, by assuming – and establishing – the brahmanical tradition as the Indian tradition, the elite reformers set in motion the process of its modernisation. Leaving aside the more-inclusive and multi-cultural Indian civilisation with its powerful undercurrents of egalitarian ideology, the tradition that was promoted by the nineteenth century reformers was exclusivist. The construction of a particular kind of tradition was the context for construction of a particular kind of nationalism. This hegemonic nationalism itself came to occupy the same place that discriminatory brahmanical religion had monopolised before.

In the context of the women's question, which formed the nucleus of the reform movement, the entire focus of attention in the nineteenth century had been on the high caste Hindu women whether it was to highlight their high status in the past or in reforming their low status in the present (Chakravarti 1989: 78). This was typical of a nationalist project that focused exclusively on high caste Hindu women and excluded the majority of shudra-adivasi and Muslim women from its ambit. However, this mass exclusion gelled well with the construction and celebration of the racial genius of the ancient Aryans. In her searching and luminous analysis Uma Chakravarti has shown how the focus on the upper sections of society to the total exclusion of all others was explicit or implicit in the nineteenth century reformist and nationalist discourse. It was evident, she argues, from Dayananda's injunctions that Arya mothers should not nurse their babies, but employ wet nurses instead so that they might recover quickly and so be ready to produce strong sons once more.

But what of the wet nurse? Who was she? What about her place in the system of procreation? Was she not required to produce strong sons too? Clearly Dayananda's injunctions were meant for one section at the expense of another. Vast sections of women did not exist for the nineteenth century nationalists. No one tried to read the ancient texts to see what rights the Vedic dasi and others like her had in the Vedic golden age. (Chakravarti 1989: 79)

The reformers never critiqued the ancient texts for handing down the worst kinds of injustices and inequalities to the lower orders and women. Some even argued that disabilities of the shudras did not reduce their happiness or well-being. Even child marriage was justified on the ground that this practice helped a girl to know whom she had to love, before any sexual consciousness had awakened in her. Likewise, the denigration and subservience of women was dismissed with selective citations to prove that they were worshipped like goddesses in ancient times, and also by arguing that a woman would make herself more uncomfortable and vulnerable if she tries to step into a man's shoes by acquiring his temperament and functions (see Sharma 1983: 13).

All unpleasant and odious aspects of social life in ancient India were swept under the national carpet by the ingenious spin doctors of the glorious past. 'Caste did not cause poverty and did not divide the city into two parts like the East End and West End of London', wrote one, while the other blithely concluded that 'in ancient India there was no concentration of the prestige of birth, influence of wealth and political office which imparts an aristocratic tinge to social organisation and sustains an aristocratic government' (cited in Sharma 1983: 15). Repeated joint notices of shudras and women depriving them of civil and property rights and frequent branding of woman with property in the ancient Sanskrit texts were not given due attention. It appears that the reformers' only motive was to establish somehow that all was good and glorious in the ancient period and that the degeneration set only in the medieval period under the Muslim rule.

As a matter of fact the didactic and narrative portions of the *Ramayana* and the *Mahabharata* and other ancient texts were often yoked together to reach at favourable conclusions. The *sanatani* and unchanging character of the Indian people was often highlighted to evade the troublesome and complex reality and the process of social development in ancient India. R. S. Sharma has pointed out how the Dharmashastras and Grihyasutras, which are works of the post-Vedic period, were included in the Vedic period in the Bharatiya Vidya Bhawan series on *The History and Culture of the Indian People*. Underlining the utterly casteist and unhistorical nature of the elitist study of the past, Sharma writes:

The study of the lower orders in ancient India has not only been ignored, but, strange as it may seem, in some cases they appear to have been held in the same contempt by modern writers as they were held by the members of the upper varnas in ancient times. It is stated that child marriage originated among the lower classes, while the Dharmashastra rules leave no doubt that it first began among the three upper varnas. It is said that women had a higher position among the upper classes, while the opposite seems to have been the case. The climax is reached when on the basis of his study of ancient Indian society a writer prescribes sexual self-control and abstinence for the 'Brahman' and the use of contraceptives for people of the lowest varna. (1983: 15-16)

The exaltation of brahmanical values grounded in the patriarchal family and varna system under the cloak of nationalism provided a potent weapon in the hands of casteist, communalist and obscurantist elements to stem the tide of social change. No wonder the reformist movement quickly lost its steam and degenerated into revivalism. As their primary aim was not to build a genuine people-centred nationalism but to strengthen their traditional clout and dominance over the masses, the reformers' agenda and orientation paved the way for Hindu revivalism, a scripture-based nationalism, and communal politics.

'NATIONALIST' VINDICATION OF CASTE IDEOLOGY

As nationalism was defined in brahmanic terms, caste was re-theorised as a glorious institution representing stability, harmony and co-operation. The valorisation of caste became the hallmark of national unity. It was argued that 'caste has its merits as the adhesive, assimilative force which holds the Hindu society together and enables to withstand attacks from outside'. No wonder there was a symbiosis between the resurgence of upper caste movements and the rise of 'national' awakening, a fact that has been erased from the history textbooks in order to build the case of a mass-based, pan-Indian nationalism. The remark of Maharajadhiraj of Darbhanga, one of the major financers of the Indian National Congress in its early days, anticipating the manifold virtues of caste in the Gandhian vein, was not his own alone. He said caste was 'the best and surest safeguard against the spirit of unrest, against the growing bitterness between the classes and the masses, between capital and labour, which is constantly menacing civilisation' (see Desai 1991: 257)

Along with the reform movements, the English-educated landlords, clerks, professionals and scholars of the Raj, who together formed the emergent middle class, also ran caste societies/organisations to strengthen caste solidarity between members of the same caste. Buildings were constructed to be rented to members of the caste and at affordable rents. Poorer members of the caste were given financial help by the rich. Scholarships were awarded for carrying out studies only to the boys and girls belonging to that caste. Co-operatives were started for exclusive benefits of the members of the same caste. Meetings and conferences were held to cement the caste solidarity. Magazines, newspapers and pamphlets were brought out to disseminate the caste ideology and consciousness (ibid.). Prominent figures took the lead in forming caste societies like the Akhil Bharatiya Brahman Sabha and the Kayastha Pathashala which had several units all over the country.

In an astonishing display of caste-class unity, the *bhadralok* rallied round the caste ideology, hailing it as the living testimony to India's social genius. It was surmised that India would not have survived as a nation without the caste system. Social hierarchy and inequality was spiritedly defended as 'natural', 'justifiable', and 'culturally uplifting'. The lowbrow apologists for caste hierarchy took refuge in religious sanctions and usually cited the Creation Hymn from the *Rigveda* and the karmic explanations in an Upanishadic verse.[5] The highbrow, English-friendly, 'modern' members of the *bhadralok* borrowed the language of Western science and social theory to prove that caste in its true sense was not divisive or dangerous, as was being claimed by radicals like Phule, but the 'product of a free people exercising dynamic political will'.

Drawing parallel between the ancient brahmanical eliticism and the modern concept of meritocracy, the caste stratification was presented as an excellent division of labour.

R. C. Dutt (1848-1909), the towering nationalist scholar, in his celebrated three-volume *History of Civilisation in Ancient India Based on Sanskrit Literature*, written in 1880s, argued that in ancient times caste never divided and disunited the Aryan people but rallied them as one man against the aborigines (Sharma 1983: 9). Such animosity against the aborigines, the supposed ancestors of the lowered castes and tribals, calls the bluff of the so-called nationalists: boasting of patriotism based on Aryan supremacy only implied the subordination of the majority of their own countrymen. Such assertions in the name of nationalism were actually directed against the Indian masses rather than the British colonialists. As Sumit Sarkar says, 'Caste inequality was asserted still in a remarkably open, indeed matter-of-fact, manner, for the potential readers of such tracts could be assumed to be entirely high caste' (1997: 373-4).

For Dutt, ancient Indian history was almost synonymous with Aryan Hindu history. The aborigines or non-Aryans were only a conquered and subjugated people. He fancied, in the introduction of his book on ancient India, that his writing would go a long way in dispelling the superstitious worship of the past! Dutt's book quickly acquired the status of a classic and was rendered into many regional languages. Other writer-scholars of the nationalist school further elaborated and illustrated his formulations. Dutt, who later emerged as a pioneering nationalist economic historian, also authored trailblazing romances about Rajputs and Marathas, in which he portrayed Muslims as tyrannical enemies of Hindu people.

Jogendra Nath Bhattacharya was another influential writer who insisted that caste was positive, uniquely Indian, and essential to the genius of Hindu civilisation. In his *Hindu Castes and Sects* (1896) he declared that the varna scheme had been forged as 'an act of large-hearted statesmanship' which had set up ideal models of conduct and morality for a diverse and conflict-prone population. The creation of varnas, he argues, united people and taught them noble ideals, and provided the means of assimilating the 'foreign hordes' who had so often invaded the Hindu homeland. He lavishes praise on the visionary ancient law-givers who helped transform descendants of the early Aryan 'Vedic singers' into 'one race under the name of Brahmans'. The fourfold varna scheme was a 'golden chain', to use Bhattacharya's striking metaphor, which Hindus had 'willingly placed on their necks, and which has fixed them to only that which is noble and praiseworthy'. Far from being 'tyrannical' and 'cruel', he stresses, caste has endowed Indians with selfless spiritual ideals and a concept of solidarity which had long united separate 'races and clans' of India (Bayly 2000: 163-5).

An early graduate of Calcutta University, Bhattacharya was president of the Bengal Brahman Sabha and also head of the Nadia College of Pandits, which was entitled, courtesy the colonial government, to give authoritative judgements on matters of Hindu tradition. Renowned as a nationalist scholar, his writings on caste and national culture – the first sociological work by an Indian – were greatly admired in the nationalist circle (Bayly, ibid.). In fact, it was Bhattacharya's views on caste that are relayed, as we shall see later, in the caste ideology of two of the greatest nationalist heroes, Vivekananda and Gandhi.

The system of social stratification was held as a divine order even by the fabled saint of Dakshineshwar, Ramakrishna Paramhans (1836-86). Ishwarchandra Vidyasagar made the saint quite angry by suggesting that God could not have been so unfair so as to give more powers to some and less to others (Sarkar 1997: 372). Ramakrishna asserted that big and small would always remain fundamentally different, adding variety to the world and leaving space for the *lila* of the gods (ibid.: 374). Sumit Sarkar has pointed out that his central message was 'one of quietistic, inward-looking bhakti', and he was 'often openly scornful of socially activist, ameliorative projects, even of philanthropy' (ibid.: 201). However, it was Ramakrishna's obscurantist and *sanatani* ideas which captured the imagination of the *bhadralok*. It was he who became a major cult figure and won the hearts of Vivekananda and other Hindu nationalists and not the rationalist-reformer Vidyasagar.

Vidyasagar, perhaps the most humane and rational face of the *bhadralok* intelligentsia, 'waged a determined but losing battle against the orthodoxy'. Propounding a thesis of rational knowledge rather than a polemic of power, he was critical of the Sanskritic philosophical tradition and boldly opposed the introduction of 'false systems of

Vedanta and Sankhya' into the curriculum at Sanskrit College on the grounds that it would encourage obscurantist self-congratulation (Simeon 1986). The *bhadralok* thronged to the obscurantist Ramkrishna – and later to his star disciple Vivekananda – and left the likes of Vidyasagar in the lurch to despair, 'If I had an idea of the worthlessness, dishonesty and lack of integrity of the *baralok* (high and mighty people) of our country, I might perhaps not have ventured on this movement' (see Simeon, ibid.: 11).

Caste – the main target of the contemporary social radicals like Phule, Iyothee Thass and Narayana Guru – was still being celebrated under the fig-leaf of varnashrama-dharma by its beneficiaries. Even the social services, ostentatiously aimed at patriotic unity, were being organised to replenish the classical caste culture. The Arya Samaj had started some educational and welfare programmes for the lowered castes, but these half-hearted measures were actually intended to take them firmly in the caste system. As the only brahmanic organisation that tried to reach out to the masses, the Arya Samaj had a dubious relationship with the lowered castes. From the very beginning it was against autonomous social and political movements among them. Many evidences suggest that various lowered caste initiatives to organise and agitate for socio-political rights in Punjab, United Provinces, and elsewhere were strongly opposed by the Arya Samaj. Prominent dalit leaders like Mangoo Ram in Punjab and Acchutanand in Uttar Pradesh, who were earlier associated with the Arya Samaj movement, had to come out strongly against its hypocritical position on the caste question.

Vivekananda's Polemics

Even the piecemeal and paternalistic Hindu reforms-from-the-top and perfunctory attempts to provide breathing space for the lowered castes within the Sanskritic parameter were necessitated by the political expediency, the growing fear of Muslim and Christian proselytisation, and the resounding reverberations of anti-caste movements all over the country. The latter half of nineteenth century saw the emergence of popular egalitarian movements, especially in south and west India. Social revolutionaries such as

Phule, Iyothee Thass, and Narayana Guru arrived on the scene (see Chapters 5 and 6). The brahman and allied castes quickly read the writing on the wall and decided to strengthen the armoury of hegemonic Hinduism. The man who played an outstanding role in this regard was none other than Swami Vivekananda (1863-1902), the charismatic crusader of Hindu patriotism. Not an ordinary revivalist or obscurantist, he launched an impressive attack on existing degeneration but combined it, far more effectively than other cultural supremacists, with a passionate evocation of the Hindu glories of the past. Anchored in the brahmanical vision of the past, his firebrand rhetoric of a rejuvenated and vibrant India was wedded to, as Sumit Sarkar says, 'a near-total lack of clarity about socio-economic programmes, methods of mass contact, or even political objectives' (1983: 73). He appealed for identification with the 'Daridra-narayana', the poor and the toiling castes, but had no idea or programme of what was to be done.

Vivekananda derided the torture of the 'lower' castes and the sucking of the blood of the poor. Yet he chastised the anti-brahman movements of the south for being in too much of a hurry and inciting 'fighting among the castes'. 'As Manu says, all these privileges and honours were given to brahmana, because with him is the treasury of virtue' (Vivekananda 1988: 89). 'To the non-brahmana castes, I say, be not in a hurry. You are suffering from your own fault. Who told you to neglect spirituality and Sanskrit learning? Why do you now fret and fume because somebody else has more brains, more energy, more pluck than you?' (ibid: 87). In the same vein, he advised the underprivileged castes that 'instead of wasting your energy in quarrels . . . use all your energies in acquiring the culture which the brahmana has, and the thing is done. Why do you not become Sanskrit scholars? Why do you not spend millions to bring Sanskrit education to all the castes in India? That (Sanskrit education) is the secret of power in India. Sanskrit and prestige go together in India' (ibid.: 87-8). Acquiring brahmanhood through learning Sanskrit, according to him, was the road to freedom for the caste-oppressed. It appears he was unaware of the commonly known fact that traditionally women and shudras were forbidden the study of Sanskrit scripture. More important, Vivekananda wanted the 'lower' caste people to emulate the brahmans in order to overcome all their miseries. The fabric of brahmanical ideology and practice weaving a system of oppression never pricked the conscience of the self-proclaimed 'Vedantic socialist'. So immersed was he in the brahmanic culture and Aryan pride that at times he even bared the fangs of his naked antipathy against the 'lower' caste masses. He cursed the British for educating them and cautioned the upper castes about the threat of a looming mass awakening:

... And the Europeans are now educating those ignorant, illiterate low caste people, who toil fields in their loin cloth, are of the non-Aryan race. They are none of us. This is going to weaken us and give benefit to both these Europeans and the low caste people. (cited in Biswas 1998: 251)

Vivekananda went to ridiculous lengths to deny the fact that caste hierarchies coincided with differences in ritual status and that theories propounded in the shastras had always been used to validate and perpetuate caste stratification. His faith in the ancient varna culture made him advocate even a return to the socio-religious system of Manu and Yajnavalkya (Sen 1993: 341). The official records reveal that the Ramakrishna Math and Mission that he founded, in its governance of the Order, placed great importance on the 'family culture' of potential recruits (ibid.: 331-2). He was also strongly opposed to intercaste marriages (ibid.).

Indeed, there are some stray references in his writings to the imminent shudra rule by which he meant rise of the 'lower' castes 'but it is quite significant that he should also think that this represented a general lowering of culture' (ibid.: 331). Contradicting what many loudly proclaim as his radical social orientation, Vivekananda himself admitted that he was merely aiming at religious and not social unity (ibid.). Conveniently picking out some isolated and out-of-context utterances of Vivekananda, his admirers go to great lengths to project him as a champion of social justice and egalitarianism. In reality, his position on caste remains deeply problematic, as is evident from the following roll of his statements:

Caste has kept us alive as a nation. (Complete Works of Swami Vivekananda, vol. II: 489)

It is in the nature of society to form itself into groups. ... Caste is a natural order; I can perform one duty in social life, and you another; you can govern a country, and I can mend a pair of old shoes, but that is no reason why you are greater than I, for can you mend my shoes. . . . Caste is good. That is the only natural way of solving life. (ibid., vol. III: 245-6)

Each caste has become, as it were, a separate racial element. If a man lives long enough in India, he will be able to tell from the features what caste a man belongs to. (ibid., vol. VIII: 54)

Vivekananda's sporadic, occasional diatribes against the 'puritanical' and 'sectarian' brahmans coupled with his famous proclamation of an imminent 'shudra revolution', which, contrary to popular perception, was actually a sign of cultural degeneration for him, was partly born out of the brahman orthodoxy's ugly challenge to his emerging gurudom. The more reactionary among the brahmans (including some prominent Brahmo Samajis of Calcutta) had questioned on several occasions Vivekananda's credentials as a religious teacher, citing the reason that he was a shudra. He came, as is well known, from a sanskritised and upwardly mobile kayastha caste, traditionally considered shudra in the varna hierarchy. After his 'triumphant' return from America and Europe, he was held 'guilty' of crossing the ocean, socialising with the *mlecchas* and eating 'forbidden' food. In fact, the brahmanic opposition to Vivekananda's leadership was symbolic of a long simmering animosity between the two dominant castes – the mainstay of Bengali *bhadralok* – for social status. While brahman supremacy was accepted by the kayasthas, the former were reluctant to give high caste status to the latter. Even Raja Pearymohun Mukhopadhyaya, who chaired the felicitation meeting in honour of Vivekananda expressed doubt as to whether a kayastha could become a *sannyasin* (Bose 1999: 298). The members of the Reception Committee had earlier requested Sir Gurudas Bannerjee, the noted educationist, nationalist, and judge of the Calcutta Supreme Court, to preside over the felicitation meeting. Gurudas Banerjee had not only refused but reprimanded the organisers saying that 'had there been a Hindu raja in the country, Vivekananda would have been hung for violating the caste rules' (B. N. Datta, cited in Biswas 1998: 237). A few years later, on Vivekananda's death, the same gentleman again turned down the request to preside over the condolence meeting.

This kind of caste chauvinism was still practised by the pandits, though Vivekananda's acceptance of Ramakrishna, a brahman, as his guru and Ramakrishna's great affection for his star disciple had greatly helped to mitigate antagonism. This also to some extent helps us understand Vivekananda's oscillation between the modern, humane outlook reflected in some of his ideas – he had himself been humiliated by arrogant brahmans for his 'low' origin – and his romance with brahmanical ideology which made him justify caste and gender inequalities. This is important because the ambiguity which afflicted Vivekananda was manifested, in greater or lesser degree, in ideas and activities of other national stalwarts as well.

Vivekananda's attitude to the gender question, too, was no different from his position on caste. He was patriarchal to the core. He was in love with orthodox elements of traditional – and his guru Ramakrishna's – asceticism 'viewing women as a positive impediment in spiritual life, finding womanhood best exemplified by Mother, and demanding absolute fidelity in the case of the wife. Such instincts considerably fashioned Vivekananda's social attitude towards gender relations and related issues' (Sen 1993: 330). He strongly disapproved of women's aspirations for autonomy and self-assertion and cynically rejected what he called the 'outlandish' feminism of the West. He suggested that the docile Sita was the paragon of feminine virtue. Defending the traditional position of women in Indian society, he could go to any extent to portray the 'happy picture' of Hindu women. In a speech at Oakland, for example, he even declared that denying the child-widow the right to remarry caused no 'particular hardship' to her. A cultured and well-instructed widow, he argued, does not consider life a hardship, because she lives a life of asceticism and devotion, which elevates her to higher levels of perfection (ibid.). On another occasion, he made the dubious statement that upper-caste Hindu widows seldom remarried because of the relative 'scarcity of men' (ibid.). On this count, he was happily ensconced in the illustrious league of people like Bankim who would brand the widow who remarried as 'unchaste'. He held that the faithfulness of widows was the very pillar on which social institutions rested (ibid.: 331).

'If a Hindu is not spiritual,' Vivekananda would thunder, 'I do not call him a Hindu.' He aggressively propagated the 'spiritual

India and materialist West' thesis, first expounded by the Orientalists. Other nationalists, too, took pride in India's religious greatness but Vivekananda's brand of spiritual chauvinism was conspicuous for its imperialist demagoguery. Proclaiming India's religious superiority over the rest of the world and overpowering the world with this spirituality became an obsession with the flamboyant monk. In a much-eulogised and oft-quoted lecture in Madras, he challenged his audience to conquer the whole world with Indian spirituality:

This is the great ideal before us, and everyone must be ready for it – the conquest of the whole world by India. . . . They are waiting for it, they are eager for it. . . . We must go out, we must conquer the world through our spirituality and philosophy. There is no other alternative, we must do it or die. (see Embree and Hay 1991, vol. II: 76)

What was the distinctive 'Indian' spirituality Vivekananda was so desperate to preach to the whole world? It was, for one thing, embedded in the brahmanical religion and philosophy. Theoretically, he had accepted every aspect of brahmanism, and was candid enough to admit that he had no religious ideology of his own. He supported caste, incarnation, idol worship, and everything written in the brahmanical scriptures. His religiosity had no quarrel with patriarchy or caste and its hierarchical division of the pure and impure, high and low. Yet he was able to impress many with the 'grandeur of classical Hinduism' as he had perfected the art of embellishing his religious orthodoxy with some grandiloquent words and phrases that he randomly picked up from his readings on the modern science and civilisation.

Like other luminaries of Hindu nationalism, Vivekananda lived more in the past than in the present. He proudly admitted on several occasions that his vision of the present and future of India was based on, and inspired by, the 'glorious past'. He wished to build the future of India on the past itself:

Nowadays everybody blames those who constantly look back to the past. It is said that so much looking back to the past is the cause of all India's woes. To me, on the contrary, it seems that the opposite is true. So long as they forgot the past, the Hindu nation remained in a state of stupor and as soon as they have begun to look into this past, there is on every side a fresh manifestation of life. It is out of this past that the future has to be moulded, this past will become the future. (Complete Works, vol. IV: 324).

For such an impassioned Hindu Indian culture and Hindu culture were interchangeable. This zealotry brought Vivekananda into bitter conflict with Christianity, Islam, and also Buddhism. His role model in the art of running down other religions was possibly the Adi Shankara, whom he greatly revered and who is reputed to have banished Buddhism from the land of its birth. Vivekananda's acolytes admired his catholicism and universal appeal, but the fact is, he could not tolerate even the mildest and most constructive criticism of his faith. In the face of criticism from Christian missionaries on issues like caste and untouchability, he retaliated with venegance, questioning Christ's historicity, and even fatuously opined that early Christians may have had Hindu origins (Sen 1993: 338).

But Vivekananda's worst bite was reserved for Muhammad's religion. He portrayed Islam as essentially irrational and violent and depicted Muslims as slaughterers and butchers. To him Muslims were not only 'foreigners' but their religion too was an unacceptable presence. His demonisation of Islam is practically unrivalled by the Hindu fascists of today:

Now the Mohammedans are the crudest in this respect, and the most sectarian. Their watchword is: 'There is one God, and Muhammad is His Prophet'. Everything beyond that not only is bad, but must be destroyed forthwith; at a moment's notice, every man who does not exactly believe in that must be killed; everything that does not belong to this worship must be immediately broken; every book that teaches anything else must be burnt. From the Pacific to the Atlantic, for five hundred years blood ran all over the world. That is Mohammedanism. (cited in Alam 1996: 73 from CW, vol. IV: 126)

This is not an isolated example of his verbal assault on the Muslims. His description of Islamic religion and its followers often borders on paranoia:

The more selfish a man, the more immoral he is. And so also with a race. That race which is bound down to itself has been the most cruel and the most wicked in the whole world. There has not been a religion that has clung to this dualism more than that founded by the Prophet of Arabia, and there has not been a religion which has shed so much blood and been so cruel to other men. In the Quran there is a doctrine that a man who does not believe these teachings should be killed; it is a mercy to kill him. (ibid., vol. II: 352)

Thus like Bankim and other nationalist luminaries of the time, Vivekananda had no difficulty in preferring the colonial regime to 'tyrannical' Muslim rule: 'Of course, we had to stop advancing during the Mohammedan tyranny, for then it was not a question of progress but of life and death. Now that the pressure has gone, we must move forward' (ibid., vol. IV: 373).

Vivekananda's injunction for the rebuilding of a new India on the basis of 'a Vedantic brain and an Islamic body', cited by Nehru in his *Discovery of India* as the best instance of the Hindu-Muslim synthesis, is quite mischievous. As Alam argues, Hinduism, in this case, is the ideological engine and Islam is at its service as the muscled handmaiden to carry out the physical work. 'It privileges Hinduism and downgrades Islam' (ibid.: 74). Such a synthesis, lapped up by Nehru as the pinnacle of India's composite culture, is very much like the brahman-shudra harmony in which the former thinks/orders and the latter follows and toils with his hands.

A lesser-known aspect of Vivekananda's ideological-religious thinking is his contemptuous and grossly distorted references to the Buddha and Buddhism. In this respect, too, he carries the tradition of the earlier brahmanical chauvinists who maintained that early Buddhism was only the extension and fulfilment of the Upanishadic teachings and, hence, an offshoot of Hinduism. Blithely declaring that the original aim of the Buddha was to preach Vedantism, he even denied that the Buddha did not believe in the existence of soul – he attributed this to the misunderstanding of the Buddha's teachings by his followers. In the course of its expansion, he said, Buddhism absorbed into its fold many different barbarous races of mankind, and all their superstitions and degrading practices were absorbed by Buddhism (*The Nationalistic and Religious Lectures* 1988: 69). He blamed Buddhism for the degeneration of Hinduism. For example, speaking before a gathering of Orientalists in 1900 in Paris, he asserted that 'the vulgarisation of many Hindu religious symbols or objects of worship was really the result of 'degenerate' Buddhism entering the mainstream of Hinduism' (Sen 1993: 335). 'From that time to this, the whole work in India is a reconquest of this Buddhistic degradation by the Vedanta. It is going on and is not yet finished (*The Nationalistic and Religious Lectures* 1988: 69).

An artful practitioner of managing contradictions, Vivekananda spoke differently to different audiences but never gave up the boast that Hinduism was the world's greatest – and only complete – religious as well as scientific system. As Alam points out, when it comes to defining Hinduism, history evaporates, practice disappears and what one gets is a distilled, idealised version of Vedantic religion (ibid.: 73). Most regrettably, it was the hegemonistic thinking and writings like Vivekananda's that gained credence among the elitist nationalists.

Taken in by the hagiography that has been spawned around the life and career of Vivekananda, many 'Hindu secularists' of today respect him as the ultimate modern moralist, and clash with Hindutva votaries over their 'hijacking' of the Swami. (Perhaps due to their innate or subconscious caste loyalties, the high-caste liberal-secularists find it difficult to identify themselves with more democratic and robustly secular shramanic tradition of Buddha, Kabir, Phule, and Ambedkar.) The so-called secular democrats and what has come to be known as the 'Hindu Left' overlook Vivekananda's supremacist rhetoric, his apotheosis of the Hindu glories, his fulsome endorsement of caste ideology, and his no-holds-barred polemic against Islam, Christianity, and even indigenous Buddhism. Vivekananda's recipe for the salvation of the Hindus lay in three Bs: beef, biceps and *Bhagvad Gita*. His call to Hindu youth to acquire 'iron muscles and nerves of steel' and his mission to spread Hinduism in all corners of the world – because of its alleged superiority over all other faiths – were in fact a portent of the Hindu fascist ideology.

It is also significant that Vivekananda disliked the 'moderates' within the Congress ranks. Persons like Ranade and Gokhale who wanted some reforms and did not necessarily see antagonism between the campaigns for social change and nationalism did not find favour with him. His favourites were Tilak and Aurobindo, the political radicals and social reactionaries, whose supreme aim was to replace the British rule with the brahmanic one. Welcoming Tilak at his Belur Math in 1901, Vivekananda showed rare bonhomie with his soulmate from Maharashtra and jocularly suggested that Tilak 'took up his work in Bengal while he could go and continue the same in Maharashtra . . . (because) one does not carry the same influence in one's own province as in a distant one.' Vivekananda considered Tilak his alter ego and for his part Tilak hailed Vivekananda as 'a person of the stature of Shankaracharya' (*Kesari*, 8 July 1902) and the real father of Indian nationalism. Their reciprocal admiration for each other is understandable as both of them championed a nationalism which was inseparable from Hindu revivalism and Aryan chauvinism. Confrontationist attitudes towards Islam and Christianity, particularly on the issue of conversion, also bonded these two leaders.

MONOLITHIC AND HEGEMONIC CULTURAL NATIONALISM

Dayananda-Vivekananda's hegemonic politics and obscurantist ambiguity on vital social issues shielded the basic tenets of brahmanical culture. Gandhi carried forward this regressive trend and took brahmanical construction of nationalism to new heights under changed times and circumstances (see Chapter 7). The control of sanskritic reform from the top was part of a grand design to arrest the rising tide of resistance from the caste-oppressed and marginalised.

With their compulsive tendency to look backward, to appeal to the problematic past, to rely on scriptural authority, the reformer-nationalists constantly undermined reason. They encouraged a self-congratulatory obscurantism and fostered pseudo-scientific thinking in the garb of patriotic pride. These leaders presented a monolithic and hegemonic discourse by portraying brahmanical religion and philosophy as the best aspects of Indian cultural heritage. No wonder 'the past became the heritage of the few as these aspects were not common heritage of all Indians'. During the nineteenth century, the norms and customs of high caste social behaviour were sought to be universalised in unprecedented ways, aided and abetted by the colonial policy. The Aryan-brahmanic discourse that was developed by the high caste male literati had an explicit or implicit anti-woman, anti-Dravidian, anti-lower caste and anti-Muslim bias. Implicit in the racist Aryan ideology was superiority of men over women, the brahman over the shudra, the Aryan over the non-Aryan. Even a champion reformer like Ranade saw brahmanism as the Aryan faith which had served to unite north and south in ancient India (Chakravarti 1998: 102). He believed the Aryan to be the chosen race in India – he blamed Aryan interaction with the 'lowly' non-Aryans for the unpalatable aspects of Hinduism (ibid.).

Besides egalitarian heterodox traditions, the art and architecture, science, technology, folk music, and popular literature in which the non-elites played a dominant role were grossly ignored in the nationalist construction of the past. The medieval period was portrayed as a dark era of depredation, decadence and deprivation due to the Islamic rule, and Muslims in general were held guilty of perpetrating all kinds of atrocities on the Hindus in that era. There was a tendency to put all the blame for India's misfortune and degradation of the native character on subjection to the Muslim rule. It was customary to project the British as saviours of Hindus from Muslim misrule and tyranny (Sarkar 1997: 19). The tirade against the supposed Muslim tyranny in the name of patriotism was not only unhistorical but socially and politically dangerous – it tended to create the notions of two separate, disparate, and mutually antagonistic peoples and ultimately gave birth to the pernicious two-nation theory and led to partition of the country. All these tendencies tended to divide Hindus, Muslims, Sikhs, Parsis, and high-caste Hindus from the lowered castes. Apart from benefiting the privileged groups, the so-called socio-cultural reawakening created neither a social climate for modernisation nor a genuine, people-centred nationalism.

The Western principles of democracy, equality and human rights that came to India in the nineteenth century with the colonial regime found favour with the elite, but instead of applying the same principles to all Indians, the privileged groups appropriated the egalitarian principle only for the 'nation' of which they were the sole representatives. The question of equality, thus, became the question of equality between nations. The issue of human dignity and equal rights were selectively utilised to bolster the demand for national self-determination: the nationalist leaders, demanding self-government and independence from the British, refused to accept that the privileged sections of Indian society should also give up their privileges and practise democracy in the social sphere and reconstruct social relations between individuals, castes, and communities on a democratic matrix. Cultural nationalism, in other words, was steeped in those ascriptive values that guaranteed the political domination of the privileged over the commonality.

In his essay 'Nabavarsha' (1902) Rabindranath Tagore, perhaps the greatest humanist of the *bhadralok* intelligentsia, argued the inevitability of inequality in all human societies. In another essay 'Brahman', published in the same year, which was aggressively brahmanical and patriarchal, he spelt out an notion of ideal Hindu society. 'He counterposed the entire society of gentle folk (*bhadra sampradaya*) who should be given *dwija* (twice-born) status, to those considered 'shudras', in ancient India as well as today – 'Santals, Bhils, Kols, bands of sweepers' – for in a proper samaj 'neck and shoulders must not be lowered to the level of the ground' (Sarkar 1997: 26). Applauding brahmans as the guardians of society, Tagore says: 'Brahmanism is a quality and it is a spiritual quality unique to the Indian nation, in contrast to Western philosophy' (cited in Basu 2002: 116). He goes on to assert that all that is sublime, all that is oriented to knowledge and wisdom, is expressed in the brahmanic qualities which are the spirit of the Indian nation. The quest of Europe-type equality and competition, he suggests, may be quietened through brahmanic prayers and pacificism. He concludes, therefore, that India in its quest of national identity needed to rediscover the essential brahman again. As he put it, 'We do not want to be Europeans but we want to be Dwijas' (ibid.).

Tilak, whom Valentine Chirol lionised as the 'Father of Indian Unrest', and other militant patriots like B. C. Pal and Lajpat Rai attacked all kinds of reform and social change as counterproductive to cultural unity and national solidarity. Grassroots social movements that were being waged by lowered castes, dalits and adivasis at various levels and in multifarious ways all across the subcontinent were opposed as 'divisive' as they would weaken the struggle against the colonial rule (Chapters 6 and 7). Such perverted nationalism encouraged all kinds of revivalist and obscurantist politics to skirt the real issues and suppress popular protest from below.

Vishnushastri Chiplunkar and Tilak were staunch social conservatives to the point of being reactionaries. Chiplunkar's essays in his magazine *Nibandhmala* (1874-81) evocative of the lost Hindu, Brahman and Maratha glory and Tilak's alliance with the Poona revivalists in the 1890s forged through opposition to the Age of Consent Bill (outlawing marriages for girls less than twelve years of age), and refusal to permit Ranade to hold his National Social Conference at the Congress pavilion in 1895 – Tilak violently disrupted the session and threatened to burn down the pavilion if the conference was held – are clear pointers to their brahmanical character (see Keer 2000; Sarkar 1983).

There was also a yawning gap between what the Tilaks of the world professed and what they practised. Addressing a conference on the depressed classes in 1918, Tilak, for example, spoke at length on why untouchability should be abolished. Soon after he was asked to sign a manifesto declaring that he would not practise untouchability. Tilak refused. He also refused to acknowledge an appeal addressed to him by Bombay's untouchables for support in their temple-entry programme. In 1918, he opposed the Bill validating inter-caste marriage on the grounds that it was anti-Hindu, especially anti-brahman. Leaders like Tilak, who had inspired a whole generation of 'fiery nationalists', had perfected the art of status-quoist politics in the name of selfless service to the motherland. He would pay lip-service to protect the interests of workers and peasants, but actually he was a defender of landlordism. He stoutly opposed, for instance, the Bombay government move in 1901 to restrict the transfer of peasant lands to moneylenders. Opposing the anti-landlord legislation, he stated: 'Just as the government has no right to rob the sowcar and distribute his wealth among the poor, in the same way the government has no right to deprive the khot of his rightful income and distribute the money to the peasant. This is a question of rights and not of humanity' (cited in Sarkar 1983: 69).

Chiplunkar and Tilak took upon themselves the responsibility of defending Hinduism and its traditions. They attacked the social reformers who questioned discriminatory practices in the name of religion. They wrote with passion and eloquence about the 'glorious' past but their writings – often verbose, vehement and laced with mordant satire – lacked insight, reason, and reality (Keer 2000). Their boasts about the 'superior' and 'grand' brahmanical tradition would not allow them to delve into societal problems and mass misery. This was a fatal flaw which afflicted the majority of nationalists and political radicals before and after Tilak. No wonder, then, that elitist nationalism became, for all practical purposes, a smokescreen to hide hideous social realities.

SYMBIOSIS OF CULTURAL CHAUVINISM AND COMMUNAL POLITICS

The pronounced brahmanic-Hindu tinge in much of the nineteenth century nationalist ideology and propaganda was exacerbated at the turn of the new century, giving rise to the unprecedented communalisation of politics amidst the clamour for freedom. The frequent use of Hindu symbols, idioms and myths for the national cause – Tilak's Ganesh Puja and Gandhi's Rama-rajya – and the tendency of major ideologues such as Bankim to portray Muslims as enemies and foreigners created an ideal atmosphere for the growth of communalism among both 'majority' and 'minority' communities.

Brahmanic-Hindu communalism was no longer confined to Bengal and Maharashtra. In the north, especially in Uttar Pradesh, major figures of the fledgling Hindi movement followed in the footsteps of the Bengali-Maharashtrian revivalists. The new, Sanskritised Hindi was very much an artificial – and divisive – creation of a self-seeking upper caste elite, nurturing hegemonic aspirations (Rai 2001). Its atavistic association with Sanskrit was combined with a fierce opposition to not only Urdu but also popular dialects – Avadhi, Bundelkhandi, Rajasthani, Brajbhasha, Maithili, Bhojpuri, Magadhi – of the region. The narrow-minded arrogance of Hindi chauvinists destroyed the immense potential of a language that was earlier creative, dynamic, and popular. Symbiotically attached to the Hindu revivalist aspirations, the campaign for Sanskritised Hindi as the potential national language injected communal consciousness in the cow belt. Bhartendu Harishchandra (1850-85), generally regarded as the father of modern Hindi, presented a strange but familiar admixture of colonial loyalty and Hindu patriotism. His vision of patriotism combined pleas for the use of indigenous articles with demands for a ban on cow-slaughter and the replacement of Urdu by Hindi in courts and government offices.

The communal formula of 'Hindi-Hindu-Hindustan' that Bhartendu's colleague Pratap Narain Mishra invented in 1882 signalled the dangerous developments that lay ahead. Bhartendu's idea that all Indians are Hindus and Mishra's argument in his journal *Brahman* that Hindus alone are real Indians helped in moulding cultural-literary discourse on narrow religious identities. The campaign for a purified, homogeneous Hindi as the sole custodian of the 'equally harmonious and unified Hindu-Indian society' not only meant a rejection of the plural character of Indian culture, but also carried within itself social and cultural exclusions of the subaltern masses (Orsini 2002). As P. D. Tandon, a top Congress leader and a champion advocate of 'official' Hindi, said, 'If you want to become national you have to forsake all attraction to other useless ideas and groups and stand under the banner of one nation, one language, one script, one culture.' (see Orsini, ibid.: 381).

The third decade of the twentieth century saw the birth of the fascist Rashtriya Sawayamsevak Sangh (RSS). A bunch of five Hindu Mahasabhites – K. B. Hedgewar, B. S. Moonje, L. V. Paranjpe, B. B. Thalkar, and Baburao Savarkar – who founded the RSS in 1925 – were all committed Tilakites and ardent advocates of brahmanical revivalism. Their role model was Tilak who had bitterly fought against Phule, Ranade, and Gokhale for a reformist and progressive agenda. These gentlemen were carrying 'a whisper campaign' against Gandhi as they were greatly agitated over the passing of the national leadership into the hands of a non-Maharashtrian non-brahman (Goyal 2000: 28). After the death of Tilak in August 1920, Hedgewar and Moonje had even gone to Pondicherry to invite the retired and self-exiled Aurobindo to take reigns of the nationalist movement (ibid.).

The RSS, apart from its anti-Muslim orientation, was clandestinely committed to crush the Satyashodhak Samaj movement that was spearheading a socio-cultural campaign for emancipation of lowered caste masses and women in Maharashtra. According to C. P. Bhiskikar, the official biographer of Hedgewar, the lower caste assertion ('Conflicts between various communities had started. Brahman-non-Brahman conflict was nakedly on view') was a danger on a par with the Muslim threat that lay behind the formation of the RSS (Basu et al. 1993: 14) The birth of Hindutva ideology and organisation in Maharashtra, the land of two of the greatest social revolutionaries, Phule and Ambedkar, where the Muslim population and the supposed threat posed by it had relatively been weak, was not without special significance.

Maharashtra (as we shall see in the next chapter) had witnessed a powerful social movement of the lower classes from the 1870s onwards, when Phule had founded his Satyashodhak Samaj. By the 1920s, the dalits had started organising themselves under Ambedkar. Nagpur, the birthplace of the RSS, was the centre of social radicalism and also the venue of the All India Depressed Classes Conference in 1920 where Ambedkar made his presence felt by challenging the paternalistic model of social reform advocated by V. R. Shinde and other moderate leaders. Later, Nagpur was also to become the *deekshabhoomi* (conversion land) where Ambedkar led lakhs of dalits to accept Buddhism as their religion. Here Phule and Ambedkar had launched their protest movements against the brahmanical culture by presenting an alternative vision of history and society from the viewpoint of the oppressed classes. This was an open challenge to the nationalist and RSS glorification of the ancient Aryans. The Phule-Ambedkar ideology rejects the basic Hindutva concept of a Hindu as one who considers India to be both his *punyabhoomi* (holy land) and *pitribhoomi* (father land). Not surprisingly, the RSS targeted Phule-Ambedkarism and touted the theory that such movements emanated from a divisive 'caste mentality'.

Like the earlier versions of cultural nationalism, the RSS respects the principle of varnashrama dharma, but pretends to oppose caste. Its total absence of involvement in the struggles of the dalits, tribals and OBCs, however, leaves no doubt that its claim to oppose caste is hollow. The RSS pretension of forging 'Hindu unity' is basically built on its antagonism against Muslims — as Ambedkar once pointed out, 'A caste has no feeling that it is affiliated to other castes except when there is Hindu-Muslim riot.' The RSS 'anti-casteism' serves the twin objectives of keeping the lowered caste people under the brahmanical umbrella on the one hand, and fighting Muslims with the unity thus achieved, on the other (see the Appendix).

The ideological moorings of the mainstream (Hindu) nationalism led by forces like the Indian National Congress – despite eloquent (and effective) claims to the contrary – was not very different from the cultural nationalism of the RSS (see Chapters 5, 6 and 7). This nationalism, though claiming to represent all sections of society, was hopelessly divided into separate campaigns by Hindus and Muslims. The term Hindu became a euphemism for the upper castes who crushed any dissenting voice from the lower rungs as 'casteist', 'divisive', and 'loyalist', all in the name of social cohesion and anti-colonialism.

A few appropriate noises made sporadically by a Tagore here or a Ranade there were drowned in the din of hegemonic nationalism. Persons like Tagore and Ranade with their critical consciousness functioned within the *bhadralok* parameter. Even when their views on social issues converged with those of the leaders of anti-caste movements, they were not willing to forge a united front with them. Actually, the noble souls and sceptics like the latter-day Tagore were deftly co-opted by the national movement. Even in the later stage of nationalism under Gandhi's leadership, barring egalitarian rhetoric and symbolic gestures, the issues and problems faced by the masses remained unaddressed and were never made part of the national movement. Gandhi and other leaders always accorded auxiliary importance to social transformation. They refused to accept that equal rights and freedom for all were intrinsic to national unity and solidarity.

Appendix

Parallel Fascist Thinking in East and West: Manu's Brahman and Nietzsche's Superman

> They [Aryans] have been the prominent actors in the great drama of history, and have carried to their fullest growth all the elements of active life with which our life is endowed. They have perfected society and morals. . . . In continual struggle with each other and with Semitic and Turanian races these Aryan nations have become the rulers of history and it seems to be their mission to link all parts of the world together by the chains of civilisation and religion.
>
> F. MAX MÜLLER
> cited in Johannes H. Voigt 1967: 6

Racism is at base the sinister idea that among the three principal races – white, black and yellow – the white is the superior. In nineteenth century India some claimed that among this chosen race the Aryan was the noblest and most powerful. All civilisation, its adherents in both Europe and India exclaimed in one way or another, flowed from the Aryan race. A parallel to brahmanic chauvinism – the glorification of the (Aryan) brahman with the concomitant debasement of the (non-Aryan) shudra – is to be found in the philosophy of Friedrich Nietzsche (1844-1900), whose theories of the 'master race' (*Harrenvolk*) and 'superman' (*Ubermensch*) were later appropriated by Hitler to form the Nazi *weltanschauung*. Nietzsche admitted that in his philosophy – which became identified with will to power and violence over a debased class of commoners – he was only following the scheme of Manu, the doyen of brahmanical ideology. In his *Anti-Christ*, he wrote:

To set up a law-book of the kind of Manu means to concede to a people the right henceforth to become masterly, to become perfect – to be ambitious for the highest art of living. To that end, the law must be made unconscious: this is the purpose of every holy lie. (Nietzsche 1968: 177)

Nietzsche was unhappy with what he termed the plebeianisation of Europe by the 'onslaughts' of democracy and the parliamentary system. For that he held Christianity responsible, despising it as embodiment of the victory of the subordinated classes over the elite. For him, Christianity was a great curse, a 'perversion . . . no more than the typical teachings of the socialists' (see Shirer 1991: 100). In his frenzied advocacy of 'will to power' to dominate and subjugate the common man, he finds inspiration from Manu's social philosophy which he wields as a stick with which to beat Christianity, which embodies 'the victory of Chandala values, . . . the undying Chandala revenge (against the elite) as the *religion of love*' (*The Twilight of the Idols*, see Doniger and Smith 1991: xx). Even the suggestion of a comparison between the *Manusmriti* with the Bible appals Nietzsche:

When I read the Law-book of Manu, an incomparably spiritual and superior work, it would be a sin against the spirit even to mention in the same breath the Bible. It has a genuine philosophy behind it, in it, not merely an evil-smelling Jewish distillation of Rabbinism and superstition. . . . And, not to forget the most important point of all, it is fundamentally different from every kind of Bible: by means of it the noble classes, the philosophers and the warriors guard and guide the masses, it is replete with noble values, it is filled with a feeling of perfection, with saying yea to life, and triumphant sense of well-being in regard to itself and to life – the Sun shines upon the whole book. (cited in Ambedkar, *BAWS*, vol. 3: 75)

In *Thus Spoke Zarathustra*, Nietzsche announced that 'God is dead' and made a prophecy that the coming elite would rule the world and from them the superman would spring. In *The Will to Power*, he proclaims: 'A daring and ruler race is building itself up. . . . The aim should be to prepare a transvaluation of values for a particularly strong kind of man, most highly gifted in intellect and will. This man and the elite around him will become the 'lords of the earth' (see Shirer 1991: 100-1). In *Thus Spoke Zarathustra*, he extols his 'superman' as the beast of prey, 'the magnificent blond brute, avidly rampant for spoil and victory' (ibid.), and in his *Anti-Christ* he rhapsodises Manu's elevation of brahmans as the 'gods on earth' and his belittling of the shudras as the helpless and servile creatures fit only to serve the 'gods on earth'. No wonder Ambedkar argued that Zarathustra is a new name for Manu and that *Thus Spoke Zarathustra* is but a new edition of *Manusmriti* (BAWS, vol. 3: 74-6).

It is interesting that in *The Twilight of the Idols*, Nietzsche, like Manu, uses animal imagery to discuss the human condition. He describes the menial race, the shudras, as 'the non-bred human being', 'the hotch-potch human being'. He speaks glowingly of Manu's treatment of the lowly chandala, the untouchable, who is antithesis of the brahman, the superman (Doniger and Smith 1991: xx). Society is 'not entitled to exist for its own sake but only as a superstructure and scaffolding by means of which a select race of beings may elevate themselves to their higher duties'. This 'rearing of exceptional men' will necessarily entail, he emphasises, the drastic curtailing of man's natural rights. There is no such thing, according to him, as a right to live, a right to work, or a right to be happy, for the ordinary beings. In this respect, he is categorical that the common man, the shudra, is no different from the 'meanest worm'. 'Men shall be trained for war and women for the procreation of the warrior. All else is folly' (cited in Shirer 1991: 100). It appears that he also inherits from Manu a vicious contempt for women. In *Thus Spoke Zarathustra* he exclaims: 'Thou goest to woman? Do not forget thy whip!'

Although there were other German geniuses – Schopenhauer, Hegel, and Wagner – whose ideas were selectively appropriated by the Nazis, it was Nietzsche's theories which fired their imagination. Hitler often visited the Nietzsche museum in Weimar and published his veneration for the philosopher by posing for photographs of himself staring in rapture at the bust of Nietzsche (Shirer 1991). The Fuehrer appropriated not only Nietzsche's thoughts but also the latter's penchant for grotesque exaggeration: 'Lords of the earth' is a familiar expression in his autobiography *Mein Kampf*. Rantings of 'superman' and 'master race' struck a responsive cord in Hitler's littered mind.

Though some friends/admirers of the celebrator of the

'magnificent blond brute' have vehemently denied any nexus between Nietzsche and Hitler, it cannot be doubted that the philosophy of Nietzsche – and Manu – was capable of producing fascism. Nietzsche's mesmerising eloquence and rage against all modern conceptions of justice and equality verges on a 'pornography of strength'. It is an inhuman view. Why should the common people continue to be suppressed for the magnificent health, power and glory of the aristocratic few? Tracing the intellectual roots of Nazism, William Shirer in *The Rise and Fall of the Third Reich* stresses that Hitler was not the originator of those megalomaniacal ideas, his monstrosity lay in the fact that he began to put those nasty thoughts into practice when he assumed power in Germany. The glorification of violence and conquest; the absolute power of the authoritarian state; the belief in the superiority of the Aryan race; the hatred of Jews and Slavs; and utter contempt for compassion and kindness – these were not original with Hitler, only the ruthless, barbaric means of employing them.

The affinity between Western and Indian fascism is also borne out by the adoration of Hitler and his imperialistic agenda by modern admirers of Manu in India. The Hindu Mahasabha and the Rashtriya Swayamsevak Sangh (RSS) explicitly modelled their cultural nationalism on Hitler's Nazism, extolling Aryan-brahmanic race, religion, culture, and language. Savarkar, whose 1923 tract *Hindutva* ignited the imagination of Hindu chauvinists, was an ardent admirer of European fascism. In 1938, as the president of Hindu Mahasabha, he congratulated Hitler during a public meeting in Delhi for having liberated the Sudetans who shared the 'same blood and same tongue' as the Germans (Jaffrelot 1997). But even earlier, some Hindu Mahasabhaites had had direct contact with their European role models, the Nazis and the Fascists. B. S. Moonje, who was president of the Hindu Mahasabha for a long time, was reported to have met both Hitler and Mussolini in 1931. Moonje came back to India and tried to transfer fascist models to Hindu society and organise it militarily on the same pattern. So impressed was he by the military institutions of the German and Italian dictators that he established a military school at Nasik with financial support from many Indian princes (Jaffrelot 1997; Casolari 2000). At the same time, *Kesari* and *Mahratta* (journals which Tilak had launched) and *Hindu Outlook* (the mouthpiece of the Hindu Mahasabha) regularly published, between 1925 and 1935, editorials and articles in praise of Mussolini, Hitler, and Franco (ibid.). The Nazism of Germany and the Fascism of Italy became the guiding force of the Hindu hard-liners. To them, nationalism meant to militarise Hindu society and to create a military mentality among the Hindus. Savarkar gave the clarion call to *Hinduise all politics and militarise Hinduism*. In the process, the continuous reference to the Nazi's racial policy and the comparison of the Jewish problem with the Muslim question in India reveals the evolution of the concept of 'internal enemy' along explicit fascist lines.

Showing solidarity with the Fuehrer and his Holocaust, top RSS ideologue M. S. Golwalkar, who became head of the organisation in 1940 after the death of its founder K. B. Hedgewar, writes in *We, or Our Nationhood Defined*, the first central text of the RSS:

To keep up the purity of the race and its culture, Germany shocked the world by her purging the country of the semitic races – the Jews. National pride at its highest has been manifested here. Germany has also shown how well-nigh impossible it is for races and cultures, having differences going to the root, to be assimilated into one united whole, a good lesson for us in Hindustan to learn and profit by. (Golwalkar 1939: 35)

Golwalkar, like Savarkar, applies this logic to the Muslim minority (what Jews and Slavs were to the Nazis, the non-Hindu communities, especially Muslims, were – are – to the RSS), then spells out the local implications of what he has learnt from Nazism:

. . . the non-Hindu people in Hindustan must either adopt the Hindu culture and language, must learn to respect and hold in reverence Hindu religion, must entertain no ideas but the glorification of the Hindu race and culture, i.e., of the Hindu nation and must lose their separate existence to merge in the Hindu race, or may stay in the country wholly subordinated to the Hindu nation, claiming nothing, deserving no privileges, far less any preferential treatment – not even citizen's rights. (ibid.: 62)

The rallying cry of the RSS, 'one nation, one culture, one people and one leader' strikingly echoes the Nazi catch-phrase 'Ein Volk, ein Reich, ein Fuehrer'. In his construction of the nation and nationalism on ethnic and cultural homogeneity, Golwalkar draws most of his inspiration from German writers whose ideas prepared the ground for Hitler's rise to power. According to Jaffrelot:

> Golwalkar's concern with the promotion of a homogenous nation whose culture would be dominated by the Hindu Great Tradition harks back to his reading of Bluntschli and similar authors and to his admiration for their ethnic nationalism which, in Germany, prepared the ground for Nazism. Golwalkar considers cultural elements as inherent to the group, collectively inherited from its forefathers. For instance, he regards a national language – such as Sanskrit, the 'mother language' of India – as 'an expression of the Race spirit', obviously an equivalent of the German Volksgeist.
> (1999: 56-7)

However, the RSS version of brahmanical revivalism which it flaunts as 'Hindutva' or 'cultural nationalism' is based on a special kind of 'race spirit'. It is social racism – appropriately termed by G. Pandey (1991) as 'an upper caste racism' – rather than bio-racism. The racism of the RSS variety takes the form of socio-cultural domination through the regulating and time-tested agency of caste, rather than being based on the rigid biological claims of the purity of blood. The RSS ideologues had inherited this theory of soft racism from their 'visionary' ancestors who had realised that this model was better suited to Indian conditions, as it was also more enduring and resilient. It is interesting that the Hindu chauvinists of the late nineteenth and early twentieth century who borrowed heavily from the European Orientalists the theory of the common racial origin of the European and Indian Aryans and its corollary, the fabled southward migration which they interpreted to prove that the Aryans who landed in India were the chosen race and that they once dominated the world, did not stretch the argument beyond a point. This was because two factors threatened to uproot their hegemonic structure. First, if the self-styled Indian Aryans insisted on racial purity they would appear to be foreigners in India; and second, the caste elites, the core constituency of Indian Aryans, are not more than 10 per cent of the Hindu population which reduces them to the status of a minority in India. So, the RSS ideologues take recourse to the hierarchical but integrative view of Hindu society. This explains why, as Jaffrelot contends, the Hindu nationalists played down the eugenic content of European fascism and focused instead on a hierarchical and authoritarian corporatist organisation of society. There was a tacit understanding among them that the Hindu variety of racism institutionalised in the system of caste is less visible but more enduring than the biological or eugenic one. Bhai Parmanand, who succeeded Moonje as president of the Hindu Mahasabha in 1933, had this to say:

The message that he (Hitler) sent on the Annexation (of Austria) in which he described himself as a tool in the hands of the Lord of Destiny for the unification of Germany reminded me of the assurance of Lord Krishna that whenever the world has need of him, He manifests Himself. Is the Unity of India complete? I submit not. British India and Indian India, to use the common parlance, are divided from each other. They are one and indivisible in every respect except politically. Where is the Hitler who will bring-about their unification? . . . Hitler's theory is National Socialism. . . . I find a great affinity between Hitler's National Socialism and the Varnashrama of the Hindus. (cited by Jaffrelot 1997)

There is nothing new in this formulation – the word for caste in Sanskrit is *jati*, which also means race. The Hindu ideologues had obviously inherited the caste model of racism/fascism from their forefathers. It was necessitated more by demographical constraints rather than any ideological differences with the Nazi version of fascism. Inherent numerical compulsions – the Hindu upper castes which the Hindu nationalists essentially represent are in a minority – do not allow the RSS to come out openly with its real ideology and intentions which are far more sinister. To cover up its hidden agenda of suppressing democratic aspirations of the lowered caste people, it tries to create a general impression in the mind of the people that something terrible is happening, that we are all falling apart due to diversities and pluralities represented by the Muslims and Christians, who indulge in fissiparous politics and dance to the tune of the external enemies – Muslim Pakistan and the Christian West.

The RSS makes a surreptitiously fascist attempt to reinforce upper caste dominance: its prime objective is to continue brahmanical control of power and the basic resources of life. It knows that it will have to devise new and more devious ways to tackle the traditionally subjugated people who are now demanding their legitimate place in society. The RSS was formed in the land of Phule and Ambedkar under the fig-leaf of Hindu nationalism. The RSS image of its own origins (as embodied in the official biography of its founder Hedgewar) locates 'lower' caste assertion on a par with the Muslim threat.

To camouflage its nefarious design, the RSS pretends to represent all Hindus including shudras, ati-shudras, and even includes adivasis and non-Hindu communities in its hegemonic notions of 'Hindu' since anyone living in India is a Hindu! The RSS is an organisation shrouded in secrecy, it keeps even its own rank and file in the dark about its real aims and objectives, only its 'inner circle' is taken into confidence. This hydra-headed organisation is authoritarian and violent. Nathuram Godse and his friends, who had close links with the RSS, shot dead Gandhi, the self-confessed 'sanatani Hindu' who throughout his long and illustrious life resorted to all kinds of half-truths to defend and even valorise exploitative and inegalitarian Hinduism, only because he was a pacifist and his pacifism was seen as 'emasculating' the Hindus.

The glaring difference between what the RSS professes and what it practises can teach a lesson or two to the likes of Paul Joseph Goebbels, the Nazi propaganda chief. The RSS claims that it strives and struggles for the unity of all Hindus, and that all castes and communities are equal in its eyes. But the unificatory thrust of its ideology revolves around 'naturalness of the hierarchical social order', which renders autonomous lowered caste assertions as inevitably divisive and anti-national. In reality, the RSS is an outfit of the Hindu elite dominated by a clique of conservative brahmans. Its ideological mentor was Savarkar, a Maharashtrian brahman; its founder was Hedgewar, a Telugu brahman; its organisational architect was Golwalkar, a Karhad brahman; and all the early swayamsevaks were brahmans. The third head of the RSS – after Hedgewar and Golwalkar – was Balasaheb Deoras, another Telugu brahman. The present head (in the year 2005) is K. S. Sudarshan, a Tamil brahman. In his diary, Moonje – himself a Deshastha brahman – referred to RSS cadres as 'brahman youths' and 'brahman lads' (Jaffrelot 1999: 45).

Of late, political commentators often speak of the hidden

agenda of the RSS-BJP, by which they mean things like construction of a Ram temple at the site of the demolished mosque at Ayodhya, and the Hinduisation/communalisation of all secular institutions. But the real game-plan of the RSS-BJP is to keep the Hindu toiling castes and Muslim masses uneducated and unempowered by raking up false issues in the name of religion, that divert attention from crucial problems such as healthcare, education, and employment. Using seductive religious symbols and slogans, the RSS and its affiliates brought the issue of temple construction at Ayodhya to the centrestage of politics in a nation where the majority of people of both communities live in oppressive poverty. They have created a fear psychosis among the dalits, adivasis, and OBCs against Muslims, Christians, and other 'aliens' by raising the bogey of 'Hinduism in danger' in a land where 80 per cent of the population is Hindu. Recent resurgence in Islamic fundamentalism in many parts of the world, and the elite-based Congress leadership's half-hearted secularism and dismal track-record in governance (which have over the years alienated and antagonised a large section of downtrodden communities) have come handy in the RSS design of creating religious mass hysteria. Muslims are targeted not only because of their religion but also due to the fact that after their disenchantment with the upper caste-dominated parties, they are now aligning with the political forces representing the lowered castes and classes, especially in states like Uttar Pradesh and Bihar.

There are many crucial items and thrust areas which are not made public but circulated privately among the select few. A case in point is the RSS secret circular no. 411, the sinister contents of which were exposed by a section of the print media in the 1990s. In their books, Oneil Biswas and Shyam Chand have reproduced some of the points of the above circular:

The RSS secret circular no. 411 has been issued to commanders and preachers. It is meant for the following actions, inter alia:

2. *Scheduled Castes and other backward classes are to be recruited to the party so as to increase the volunteers to fight against the Ambedkarites and Mussalmans.*

5. *Hindutva should be preached with a vengeance among the physicians and pharmacists so that with their help, time-expired and spurious*

medicines might be distributed amongst the Scheduled Castes, Mussalmans and Scheduled Tribes.

10. Special attention should be given to the students of the Scheduled Castes and Scheduled Tribes so as to make them read the history written according to our dictates.

11. During riots the women of Mussalmans and Scheduled Castes should be gang-raped. Friends and acquaintances cannot be spared. The work should proceed on the Surat model.

15. All literature opposed to Hindus and Brahmans are to be destroyed. Dalits, Mussalmans, Christians, and Ambedkarites should be searched out. Care should be taken to see that this literature and writings do not reach public places. Hindu literature is to apply to the backward classes and Ambedkarites.

16. The demand by the Scheduled Castes and Scheduled Tribes for filling in the backlog vacancies in services shall by no means be met. Watch should be kept to see that their demands for entry into and promotion in government, non-government or semi-government institutions are rejected and their service records are destroyed with damaging reports.

18. Measures should be taken to make the prejudices amongst Scheduled Castes and backward people more deep-rooted. To this end, help must be taken from saints and ascetics.

20. Attacks should be started with vigour against equality-preaching communists, Ambedkarites, Islamic teachers, Christian missionaries and neighbours. (see Biswas 2001: 121-3; Shyam Chand 2002: 154-5)

The RSS, according to Shyam Chand, has not denied the existence of such a circular.

5

Phule's Struggle against Brahmanical Colonialism

> Let others go where they will. We will follow the path of Jotiba [Phule]. We may or may not take Marx with us but we will certainly not abandon Jotiba's philosophy.
>
> B. R. AMBEDKAR
> in a speech on 28 October 1954
> cited in Dangle, ed., 1992: 259

Jotirao Phule (1827-1890), or Mahatma Jotiba Phule as he is commonly known, was the first man in modern India to launch a movement for the liberation of caste-oppressed, toilers, men and women. What Rammohun Roy, Dayananda Saraswati and Vivekananda were to the elitist cultural nationalism, Phule was to the freedom struggle of India's long-suppressed humanity. This Maharashtrian social revolutionary presented a socio-cultural analysis that was fiercely critical of domination. Based on his pioneering historical-materialist critique of caste and brahmanism, he spearheaded a multi-pronged struggle to rebuild society on the matrix of equity, justice and reason. The ideological-political founder of the anti-caste movement, Phule also, as some social scientists have argued recently, clearly saw a close relationship between knowledge and power much before Foucault and Edward Said did.[1] He saw brahmanism as the ideological and institutional system of monopolising knowledge and power by a particular class which uses these to exclude, divide and dominate other groups in society. He argued that 'even before trying to overturn the material power of the upper castes over the lower castes, and over their own women, it was necessary to step out of the ideologies of brahmanism for which access to knowledge was an essential prerequisite, that is one had to understand a system before one could dismantle it' (Chakravarti 2002: 115). He termed this understanding of knowledge as *tritiya ratna*, the 'third eye', which was the means to end brahmanic hegemony and towards this end education, 'not mere alphabetical competence but the power to see through hegemonic ideology', was to play a crucial role (ibid.).

In 1848 – the same year which saw the publication of the Communist Manifesto in the West – Phule, at the age of twenty-one, dared to establish, defying the high caste backlash, a school in Pune for untouchable women, the most oppressed and desolate segment of Indian society. In striking contrast to the high caste social reformers of the time, Phule believed that one's radical ideology must be complemented by radical practice. He waged struggle at all levels, developing a radical re-interpretation of Indian history and mythology, and communicating it to people through popular plays, songs, tracts, and organisation-building. Leading a campaign to debunk the myth of the golden Hindu era that was being valorised by the contemporary nationalist leadership, he exposed the brahmanical self-interest in apotheosis of the past and maintenance of the traditional order. He confronted the nascent elitist nationalism, contending that a society divided by caste and social slavery could not constitute a genuine nation. Those claiming to represent the nation were actually its destroyers since they not only ignored these hierarchical divisions but actually sought to maintain them as a basis for their power (Omvedt 1994: 15).

Phule's radical ideology combined with its distinctive brand of politics announced the arrival of a new factor in India's social chemistry. His understanding of the cultural power of brahmanism was of historic significance. Through his popular writings and mass campaign, he unravelled the brahmanical pseudo-religion and the inhuman conditions and indignities that were systematically thrust upon the toiling people. Laying bare the *gulamgiri* (slavery) of the toiling castes and all categories of women, he stressed that those who did not admit of their enslavement could never be free. He made mass education the focal point of his movement, with the belief that knowledge would generate forces that would sound the death knell of the old order and emancipate the subjugated.

An ideologue-activist unlike any other in India of his time, Phule grappled with almost all important questions facing society – religion, caste, politics, education, language, literature, history, mythology, the gender question, mass poverty, the state of agriculture, and the lot of the cultivators. His range of concerns and ideas, Deshpande (2002) emphasises, was broader and deeper than that of any other leader of the nineteenth century. Contending that he had a complete system of ideas, Deshpande has argued that Phule was the first to identify and theorise the bipolar *(dvaivarnik)* structure of Indian society, marked by the dichotomous relationship between the oppressors (the brahmans) and the oppressed (the shudra-tishudras),[2] and he wanted the community of the oppressed to lead a revolution for all-round change:

Phule . . . was amongst the early thinkers to have identified, in a manner of speaking, classes in Indian society. He analysed the dvaivarnik structure of Indian society, and identified the shudratishudras as the leading agency of a social revolution. And the shudratishudras will lead the revolution on behalf on the whole society, to liberate the entire people from the shackles of brahmanism. What they will lead, then, is not a movement for some reform in the present structure, some tinkering here and there, but a total smashing up of the entire oppressive structure, ideological and material. Phule was the only thinker of the nineteenth century who insisted that this is both necessary and possible. (ibid.: 20-1)

To understand Phule, his concerns and his struggle in appropriate historical-sociological context, a quick look at the chronology of his life and career may be of some help. Phule was born in 1827 in a family of fruit-and-vegetable growers (Mali) in Pune. He was educated in a Marathi-medium school during 1834-8; married Savitribai in 1840; continued education in an English-medium secondary school during 1841-7. In 1848, he established a school – the first in anywhere in India – for downtrodden girls; shocked and fearing a high-caste backlash, his father turned his son and daughter-in-law (who taught in the school) out in 1849. Undeterred, Phule ran the school and set up more schools between 1848 and 1852, which admitted girls of all castes. Felicitated by the Department of Education for his educational work in 1852, in 1855, he established a night school for working people. Outraged by his 'subversive' activities, the reactionary elements made an abortive attempt on his life in 1856. In the 1860s, he joined the widow remarriage campaign. In 1863, he established a home for illegitimate children and their mothers. Phule's father died in 1868; the same year he threw open the water-tank in his compound to the untouchables. *Gulamgiri* was published in June 1873 and followed up with the founding of Satyashodhak Samaj (Society of the Seekers of Truth) on 24 September 1873. He worked as a member of the Pune Municipal Council in 1876-82. He deposed before the Hunter Commission for Education on 19 October 1882. Honoured in a massive public meeting with the title of Mahatma on 11 May 1888, he died in Pune on 28 November 1890 after a prolonged illness.

In his battle against discriminatory brahmanism, Phule was inspired by the egalitarian philosophy of the Buddha and Kabir. He was an admirer of the emergent liberal democracies of the West, but he consciously built his protest movement on the ideological and cultural bedrock of the indigenous shramanic tradition. In fact, he saw his own movement as a continuation of those of Buddha, Kabir, and Tukaram.[3] Phule hailed the Buddha as the saviour of the masses and accused the brahmans of 'nursing a grudge against the Buddha' for their defeat at his hands (Phule 1991, vol. II: 85), of absorbing some Buddhist tenets in their scriptures and later defeating Buddhism by cruelly persecuting its followers (Keer 2000: 119). Phule and his colleagues also felt a deep bond with Kabir: they regarded the rebellious saint-poet as one of their ideological mentors. Many of Phule's friends, including Gyanoba Krishnaji Sasane, were staunch Kabirpanthis. Kabir's poems, especially those that presented a radical critique of brahmanism, played a sparkling role in shaping their social radicalism. According to Phule's close associate Tukaram Hanumant Pinjan, it was Kabir's defiant verses which ignited the spark for formation of the Satyashodak Samaj.[4] Similarly, the profound humanism of another shramanic stalwart, their very own Tukaram, was also a source of inspiration for Phule and his colleagues. They were said to be particularly fond of Tuka's famous dictum *satya asatyashi man kele gwahi* – 'know truth and untruth through voice of conscience' – whose obvious implication is a quiet yet firm rejection of the authority of the priestly literature and institutions.

Brahman Power and Oppression of the Time

Phule was a product of the oppression of his social environment. Born into a shudra family in Maharashtra within a decade of the collapse of Peshwa rule in 1818, Phule faced the indignities and humiliations routinely heaped on the lowered castes. The power and glory of the brahman Peshwas who had become de facto rulers of the Maratha kingdom after Shahu's death had declined, following the ascendancy of the British, but the brahmans still fancied themselves as the chosen caste. Acceptance of the 'divinely-ordained' superiority of the brahmans was still the norm. Most of the posts in the fading Peshwa administration were reserved for them. Bajirao II (1796-1818), the debauched and profligate last Peshwa, was venerated by the brahmans as 'an incarnation of Krishna and Shiva' (Keer 2000: 4). That was so because under the Peshwai they had become very powerful, with all kinds of privileges and exemptions, which had not existed under the original Maratha system founded by Shivaji. The *dakshina* for brahmans had become enormously inflated during the rule of Bajirao II. The Peshwas also provided generous financial support to scores of brahman scholars to enable them to pursue scholarly pursuits.

The brahmans, especially the Chitpavans, dominated the society at every level. They controlled economic, administrative, and cultural functions to such an extent that the Peshwai had come to be known as the 'Brahmanya raj' (Chakravarti 1998: 5). The Peshwai strove to create, ideologically and materially, the brahmanical Hindu kingdom whose prime objective was to uphold the existing social order. 'In this situation privileging brahmans and suppressing other castes went together' (ibid.: 13).

The caste system had become more rigid during Peshwa rule. The brahmans perpetrated the worst kinds of atrocities on the lowered castes. Narayan Vishnu Joshi has written that the rules of purity-pollution were strictly observed in those days. People of lowered castes such as mahars, mangs, chambhars, bhangis, dhedhs had to tie earthen pots to their waists while walking on roads. They had to sit down on noticing a brahman on the road, for their shadow was polluting. The untouchables were allowed to walk on roads only if they tied the branch of a tree to their wrist: the branch served the purpose of sweeping the earth and erasing their vile footprints! The untouchable mahars were not allowed to build their huts too close to an upper caste village.

Prominent reformer Gopal Hari Deshmukh, the Lokahitavadi (1823-92), has described the horrors of the time in his *Shatapatre* (One Hundred Letters). Written in the late 1840s, it gives a graphic account of the social degradation and depravation under the last Peshwas. Himself a brahman, he views the deplorable situation as the by-product of centuries-old ascriptive values and holds the brahmans responsible for promoting all kinds of retrograde ideas in order to safeguard their hereditary privilege. The social effects, he argues, of upholding ascriptive values has been disastrous as they stifled individual enterprise and merit, with the decline of the social leadership in Indian society (see O'Hanlon 1985: 93). The verdict of the Lokahitavadi was quite uncomplicated: 'The brahmans ruined the country' (cited in Keer 2000: 6).

British rule brought an altogether new system of governance, but strengthened the entrenched brahmanical leadership within the society. As we have seen in the previous chapter, the British rulers cemented a conscious alliance with the native elites. The collaboration and collusion between the foreign and native elites, vital for the construction and survival of the colonial order, was advantageous to both. This was, however, a complex process; it ruined many traditionally powerful elites, but usually patronised and empowered the information-providing brahmans who acted as interlocutors of a sort between the colonisers and the colonised. On the one hand, the British knocked off the traditional revenue and administrative system along with a host of feudal positions or offices; on the other, they carefully cultivated a section of the Indian elite, especially the brahmans with certain literary skills, to act as intermediaries and facilitators. The colonial rulers had to build a well-organised revenue collection system and a new administrative and legal structure to rule over the subcontinent. This mammoth task involved the creation of new job opportunities, for which knowledge of certain literacy skills was necessary. Thus, the brahmans who traditionally enjoyed the privilege of learning were able, despite the eclipse of the Peshwai, to make a smooth transition to the colonial order and corner almost all employment opportunities. Moreover, the Peshwai system of giving *dakshina* to the brahmans for education was upheld by the British for a very long time.

In other words, the British co-opted the literate and articulate priestly-feudal elites and gave them new opportunities. At the village level in the western India, the colonial legal system elbowed out the traditional role of the patil (village headman) as custodian of law and order, and now empowered the brahman kulkarni (village accountant) whose help was required in the maintenance of revenue records. The introduction of the private ownership of land in the village economy and the gradual penetration of monetary economy in rural areas enhanced the power and prestige of the literate Joshis (village priest-astrologers) as never before. In the new expanded monetary and political economy, the brahmans emerged as clear winners as they established a virtual monopoly over colonial jobs. Additionally, caste-based societal rules still guided the daily life of the people. Economic exploitation was implicit in the caste structure, but it was still validated on religious grounds. In a word, the brahmanical hegemony far from slackening hold on the society even got invigorated under the colonial regime (Frykenberg 2001; Aloysius 1997).

Such was the social environment of Phule's time. Though learning was not formally prohibited to the lower orders during this period, the privileged class did everything in its capacity to stop children of the lower classes from getting educated. When Govindrao, for example, sent his son (the young Phule) to a school, his brahman clerk argued that learning was not the *dharma* of a shudra, and persuaded him to take the child away from school. The Lokahitavadi commented on this incident in his *Shatapatre* (1850):

If a Brahmin were to come across a clerk of the Maratha caste or of a caste other than his own, he would get livid. The Brahmin would say that kaliyug was here, and learning (which had been held sacred) was being polluted by being imparted to the lower castes. Thus we see that the Brahmins held the belief that the other castes should not be imparted education; hence, the Brahmin clerk's advice to Govindrao to withdraw Joti from school. (cited in Joshi 1992: 6-7)

The mischievous clerk had almost succeeded in stopping the education of Phule. Had it not been the timely intervention of a Muslim clerk, Gaffar Beg Munshi, and a British officer, Liggit, Joti like other children of his community would not have gone to school again.

Another shattering incident occurred in 1848 when the twenty-year-old Phule was publicly humiliated for daring to join the marriage procession of his brahman friend. On learning of the caste of Phule, the incensed relatives of the bridegroom abused the 'lowly shudra' for rubbing shoulders with brahmans. Deeply hurt and with tears in his eyes, Phule returned home. He narrated the humiliating experience to his father, who tried to pacify his son by suggesting that he should not take this incident to his heart: 'How could we, the lowly shudras, aspire to be equal to the brahmans? Was it not very kind of them just to drive you away instead of giving you a good thrashing?' His father gave many examples of such indignities inflicted on persons of 'lowly origin', and added that he had himself seen non-brahmans humiliated and trampled under an elephant's feet for such offences.

But Phule was not like his father; he was educated in a missionary school and by now had read Thomas Paine's *The Rights of Man* – the French Revolution of 1789 and the democratic upheaval in America had become part of his mental furniture. He felt through his personal humiliation and his father's pathetic response to it, the full force of social oppression. In that moment of despair and outrage at the extent and enormity of inhuman subjugation of one man by another, he resolved to work for liberating people. Until then he used to dream to drive out the alien English from the Indian soil. Now he realised that caste slavery was the worst enemy of Indian society and culture, and that true patriotism could not be inculcated in Indian people unless they abolished discriminatory and divisive institutions.

Realising that his social engagement would require a great deal of time and freedom, Phule decided against taking a government job and instead stuck to his family horticultural business. His business brought him into a widening market circuit of rural-urban interlinkages. Phule now also ventured into contracts for various construction work. Shady transactions at these sites gave Phule a first-hand experience of brahman nepotism and corruption at the intermediate and local levels of British bureaucracy. When Phule began an ideological battle against the brahmanical privileges in the old as well as emerging economy and social order, the old historical background of Peshwai together with his bitter personal experiences played a crucial role in formation of his radical critique (Gavaskar 1999).

Phule's exposure to modern intellectual currents after coming in close contact with Christian missionaries in his school days, and his reading of Paine's *The Rights of Man* and *The Age of Reason* in 1847 had left a deep imprint on him. Significantly, he was more influenced by the robust American democracy of the time rather than the tradition of feeble English liberalism.[5] Phule's critique of brahmanic Hinduism drew sustenance from different sources including the Christian and European rationalism but the most critical input, as stated earlier, was provided by the home-grown shramanic tradition of equality and reason coupled with Phule's own experiences and observation of socio-economic realities. Also, the British colonialism and its various spin-offs, its impact on social and economic relations, the transformation of caste elites into an emergent middle class, modern European ideas of society and democracy, and the Christian missionary campaigns against inegalitarian Hinduism provided the background and context in which Phule's anti-caste ideology took radical shape.

EMERGENCE OF ANTI-CASTE RADICALISM

Despite the demise of the Peshwai and advent of the British rule, society was still dominated by brahmanical values and forces. Phule and his friends realised that their challenge was to create an ideological basis for revolution in people's minds, and on this foundation bring about revolutionary changes in socio-religious values. Delving into the nature and sources of caste ideology, Phule analysed that brahman religious authority and monopoly over knowledge enabled them to establish their cultural hegemony over the rest of society. He always used the word brahmanism for Hinduism, as he saw the latter as the world-view of the brahmans. 'As the toiling castes lived and worked within the political, social and ritual relationships laid down by the brahmans, they unwittingly succumbed to the interests of the brahmans themselves.' With this understanding, Phule's attack on brahmanism was radically different from earlier sporadic attempts to fight caste discrimination.

Phule shifted attention from social mobility within the caste system to a total rejection of the system itself. In 1865 he published a remarkable book, *Jatibhed-Viveksar* (A Critique of the Caste Divisions), written by his friend Tukaram Tatya Padwal (1839-98) (see O'Hanlon 1985: 42-5). It is the first modern Marathi work, or for that matter in any Indian language, which challenges the religious world-view and social hierarchies of brahmanism from an anti-caste perspective. It brilliantly brings out the arbitrary and insidious nature of caste distinctions and the obnoxious notions of purity and impurity, and goes on to argue that divisions of labour and occupations should be based on the merit and aptitude of each individual.

Importantly, *Jatibhed-Viveksar* also describes attempts at upward mobility by several lowered castes claiming kshatriya or vaishya status, and the strong brahman resistance to these attempts. Anticipating D. D. Kosambi (who about a century later unravelled the *hiranya-garbha*, the 'golden womb', phenomenon[6]), Padwal lays bare the cunning of the brahman on the grant of high caste kshatriya status to powerful social groups. Shivaji and the Marathas, who were earlier despised as shudras, were recognised as kshatriyas after they assumed power in order to co-opt them in the brahmanical order.

Padwal's penetrative analysis of caste was carried forward in Phule's actions and thinking. He strongly opposed brahman practices such as the wearing of the sacred thread, and mocked at attempts claiming higher social status by adopting customs and practices of the high castes. Such moves, Phule argued, obscured the reality that all social divisions were part of the 'same engine of social oppression'. Pointing out the dangers that accompanied such initiatives, he argued that identifying with the higher castes amounted to the acceptance of caste ideology and implied a distancing from other castes regarded low in the hierarchy. He stressed the need to reject outright all sanskritising tendencies which led people into the trap of brahmanism and ensured the continuation of divisions among the marginalised. Phule's target was to subvert the brahmanical *bhedniti*, the policy of divide and rule. While the brahmans, he pointed out, have kept themselves united in one varna and jati, they conspired to divide – on a hierarchical basis – the toiling masses, the shudras and atishudras into thousands of jatis, creating dissension and disunity among them (see O'Hanlon 1985; Chakravarti 1998).

Phule stressed that the sacerdotal literature was produced to establish cultural hegemony, distinguishing markers like the *Gayatri Mantra* and the sacred thread were devised to legitimise birth-based superiority, and *dharmagurus* like Shankaracharya preached and philosophised theories that reinforced the brahmanical world-view (*Collected Works*, vol. I). Phule's mission, therefore, was not to 'modernise' the brahmanical distinguishing markers by making them accessible to some upwardly mobile castes, but to construct an alternative culture and society based on equity and reason. Universal brotherhood was to be the guiding principle of his future society. At the same time, he was aware of existing power relations, and the fact that the inegalitarian social structure could not be dismantled without a struggle: 'We know perfectly well that the brahmin will not descend from his self-raised pedestal and meet his kunbi and low-caste brethren on an equal footing without a struggle' (ibid.: xxxvi).

Phule published in 1873 his controversial and hard-hitting book *Gulamgiri* which was a virtual declaration of war on the brahmanical culture. It was a manifesto of revolt against the caste society. Phule, in fact, even included in the book a manifesto exhorting everyone to discard caste and declaring that he was willing to dine with all regardless of their caste, creed, or country of origin (ibid.: xviii). *Gulamgiri* created a storm and several newspapers refused to give publicity to the manifesto because of its contents (ibid.). Written in the form of dialogue, the book traces the history of brahmanical domination and goes on to examine the motives and objects of cruel and inhuman laws framed by the priestly class. The main objective of framing these falsehoods under the cloak of religion, Phule contended, was to dupe the mind of the ignorant masses and chain them to a system of perpetual bondage. The severity of the laws against the shudras, according to Phule, can be explained only in terms of a 'deadly feud' between the two arising out of the advent of the Aryans into this land. Phule depicts Aryan-brahmans as outsiders who gradually usurped everything belonging to the aboriginal shudras. Justifying his no-holds-barred attack on brahmanism, Phule insisted that 'no language could be too harsh by which to characterise the selfish heartlessness and consummate cunning of the brahmanic ideology by which India has been governed so far'. He asserted that what he had described in his book was 'not one hundredth part of the rogueries' that were practised on his 'poor, illiterate and ignorant shudra brethren'.

Though written in Marathi, Phule's eloquent preface to the book is in English. The remarkable Dedication that celebrates and salutes the American abolition of slavery in 1863, too, is in English.

Satyashodhak Samaj: The Vision of a New Society

Phule had a vision of fundamental change in society. He believed that the toiling castes who constitute the overwhelming majority of Indian population should not be associated with brahmanic organisations but strike out on their own to form a new society on the principles of equity/castelessness, rationality and justice. Such a society – the Satyashodhak Samaj – Phule and his colleagues founded in 1873. The set of principles that the Samaj drew up shortly after its formation included belief in equality of all human beings. Members were exhorted to spread truth and right-thinking among people, and make them aware about man's natural rights and social obligations. All kinds of social evils and malpractices were to be targeted. Public education was accorded the highest importance. Members were urged to make every effort to spread education by teaching women and children, and by helping those who wanted to go to school and college. Dissemination of improved techniques in agriculture was also among the priorities. Membership was extended to all castes and communities including brahmans, mangs and mahars, and even some Jews and Muslims were its members in its early phase (Keer 2000: 128). Weekly meetings of the Samaj were held in Pune where issues like social reform, widow-remarriage, mass education, the encouragement of swadeshi goods, freeing people from beliefs in superstitions and astrology, and the encouragement to simple marriage ceremony at minimum expense were regularly discussed.

With its avowed aim to save the people from the 'hypocritical brahmans and their opportunistic scriptures', the Samaj insisted that performance of any religious ceremony by a brahman priest for a member of another caste validates the ritual purity of the brahman, that he alone has the power to mediate between the human world and that of the high gods. This implies that it is the brahman priests who control the entry of divine power into the world – the belief which provides the basis for Hindu religious and social hierarchy and the notions of purity and impurity. Therefore, Phule activated the Samaj to organise and conduct religious and marriage ceremonies in people's language without brahman priests and their 'mumbo-jumbo in Sanskrit' (Keer 2000: 126-42; O'Hanlon 1985: 220-50).

The reactionary backlash was swift in coming. Orthodox brahmans launched a vicious propaganda campaign against the Samaj as they wanted to nip the 'subversive' movement in its bud. They brought all kinds of pressures upon the simple adherents of the Samaj to leave the organisation. How would your prayers reach God if they were said in Marathi and not Sanskrit, they asked the gullible folk. Phule had to pacify his supporters that God knew everything and understood the yearnings and prayers of every human soul, however expressed (Keer 2000: 128). The reactionary groups tried to intimidate the people that their association with the Samaj would destroy their family and fortunes on account of the curses of brahmans and their gods. Many Satyashodhaks had to bear the brunt of brahmanic wrath. Those who became its members were harassed, and some of them were even forced, on flimsy charges, to leave their jobs in government service by their superior officers, mostly brahmans (ibid.). Such pressure however failed to dampen the spirit of the most Satyashodhaks, who continued their march, defying the brahmanical roadblocks.

As Deshpande (2002) has argued, Phule was the first to think of Indian society in terms of class. He was categorial that all those who produce society's wealth were shudra-atishudras as they had to suffer oppression at the hands of the elite, the parasitical consumers of society's resources. He strove to bring together all labouring classes – kunbis, malis, dhangars, Muslims, bhils, kolis, mahars and mangs – under one umbrella to wage a morality-driven and knowledge-based struggle against brahmanical falsehood. His movement was based on the idea of uniting the peasant castes with the untouchables and Muslim masses without which the oppressed could never gain strength to subdue their common oppressors. His broad-based community of the oppressed consisted of all those who were at the receiving end of the brahmanical system. O'Hanlon has noted (1985: 131) that one of the aims of his play, *Tritiya Ratna*, was to convince his audience that the heterogeneous collections of social groups that fell within the category of exploited did, in fact, share common interests and a common social position:

This was to be done by the ideological construction of a social grouping that would be both socially credible and attractive. The latter was particularly important, so that elite non-brahman castes might not feel that they were losing by their association with traditionally low castes. This new social construct was to be the community of the oppressed itself, with its explanation of social evils in terms of the exploitation of all by one group, and its atmosphere of hope and striving for change.

As victims of the brahmanical system, Phule places both 'clean' shudras and 'untouchable' ati-shudras in the community of the oppressed, and gives mahars and mangs 'the central place in the fused group of the oppressed'. He explains that the disabilities suffered by the untouchables and the exploitation of the cultivators are the result of the same phenomenon. This was a revolutionary interpretation of Indian society.

Emphasising bipolarity had radical implications. First, it meant that Phule was rejecting the system of regressive hierarchy which engineers divisions and schisms among the oppressed. And second, while rejecting the notions of high and low, pure and polluted, the main thrust of his attack was on the inhuman and oppressive nature of brahmanism (Deshpande 2002: 8). His notion of community of the oppressed was informed by the idea of universal brotherhood amongst all those who believe in the principle of human equality and dignity. This brotherhood transcends all artificial divisions of social position, language, religion, and nationality. That is why he felt closer to a liberal foreigner than to the self-serving conservative compatriot. It was for such radical thinking and activities that Phule was branded by his opponents as a semi-Christian and a hater of Hinduism. No doubt he was an admirer of some of the humanist and egalitarian aspects of Christianity and Islam – he had the highest regard for Jesus (who frequently figures in his writing as a champion of justice and equality, a sort of Western alter-ego of his

Bali Raja, the mythical Indian king whom Phule idolised as embodiment of justice and benevolence) and Mohammed (in a laudatory poem Phule hails him as the prophet of brotherhood) – but he had made it clear that he did not believe in the idea of revealed truth or divine sanction, and as such had nothing to do with the fundamentalism of any creed or religion.

For Phule, the subversion of brahmanical religion and culture was not an end in itself. It was the starting point of an alternative reconstruction. This could not be done without replacing the religion of the old with a new universal religion. He was of the view that man and society needed religion but he used the term as a synonym for humanity and morality, stressing on an ethical conscience in human relationships. His *Sarvajanik Satya Dharmā Pustak* (The Book of True Faith), written just before his death and published posthumously, is like his final testament, containing the gist of his thoughts on religion and culture. Here he attempts to articulate his vision of a rational, compassionate and egalitarian religion. Phule was not an atheist, but his God, like Kabir's, was conceived in radical monotheistic terms. He did not believe in the God and his prophets as propounded by institutionalised religions nor did he believe in theories of hell and heaven, incarnation and pre-destination. His own mind and conscience, to paraphrase Thomas Paine's maxim, was his temple. In this sense, his God was not transcendental, but resided within his own being. Though Phule coined the word *Nirmik* – Creator – for God, he believed that *Nirmik* has no role to play in man's life after creating him; so man has to take full responsibility of his own life.

Thus, the natural and social worlds, devoid of supernatural intervention, were left open to investigation by secular reason in all its empirical, logical and scientific implications. Blind beliefs, superstitions and rituals have no place in Phule's religion. The brahmanical religion claimed the varna order to be divinely-ordained and eternal, and, therefore, unalterable and unassailable. Phule rejected this pseudo-religion along with its false gods and shastras. He dismissed the notion that the Vedas and other brahmanical scriptures upholding the caste system are God-inspired and based on religion; on the contrary, he argued, they are utterly unethical and political.

His *Nirmik* is *sarvajanik* – equally available to all as he resides in every heart – and not hidden or esoteric or available only to the chosen few. His was an attempt at eliminating the middleman between man and god, a role traditionally played by brahmans. In a radical shift from the brahmanical position, he tried to make religion casteless, monotheistic, and humane. He believed that man could never be happy in the world unless his conduct was truthful and righteous towards one another. His attempt to persuade everyone to strive for moral excellence by adopting right kind of conduct towards others is reminiscent of the compassionate illumination of Gautam Buddha, who was an inspirational figure for Phule. Phule's religion is awash with egalitarianism as he sublimely exhorts everyone to 'hug brotherly Christians, Muslims, Mangs, Brahmans'. He defines ethics as truthful human conduct. It does not matter, then, whether the one who practises it is a Christian, a Muslim, or a Satyashodhak.

Phule believed that a progressive ideology must be followed by progressive practice. He set a personal example by throwing open the well in his courtyard in 1868 to the 'untouchables' in the teeth of resistance from his caste fellows. It was even rumoured that he had converted to Christianity, because only Christian missionaries were not supposed to believe in being polluted by the untouchables. Earlier, the conservatives had forced his father to banish him and his wife Savitribai for their 'sin' of setting up a school for untouchable girls. Not one to cave in easily, Phule and his wife chose to leave the comforts of his father's home but did not close the school. Phule and Savitri, to cite another example, were childless and he was being pressurised even by his father-in-law to remarry; he rejected the suggestion with disdain and instead chose with his wife to adopt the 'illegitimate' child of a brahman widow. Similarly, on the death of his father, he performed the last rites differently – by feeding orphans and the physically challenged. On his father's first death anniversary, he distributed books among students and gave food to the poor.

Phule's congruity of principle and practice stands in clear relief from the dubious track-record of the top leaders from the other spectrum. In 1873, M. G. Ranade, then aged thirty-two, a scholar and champion reformer, the toast of elitist reformers, lost his wife and immediately married a girl of eleven. This appalled Phule. He wrote a scathing article in *Vividhadnyan Vistar* in which he asked Ranade not to preach what he himself could not practise (Keer 2000: 136). Earlier in 1871, when Ranade's young sister was widowed, he said that if she remarried, his father would be devastated and the Pune brahmans would ostracise him. To which Phule replied, 'then, don't parade yourself as a reformer and a champion of widow-remarriage' (ibid.). Later, the great Ranade in his capacity as a judge also earned the distinction of passing a verdict against the Satyashodhak marriage ceremonies without brahman priests. In his 'enlightened' opinion, it was wrong to perform a marriage ceremony without a brahman priest, and even if the priest had not been invited to the wedding, he should still be given *dakshina*, the traditional gifts. Phule had to challenge the verdict – the lower court rejected his case but the higher court ruled in his favour.

The Lokahitavadi was another great reformer, widely respected for his progressive ideas, but one who meekly surrendered to the conservatives. His impressive reforming career came to an inglorious end when he accepted to undergo an expiation for having sent his son to England for education in defiance of the scriptural ban imposed on crossing the seas; and, he himself caved in to the caste prohibition to cross the black waters when he was required to go to England. Much worse, the Lokahitavadi married his grandchildren when they were barely six or eight years old (ibid.: 136-7). Phule was aghast at the betrayal. Such double standards, Keer stresses, strengthened the hands of reactionaries like Chiplunkar and Tilak who felt vindicated by the reformers' inability to put into practice what they were preaching. They sniggered, 'In what way are the reformers who plead for social reforms different from us?'

THE REWRITING OF HISTORY AND MYTHOLOGY

Phule's vision of reordering the society was radical; the challenge, however, was how to bring about the desired transformation. Brahmanism presented the biggest obstacle. The ideological mainspring of brahmanical power and hegemony lay in the ancient scriptures and religious literature. For Phule, there was nothing sacred or religious about brahmanism but because it paraded itself as divinely ordained, it was necessary to expose its design of dominance. Over the centuries, the ignorant masses had been mentally enslaved through extensive integration of the Dharmashastras and *itihas-purana* into the popular culture and oral traditions. The battle for the mind could not be won without launching a counter-cultural movement. With this thinking, Phule came up with contestatory accounts of brahman histories, scriptures, myths and stories. Most ingenious was his attempt to link his subversive interpretation of the past with symbols and stories from the contemporary local milieu. The reconstruction of the history and mythology was propelled by the purpose of uniting all women and labouring classes, traditionally divided into hundreds of castes, against their common historical and cultural adversaries.

During the four decades of his public life, Phule brought out various prose and poetic works that presented a broad paradigm of a myth-history from the viewpoint of the toiling castes. Through tracts, magazines, plays and leaflets, and aided by attempts at organisation-building, Phule launched a cultural broadside against the entrenched culture which allowed a particular class to monopolise education and power. In a brilliant display of imagination and insight, he linked present oppression with past atrocities and portrayed the ancient history of India as an endless struggle between the brahmans and the shudratishudras. He analysed and theorised the genesis and growth of caste system in an historical and materialist perspective. Prior to this, scholars of both Indian and foreign origins had portrayed caste as an eternal social organisation that existed from 'time immemorial'. In a paradigm shift, Phule presented brahmanism and the caste order as symbiotic and historical. Constructed over time, they represented for him a hegemonic system of oppression that had to be fought and crushed.

Since Phule wanted to dismantle the whole structure of the exploitative system, he produced subversive tracts against brahmanism and vehemently contested its philosophical and metaphysical formulations. He rejected the doctrine of karma which traces everything including individual suffering and social or caste status to the karma of previous births. While repudiating such ideas, he accused the brahman of imprisoning the gullible people by indoctrinating notions like *daiva* (fate), *sanchit* (accumulated merits/demerits of previous births), and *prarabdha* (predestination) which have made them lose their dialectial relationship with the world, resulting in their meek submission to the external forces. In the same vein, he dismissed the incarnation theory which postulates that Vishnu took different incarnations at different times to 'save' the society from chaos and anarchy. This thesis, as Deshpande (2002) has underlined, is at the heart of brahmanic religious system as it dissolves the contradiction between polytheistic religious practices and monotheistic Vedantist metaphysics. In a radical departure from traditional meaning, Phule interpreted the various incarnations of Vishnu as different stages of Aryan onslaught on the original inhabitants of India, and unmasked the atrocities of various godheads. Thus, by rejecting the two core doctrines of karma and incarnation, Phule tried to uproot the very foundation on which brahmanism was founded and sustained.

His *Gulamgiri* is an attempt at such revolutionary deconstruction. Here, he discards the brahmanic caste ideology, supports the Dravidian theory to counter the prevalent Aryan mythology, and dreams up a Bali-rajya of equality and justice in opposition to Ram-rajya based on the varna-dharma. Blazing a new trail, in stark contrast to the brahmanical historiography which traces the first colonial encounter to the Muslims and then the British, Phule portrayed the Vedic Aryan as the original coloniser of the indigenous people. He expounded that the upper strata of Indian society were descendants of the savage aliens who cruelly subordinated the peace-loving aborigines by usurping their land and property. The violent invaders imposed inhuman social and religious practices on the local populace in order to keep them in permanent subjugation.

While expostulating this Phule insisted that the introduction of caste system was a critical instrument by which the brahmans concealed their original act of usurpation and ensured the perpetuation of their own privileged position. Rewriting many of the central episodes of the brahmancial mythology – the incarnations of Vishnu; the story of King Bali and the dwarf Vaman; the legend of Parashuram's extirpation of the kshatriya, etc. – Phule argued that these symbolised the real history of ancient India, deliberately garbled by later brahman writers, in order to conceal their misdeeds and consolidate their power over the lowered castes. He also illustrated this by reinterpreting core elements in the social structure and popular culture of contemporary Maharashtra, presenting them as survivals from the remote past. Towards the end of the book Phule tries to show how the wily brahmans shifted their position in recent times and kept intact, even enhanced, their power during the British rule which allowed real power to slip from its hands into those of the high caste professional and administrative elite which served it.

Phule wrote a ballad on Shivaji – *Shivaji Pavada* – in 1868. In it he depicted Shivaji as a shudra king and social rebel against caste tyranny whose descendants were robbed of their power by the treacherous brahman Peshwas.[7] As if anticipating the brahmanical, especially Tilak's, resurrection of Shivaji in the 1890s as the orthodox anti-Muslim and saviour of the brahmanic culture – *gau-brahman-pratipalak* (protector of cows and brahmans) – Phule placed Shivaji within the anti-brahmanical tradition of Maharashtrian history and culture. The ballad portrays lowered castes and untouchables as the descendants of the original kshatriyas, who were led by the legendary King Bali. Phule argues that the kshatriyas had been destroyed at the time of the Aryan invasions, and they remained in pitiable condition ever since. He supported his thesis by explaining that the term kshatriya was derived from the word *kshetra*, which means a field or land. His explanations was that all those who lived or worked peacefully on their land were kshatriyas. Using Shivaji's 'low' caste status to his advantage, he portrayed Shivaji as leader of all shudraatishudras – the descendants of the forgotten kshatriyas. He draws a parallel between Shivaji and King Bali as the brave and just leaders of their communities against the alien oppressors.

Not unexpectedly, reviews and comments laced with scorn and contempt lambasted the 'unknown' author who dared to venture into history-writing (Keer 2000). Drunk on the 'glorious past' and blissfully oblivious of the social evils of their time, the learned custodians of Indian culture were aghast at the audacity of a 'semi-literate' shudra to contradict their cherished understanding of the past. Leading the pack of such scholars was Tilak's soulmate Vishnushastri Chiplunkar who derisively dismissed Phule as a 'Shudra Religious Teacher' and a 'Shudra World-Teacher' (Keer 2000: 146). However, Phule's colleagues were not prepared to take things lying down any more – they decided to join the issue and *Deenbandhu*, the journal of the Satyashodhak Samaj, carried a sustained campaign against the reactionary ideas of Tilak and Chiplunkar. Later, Phule's fellow Satyashodhaks wrote two devastating books – Dinkarrao Javalkar's *Deshache Dushman* (Enemies of the Nation) targeted Tilak and Chiplunkar while *Marathyanche Dasiputra* (Maratha's Bastards), written by R. N. Lad, mounted a frontal attack on the Chitpavan Peshwa dynasty that fraudulently wrested all power from Shivaji's descendants and headed the Maratha confederacy in the eighteenth and early nineteenth centuries. (Peshwas, it may be noted, were the inspirational icons for Chiplunkar, Tilak and other revivalists in Maharashtra.)

EDUCATION AS EMANCIPATION AND EMPOWERMENT

Phule's reconstruction of the past and linking it to the oppressive present was one aspect of the attempt to fight the inegalitarian system and brahmanical ideology. A more essential and enduring way to change the existing power structure was through education. Phule laid maximum emphasis on spreading education. The kind of education he stood for was modern and scientific, which could work as a catalyst for social change and transformation. It is significant that he opposed, as Uma Chakravarti has pointed out, the obscurantist attempts of his elitist contemporaries to yoke together modern science and technology with Vedic knowledge. A staunch rationalist, he wanted to use knowledge as a weapon to bring about an attitudinal change leading to 'a kind of cultural revolution as well as a technological one'. For him, the acquisition of knowledge by the oppressed was emancipatory and his pedagogy was informed by a clear understanding of knowledge and power:

> Phule was the first Indian 'system builder' . . . (the) first to attempt at transforming plural categories of history into singular or universal. Phule talked about knowledge and power much before Foucault did. In fact, Foucault's post-modernist analysis came at a time when Europe has literally seen an 'end of history' whereas Phule's efforts were to change the world/ society with the weapon of knowledge. (Deshpande, cited in Omvedt 1994: 23)

How important education was in Phule's scheme is evident

from the fact that the major theme of his maiden venture (1855) into literary writing – *Tritiya Ratna* (The Third Eye) – was education. In this play, he argues that by denying knowledge to the shudras, the brahmans might be held responsible for the condition of masses and for the backwardness of Hindu society itself. His differences with his brahman colleagues, working with him in the 1850s, who stressed the general backwardness of Hindu society as the cause of the sufferings of the lowered castes, rather than attributing these to any particular social group, were precisely on this point. The matter came to a head when the brahman activists insisted that it was enough to give the basic skills of reading and writing to the 'lower' caste people, while Phule maintained that 'they should be given a thorough education, and get from it the power to distinguish between good and bad'.

The high expectation he had from public education was not unrealistic. The 'potential explosiveness' of education was evident when Muktabai, a fourteen-year-old Mang girl in Phule's school, wrote the essay *Mang Maharachya Dukha Visaiyi* – 'About the Grief of the Mangs and Mahars' (1855). In this she presented a heart-rending description of the dismal conditions imprisoning the untouchables, and caustically critiqued the heartless, inhuman brahmanical social system. Analysing the poignant essay, Uma Chakravarti writes:

> ... *Muktabai presents the best example of Phule's belief that a special vision, a tritiya ratna, would be the outcome of education and would have the means to strip the falsity of Brahmanic ideology. It enabled her to proclaim, 'Let that religion where only one person is privileged and the rest deprived, perish from the earth, and let it never enter our minds to be proud of such a religion'.... Muktabai's essay ends abruptly, 'Oh God! What agony is this! I will burst into tears if I write more about this injustice.' Even so, the anguished Muktabai understood and rejected the existing social order and provided a scathing critique of Brahmanical power in nineteenth century Maharashtra. The newly acquired skills of literacy for this untouchable woman had made it possible to question, in print, the most 'sacred' person in the social hierarchy, and reject unequivocally his 'knowledge' and his authority.* (1998: 74-5)

Phule and his associates spearheaded a spirited campaign for mass education. But their individual and collective efforts were not enough. Phule wanted the government to spend the people's money – collected through taxes – on developing an infrastructure for universal education. Phule repeatedly asked, advised and (in exasperation) warned the government to shoulder more responsibility in this regard. He was sharply critical of the British policy on education because, as he put it, it grossly neglected primary education in its eagerness to promote higher education (in order to produce a class of professional and administrative allies) which only benefited the elite. In a petition in 1882 to the Hunter Commission, appointed to examine the question of education, Phule pointedly accused the government of ignoring the education of the lower classes by toeing a trickle-down theory. The government, he said, was under the illusion that people from the higher classes would spread education among the lower classes. The government squandered the taxes it earned from poor farmers on educating the upper classes. But the children of the rich, he pointed out, who availed of free education and achieved material success on its strength, did nothing to assist the uplift of their underprivileged countrymen. The British education policy ensured 'monopoly of education by the Brahmins' and as a result 'all the senior government posts are monopolised by them'. He suggested that if the government was serious about doing something about it, primary education should be made compulsory up to the age of twelve. Higher education, to which the government had already devoted very generous resources, might be better left to the efforts of private individuals.

Phule wanted the Commission to meet the poor and the unlettered, and then frame an appropriate policy aimed at universal education. But this was not to be, and an embittered Phule was left to remark: 'The Hunter Commission did not interview farmers. It relied solely on the discussions it had with Parsis, Christians and Brahmins and accepted their word as final. Hence, the report of this Commission will not benefit the illiterate and the poor.'

In his ballad *Vidyakhatyatil Brahman Pantoji* (Brahman Teachers in the Educational Department) and in his introduction to *Gulamgiri*, Phule attempted to show how the caste elite on the strength of religious authority and monopoly over education appropriated all positions in administrative and educational institutions under the

British regime. Explaining how social and material conditions had kept the lowered castes illiterate, and why the brahmans were unwilling to impart education to the other castes, he demanded education for all and recruitment of teachers from other castes as well:

> *Appoint teachers from other castes*
> *Appoint those with a knowledge of the truth*
> *Prepare a class of schoolteachers*
> *Only of Malis and Kunbis*
> *Another for Mahars and Mangs.*
>
> (cited in O'Hanlon 1985: 215)

Phule could see the gradual formation of a class of English-educated native administrators who were continuing the traditional policy of exclusion of the lowered castes by convincing the British that these people had no liking and aptitude for learning. His repeated exhortation to the British to democratise education was based on an anxiety that the traditional educational disabilities of the underclass were being confirmed and reinforced by the colonial power structure.

Phule's stirring concern for public education was of course not shared by the powers that be – whether foreign or Indian. Deploring the existing education system, he gave vent to his frustrations by depicting, in Gavaskar's words, the 'drain of wealth' within the country wherein the taxes paid by the working class go into educating the sons of the rich and powerful:

> *He who owns goods suffers the most*
> *goes the Pathan saying,*
> *children of queer people study;*
> *Mali, kunbi slog in the fields to pay taxes,*
> *don't have enough to clothe.* (see Gavaskar 1999)

Phule did not let go any opportunity to promote the cause of public education. As a member of the Pune Municipality in the 1880s, he opposed a proposal of the president of the municipality to spend money on decorating the city on the visit of the Governor-General, arguing that the money would be better spent on the education of poor in the city. In another instance, the Prince of

Wales was greeted on his visit to Pune in 1889 by the boys and girls of Phule's school with a jingle:

> *Tell Grandma we are a happy nation,*
> *But 19 crores are without education.* (Keer 2000: 245)

GENDER INEQUALITY AND WOMEN'S SUBORDINATION

In the nineteenth century, Rammohun Roy was followed by many reformers who engaged in the women's problems. They tried to build positive public opinion on issues like sati, widow remarriage, child marriage, women's education, etc. Their approach, however, was paternalistic, caste-bound and brahmanic in character. Unwilling to step out of the Vedic-brahmanic world-view, their high-caste prejudices were apparent in much of their activities and pronouncements. Phule's position was drastically different from such reformers. He presented women in common with the oppressed lowered caste men as victims of brahmanical power. The brahmanical system, he argued, treats all women – irrespective of caste – as inferior creatures; the Dharmashastras invariably club them together with shudras or dasas. Therefore, he included women of all castes and communities in his notion of the oppressed, and contended that the subordination of women and toiling castes and denying them the right to education were the main causes of the appalling backwardness of Indian society.

Like the elitist reformers, Phule was also a forerunner of female education and women's rights, but he was unique in asserting equality between the sexes. As he saw subjugation of women as a part of the larger hegemonic design inherent in the ideology of caste, his critique necessarily implied the view that the end of the brahmanical system would ensure the end of patriarchy as well. According to Uma Chakravarti, while reinterpreting the past and exploring caste as a cultural hegemonic system, Phule emerges as a trenchant critic of brahmanical patriarchy:

He alone, among nineteenth century social reformers, was able to stand outside Brahmanical patriarchy and, although gender was not a central factor in his analysis of caste and the reproduction of inequality, his rejection of the caste system and of brahmanic Hinduism enabled him to adopt a

more radical approach to gender inequality than any of his contemporaries.
(1998: 65)

Phule was not merely for improvement in women's position, he believed in gender equality and wanted nothing less than equal and common human rights for men and women. In the context of widowhood and sati, Phule says that when a husband dies, it is the woman who leads a life of suffering, burdened by widowhood for the rest of her life. Earlier they even burnt themselves and became sati on the funeral pyres of their husbands. But 'has anyone ever heard of a man burning himself alive in the event of his wife's death and become a sata?' (*Selected Writings* 2002: 231). Sata was of course an ironical coinage by Phule to suggest a male sati. He wanted that the traditional family and marriage system be changed in the light of reason and gender justice. His *Sarvajanik Satya Dharma Pustak* suggested new marriage rites laying emphasis on man-woman equality. He was also the first, as Deshpande points out, to draw attention to the fact that the labour of the young bride is used as bonded labour by the family the girl marries into.

Since exclusion from knowledge was the main cause behind women's subordination, education was to be his main resource to liberate them. Not surprisingly, the first school he and his wife Savitribai established in 1848 was for girls. Despite economic hardships and fierce opposition, Phule set up 18 schools between 1848 and 1852. Out of these six were in Pune town, six in rural areas of Pune district, three in Satara and three in other places. His educational campaign was causing consternation among the conservative elements. His wife was often greeted with insults and abuses while going to teach in these schools. Also, an attempt was made on Phule's life in 1856.

The 1860s saw Phule actively campaigning for widow remarriage and banning the practice of child marriage. He arranged the remarriage of a brahman widow in 1864. He took a more daring initiative when, moved by the plight of victims of enforced widowhood, he set up a sanctuary in his own home compound in Pune for pregnant brahman widows, which was boldly advertised by means of notices pasted up publicly in the brahman locality. It is to be noted that enforced widowhood was a problem largely confined to the brahman and allied castes; the remarriage of lowered caste widows was quite common in Maharashtra and elsewhere.

As O'Hanlon (1985) and Chakravarti (1998) have shown, the material and sexual consequences of enforced widowhood were responsible for a large number of young brahman women becoming pregnant. Faced with the fear of excommunication or even worse, many of them resorted to abortions or threw their illegitimate children to their cruel fate. Abortions or desertion of newly-born babies were common, but if the matter became public, murdering the 'fallen women' to uphold family honour was also quite common within the cloisters of high-caste homes. Phule's decision to establish a foundling home to save the widows and prevent infanticide picked on 'one of the most vulnerable spots in brahmanism, the linchpin of upper caste gender codes, enforced widowhood and its consequences' (Chakravarti 1998: 76). Phule and Savitribai gave protection to frightened pregnant widows and assured them that the orphanage would take care of their children. It was in this orphanage that a brahman widow gave birth to a baby boy Yashwant in 1873 whom Phule and Savitri adopted as their son.

Along with other routine humiliation, the widows were also forced to shave their heads. Against this Phule organised a successful barbers' strike where the barbers refused to perform the customary tonsure of widows. O'Hanlon (1994) has written about his way of highlighting women's issues in a provocative way. Quoting one of Phule's friends, she recounts how he employed a brahman woman, Gangubai, as a domestic helper on very high wages, as a way of helping the deserted woman and mocking the wealthy brahmans who usually employed poor women from other castes to do their menial work. He seemed to have succeeded in this case, for the brahman woman's relatives came and took her away.

While Phule was sensitive to common gender problems faced by all women, he was also conscious of crucial differences among women based on caste and their place in the system of production. In *Shetkaryacha Asud* (The Cultivator's Whipcord), Phule has shown how the women of toiling castes had to labour at home and in the fields, whereas the brahman women work only at home and lead a relatively comfortable life. Thus 'the brahman women are subject only to the power of the brahman men, while the labouring women are doubly crushed as they are dominated by both the upper caste men and the men of their own families'. He has brought out this glaring contrast vividly and poignantly in his poem *Kulambin*, 'The Peasant Woman'. Here, Phule compares the hardships of a shudra woman – clad in rough, tattered sari, balancing her tiny child on her back, who slogs from early morning to late evening both at home and then in the fields with the men, who has no time to comb her hair or bathe – with the cosy life of the 'bejewelled *bhatin*', the brahman woman, 'who does not have to work as a labourer, to tend to the cattle, to collect cow-dung, to carry the sheaves of corn to the threshing floor'. A shudra woman more often than not has to work as a dasi in a brahman's home but the brahman woman 'does not grind the corn in the shudra's house nor does she sprinkle water in the courtyard of the shudra, to earn her livelihood'. While the kulambin's labour nourishes and sustains the whole society, including the 'brahman beggar', the bhatin 'does not look after shudra children, does not kiss them.' Phule is thus aghast that the brahman woman, like her menfolk, despises the toiling woman as an inferior being and addresses her by various disparaging names.

Later, however, Phule's understanding of women's oppression changed somewhat as he tried to link subordination of women with a structure of relations that might be recognised as akin to patriarchy (Chakravarti 1998: 77). Phule perceived the close dependence of caste and gender hierarchies as 'the safeguarding of the caste structure is achieved through the highly restricted movements of women or even through female seclusion'. This understanding was expressed when he stoutly defended feminist pioneers like Pandita Ramabai and Tarabai Shinde against attacks from the male orthodoxies of all stripes. 'In Ramabai's case he mounted an attack on brahmanism, in which much of the high-caste woman's oppression was located. In Tarabai's case he went further, as he was critical of his own compatriots in the non-Brahman movement with regard to recognising women's subordination' (ibid.).

Pandita Ramabai (1858-1922), one of India's earliest feminists, was an outstanding scholar of Sanskrit. In 1882, she founded the Arya Mahila Samaj to promote the women's cause. She was the first Indian woman to declare, on the basis of her study of the shastras, that 'the Sanskritic core of Hinduism was irrevocably and essentially anti-women'. Later, she embraced Christianity, denouncing the Hindu shastras, epics and contemporary preachers for portraying women as 'bad, very bad, worse than demons, and unholy as untruth, and that they could not get *moksha* as man (could)'. Her conversion and increasingly bold espousal of women's issues had made her a pariah. Accused of committing an unpardonable sin against Hindu society, she was damned – and deserted – not only by her conservative friends and relatives but also by the reformers and nationalists of many hues. Among Ramabai's detractors were Ramakrishna and Vivekananda[8] (ibid.: 319-20).

Ramabai's renouncement of Hinduism for Christianity was seen by the upper caste public intellectuals like Vivekananda as an attack on the brahmanical tradition within which they had comfortably pitched their tents of social reforms and cultural nationalism. Uma Chakravarti has pointed out that after her conversion Ramabai represented not the supposed glory of the ancient Hindu women but a discordant voice who spoke, much to the chagrin of the so-called nationalists, for the subjugated women of the nineteenth century India. She became a thorn in the flesh of the upper caste nationalists since her standpoint on gender and religion could not be accommodated in their construction of the nation which was exclusivist – Hindu, patriarchal and upper casteist – in orientation.

Phule was the only person who came forward to support Pandita Ramabai's struggle. He applauded her efforts for education among high-caste women. In his booklet *Satsar* (The Essence of Truth), Phule argued that Ramabai, as a truly educated woman, had seen for herself the discriminatory orientation of shastras against lowered caste masses and women and therefore rightly decided to break away from the 'tyrannical' religion. He went on to argue that the brahmans had always invented all sorts of 'malicious lies about women', and prevented them from acquiring education because the educated ones like Ramabai would then 'throw away the scriptures' and revolt against the male authority.

Phule also pointed out that Ramabai was not the first to defend women's rights and dignity; even before her, Tarabai Shinde of Buldhana in Berar wrote a book against the patriarchal order. Tarabai's 1882 tract *Stri-Purush Tulana* (A Comparison between

Women and Men, tr. O'Hanlon 1994) was the first feminist work in India. Written in biting language, the book presented a searing criticism of the way that men depicted women and excluded them from power. Tarabai came from a Satyashodhak background and shared much of its radicalism against the orthodox religion. Her rebellion against women's subordination among non-brahman castes was not taken kindly by many Satyashodhak activists. Phule intervened and presented a stirring defence of Tarabai, arguing that women of non-elite castes suffered doubly from discrimination and as such they were far more victimised than the caste-oppressed men. He referred to Tarabai as *chiranjivi*, 'our dear daughter', and lauded her work.

AGRICULTURE, PEASANTRY AND LABOUR

In Phule's time, much more than now, India was a predominantly agrarian society. It was natural for someone like Phule who wanted to build a mass movement to be deeply interested in rural life and labour. Indeed, the question of agriculture and cultivators was at the centre of his thought and concern. Phule comes across as an authentic and extraordinary spokesman of the poor peasantry (O'Hanlon 1985; Deshpande 2002). Cultivators, he argued, are the producers and sustainers of society, who themselves lead a wretched life of poverty and indebtedness due to an exploitative system made worse by abysmally low productivity in agriculture. In his later years, he increasingly used the terms 'shudra cultivators' and 'shudra labour' in his ideological construction of the community of the oppressed. He took note of issues such as frequent drought, lack of irrigation facilities, primitive tools, ignorance about new agricultural tools and techniques due to lack of education, excessive taxation, and the callous negligence of the rural sector by the state.

This period witnessed considerable agrarian unrest in western Maharashtra. In 1875, the impoverished peasants in Deccan, particularly in the districts of Ahmadnagar, Pune, Satara, and Sholapur, rose in revolt against the moneylenders. In 1877, the region faced a devastating drought, but there was no state or community-level support for the famine-stricken people. There was hardly anyone among the reformers and national leaders who bothered about the lot of peasantry and appalling conditions in agricultural production. Phule was the first social activist who made agriculture and the lot of cultivators one of his central concerns (Deshpande 2002). During the uprising of 1875 he came out in solidarity with the peasantry, and in the wake of the 1877 famine he and his Satyashodhak friends set up an orphanage for the destitute children. His engagement with rural life and labour intensified after 1880. He and other Satyashodhaks extensively toured in rural areas, addressing large gatherings of peasants, and helped organise a boycott of the exploitative brahmans and moneylenders. During this period he wrote a series of speeches. His writings constitute one of the most elaborate and minutely observed pieces of social reporting of the contemporary rural society (O'Hanlon 1985). In 1883, Phule reworked them into a single volume entitled *Shetkaryacha Asud*, 'The Cultivator's Whipcord'.

In *Shetkaryacha Asud*, Phule not only details the material life of cultivators but also raises important social and economic concerns, against the historical background of exploitative brahmanical system and indifferent British regime. Comparing the cultivators of India with the farmers of other countries, he notes with concern that the lot of Indian peasantry is far worse, 'even worse than that of beasts'. For this he pins the blame on cultural and economic exploitation by brahmans, and on the callous British rulers who go by the dictates of their subordinate brahman officials. The British government is an utterly incompetent and highly expensive government which does not do anything to improve the situation, he claims. He points the finger at the vicious nexus that exists between the local exploiters – brahmans and moneylenders – and the distant one, the indolent British officials who make merry by drawing exorbitant salaries:

Because the white government officers are mostly engrossed with luxury, they do not have time enough to enquire into the real conditions of the farmers and because of this negligence most government departments are dominated by brahman employees. Both these causes have the effect that the farmers are looted, and are without enough to fill their bellies or cover their bodies. (*Selected Writings* 2002: 131)

Being fleeced thus, the cultivator is in no position to send his children to school. Even if some lucky cultivator, Phule contends, has the necessary means he is dissuaded by the wily brahmans from sending his little ones to school.

Besides depicting the peasant pauperisation, Phule puts forward several plans and suggestions for structural change in rural society. He suggests a productive partnership between the community and the state. Despite severe shortcomings – and the hitherto extremely bad track-record – of the government, he wants it to play a pro-active role in agrarian transformation. However, his rural reconstruction rests, more than anything else, on educating the public. Cultivators must get some science education about agricultural production and operations but greater emphasis, he insists, should be given to their children's education in agriculture techniques. Their teachers should be selected from their own communities, and such teachers must have first-hand experience of agricultural activities and operations. Proposing a sort of vocational education, Phule suggests that children should get professional training in trades like iron-smithery and carpentry, and those who excel in these areas should be sent abroad to the agricultural schools. Talented boys from these schools, who also show good leadership qualities, should be made the patils or village heads.

He hopes that the non-hereditary, qualified and impartial patils will also help in breaking down divisions along caste lines and stopping infighting and expensive, though thoroughly avoidable, legal wranglings among the ignorant farmers (generally created by the village elites for selfish ends). Phule also wants the government to give employment to cultivators' educated children in different departments, particularly those concerned in any way with rural and agricultural sector. There should be fair representation of all communities in proportion to their number in all government offices. This is especially required, he argues, as the elites who have monopolised most jobs in all departments are only interested in feathering their own nests.

Beyond committed writing and public campaigns to highlight the cultivators' cause, Phule employed his talent for using symbols to identify the Satyashodhak Samaj as the natural representative of the peasantry (O'Hanlon 1985). The Duke of Connaught visited Pune in 1888 and the city dignitaries hosted a dinner in his honour, to which Phule was also invited. He arrived after all the other guests, who were startled to see a poor, ragged farmer in their midst. Phule was dressed as a typical Maharashtrian cultivator – a torn turban on his head, a tattered blanket round his shoulders, a rustic dhoti, a sythe at his waist, and a battered old sandals tied with string on his feet. After dinner, he created quite a stir, by delivering an impassioned speech in fluent English. He contrasted the grinding poverty of the cultivators with the affluence of the rich invitees, and pointed out to the British guests that the people gathered here did not represent India, the real people of India were to be found in villages and city areas inhabited by the untouchables. He told the visiting dignitaries to go home and say that they had met a real villager, a representative of millions of Indians, whose protection and advancement were the first duties of the government (O'Hanlon 1985: 272-3).

Throughout his life Phule fought for peasants' and workers' rights. *Deenbandhu*, the weekly published by the Satyashodhak Samaj, regularly highlighted the plight of workers and peasants. N. M. Lokhande and Krishnarao Bhalekar, Phule's close associates, were among the first to build an organisation of workers in India (Keer 2000). From 1880 onwards, Phule and Lokhande addressed several meetings of the textile workers in Bombay. They played a pioneering role in building a trade union movement for the redressal of the workers' grievances (ibid.).

A champion of the labouring people, Phule was also the one to invest labour with dignity, beauty and positive value. His thinking on this evolved over the years in a significant way. While earlier he portrayed the labour of the masses as a tool of brahman oppression, later he attached positive value to productive labour, contrasting it consistently with the worthlessness of the brahmanic life-style. Nowhere does Phule's glorification of labour as value come out as powerfully as in his poem *Kulambin*, in which he pays a touching tribute to a poor peasant woman who labours tirelessly near the hearth and in the fields. By showering praise on the uncombed, untidy labouring woman and speaking negatively of the slothful brahman woman, who idles away her time on titivating herself, Phule appears to be crying for a radical change in the traditional criteria of value, beauty and aesthetics.

At a practical level too, Phule tried to bring about an

attitudinal change towards labour. O'Hanlon has narrated an anecdote which underlines his fascination for labour. On a particular day Phule was with the workers on his orchards outside Pune. When all the labourers had stopped for their midday meal, Phule got up and started to drive the well-bucket himself, cheerfully singing as he worked. When the workers laughed, he stopped to explain that he was proud to be a cultivator and all real cultivators had to make their music as they worked – it was only those who did not toil with their hands who had the leisure to sit with musical instruments. Another incident is recorded by his biographer Keer describing how on finding a little snotty-nosed poor boy crying for food, Phule lifted him, washed him, and purchased some food for him. A person passing-by recognised Phule and asked him how could he bear to fondle the dirty child. Phule replied that the poverty and helplessness of the boy's parents was the reason why such children were dirty. It was not their fault, it was the responsibility of society to provide them with water, soap and clothes. He also reminded the gentleman that the boy's body wanted washing, but the mind of the questioner needed thorough cleaning.

CRITIQUE OF NATION AND NATIONALISM

Phule was scathing in his criticism of the elite-based socio-political movement that was being spearheaded by the so-called nationalists, because as he saw to his horror, they were actually constructing a neo-brahmanism under the cloak of nationalism. Their vindication of caste and their glorification of a tradition that was deeply regressive represented for him an outright treachery to the nation and toiling masses. The basic postulate of these nationalists was that their earlier domination by the Muslims and more recent conquest by the British had been the result of weakness caused by the corruption or degeneration of the classical caste system and original religion of the Aryans. The remedy for this degeneration was for all castes to unite – through faithful adherence to their respective caste duty – and return to the purity of their ancestors. The unity thus achieved, they urged, would make Hindu society strong enough to drive away the foreigners and establish swaraj. Phule was utterly dismissive of this brand of patriotism, seeing in it subtle elite attempts to preserve traditional socio-religious hierarchies from the reforming and radical influences that accompanied British rule. For him, the oppression and violation of the rights of the Indian masses inherent in the conventional brahmanism was far more sinister than that in the British rule. His persistent insistence was on equality or universal brotherhood, which he held up as the criterion to unite not only the community of the oppressed but society as a whole for any larger political projects (O'Hanlon 1985: 202-3). The image of universal brotherhood which he presented as the standard by which contemporary expressions of patriotism were to be judged necessitated a decisive break from the socio-religious distinctions and hierarchies of the conventional Hinduism, which the brahman 'patriots' wanted to strengthen in order to achieve 'harmonious unity' of the past.

In a far-sighted insight and anticipation, Phule spoke sharply of 'a few half-baked shudra scholars' and some 'belly-filling clerks from amongst the shudras' who might be duped into entering a false national alliance by the wily brahmans. Such fraudulent unity, he warned, would neither be fruitful nor long-lasting. As he writes in *Shetkaryacha Asud*:

... If the brahmans really wish to unite the people of this country and take the nation ahead, then first they must drown their cruel religion, which is customary amongst both the victors (brahmans) and the vanquished (shudras), and they, publicly and clearly, must cease using any artifice in their relationship with the shudras, who have been demeaned by that religion, and trample on inequality and the Vedanta opinion, and till a true unity is established, there will be no progress in this country. If by chance, in their inherited and customary cunning the Arya brahmans join hands with a few half-baked shudra scholars and manage some progress, that improvement will not last for too long. (Selected Writings 2002: 178)

To understand Phule's critique of nationalism, it is imperative to discern the basic orientation of *bhadralok* reform movements which were a kind of prelude to the rise of 'nationalism'. Conceptualised in entrenched brahmanical tradition, the high caste reformer-nationalists (as we have seen in the last chapter) concentrated only on those practices and custom which were concerned with the traditionally privileged classes who were now emerging as the new middle class under colonial patronage. The toiling castes and oppressed communities hardly figured in their national discourse. It was this continued exclusion that forced the subjugated people to come out against the entrenched interest groups in various hues and garbs in region after region, writing in the process a subversive chapter in India's social history, popularly known as the non-brahman or anti-caste movement. At the root of the anti-caste movement lay the centuries-old oppression and injustice carried out in the name of shastras and sanskriti, which was now being renovated and replenished under the seductive rhetoric of 'nationalism'. Phule was the pioneering leader of this movement which not only denounced the basic tenets of brahmanic culture but also challenged the elite-based nationalist project that glorified that regressive tradition.

Through his contestatory renditions of history, politics, education, religion and ethics, Phule tried to repoliticise diverse arenas of public discourse, and asserted that mindless glorification of Vedic-brahmanic tradition was part of, and not the solution to, the national problem. He challengingly asked the Veda-worshipping nationalists to bring the Vedas out in the open – *brahmananache Veda maidani aana na*. To those who sang the glories of the past and cited European scholars' rapturous rhapsodies about the religion of the Vedic Aryans, he asked why Orientalists like Max Müller were not embracing the Vedic religion if they were so convinced of its sublimeness. In sharp contrast to the high caste reformer-scholars, who were selectively modernising brahmanism in the name of Hinduism and nationalism, Phule's agenda was to smash up the whole edifice – ideological as well as material – which supported the base and superstructure of the ascriptive order. It was for this reason that Phule was sharply critical of Brahmo Samaj, Arya Samaj and Bombay-based Prarthana Samaj, and had derisively dismissed them as *Aryan-Brahman Samaj-es* (Keer 2000: 119, 129-31; O'Hanlon 1985: 268-9). Phule was of the view that the notions of 'Brahma' and 'Arya' were essentially anti-shudra. He had termed elite-based organisations such as the Sarvajanik Sabha[9] as 'Naradachi Sabha' (Narad being the fabled brahman mischief-maker who was emissary between men and gods).

Phule's analysis of brahman power penetrated several layers of 'conspiracy' worked out by the modern votaries of the brahmanical order. He was unique in establishing – through historical and contemporary facts and their reinterpretation – the interconnectedness of all kinds of brahman power in modern times:

The different areas of Brahman activity – in the religious and economic life of the village, in the new local and provincial political institutions, in the religious reform societies and the social reform movement amongst Brahmans – were but varying manifestations of an essentially unitary force. This force waged a hidden war on these different fronts to maintain the power of Brahmans as against other social groups, and appeared in different guises the better to confuse and mislead its victims. (O'Hanlon 1985: 206)

Exposing the brahmanical orientation of the emerging nationalism, he pointed out that, for all practical purposes, its politics were hegemonic, and, thus, a negation of the vision of a just and egalitarian society. The casteist and selfish world-view of the high caste patriots who were now in the forefront of the newly-formed Indian National Congress provoked Phule to question their 'nationalist' credentials. He argued that the Congress did not represent the nation, because it did not represent the interests of the majority of Indian people. The Congress, he stressed, could not become truly national until it engaged itself with wider social issues and emancipation of the oppressed within Indian society. The Congress indeed did not take up any social issues like the question of caste oppression and untouchability for a long time (see Chapter 7).

Some reformer-nationalists led by Ranade had made a half-hearted attempt in 1887 to form a Social Conference as a separate platform for the discussion of social questions. The idea was that this body would meet after the annual session of the Congress. The intent was not bad but even this slender connection between the Congress and social concerns remained merely a fond dream because most top leaders like Dadabhai Naoroji, Surendranath Banerjee, and Tilak opposed any such initiative, arguing that mixing up social issues with political matters would divide society and weaken the Congress. The matter came to a head in the 1895 Congress session in Pune when Tilak, on his home turf, threatened to burn down the Congress pavilion if such a meet was held after the session. The reformists beat a hasty retreat; conservatives won the day; the

Congress snapped its ties with the Social Conference.

Phule, on the other hand, wanted a symbiotic relationship between national politics and social questions. The politics that was divorced from the social reality was to him a self-seeking exercise by certain vested interests. He was blunt in branding such elements as anti-national loudmouths who pretended to represent the nation and nationalism without bothering to resolve what Phule perceived as the 'main contradiction in Indian society' by which he meant to bring the hitherto excluded and oppressed people into the sociopolitical mainstream. His own politics was conceived and embedded in such a radical social agenda. Nowhere was this more clear than in his response to an invitation by Ranade to participate in the plenary session of the Conference of Marathi Authors in 1885. In his reply, Phule expressed his inability to participate since his taking part in such conferences – where the people with their heads in the clouds have no idea of the oppressive reality on the ground – would not benefit the downtrodden classes:

The conferences and the books of those who refuse to think of human rights generally, who do not concede them to others and going by their behaviour are unlikely to concede them in future, cannot make sense to us, they cannot concur with what we are trying to say in our books. These upper caste authors who are forever miles away from reality and who can only make ceremonial and meaningless speeches in big meetings can never understand what we the shudras and atishudras have to suffer and what calamities we have to undergo. . . . If these leaders of men are genuinely interested in unifying all people they must address themselves to the discovery of the root of the eternal love of all human beings. Let them discover it and may be formulate and publish it as a text. Otherwise to turn a blind eye to the divisions among the human beings at this hour is simply futile. (Selected Writings, ed. Deshpande, 2002: 200-1)

Phule's castigation of ivory-tower intellectuals/writers and his impassioned advocacy for a new brand of literature that is universal, all-embracing and truly representative of people, was emblematic of his brand of politics, nation and nationalism. For him, nation was a democratic society. The birth of a nation required the growth of a civil society, the celebration of citizenship, and beginning of the process of empowerment of the marginalised. Thus, his concept of nation was based on the theory of 'change from a hierarchical to an equalitarian type of society' (Aloysius 1997). No wonder Phule dismissed the Congress brand of elitist nationalism:

There cannot be a 'nation' worth the name until and unless all the people of the land of King Bali – such as Shudras and Ati-shudras, Bhils (tribals) and fishermen etc., become truly educated, and are able to think independently for themselves and are uniformly unified and emotionally integrated. If a tiny section of the population like the upstart Aryan Brahmins alone were to found the 'National Congress' who will take any notice of it? (Phule, Collected Works, ed. Patil, vol. II: 29)

Phule did not miss the collusive and conniving nature of brahmanical (internal) colonialism and British imperialism. As he wrote in *Satsar*: 'Our wise rulers have until now spent crores of rupees from the royal and local fund on educating the brahmans. Then they appointed them on responsible posts and made them happy in every way. The reason must be that the scholar brahmans would come to the aid of the government in times of crisis' (*Selected Writings*, op. cit.: 212). His writings, *Shetkaryacha Asud* in particular, were interspersed with trenchant criticism of colonialism. Though it is not generally understood, he often bitterly criticised the British for adopting anti-poor and pro-rich policies. He tried to explain how feudalism and capitalism in India (though he did not use these very words since they were not available to him at the time) were fused into a caste/class mode of brahmanism. And since brahmanism and colonialism fed on and fattened each other, the thrust of his argument was that without fighting brahmanism the so-called anti-imperialist nationalism would only strengthen the oppressive and retrogressive forces in Indian society. With this ideology, he was the first to challenge the elitist agenda of the Congress. The Satyashodhak activists had built an effigy of a poor, emaciated farmer near the venue of the third session of the Congress in Bombay to drive home this point (Keer 2000: 246).

Phule's main charge against organisations like the Congress was that despite their declared policies and programmes of public welfare, in reality they did nothing to improve the lot of the poor as these organisations were dominated by the self-serving elites and were not representative in character. He pointed out that the larger people, peasants and 'untouchables' were not members of these bodies. Criticising the kinds of demands made by the Congress, he argued that Indianisation and brahmanisation were not the same thing (Phule, CW, vol. I: xx). He vehemently contested Ranade's 'shallow advice' that caste distinctions did not hinder the social goal and national advancement. In his opinion as long as traditional restrictions on meeting, dining and marrying outside the caste remained, it was not possible to create a sense of nationality among the people. Phule argued that social equality and massification of education were necessary prerequisites of nation-building (ibid.: xx-xxi). The elites who talked of nation-building, he stressed, without bothering with the vital question of democratisation of society were selfish pursuers of monopoly power and not nationalists.

There is a tendency in the elitist historiography to portray Phule as a British loyalist. This criticism is based on some laudatory references to the British rule in his writings. But these are also interspersed with severe criticism of colonialism as he often — and instinctively — sees it as anti-people and pro-elite. For instance, he held the British responsible for the deteriorating condition of the people, and blamed them for neglecting the primary education while promoting the higher education which mostly benefited the elite. He also refuted Ranade's claim that the condition of the agriculturists was fairly good during the British period (ibid., vol. II: 48-9). Ranade had also shown his fondness for feudalism by showering praises in some of his speeches on the hereditary land-owning class 'as they served a useful purpose in society'. Phule wrote a booklet in 1885, appropriately titled *A Warning,* to rubbish all such claims, and to highlight the plight of the toiling people who were leading a hand to mouth existence in the caste-feudal order patronised by the colonial power. He consistently opposed the exploitative nature of the state and excessive taxation, all kinds of cesses, and in many cases takeover of farmer's lands reducing peasants to paupers.

6

Guru, Iyothee, Periyar, Acchutanand: Different Strategies, One Goal

> India is a strange place which collects all sorts of social groups, divided by different religions, thoughts, practices and understandings. But broadly speaking, they can be categorised into two – the majority low castes who have been devoid of humanity for centuries and a handful who take their pleasure, call themselves superior and live at the cost of the majority. One's welfare is another's misery; that is their connection.
>
> MUKUNDRAO PATIL
> *Din Mitra*, June 1913
> cited in Omvedt 1976: 157

The high caste nationalist leadership never took into consideration institutionalised discrimination against lowered caste masses, untouchables and tribals, nor did it recognise the existence of multiple traditions and faiths within and without the larger Hindu fold. Beyond the rhetoric, the monolithic-hegemonic nationalism they espoused was propelled by two objectives: first, to wrest rule in the state from the British, and, second, to maintain their privileges and dominance over the masses within the traditional caste-class structure (Omvedt 1994; Aloysius 1997). The construction of scripture-based Hinduism as the cultural basis of nationalism was in essence the assertion of upper caste hegemony. If we set aside inconsequential semantic quibbling between the so-called progressives or secularists and the conservatives or revivalists, the foundational basis of Indian nationalism in both its secular and communal versions was the same – Sanskritic culture and ideology. While many openly valorised caste as the fundamental basis of Hindu or national unity, the 'progressives' among the nationalists fine-tuned the art of either keeping absolute silence on caste or spouting casteist platitudes on social harmony and unity in diversity. Such a strategy gave the caste elites a double-edged sword: it enabled them, on the one hand, to assume national leadership in the name of anti-colonial struggle, and on the other, also provided them with an attractive polemic to dismiss the protests and uprisings of the lower classes, the adivasis, and the Muslim masses, as divisive and anti-national.

Phule, Periyar, and Ambedkar who struggled against slavery and subordination of the commoners and demanded socio-economic reconstruction as an indivisible part of patriotism were branded as enemies of the nation. Anti-caste movements which aimed at people's liberation not only from colonialism but also from the native ruling classes, capitalists and landlords, were conveniently relegated as the casteist and anti-national assertion of the illiterate lower classes. Baburao Bagul has critiqued this narrow, obscurantist nationalism in these terms:

The intelligentsia, that is the Indian national leadership, divided the national liberation movement . . . into two warring factions: a political movement and a social movement. They also declared those who organised social movements, those who theorised on agriculture and industry, to be stooges of the British and traitors. The national movement was turned into a form of historical, mythological movement and ancestor worship. . . . Those who propounded inequality and did not wish society to be democratic, started eulogising history, mythology and ages gone by because, in those mythological and historical ages, they were the supreme victors and leaders. (see Omvedt 1994: 88)

The emergence of social movements from below – rooted in the millennia-old non-brahmanical traditions – was a slow and tortuous process. Colonial rule had accepted the traditional brahmanical caste and community relations, which meant further exploitation of the toiling castes who were now burdened with additional 'caste duties' for new forms of surplus production for the foreign rulers. As colonial exploitation operated through the vigorous implementation of caste relations, the British had no option but to depend on the native elite as intermediary. The colonial rule, thus, rested on the collusion and convergence of interests between the imperial and indigenous elites. As Aloysius (1997) has contended, colonial rule in fact empowered, enlarged, elevated and even nationalised the upper strata of society. The lower strata, for all practical purposes, were further marginalised under the colonial dispensation. British rule, however, unwittingly opened some unprecedented channels of physical mobility for the lowered castes, with far-reaching consequences.

The colonial masters encouraged migration to buttress their own interests. It ensured them a cheap supply of labour for various projects, and also served them land revenue. Now the lowered castes could escape the caste stranglehold by migrating to distant places both within the subcontinent and the overseas colonies to become plantation, factory, or mine workers. In addition to this, the doors of the British armies and factories were open for the lowered caste people for employment. The growth of the colonial elites, opening up of the economy with the introduction of industrialisation, and the arrival of the railways helped the caste-oppressed escape village tyrannies. The British had also brought with them a proselytising religion which held promises of equality, dignity, and economic freedom. The poor and the despised now had the option to convert to Christianity. The changed times had also opened for them a small window of educational opportunity, especially in towns and cities. A few educated, semi-educated persons from the lower orders acquired a consciousness of their degraded and deprived status; and, some of them even rose in revolt – Phule was an outstanding example – against the culture of oppression.

The stirrings of awakening among the lowered castes were manifested in the emergence of various forms of activities, protests and organisations. Varying from place to place, community to community, issue to issue, both in intensity and spread, as Aloysius says, the struggles took different forms in different places, depending on the circumstances. There was, however, a common thread running through all these struggles as the oppressed masses attempted to throw out all civic-religious-educational-economic-administrative disabilities imposed on them by the indigenous elites. As the oppression rested on traditional ascriptive order and 'because colonial exploitation involved the extraction of surpluses mediated through caste and community relations, very often caste and community became, in reaction, issues and weapons of resistance for the exploited' (Omvedt 1994: 93). The scattered and uneven movements of the toiling castes – Shanar-Nadars, Parayars in Tamil Nadu; Ezhavas, Pulayas in Kerala; Mahars, Malis, Kunbis in Maharashtra; Malas, Madigas in Andhra Pradesh; Chamars, Ahirs, Koeris, Kurmis in Bihar and Uttar Pradesh; Kaibarta, Rajbansi and Namashudras in Bengal; Dheds, Bhangis in Rajasthan; Chamars-turned-Adi-Dharmis in Punjab, etc., along with similar struggles among Muslim and other communities all across the subcontinent – were economic-political as well as civil and human rights movements (Aloysius 1997).

Dynamics and Dimension of Egalitarian emergence

The issues the lowered caste people raised and fought for centred on citizenship rights. While the privileged 'nationalists' were organising themselves first to demand a greater share in colonial rule and then to launch a movement for total independence, the lower orders had to agitate to ensure their right of access to public places – roads, markets, schools and offices – the right of their women (like in Tamil Nadu and Kerala) to cover their breasts; the right of access to religious places and educational centres; the right to give up agricultural bondage and hereditary occupations and the liberty to choose any other. These struggles were waged not against the white imperialists of the West, but against their own countrymen. Sometimes they had to seek state protection from the indigenous oppressors – brahmans and allied groups of zamindars and moneylenders – who would try to stifle protest and advocacy of civil rights. Many times the agitating masses had to bear the brunt of murderous attacks by the henchmen of local elites.

The emergent 'national' leadership was hand-in-glove with the native colonisers who formed the core group of its supporters. In fact, the 'middle class' nationalist Congress leaders of various professions were also upper caste people, overwhelmingly brahmans, and they invariably had a connection with the land. 'Thus power-holders in the Congress up to the very end tended to oppose anti-landlord legislation and the efforts to protect peasants and tenants' (Omvedt 1994: 89). Not surprisingly, the high priests of cultural nationalism vehemently denounced lower class movements as anti-national attacks on Indian custom and tradition, alleging that the fabric of harmonious and spiritual India was being torn apart. The ascriptive tradition in India that had empowered brahman and allied castes for centuries to operate a very rigorous scheme of domination, internalised through varnashrama-dharma, was the main target of pro-equality social movements.

Education, which had for centuries been the monopoly of a few, became the major thrust of these struggles. Leaders of pro-egalitarian movements stressed that the aquisition of knowledge would enable the oppressed to look critically at the social situation, which in its turn would inspire them to transform a society that had relegated them to a sub-human status. Education was seen as a liberating weapon capable of breaking, to use Paulo Freire's expression, the 'culture of silence' imposed on the dispossessed. As early as 1848 Jotiba Phule had set up a school for untouchable girls, making it clear that education would be his foundation of a cultural reconstruction. Throughout his life Phule stressed the necessity of modern education and scientific knowledge. He was the first leader in modern India to demand mass education. A few years later, Narayana Guru, the chief architect of modern Kerala, advised his people: 'Educate that you may be free and organise that you may be strong'. *Mitavadi*, a journal brought out by his supporters, adopted this maxim above its masthead. Ambedkar's clarion call to depressed classes at the time of founding his first organisation, the Bahishkrit Hitkarani Sabha, in the early 1920s, was: 'Educate, Organise, and Agitate'.

Aloysius has, after Ernest Gellner (1983), argued that mass literacy and education is at the heart of the transition from the pre-national to the national form of society. It is one of the foundations upon which the modern nation is erected. 'The significance of the battles fought all over the length and breadth of this country during colonial times by the shudras and untouchables to gain entry into schools and other educational institutions, much against the resistance, atrocities and oppressions of the powerful high caste, could be better grasped if they are seen as the birth pangs of a modern India' (1997: 82). The non-brahman movements, insofar as they promoted egalitarianism as a social ethos and citizenship rights as the basis of the new polity, contrary to what the elite nationalists would like us to believe, were actually struggling for and strengthening the process of the brith of the nation (ibid.: 80-1).

Thus the colonial period actually saw two nationalisms, two struggles: one for freedom from British rule, for transfer of power from the British to the Indian elite; and one against all kinds of oppression and discrimination. It was the latter that necessitated a structural change in society. These social movements for homogenising and democratising the emerging civil society were

. . . *national in the primary sense of the word; their thrust, in all their unevenness and in spite of their partial nature, was towards the creation of a national socio-political community as distinct from the colonial society on the one hand, and from the society based on ascriptive status on the other. Their discourse is homogenisation or equitable distribution of social power within culture; the main component elements of this discourse are political democracy or citizenship, mass or universal literacy, social mobility and on the agrarian front, denial of ascription in determining social status.*

(Aloysius 1997: 80)

Nationalism from below had a bigger agenda and was a more authentic nationalism in the sense that it demanded equity and justice not for a few, but for all. In a significant way it incorporated people's struggles for education, employment, social mobility, and political power, besides tenancy rights, land, and water which alone could give meaning to freedom. This nationalism was embedded in multiple local struggles and anti-caste movements which erupted in varied forms in all parts of the land during the colonial rule. These struggles revolving around the issues of oppression and emancipation reflected the birth pangs of a civil society.

As early as 1800, a defiant group of Ezhavas, the lowly toddy-tappers of Kerala, claiming equality, tried to enter the famous Vaikkom temple. For challenging the 'sacred tradition' of brahmans, they were brutally killed and their bodies buried in a corner of the temple compounds (Rao 1979: 58-9). This is the first recorded instance in modern India of an agitation against civil and religious disabilities.[1]

In the first half of the nineteenth century, Ezhavas in Kerala and the Tamil counterparts of the Ezhavas – known as Shanars or Nadars – had a running battle with the higher castes for asserting their women's right to wear blouses. Known as the breast-cloth controversy, the struggle against the degrading custom of partial nakedness of their women as a mark of respect to the dominant castes sparked off a determined socio-political fight to throw off the oppressive yoke of caste elites.

In the 1850s, a Mahar boy from Dharwar was refused admission in a government school. He took the matter to the Education Department of Bombay Province, and later to the Government of India at Calcutta. His petition was rejected on the grounds of stiff opposition from the higher castes.

Balak Das, son of Guru Ghasi Das (1756-1836), who transformed the much-despised Chamars of Chhattisagarh into Satnamis, a sect preaching monotheism and the equality of all men, was killed in 1860 for daring to wear the sacred thread. The oppositional order which appropriated some brahmanic symbols to challenge the caste system and relations of power, again organised a thread-wearing ceremony in 1917. This invited the wrath of the upper castes who 'punished the rebels' with violence, beheading several of them and branding sacred threads on their chests and backs. In the teeth of such atrocities, a Satnami Mahasabha was founded which demanded a new identity for the Satnamis and their democratic representation in socio-political sphere.

In 1872-3, a 'Chandala movement' erupted against untouchability, social disabilities and segregation in Faridpur and Bakarganj districts of eastern Bengal. Protesting against social humiliation and material deprivation, the toiling castes refused to serve their tormentors, the higher caste people. After a few months, the social boycott movement petered out as their poverty forced them to return to work. Yet they again rallied during the 1880s to develop the Matua cult, an egalitarian, non-brahmanic form of Vaishnavism, and renamed themselves Namashudras. The man who led the movement was Guru Chanda, who constantly emphasised the need of education for social emancipation and economic betterment. The Namashudras claimed equality, set up schools for their children, and sought new job opportunities in defiance of upper caste resistance.

With equalitarian aspirations, the tribal community in Orissa revived an earlier Mahima or Alekha Dharma under the leadership of Bhima Bhoi (c.1855-94). The tribal poet-prophet Bhima led an ideological struggle against prevailing social and cultural oppression of his people. He often had to face insults, humiliation and hostility due to his radical monotheism and opposition to idolatry and caste system. In 1881, he led a march to the seat of brahmanical power – Puri – to reclaim the supposedly hidden Buddha image beneath the statue of Jagannath from priestly clutches. The villagers from nearby areas who unsuccessfully tried to enter the Puri temple were detained and tortured.

At the turn of the twentieth century, the Moamaris and other lowered castes in Assam organised themselves into political bodies to overcome various civil disabilities and promote education among their children. Several despised castes discarded their traditional names and identities and demanded education, social equality and diversification of occupation.

The early years of the twentieth century witnessed spontaneous as well as organised protests from lower orders in Bihar and Uttar Pradesh. Tribeni Sangh, an association of Koeri-Kurmi-Yadav castes in Bihar, and several lowered caste bodies in Uttar Pradesh were fighting against *begar* (forced labour) and defying prohibitions about the wearing of the sacred thread, footwear and the use of horses and palanquins. In village after village they refused to perform *begar* for zamindars and also refused to pay the increased taxes imposed on them. The Yadavs at many places refused to sell cow-dung cakes, curd and milk to landowning higher castes at concessional rates.

Anger and revulsion against caste-feudalism and human bondage was building up among the oppressed across the subcontinent from the early nineteenth century. It found expression in myriad ways – sometimes under religious garb, at other times directly confrontationist under purely secular agenda. In region after region, the exploited peasantry and labour consisting mainly of lowered castes and untouchables were rising in revolt against servitude (forced or free labour and *nazrana* or gifts). High caste zamindars, appointed by the British to collect revenue, and *mahajans*, the exploitative moneylenders, had become the terror of the poor living in villages.

The tenants and landless workers had to bear the brunt of the practice of 'free labour, rent-farming, arbitrary evictions, cheating, juggling of accounts, and all forms of physical maltreatment including not too rarely murder' (Aloysius 1997). It was in such oppressive circumstances that the nineteenth and early twentieth centuries witnessed a series of peasant revolts – the Deccan grain riots, the Pabna agrarian agitation, the Mapilla revolts, and the tribal revolts of the Santhals and the Mundas, and the cultivators' agitations in the plains of Bihar and Uttar Pradesh. These movements along with the anti-caste agitations all over the subcontinent, 'more than any other, systematically exposed the collusive and collaborative nature of colonialism – a product of complicity between the imperial and indigenous elite against the lower castes and tribes who constituted the majority' (ibid.: 74).

Thus, the late nineteenth and early twentieth century – a period of spectacular rise of cultural nationalism and movement for transfer of power – witnessed widespread awakening of political consciousness among the lowered castes and communities all over the country. Their egalitarian aspirations produced several streams of movement against the stranglehold of ascriptive hierarchy, slavery and caste-feudal exploitation. These struggles threw up a determined lot of leaders who were unrelenting critics of caste and its consequences. These anti-caste campaigners confronted the hypocritical nationalist leadership for keeping pro-equality social movements out of the 'national agenda'. Phule, Shahu Maharaj and Ambedkar in Maharashtra; Iyothee Thass and Periyar E.V. Ramaswami Naicker in Tamil Nadu; Narayana Guru, Dr. Palpu, Kumaran Asan, K. Ayyappan and Ayyankali in Kerala; Bhagyareddy Varma in Andhra; Mangoo Ram and Chhotu Ram in Punjab; Acchutanand and Ram Charan in Uttar Pradesh; Hari Chanda Thakur, Guru Chanda and Jogendranath Mandal in Bengal; Sonadhar Senapathy in Assam; and many lesser-known social crusaders all mocked the patriotic pretensions of indigenous elites, and attacked the system of exploitation at every level. They rejected the high caste culture tradition and tried to create socio-religious practices embedded in India's non-brahmanic culture. It is remarkable that all of them underlined, in their own distinctive idioms, Phule's basic contention that 'just as India went through a phase of British colonisation, it had previously passed at various stages of its history through brahmanical colonialism'. Linking the present hierarchy and exploitation to the historical past, they pointed out that the internal colonialism has its roots in a false philosophy and a pseudo-religion which sanctify caste-based discrimination and domination. In the course of their struggle against the priestly-feudal tradition, they tried to underscore the existence of a parallel – many identified it as the Buddhist/shramanic – tradition which, they reckoned, was more conducive for the development of a new, democratic and egalitarian culture.

Narayana Guru and Kerala's Liberation Movement

Today, Kerala is hailed as a model of modern progressive state with 100 per cent literacy and spectacular achievements in terms of socio-economic advancement and human development. But not long ago, the state was a hotbed of appalling backwardness, untouchability and unapproachability, where the lower classes were subjected to the most degrading and dehumanising practices. The notorious practice of *theendal* or 'distance pollution' was reflective of the subhuman status of the lowered caste people who suffered worst kinds of atrocities at the hands of the high caste Hindus like Nambudiris and Nayars.[2] The Ezhava community which form a major chunk of the state population is regarded today as an affluent OBC, but at the turn of the twentieth century its members were considered no better than the untouchables. Like other depressed castes, they suffered from several social-cultural disabilities. They were not allowed to use tanks and wells, or roads and bridges that ran near upper caste homes and temples. They were not allowed to wear footwear or carry an umbrella. Their women were not permitted to use any upper garments to cover their breasts. Forced to render free services to the higher castes, they were denied admission to public schools, and were kept away from administrative services (Rao 1979: 24). The prevailing idea among the dominant castes, who enjoyed many privileges and on that strength had lately monopolised access to English education and government jobs, was that the lowly Ezhavas should confine themselves to their traditional occupations like farming, toddy-tapping, and weaving.

Resentment was simmering for quite sometime against the oppressive situation that obtained in Travancore, Cochin and Malabar. As early as 1885 Dr. Palpu (1863-1950), the first Ezhava graduate who could not get a government job due to his caste, demanded the removal of social and civil disabilities against lower orders. He led a popular campaign for lowered caste entry to public schools and employment in civil services. A memorandum signed by 13,176 Ezhavas was, for example, given in 1896 to the ruler of Travancore, asking that government schools and the public service be opened up to them. The request was turned down on the presumed grounds that the Ezhavas did not require to aspire for education or government jobs! This response only steeled the determination of Dr. Palpu and his associates to intensify the movement. Society was in ferment – the new forces were surging ahead for change, while the old order was refusing to die down. It was at about this time that Narayana Guru (c.1854-1928), an ascetic belonging to Ezhava caste, appeared on the scene, and through his imaginative public activities and campaigns played the role of liberator.

Narayana Guru was a multi-faceted moral warrior who believed that true spirituality could flower only in a humane, harmonious and congenial atmosphere. What he saw around him – widespread misery, ignorance, and the negation of basic human rights to a vast majority of people in the name of traditional religion – appalled him. Shudras and avarnas who together form more than 80 per cent of the total population were debarred from entering the sacred domain of religion. This meant they had no right to become religious aspirants or leaders. Narayana Guru created history by establishing scores of debrahmanised temples, ashramas and academic institutions. His initiative released socio-cultural forces that not only challenged the material aspect of upper caste domination, but also set in motion the subversion of the brahmanical hierarchy. The movement Narayana Guru led proved momentous and marked the beginning of the end of the old regime.

At the time of the first consecration on 10 February 1888 at Aruvipuram in south Travancore, he simply picked up a stone from a nearby stream and installed it as a Shiva shrine. The incident sent shock waves among bigoted brahmans who angrily demanded what right Narayana Guru had as an Ezhava to consecrate an idol of

Shiva. Guru silenced his detractors with the minimum fuss: 'I consecrated the Ezhava Shiva – not the Brahman Shiva – and I did it for the untouchable Ezhavas.' His devastating play of wit was again at its sparkling best when the purists accused him of committing a grave mistake by not consulting astrologers for ascertaining the auspicious time for consecrating the idol. 'We cast a horoscope only after a child is born, and not the other way about, don't we? The idol has been sanctified. Now you may please cast the horoscope' (Kunhappa 88: 25-6). Subsequently, Guru set up a parallel chain of temples in different parts of the state where everyone was welcome, including the lowest-of-the-low Pulayas and other untouchable castes. When a memorial temple was built at the site of his first consecration at Aruvipuram, Guru got the following message engraved there:

Here is a model abode
Where men live like brothers:
Bereft of the prejudice of caste
Or the rancour of religious differences. (ibid.: 23)

Guru was born and brought up in a conservative milieu. The ordinary people of that era had enormous faith in established religious practices; he did not fail to fill those symbols with altogether new, radical and egalitarian human values. In other words, his vision was not to set up places of worship for the downtrodden communities – in later years, he even had to face flak from several of his radical associates for promoting idolatry and irrationality on this count – but to make an egalitarian society where new forms of creativity and compassion could evolve on the ideological foundation of 'One Caste, One Religion and One God for Man'. On one occasion, for instance, he spelt out the purposes of undertaking a pilgrimage as general education, human understanding, organisation of the followers of his faith, besides devotion to God.

The temples Narayana Guru established were harbingers of social change as the officiating priests in all these temples were considered impure in the varna hierarchies. More important, he visualised these temples as centres of constructive activity and educational opportunities for the deprived people. Guru was particular that every temple should have gardens around it, there should be schools as well as vocational and technical centres too as ancillary to these temples. The money received as offerings should be utilised for the greater public good, promoting the cause of mass education. The fact that he envisioned these temples as parallel institutions is evident from his insistence on many occasions that the temple buildings and premises must be used as schools, libraries, meeting halls, or even weaving sheds.

He constantly emphasised the need of modern education in both English and Malayalam with a view to promoting a modern outlook and employment opportunities in new fields. The motto he gave to his followers was: 'Educate that you may be free, and organise that you may be strong'. In a speech in 1910, to the Vijnana Vardhini Sabha at Cherai, Guru also underlined the need for women's education and for technical training to establish industries. He stressed that the setting up of temples was not an end in itself. He was unhappy that temples did not play the desired role of bringing people together; instead, he noted with concern, they only heightened caste divide. This made him declare in a message in 1917 that he considered educational institutions to be the real temples which would educate people into sinking caste differences:

People are likely to regret the spending of money on construction of temples. . . . The major temples should be educational institutions. . . . It was thought that through temples, all people could be brought together without caste distinctions. But the experience doesn't justify the hope. Temples increase caste barriers. Now we must try to educate the people. Let them have more knowledge; that is the only way of improving them. (George 1991: 17)

Guru was a social revolutionary beneath his religious garb, a revolutionary whose heart overflowed with compassion for his fellow beings, a revolutionary who never raised the pitch of his voice in his struggle to raise public consciousness. Some scholars see Guru's socio-cultural movement within the parameter of orthodox Hinduism because of his love for Sanskrit and Vedanta philosophy. It may be noted, however, that his system of thought and multi-pronged activities, oriented as they were towards socio-cultural transformation, was embedded in a strong denial of caste, which was the actual sum and substance of the Vedic-brahmanism in terms of social vision. Unlike Gandhi, he was sensitive to the cultural implications of the co-option of the caste-oppressed into brahmanical modes of worship. That was why he sought to create new places of worship rather than initiate a campaign for the entry of lowered castes into brahmanical temples. Through the debrahmanisation of religion, the democratisation of education, the diversification of occupations, and the adoption of a generally rational approach to society and culture, Narayana Guru strove to build an egalitarian and enlightened social order which necessarily implied a determined struggle against discriminatory brahmanism. As such Guru was a standard bearer of India's non-brahmanic tradition. He carried forward the legacy of the counter-culture which had challenged the system of inequity and injustice since the Buddha's time.

Guru's greatest ambition was to resurrect and revitalise a demoralised and dangerously divisive society through cultural-educational empowerment of the masses. For this greater common good he was willing to embrace anyone, irrespective of differences in ideologies and strategies. An ever-evolving saintly figure, he respected democratic dissent and the divergence of opinions which enabled him to carry along a motley band of creative thinker-activists with wide differences in mental make-up and temperament. The leading associates whose talents and hard work took the movement to glorious heights included Dr. Palpu, the learned social activist and an impassioned campaigner for education; Kumaran Asan (1873-1924), one of the greatest poet-visionaries of modern Kerala who considered – and preferred like so many of Guru's colleagues – (egalitarian) Buddhism as the anti-thesis to discriminatory Hinduism; C. V. Cunhuraman (1871-1949), the supreme rationalist who refused to accept anything unless he was intellectually convinced about it; K. Ayyappan (1889-1969), an agnostic and a thorough-going radical who changed Guru's slogan of 'One Caste, One Religion and One God for Man' to 'No Caste, No Religion, and No God for Mankind'; and T. K. Madhavan (1886-1930), a moderate who resorted to satyagraha for rights and dignity for the untouchables.

A brilliant organiser and institution-builder, Guru felt the need for a powerful secular body to reach out to the masses, and encouraged some of his closest colleagues to set up such an organisation. A society called the Sree Narayana Dharma Paripalana Yogam, popularly known as the SNDP, was founded in 1903 for the dissemination of ideals of Sree Narayana Dharma, for the empowerment of the backward and oppressed communities. Open to everyone without caste distinction, the SNDP soon became a hugely popular organisation. Its annual gatherings attracted thousands of volunteers. Palpu and Kumaran Asan played a leading role in galvanising the organisation into a powerful vehicle of socio-cultural transformation. Palpu organised a women's conference which became a regular feature at the annual meetings. A great votary of science and technology, he also organised an industrial exhibition in 1905 as part of the SNDP annual conference.

Palpu and Asan led a popular agitation to secure the admission of Ezhava boys and girls to public schools. This resulted in a series of violent clashes between Ezhavas and high caste Nayars. For instance, when a school at Haripat was thrown open to Ezhavas by the then Dewan of Travancore in 1903, the infuriated Nayars went on a rampage, robbing Ezhava houses and attacking Ezhava school boys (Rao 1979: 49). The lowered castes' right to enter the educational domain was thus won in a protracted struggle waged by the SNDP. The Ezhava agitation for educational rights inspired other deprived and oppressed communities to launch similar struggles. Several lowered caste organisations sprang up at the turn of the century to promote education of their men and women. New schools were set up and pressure for the admission of depressed classes to state-run schools mounted. The spread of education among the deprived did not wait for sarkari action, much of it came through peoples' own efforts.

Traditionally, Ezhavas were divided into several sub-castes, Thiyyas, Chovans, Thendans, etc., who did not intermarry and indulged in many superstitions and unsavoury practices. Guru's movement helped mould them into one community, and made them amenable to shedding meaningless customs and expensive rites. Guru urged his followers to give up alcoholism and traditional jobs like toddy-tapping, and instead seek employment in new industries, crafts and trade. For this purpose, the SNDP organised industrial exhibitions, and conducted several vocational training programmes. It must not be construed, however, that the SNDP's activities and concerns were confined to Ezhavas. Its leaders made a conscious and concerted endeavour to break barriers among castes. The society's temples, institutions, hostels, etc. were open to all people, including the Pulayas, Parayas, and Cherumas. And as Guru's biographer, Murkot Kumaran, has puckishly put it, 'Even brahmans were permitted temple entry!' The SNDP took the shape of a popular movement and had a cascading effect on all castes – including Nambudiris and Nayars – by making them realise the need to discard the vestiges of the past and replace them with values and institutions appropriate for the modern time. Above all, it launched a vigorous campaign against the disabilities suffered by the depressed castes by rousing public consciousness and warning the orthodox to change their ways. Poet Asan put the high-and-mighty on notice with the prophetic call:

> *Change you the laws yourselves, or else,*
> *The laws will change you indeed.* (George 1991: 66)

The SNDP's call was bold and categorical: either the ascriptive rules should be drastically changed or else those who upheld them would be put in their place, that is, the dustbin of history. The radical prophecy came true as the entrenched interest groups had to yield ground to the awakened masses. This heralded the dawn of a new era marked by the arrival of the hitherto excluded people in the public sphere. Now, lowered caste people could fearlessly walk on public roads; it was no longer possible to stop them from entering schools, colleges, and other public domains.

Kumaran Asan, the executive secretary of the SNDP for a long time, used his creative talent to a give a strong cultural base to the movement. Reckoned as one of the three greats of modern Malyalam poetry – the other two being Vallathola and Parameswara Iyer – Asan blazed a new trail in the literary arena with his innovative techniques and radical content. Many of his poems were inspired by a passion for social reconstruction. He wielded his pen to arouse profound patriotic feelings and revulsion against caste among the masses. In 1908, he wrote with anguish:

> *Thy slavery is thy destiny, O Mother!*
> *Thy sons, blinded by caste, clash among themselves*

And get killed; what for is freedom then? (Sarkar 1983)

In *Duravastha* (The Deplorable Condition), he brings out the inhumanity of the caste system. The poem shows how the Mappillas, converts to Islam from outcastes, had embraced the new religion to escape the atrocities of the Hindu upper castes. And then, as a poetic justice, he weaves a suitable narrative to bring together in matrimony a Nambudiri woman and a Pulaya man. The marriage between the highest and the lowest in the hierarchy invited the venom of many savarna critics, but Asan defended himself by saying that the poem was inspired by the ideal of a casteless society.

Asan saw the Buddha as a historical role-model against inegalitarian brahmanism. In his view, after the Buddha 'there have not appeared great men who fought against the caste system and won the victory' (Awaya 1999). No wonder, some of his most celebrated poems, especially those containing the poignant criticism of caste like *Chandalabhikshuki* (The Untouchable Nun) and *Karuna* (The Compassion), are anchored in Buddhist narrative. His enthusiasm for Buddhism also made him render Edwin Arnold's *The Light of Asia* into Malayalam under the title *Sri Buddha Charitam*.

Asan's ardour for Buddhism was not an isolated case. The urge to embrace Buddhism among Kerala's lowered caste intelligentsia was quite strong, and manifested itself in various forms throughout the movement. Linking their present condition to the history of Buddhism in the region, they asserted that because of lowered caste attachment to Buddhism even after the spread of brahmanism in Kerala, their social position was pushed down to the lowest rung of caste hierarchy. In this light, their social marginalisation, they argued, could be interpreted as a result of their historic resistance against the onslaught of brahmanism (Awaya 1999).

Amidst the social ferment and quest of an alternative culture, many intellectuals associated with SNDP activities presented Buddhism as the anti-thesis to discriminatory Hinduism. Stalwarts of the movement were opposed to the fight-from-within-the-Hinduism line adopted by Guru. In line with outstanding subaltern theoreticians elsewhere in contemporary as well as later periods (Phule, Iyothee Thass, Ambedkar et al.), they believed that so long as they remained within Hinduism they would not attain dignity and equality. One Sivaprasada Swami, for example, wrote an article in *Mitavadi* (February 1917) in which while reflecting on the SNDP activities, he deplored its strategy of remaining within Hinduism: '. . . So far as we remained within Hinduism, we who were born to a depressed class would remain depressed.' He also dashed off a letter to Narayana Guru in which he stressed the fact that the more Guru spread Vedic teaching, the more caste consciousness was strengthened. His suggestion to Guru was to start a new religion, preferably such a religion as Buddhism which denied caste. Siva Swami was not the only one who was inclined to convert to Buddhism. It was a view championed by top leaders like K. Ayyappan and C. Krishnan, and supported by the Ezhava youths (ibid.).

Enthusiasm for revival of Buddhism was considerable, but there was no unanimity on the issue. There were people like Cunhuraman who preferred Christianity, while a few others like T. K. Madhavan were against conversion to any other religion. But the principal factor that tilted the scale against large-scale conversion to Buddhism was Guru's own inclination against the adventurous project. In his characteristic style, he offset the tide of conversion, and pacified the Buddhist enthusiasts by arguing that 'whatever is one's religion, it is sufficient that man be good'. Nevertheless, many of his followers remained committed to Buddhism as an emancipatory religion, and some of them – C. Krishnan and R. Sugatan are two prominent examples – actually converted. In his book *The Light of Buddhist Teaching* (1929), Krishnan interpreted Buddhism in a radical light and laid emphasis on its rational and ethical aspects. He contended that Buddhism, unlike Hinduism, only gives the principle or method of how to lead a meaningful life without the externalia, dogmas, rituals, and practices like offering money and food to deities and priests. A similar approach was adopted by R. Sugatan, who was to become an outstanding leader of the trade union and communist movement in the state. Sugatan and his friends went on to establish an organisation called the Buddha Mission in their native place Alleppey to spread Buddhism.

A significant fallout of the elusive quest for an emancipatory religion was the socio-political radicalisation in the 1920s and 1930s that led to the remarkable growth of rationalism and socialism in the state. The rationalists held a meeting in 1925 at the Advait

Ashram established by Guru in Alwaye, and started a Malyalam magazine called *Yuktivadi* (The Rationalist) with K. Ayyappan as its editor. Another important development in the 1930s was the Swatantra Samudayam (Independent Community) movement that rejected all religions and stressed the need to restructure society and economy on modern and egalitarian values. The leaders of the movement held the view that the Ezhava and other lowered castes should declare that they were an independent community – not Hindus – and that without converting to any religion they should opt for an enlightened atheism. They attacked institutionalised religions, especially caste-ridden Hinduism, for promoting injustice and obscurantism. E. Madhavan wrote *Swatantra Samudayam* in 1934 in which he held religion responsible for chaining man to ideas that gravely harmed his progress. He saw organised religion as a threat to advancement of science and education, freedom of expression, and peaceful co-existence. Hinduism, he argued, had promoted additional evils such as the institutionalised disenfranchisement of women and lowered castes. The temple down the ages had been a hotbed of discrimination and superstition, stunting the growth of social and moral values, Madhavan contended. He also took Gandhi to task for supporting varna ideology and promoting hypocritical temple-entry as the panacea for the caste-oppressed (Awaya 1999: 155).

The SNDP movement always raised its voice against injustice and discrimination. Guru's unitarian doctrine – One Caste, One Religion, One God for Man – was often held up as a strong repudiation of caste and hierarchical social order. Its leaders not only protested against the injustices suffered by the Ezhavas but also challenged the whole issue of discrimination based on birth. They pleaded with their caste members and others to treat the castes considered inferior to them with equality. An outstanding figure in this regard was K. Ayyappan, the man who took up the issue of freedom, dignity and human rights of the most despised castes with a revolutionary zeal. His organisation, Sahodara Sangham (The Association of Brotherhood), celebrated its first anniversary by burning the effigy of a monster symbolising caste. He identified himself with the plight of the untouchables, and wanted all the lowered castes to mix together, interdine, intermarry, and move forward together. More important, he practised what he preached, actively promoting brotherhood among all people. His commensality activities with Pulayas and other radical measures incurred the wrath of the conservative elements of his own caste. He was even excommunicated for a while, and accused of taking too much liberty with Guru's teaching. Nicknamed 'Sahodara Ayyappan' and jeered as 'Pulayam Ayyappan' for his thoroughgoing humanism, he was made to suffer so much that he had to approach Narayana Guru for advice. Guru, however, was very pleased with Ayyappan's activities. Showing full solidarity with him, he even gave him his support in writing: 'Whatever be the religion, language, custom, caste or dress of individuals, since they are all human beings, there can be no objection to their interdining or intermarrying' (Kunhappa 1988: 56). This silenced Ayyappan's critics.

The SNDP movement preceded the Congress-led national movement by a few years in Kerala. When Congress nationalism gained some ground in the state in the early 1920s, its elitist orientation did not enthuse the lower class leadership. Though they had high expectations from Gandhi, they soon became disillusioned with him. They attacked the upper caste national leadership for neglecting social issues and caste discrimination. Ayyappan pointedly asked Gandhi why he did not call such Indians devilish who were treating Pulayas, Parayas and other lowly castes as sub-human beings, though he fulminated against the British and called them 'devil-like' and 'satanic' for their oppression of Indians. Ayyappan gave voice to the general anguish of the lower classes when he bitterly remarked that neither Gandhi nor other leaders of the national movement had comprehended the evil of caste and cultural oppression.

However, the SNDP leadership was quick to seize Gandhi's distinctive use of satyagraha as a political weapon. In fact, the Ezhava leaders reinterpreted and adopted satyagraha in more radical light, and innovatively deployed it against caste discrimination in the region. As early as October 1918, the Passive Resistance League was established in Kozhikode to fight social evils like *theendal*. The Congress' temple satyagrahas in the 1920s, particularly at Vaikkom and Guruvayur, were not only inspired by the SNDP movement but the bulwork of mass support also came from its cadre.

T. K. Madhavan, the organising secretary of the SNDP during the 1920s, was the main proponent for passing the temple entry resolution at the 1923 Kakinada Congress Conference. And it was he who led the Vaikkom satyagraha from the front. Even before that, Madhavan and Ayyappan had themselves entered the prohibited area, defying the exclusion of lowered castes from the temple and surrounding areas. For the Congress, temple-entry was little more than a political ploy to win the mass support for its hegemonic ambitions, while the SNDP leaders viewed it as a step towards a bigger social movement. Irrepressible leaders like Ayyappan, for example, soon got tired of this non-issue, and went on to criticise Madhavan for exhausting people's energies for a minor issue like temply-entry.

Even Narayana Guru was utterly unsatisfied with the mild Vaikkom satyagraha as he wanted the agitationists to 'scale over the barricades' and not only walk along the prohibited roads but enter all temples (Sarkar 1983: 244). On the other hand, the Congress remained obnoxioulsy conservative on caste while paying the lip-service to issues like temple-entry. Nowhere was it more evident than Gandhi's famous conversation with Narayana Guru in which the former shamelessly defended caste categories saying that all leaves of the same tree are not identical in shape and texture. To this, Narayana Guru pointed out that the difference is only superficial, but not in essence – the juice of all leaves of a particular tree would be the same in content. But the sanatani Gandhi was not convinced; his faith in varnashrama-dharma remained unshakeable to the last.

The SNDP movement galvanised the 'untouchables' into collective action to throw off the yoke of slavery. The lowly Pulayas came forward to assert their civil rights, walking on main roads, entering market places, attending schools, and claiming right to own land. In a dramatic fashion, Ayyankali (1863-1941) led Pulayas, driving their bullock carts, through the thoroughfares of town after town, defying the tradition that denied them access to public roads. Under his leadership, Pulaya women gathered at several places to publicly assert their right to cover their breasts and cast away the *kallumalai*, the garland of stone – the symbol of their social slavery – that was their only sanctioned covering above the waist (Saradmoni

1980: 152-3). In 1907, he organised the Sadhu Jana Paripalan Sangham, the membership of which was not confined to the Pulayas. Though himself illiterate, he led a movement for modern education and vocational training for all communities, particularly among the Cherumas, Parayas, and Pulayas and their womenfolk. He set up several schools for untouchable girls in the teeth of resistance by the higher castes. Ayyankali created history around 1915 by organising the first-ever landless agricultural workers' strike in the subcontinent, which was not for any economic demand but to insist on the right of untouchable children to attend schools (ibid.: 149).

Later, the Ezhava-Pulaya struggle expanded to include Christians and Muslims in a bigger alliance, and together they formed the Civil Rights League in 1919, which demanded, among other things, universal franchise and equality of citizenship. All in all, the SNDP movement 'effectively laid the first foundation stones for the new civil society in Kerala through promotion of education both literary and technical, diversification of occupations and vertical social mobility' (Aloysius 1997). Narayana Guru's middle-of-the-road approach, as against the more radical course advocated by firebrand leaders like Ayyappan, did not raise much dust, but shifted the pyramid of social and cultural hierarchy. It started a state-wide social process which gave a body blow to the old order.

DRAVIDIAN UPSURGENCE: IYOTHEE THASS AND THE JUSTICE PARTY

In the Tamil land, the second half of the nineteenth century witnessed sporadic yet determined attempts by lowered castes to articulate their deprivation and humiliation, and also a sense of longing to belong to their original Dravidian culture. Here, it was easy to give linguistic, ethnic, and indigenous identity to the non-brahmans who had a language with non-Sanskrit origin, recognised as Dravidian or Tamil.[3] Their oppressive present and distorted past were attributed to the alien invasion of brahmans, descendants of the Aryan conquerors. Such reinterpretations of the past was buttressed by the situation that obtained in the region, strengthening the suspicion that the south India's brahmans were still conspiring to suppress the Dravidian people and their culture.

Here, the Dravidian radicals adopted their indigenous and autonomous Tamil literary traditions in a battle for social and political equality. Emphasising the pre-Sanskrit and non-Aryan Dravidian heritage of the south, several Tamil Sangams were formed in cities like Madurai and Madras. The revival of interest in ancient Tamil classics spurred the publication of many journals which attacked the alien and oppressive brahmanic culture. The *Ramayana* was turned on its head by glorifying Ravana and depicting Rama as the villain; the murder of Shambuk the untouchable boy by Rama was mourned and roundly condemned. The Dravidar Kazhagam of 1882 raised and debated the ideological matrix of Dravidianism. At the turn of the new century, the stage was set for emergence of a powerful non-brahman movement in the region.

Iyothee Thass (1845-1914), a dalit by birth and a Buddhist by conviction, was an outstanding figure in the socio-cultural awakening which preceded the spectacular rise of a non-brahman movement in the Tamil land (Geetha and Rajadurai 1998; Aloysius 1998). An idealogue and a cultural crusader, Iyothee Thass' novel ideas and activities broke new ground in the subaltern struggle for identity, human dignity, and justice.[4] Realising the liberatory potential of Buddhist tradition and drawing on the Tamil-Buddhist connection in the past, Iyothee was the first to interpret the history, religion and literature of the Tamils from the viewpoint of a Buddhist presence in the region. His writings taken together with the work of some of his associates like Masilamani comprise a corpus which represent a Buddhist vision of the Indian past. Part history and part polemic, their writings anticipated, in many ways, the historiograhical writings of Ambedkar (Geetha and Rajadurai 1998). 'More important, they prefigured and, to an extent, overlapped with an emergent Dravidianism which . . . provided a wholly new historiographical tradition. Directed against the Aryan version of history, this latter came to articulate a historical sensibility that was assertive in its Tamilness and scornful of what it considered the Aryan element in India's culture' (ibid.: 92).

It is not well-known that Iyothee Thass was the pioneer of what is now known as neo-Buddhism in India. Based in Madras, he founded the South Indian Buddhist Association which by 1910 had many branches in India and abroad (Aloysius 1998). Tamil Buddhism was constructed on the matrix of castelessness since the Aryan-brahmanic introduction of caste system in a casteless region was perceived as the crucial factor that led to 'discriminatory distinction in public life, both secular as well as sacred'. What was remarkable about Tamil Buddhism, according to Aloysius, was its ability to evolve and articulate the concerns of the marginalised and caste-oppressed into a universal vision of emancipation for all. 'Subaltern concerns – such as the welfare measures for the upliftmen of the poor, removal of civil disabilities of the 'outcaste', etc. are, here, seen as being inseparable from those of the social whole; and sectional emancipation is unthinkable without simultaneously effecting an overall structural change. And this was done through subtle shifts in emphasis: from ascriptive groups to organising principles and from sectarian obsession to universal vision. The emancipatory strategies of a religion of the oppressed are necessarily the opposite of those of the oppressors' (ibid.: 153-4).

Iyothee Thass who led this movement from the front also spearheaded a campaign for education among the 'untouchables'. Along with his colleagues he set up several schools in lowered caste enclaves in urban centres. A Tamil scholar and Siddha medical practitioner, he ran a popular weekly, *Tamizhan,* for years. Besides, he published scores of pamphlets and tracts by him and his associates which were widely circulated among Tamils everywhere. The articles he wrote for *Tamizhan* give an idea of the astounding range of his concerns: caste hegemony, untouchability, indigenous medicine, agricultural rituals, folk deities, issues involved in a census and conversions, Buddhism and Jainism in the Tamil land. His writings are remarkably modern not only for their insight into the nature of society, but also for espousing the cause of social emancipation, Buddhism, rationalism, and the new egalitarian Dravidian identity.

Iyothee Thass was among the earliest non-brahman, Adi-Dravida intellectuals who presented a systematic and sharp critique of brahmanical power, the brahman's role in the modern society and polity, and above all, the brahman's espousal of a problematic nationalism (Geetha and Rajadurai 1998). He drew attention to rampant civil injustices and various acts of social and ritual discrimination that ensured brahman exclusivity. He cited several instances of prejudice and discrimination practised by not only brahman proponents of nationalism, but by the largely brahman-owned press and the brahman publicists who mediated and engineered public opinion. It is remarkable that he located the power of the moden, secular brahman in the control he excercised over the construction of public opinion (ibid.: 63). On many occasions, he pointed out the caste bias and rancour prevalent in the orientation and presentation of events or opinions in the brahman-dominated nationalist press. Appalled by the brahman's proclivity to fortify his caste status and promote their own castemen whenever in position of power, he asserted that a caste, so possessed of its own interests and forced expropriation of the interests and concerns of others, could hardly be considered national or representative (ibid.).

Iyothee Thass linked the unrepresentative nature and content of the brahman-piloted swaraj and swadeshi projects to 'a flawed epistemology and a jaundiced world-view' (ibid.: 66). Probing into the brahmanical world-view and its deleterious implications, he held all brahmanical learning to be unproductive and passive because, he insisted, it induced laziness and reduced knowledge to a concern with the superficial. According to him, the brahman's contemplative knowledge deters him from aligning that knowledge to work and action. Divorced from the creative realm, his intellectual energy is expended on gratuitous tasks such as defining the rules of touchability, seeability and approachability. Second, his age-old indulgence in the art of religious inquiry keeps breeding new creeds, each advancing its own claims on truth and wisdom through endless hair-splitting and convoluted arguments. This world-view and knowledge-system, Iyothee Thass argues, has not changed with the brahman's acquisition of modern education: he is more interested in flaunting his mastery over English grammar than expressing an intelligible, useful, and relevant thought or idea. Not surprisingly, the new political ideal produced by the grotesque and insular knowledge-system of the brahman seemed to Iyothee Thass as deeply problematic and deficient as the tradition which informed it (ibid.: 66-7). Highly critical of the elitist nationalism, he was categorical that unless this nationalism heeded the concerns and anxieties of the producing masses and until it learnt to express itself in people's language, it could neither be representative nor effective.

Led by a host of civic leaders and social critics like Iyothee Thass, the southern people began a battle for the recovery of their past as well as establishment of their rights in the present. The intellectual ferment thus generated unleashed forces that led to the emergence of a powerful political non-brahmanism in the then Madras Presidency consisting of Tamil Nadu, Karnataka, Andhra and Malabar Kerala. The South Indian Liberal Federation, commonly known as the Justice Party, was formed in 1916, on an anti-Congress, anti-brahmanical plank with the objective of radical redistribution of socio-political power. Thyagaraya Chetty and T. M. Nair played a pivotal role in the 'shudra movement' by issuing in December 1916 the Non-Brahman Manifesto against the overwhelming preponderance of brahmans in the fields of education, public service, and politics. Brahman domination in the public sphere was clearly reflected in statistics. While 80 per cent of the brahman populace was literate, barely four per cent of non-brahman people had learnt the alphabet, let alone derived the benefits of higher education. According to the 1901 census, brahmans accounted for only three per cent of the Presidency population, but between 1897 and 1904 they had secured 94 per cent of positions in the Provincial Civil Service. In 1914, 450 out of the 650 registered graduates of the Madras University were brahmans. In 1914, out of 16 individuals elected as delegates of the Congress from the region 14 were brahmans. Up to 1901, there was not a single non-brahman representative in the Madras Legislative Council (Irschick 1969).

Leading Justicites hammered home the point that the brahmans had usurped all real power, while the toiling masses, cultivators and others who constitute 97 per cent of the population had not even a semblance of power in their hands. Demanding democratic representation for non-brahman castes in the fields of education, administration and legislation, Justice leaders lashed out at the brahman-dominated Congress nationalism, and claimed that the non-brahman movement cherished very different ideas about Indian nation-building and national representation. To the non-brahmans, the progress could not mean the 'development along modern lines of any particular class or section' (Geetha and Rajadurai: 127). Implicit in this assertion was the view that nationalistic imperative to free the country from colonial rule should not obscure and subsume the vital question of internal discrimination and subordination. The Justicites, therefore, insisted that if democratic ideals were to be realised in practice, mere affirmations of equality without any change on the ground would make no difference. The non-brahmans, who constituted the 'producing communities', they asserted, would have to come forward to wrest power from the entrenched interests of a tiny minority. Declaring caste as antithetical to the national unity, M. V. Naidu, a prominent Justicite, underlined the fact that the practice of democracy required the substitution of caste sentiment by a truly national sentiment. Caste differences in India, he stressed, had thwarted the growth of common sympathies and the spirit of cooperation which bound people together into a political community. Efforts to blend different communities into a homogeneous whole had not succeeded, he contended, because of systematic opposition by orthodox Hindus (ibid.: 127-8).

Presenting the Justice road-map, leaders like Thyagaraya Chetty and Nair exuded confidence that the non-brahmans could attain a unity and wholeness, both in their resistance to the brahman power and through assertion and practice of an alternative culture and community with their own values and conventions. Chetty extolled the 'genius of Dravidian civilisation', and held that it does not recognise difference between man and man by birth (ibid.). Significantly, the Justicites suggested four lines of action for putting democratic principles into practice. First, non-brahmans were to educate themselves in large numbers. Second, they were to work for their and the country's economic development. Third, they were to come together and work to ensure proportional representation for all communities in administration and in the legislative bodies. Last, they were to make efforts, through their unified interaction, to build a casteless fraternity of people that abided by modern values and ethos (ibid.: 128-9).

This was a tall order. While it was relatively easy to work, through both legislation and action, on issues like mass education and proportional representation, no purposive action on the question of economic advancement and social transformation was possible without a programme of systematic and structural change. Given the formidable socio-historical circumstances and very limited power under the dyarchy under which the Justice Party was constrained to operate, it could not bring in any structural changes. Moreover, the city-based and English-educated Justice leaders, notwithstanding their claim to represent the entire non-brahmans, peasants, workers and artisans were not in a position to galvanise the depressed masses living in remote villages or towns. However, it was in respect of education and affirmative action in government jobs, the Justice Party indeed played a historic role. Here the Justicites were able to address – and bring together – the non-brahman masses, all of whom were sensitive to the historical wrongs done by brahmans. Even in this instance, the Justice Party had to face up to an extremely hostile brahman press and a brahman-dominated public sphere (ibid.: 129). 'They literally had to unmake public opinion with respect to caste and the question of representation, and their successes in this regard, constituted no mean achievement. For, they amounted to nothing less than a re-drawing of the limits of civil society in the Tamil country' (ibid.).

In 1920, the Justice Party won a remarkable victory in the elections to run a diarchic government in the Madras Presidency. On assuming office, it passed a Government Order on 16 September 1921 directing an increase in the proportion of posts in government offices held by non-brahmans. This was the expansion of the 1851 Standing Order (No. 128, Clause 2) of the Revenue Board of Madras instructing all district collectors to be careful to see that subordinate appointments in their districts were not monopolised by a few influential families (Irschick 1969). Standing Order 128 was the first recorded attempt to remove the upper caste monopolisation of government jobs. The order however was hardly implemented at any stage: half-hearted efforts to enforce it proved unsuccessful in the face of dogged opposition by the privileged few who stood to lose by the order. The vested interests had projected the move as an attempt by the British to 'divide and rule'.

The Justice's fresh initiative to ensure the representation of various castes and communities at all grades and levels in government appointments was again derided by the brahman lobby as divisive and dangerous. Brahman opinion-makers like C. P. Ramaswamy Iyer organised protest meetings which resolved that such reservation was 'detrimental to the best interests of the country' and as regards the Hindu community, 'such divisive move would prove highly injurious to the integrity of Hindu society' (Geetha and Rajadurai 1998: 158). The Justice government, however, refused to be deterred by such outbursts and brought another – and a far more comprehensive – order on 22 August 1922 to ensure that representation from below was extended both to initial recruitment and at every point in promotion. This initiative, through hamstrung by the British government's opportunistic ambivalence on the issue and stiff opposition in implementation posed by the powerful brahman lobby, had a historic bearing as it effectively laid the foundation of affirmative action.

During its tenure the Justice Party also brought in progressive legislation pertaining to intermarriage, franchise for the common man, abolition of the devadasi system, throwing open temples to depressed classes, regulating temple administration and bringing it under the control of the state, and educational facilities and reduction of fees for weaker sections. Above all, it did a splendid job in promoting primary education, women's education and a more viable technical, industrial and agricultural education. For instance, by 1925, in about 18 out of 25 municipalities, free and compulsory school education was introduced. The Education Act of 1920 was amended with a view to offset high drop-our rate and keep poor children in school (ibid.: 133). The Justice Party also introduced a scheme to feed deprived children in schools. It was held that children, once in school, could not be taken out within the period of their school age and parents who attempted to do so were liable to pay a penalty. It also paid special attention to the spread of education among Adi-Dravidas and insisted that all public schools admit them, failing which the managements would forfeit grants-in-aid. Adi-Dravida students were also given concessions in fees, besides other facilities (ibid.: 134).

The Justice's legislation regarding social and educational reforms was bold and imaginative, though their implementation left much to be desired. One reason was an acute financial crunch, aggravated by the fact that, though elected, the government under dyarchy could not resolve on problems of finance (ibid.). Secondly, the brahman-dominated bureaucracy was prejudiced against the implementation of any pro-people legislation. The status-quoist officials tried their best to sabotage the measures which they thought did not augur well for their privileges. More important, the Justice Party's own inability to link its progressive legislation to an ideological and social struggle against discrimination rendered its transformatory agenda more rhetoric than reality. Not only did it fail to build a credible ideological alternative to brahmanism, some of its leaders also exhibited an elitist orientation, which prevented them from taking the movement to the grassroots. The hegemonic forces proved to be too strong for its reformist measures. The task of mass mobilisation for a radical anti-brahmanism was left to social revolutionaries like Periyar.

PERIYAR AND THE SELF-RESPECT MOVEMENT

E. V. Ramaswami Naicker (1879-1973), better known as Periyar, a title meaning 'great man' that was conferred on him by the people during his heroic struggle, was a relentless critic and campaigner against the brahmanic culture and ideology. His extraordinary life and career puts in bold relief the problematic history of Congress politics and nationalism. Periyar had joined the Congress in 1919, rose quickly to become a prominent figure in the Tamil Nadu Congress, and then became disillusioned with what he saw as its hyprocritical politics. He left the 'brahmanic Congress' to organise a 'Self-Respect movement' for Dravidian people which represented not only the radical phase of the non-brahman movement but also a response to the 'politics of piety' as espoused by Gandhi (Geetha and Rajadurai 1998). The Self-Respect League that he formed in 1926 bore a striking similarity – in its objectives – to that of Phule's Satyashodhak Samaj, calling for the annihilation of caste, opposing brahmanical hegemony, and championing the liberation of subjugated classes and women. A trenchant critic of caste hierarchy, ritualism and idolatry, Periyar – like Phule and Ambedkar – conflated Hinduism with casteism and brahmanism, and lambasted Hindu laws and institutions as inhuman instruments of 'brahmanic', 'male' and 'Aryan' exploitation. His militant, mass-oriented movement attacked the Congress nationalism as the political front of brahmanical ideology that put aside vital issues such as power, difference, and discrimination within the country.

The Self-Respect movement was 'fundamentally opposed to the holy alliance of religion, caste and nationalism, an alliance which it understood as embodying a social and political order that was inherently inegalitarian' (ibid.: 303-4). Periyar was highly critical of the way the brahmans continued to 'conflate ritual scruple with national principle', and deeply felt the slights brahmans routinely handed out to non-brahmans in the emerging public spheres of Madras and elsewhere. The most crucial episode in his early public life was his clash with the Congress leadership over the question of separate dining for brahman and non-brahman students in a Congress-sponsored residential school (*gurukulam*) near Madras. It was a galling – and eye-opening – experience for Periyar that the school, set up with the aim of imparting traditional religious education in the larger context of a commitment to social service and patriotism, was practising untouchability by arranging separate dining for non-brahman boys. The general position of the Congress nationalists and Gandhi was supportive of this practice under the pretext of maintaining traditional harmony. Periyar unsuccessfully tried to reason with the 'nationalists' that 'the gurukulam must stand for an ideal – for Indian nationalism – and there should be no invidious distinction between man and man' (Viswanathan 1983: 49). Nationalism, he argued elsewhere, should be nurtured by citizens without bargaining their dignity and conscience on a common agenda which must include

all round growth of knowledge; spread of education; the cultivation of rational thought, work, industry, equality, unity, initiative and honesty and the abolition of poverty, injustice and untouchability. (cited in Geetha and Rajadurai 1998: 472)

Before all else, such a nation to exist, Periyar insisted, required the abolition of varnashrama-dharma and its discrimination based on birth.

Periyar's relationship with the 'brahmanic' Congress was stormy and short-lived. In 1920, he had presided over a separate session of non-brahmans at the 26th provincial session of the Congress at Tirunelveli. In this conference, resolutions were adopted demanding the reservation of constituencies and government posts for non-brahmans. But Srinivasa Iyengar, the Congress president, did not allow these resolutions to be taken up in the open session, vetoing them in the 'public interest'. Again, in the 1924 provincial Congress session at Thiruvannamalai, Periyar in his presidential address emphasised the need for proportional representation to weaker sections in all fields. He was for abolition of the caste system, he stressed, but unless that was done members of all castes and communities should get representation in every field as caste remained a reality. Periyar attempted to convince the Congress leadership that until the evolution into castelessness, the only way out should be to balance the wrongs of history in a democratic manner that would empower the caste-oppressed. Reservation, he pointed out, was one of the ways to reach out to the unreached and redistribute existing socio-political power in a democratic manner.

The irrepressible Periyar again piloted a resolution demanding representation to all communities at the Kanchipuram Congress session in 1925. He was informed that his resolution would be considered if the demand had the approval of 30 delegates. Periyar enlisted the support of 50 delegates, yet it was not allowed to be taken up in the open session (Sunil 1991). This led to pandemonium, and amidst the babel of angry exchanges, Periyar had to walk out of the Congress with his supporters. Before leaving he said:

We are talking of sacrificing all for swaraj. If we attain swaraj, it must be a swaraj for all the people. Today, there is a growing fear in the minds of the people that swaraj would be brahman raj in toto. We must create confidence in people. Every community should be cordial to others. We must ensure that every community is safe and prosperous. Today, crores of people are in a pitiable state. They are dumb. The only way is to give legitimate representation to all the communities. (cited in Sunil, ibid.: 17)

Periyar unmasked Congress hypocrisy again in 1928, when the Justice Party-supported S. Muthiah Muddaliar cabinet issued a government order giving adequate representation to all the communities. The Congress leaders, furious at this 'divisive' move 'taken at the behest of the British', were challenged by Periyar: non-brahmans would be ready to forgo the benefits of the GO if brahmans came forward to give up all caste and community distinctions in society. As expected, the self-righteous brahman nationalists did not respond. Periyar's poser exposed them thoroughly. The GO was finalised and passed on 27 December 1929, paving the way for the present reservation policy.

Here we have to digress a little to tell the story of how Periyar had to wage a harder battle after Independence to defeat the upper caste design to bury the reservation policy (for backward classes) once and for all. When the Constitution was adopted on 26 January 1950, it did not single out any particular class as a backward caste. The Nehru-led government at the Centre got the perfect excuse and called for the abrogation of the GO on reservation. The representation issue was also challenged in the Madras High Court which ruled in August 1950 that it was unconstitutional. The Supreme Court too took the 'unconstitutional' line, upholding the high court decision. An enraged Periyar took up the challenge and deplored the Constitution as the hand-maiden of brahmans. He pointed out that though Ambedkar was the chairperson of the drafting committee, he was the lone representative of dalits and backward classes and had to capitulate before the four brahman members of the panel – three of them (A. Krishnasamy Iyer, T. T. Krishnamachari and Gopalasamy Iyengar) hailing from Tamil Nadu itself. Popular protests erupted everywhere. The people were furious and tempers were running high. Wave after wave of people spontaneously took to the streets; dharnas and strikes became the order of the day. At Periyar's call, August 14 was observed as GO Day which brought the state to a complete standstill (Sunil, ibid.). The writing on the wall was clear: the people were solidly behind Periyar who even threatened to separate from the Indian union 'ruled by the brahmanical and north Indian elite'. These protests forced the Union government into the very first amendment of the Constitution to incorporate Article 15(4) which enabled the state to make any special provisions, notwithstanding Articles 15(1) and 29(2), for the advancement of the socially and educationally backward classes as well as the scheduled castes and tribes. It was under this provision that the reservation policy was reintroduced in Tamil Nadu and also adopted at the Centre and in different states in subsequent years in different forms.

Unlike the Justice Party, Periyar's movement was multi-pronged and by no means confined to the reservation issue and political non-brahmanism. Though its rhetoric was built on the ideological moorings of the earlier movement against the brahmanic dominance, the Self-Respect movement set for itself a much broader task. Its non-brahmanism was a radical blueprint for societal and cultural transformation. It visualised the term 'non-brahman' as a grand fraternity comprising all those whom the brahman and brahmanism held to be low, despised, and less than human. In the words of Periyar:

Even Christians, Mohammedans, Anglo-Indians and other non-Hindus are non-brahmins. Amongst the Hindus all those, excepting those of the brahmin caste . . . are non-brahmins. Those referred to as untouchables and who therefore are marginalised as unseeable and unapprochable are also non-brahmins. If all those communities are to escape ensnarement by the magic web of Brahminism, and live in self-respect, they have to transcend minor sectarian differences, shed their self-interest and cease to be the brahmin's spies. . . . They need to trust in universal progress and unite to achieve this objective and meanwhile should eschew prejudice and falsehood.
(see Geetha and Rajadurai, ibid.: 290)

The basic thrust of the Self-Respect movement was to free non-brahmans from their shudrahood and to prepare them to come together with the ati-shudras and others to realise an ideal society in which caste would have no place. Like Phule, to Periyar the abolition of untouchability 'required nothing more or less than the abolition of the caste syatem itself' (ibid.: 288). He said that not only was the progress of non-brahmans linked to the progress achieved by the untouchables, but the sorrows of the latter were a matter of concern and feeling to the non-brahmans as well. And while underlining the importance of securing proportional representation for all non-brahmans, he deemed it more necessary for the untouchables since the latter had to endure more ignominies than the rest of non-brahmans. Assuming positions of authority, he said, would enable the untouchables to prevent atrocities and civil disabilities inflicted against them (ibid.: 290).

In other words, whereas the Justice Party had been mainly concerned about ending the brahman raj in public spheres through its politics of proportional representation, the Self-Respect movement aimed at bringing about a cultural revolution on the bedrock of casteless egalitarianism and rationalism. Stressing egalitarian social relations across caste, community, and gender lines, Periyar advocated the overthrow of caste and instituted non-brahmanic forms of marriage celebrating the equality of woman and her right to choose life-partner and other such practices designed to give a death blow to the brahmanical order. Presenting a radical critique of the religious beliefs and practices in a variety of ways, Periyar wanted to demolish the whole brahmanic structure of society which he saw as the root cause of the degradation and subordination of women and the non-brahman populace. In contrast to the Justice Party, which could not mobilise the masses at the grassroots, Periyar's movement attracted thousands of non-brahman youth, in both urban and rural localities, who were mostly poor and first-generation learners. The movement's central agenda of restoring self-worth, pride and dignity to the long-humiliated men and women had obviously caught the imagination of the Dravidian people. At various points, the mass movement organised dramatic assaults on brahmanical symbols: its members burnt hate-filled texts such as the *Manusmriti*, proclaimed that Rama's glorification was a brahmanic myth that symbolised the Aryan conquest and the denigration of the Dravidians, showered discriminatory gods and priests with shoes, and marched defiantly on the prohibited temples in mass demonstrations.

To counter the dominant role the caste elites were playing through the so-called nationalist press such as *The Hindu*, Periyar founded his own journals and newspapers in Tamil like *Kudi Arasu* to popularise radical critiques of brahmanism, Congress and its brand of nationalism. Through these journals written in racy Tamil, he reached new audiences well beyond the elite-based Justice constituencies. Periyar developed the Self-Respecter's engaging style of social activism and distinctive acts of social protests as a counterforce to Gandhi's politics of piety in the cultural and political domains. Periodically, Periyar had to resort to strident rhetoric to draw attention to the issues.

In the beginning of his public life, Periyar was impressed by Gandhi's espousal of constructive programmes and social reform. But soon he saw through Gandhi's position on caste, culture, and nationalism, and his respect for the Mahatma metamorphosed into a bitter resentment. In 1924, he had participated in the Vaikkom temple agitation, and clashed with Gandhi, questioning the latter's mealy-mouthed ambiguous approach regarding socio-religious oppression against the untouchables and lowered castes. In the decade of the 1920, Periyar, despite his avowed atheism, pressed for the right of temple entry for the untouchables with the understanding that the 'temple was a civil sphere as well as a religious one'. But as Gandhi and Congress embraced the cause – especially after the showdown with Ambedkar on the question of separate electorates for depressed classes (in which Periyar stood firmly with Ambedkar) – with the intention to 'kill the depressed classes with kindness', the Dravidian leader lost all interest in the movement for temple-entry, dismissing it as 'hankering after a worthless dream' which, he asserted, would only strengthen the brahmanical order.

His final break with Gandhi, however, came earlier, when during a tour of the south in 1927 Gandhi openly defended varnashrama-dharma and praised the brahmans as worthy custodians of 'holy' Hindu life. Rubbing salt into the wounds of social radicals like Periyar, Gandhi also maintained that a ban on intermarriage or interdining was essential to the ideal Hindu system. Even earlier, in April 1921, addressing a public meeting in Madras, Gandhi had said that Hinduism 'owes it all' to the great traditions established by the brahmans. In the same speech, in an obvious reference to the non-brahman movement in the south, Gandhi had reprimanded the non-brahmans not to attempt to 'rise upon the ashes of brahmanism'. Coinciding with Gandhi's visit to the south, a 'Brahman Sammelan' organised at Tuvar in the district of Thanjavur approved the continued validity of varna-dharma, observing that at present there were only two varnas – the brahman and the shudra – and it behoved both to stick to their varna vocation with sincerity and responsibility (Geetha and Rajadurai, ibid.: 299).

As expected, Periyar responded angrily. If shudras were to follow Gandhi's advice, he said at a public meeting in Tinnevelly, they would end up only serving the brahmans. He reiterated the same point in an editorial, cautioning the public that Gandhi's observations and attitude would only help the brahmans, and clearly stressing that the Mahatma's obscurantist ideas needs to be exposed and countered:

Though the public believes that Mahatma Gandhi wishes to abolish untouchability and reform religion and society, the Mahatma's utterances and thought reveal him to hold exactly the opposite views on this matter . . . if we are to follow the Mahatma's untouchability creed, we will slip into the very abyss of that untouchability we are attempting to abolish. We have been patient, very patient, and tight-lipped but today in the interests of abolition and self-respect we are, sadly enough, forced to confront and oppose the Mahatma. (ibid.: 299)

The editorial went on to dissect Gandhi's views on caste and varna in detail, and found them indistinguishable from the standard brahmanic position on the issue. Not surprisingly, this editorial created a storm as it had ruffled the feathers of many devoted Gandhians who vented their ire on Periyar's 'distortion' of Gandhian views. Periyar, in his inimitable style, pitied such carpers and confused patriots, holding them in ridicule for parrot-like protests such as 'He meant this, not that' or 'He did not intend to be understood thus'. Periyar and his associates asserted that they could easily see Gandhi for what he was: 'a crucial player in the construction and deployment of Congress-brahmin hegemony' (ibid.: 300). From now onwards, Periyar consistently and caustically critiqued Gandhi and his politics as an indivisible part of the bigger brahmanical problem.

It is interesting that on Gandhi's assassination in 1948, Periyar wrote a unique obituary, condemning his murder but also noting that 'Godse was not an isolated bigot or madman but rather an expression of the very forms of Hindu nationalism that Gandhi himself had done so much to cultivate, and that had become pervasive in India at large' (Dirks 2002: 263). Gandhi, to quote Periyar's own words, was struck down by a cancer within, a scourge that the Dravidian leader saw as fundamentally about the cloying connection of brahman privilege to Hindu ideology (ibid.).

At the time, Periyar's anti-caste crusade, egalitarian radicalism and atheistic rationalism had galvanised not only lowered caste youth in thousands, but had also fired the imagination of a host of creative talents. Among them was Bharati Dasan whose poems presented the Self-Respect idealism not in the terms of seeking a revivalist return to the supposed golden age but as an inspiration for socialist modernity that shatters the darkness of regressive tradition:

> Is it greatness to refuse the right of women?
>   Or is it great to be happy with the progress of women?
> . . . Is it right to believe in the Vedas, in God, in all this decay?
>   Or is it right to establish socialism on earth?
> Will we live continuing the divisions which surround us?
> Or will we live rising up through self-respect?
>   (cited in Omvedt 1995: 56-7)

As Omvedt says, Dasan's socialism reflected a new radicalism and a short-lived alliance of anti-caste and class themes in the early 1930s. In 1932, Periyar visited the Soviet Union, and was enthused by what he saw in the nascent socialist society. He now started speaking against the Indian elite and British imperialists as agents of world capitalism in his usual subversive language. This attracted close monitoring of his activities by the British government. M. Singaravelu, a Buddhist scholar and pioneering labour leader with the reputation of being the 'first communist of south India', encouraged Periyar's growing fondness for socialism. He wrote a series of articles in *Kudi Arasu,* expounding socialism and a materialistic interpretation of history (Omvedt 1995: 57). Periyar joined hands with Singaravelu, and the Self-Respect Samadharma Party was launched in December 1932.

For the Self-Respecter radicals, the term *samadharma* was not merely the Tamil equivalent of socialism, it assumed equality amongst men and between men and women as a given. More important, it required that this equality be realised through an affirmation of each individual's self-worth and self-respect. As such, the principle of samadharma stood not only for a new age of economic equality and public ownership of property, but the realisation of a millenarian dream whereby caste society in its entirety and in all its complex ways of being would be transformed (Geetha and Rajadurai 1998: 420-1).

On the other hand, persons like Singaravelu and Professor Lakshmi Narasu, both Buddhist scholars of distinction, used and interpreted *samadharma* in a different light, though with the same objective. They sought out its Buddhist origins as a word and as an ideal, emphasising the revival of the socialistic spirit of Buddhism that had long been the moral-spiritual basis for countering discriminatory Hinduism (ibid.: 421-2). Adi-Dravida thinker-activists simply identified a caste-free society as a samadharmic society. The ideal of samadharma was not yet clearly enunciated, it was left theoretically open-ended though the Self-Respecters at different times and contexts identified its ideal with a set of clearly defined material attributes necessary for building a socialist society (ibid.). But it certainly marked an upsurge in the radicalisation of the non-brahman struggle. Socialism now began to be advocated from its platforms, and several anti-capitalist and anti-landlord conferences were held by the Self-Respecters.

However, this coming together of the anti-caste struggle and the leftist movement did not last long. The conservatives in the non-brahman movement remained unenthusiastic about the development, but more than that the brahmanic communist leaders with their gross and orthodox Marxism opposed the anti-caste movement as casteist dilution of the class war. As Omvedt has pointed out, Singaravelu's type of indigenous socialism was found to be dangerous by the communist bosses in Bombay. The real split finally occurred on a straightforward political issue. On the eve of the 1934 elections, the Self-Respect movement was faced with the choice of supporting either the Justice Party or the Congress, as there was no socialist party at the time. While Periyar saw the Self-Respecters' future in a revival and radicalisation of the Justice Party, the left could see it only in the Congress, which by the mid 1930s they identified as the 'anti-imperialist united front'. In 1936, the communist bosses ordered Singaravelu and his comrades to diassociate from Periyar's movement and instead join the Congress Socialist Party, part of the Congress within which the communists were working (Omvedt 1995: 58).

The result of the split proved disastrous for both Periyar and the left. Hereafter Periyar hardened his attitude towards the 'brahmanic' left and Congress nationalism, and increasingly identified with a linguistic-regional nationalism. While the majority of high caste Indian Marxists in their mechanical interpretation of the class war in purely economic terms completely ignored the necessity of struggling against social and cultural oppression, the others – more hypocritical and opportunistic comrades – saw their revolutionary salvation only in toeing pro-Congress nationalism.

In 1936, Periyar assumed the leadership of the fading Justice Party and endeavoured to make it not only a movement of social change but also a cultural-political vehicle of Dravidian language, culture, and nationalism in opposition to what he termed the Aryan-brahmanic-and-north-dominated nationalism. Periyar led a militant agitation against the imposition of Hindi in government schools effected by the Congress soon after the latter came to power in 1937, citing it as yet another instance of the oppressive character of 'Aryan nationalism'. Imprisoned for a while for his vociferous opposition to the Congress government on the issue of Hindi, which he saw as a part of the bigger Hindi-Hindu-Hindustan conspiracy of the brahmanic north, he now demanded the creation of a separate state for the Tamil, Telugu, Kannada, and Malyalam speaking people of the south.

In the 1940s, Periyar's politics came to be dominated by the demand for an autonomous casteless federation of Dravida Nadu. In 1944, he established the Dravida Kazhagam, which had as its prime objective the establishment of a non-brahman, Dravidian state. It must be noted, however, that it was his zeal to build a truly casteless community that propelled him to raise such demand. His was a struggle for a new community, and his polity was committed to that larger objective. Periyar's society was to be 'distinguished from the brahmanic caste order by its civilisational and cultural differences' (Geetha and Rajadurai 1998: 327). Dravidian in its ethos, the new society that Periyar envisioned and struggled for was fuelled by a desire to build a world free of caste. In a significant way, the word 'Dravidian', the antithesis of 'Aryan', signified the acceptance within its fold of all those who consented to the rejection of caste culture. Thus, when Ambedkar met Periyar in 1944 to discuss joint initiatives, the former claimed that the idea of Dravidasthan was in reality applicable to all of India, since brahmanism was a problem which afflicted the entire subcontinent (ibid.).

The non-brahman movement of Tamil Nadu spread to the princely state of Mysore. Here too, brahman dominance in the fields of education, government service, and politics began to be contested by the deprived castes and communities. The major ethnic groups of the region, the Lingayats and Vokkaligas, along with the Muslims took the lead in challenging the brahman monopoly of the public sphere. The Vokkaliga Association was formed in 1906, and the Virashaiva Mahasabha (representing the interests of Lingayats) in 1909. Other organisations founded during this period included the Adi-Dravida Abhi-Vruddhi Sangha, the Kuruba Association, and the Central Muslim Association. By 1917 various ethnic groups formed an alliance called the Praja Mitra Mandali. In 1918 they submitted a memorandum to the government asking for adequate representation of non-brahmans in public service, educational institutions, and legislature. The Miller Commission appointed to examine the demands issued a report – recommending representation to the backward castes – which was accepted by the government in 1919 (Omvedt 1994: 127). This enabled the non-brahmans, particularly the Vokkaligas and Lingyayats, to enter the domains of education, employment, and politics.

The lowered caste people raised the banner of revolt in Andhra Pradesh too. Unlike Mysore, where the anti-brahman ideology did not assume the form of an anti-Aryan, pro-Dravidian image, the dalits in Andhra, especially in the coastal areas, were influenced by the militant Dravidianism of Tamil Nadu. While the dalits of Tamil Nadu and Karnataka constructed their cultural identity as Adi-Dravidians and Adi-Karnatakas respectively, Telugu-speaking Malas and Madigas proclaimed themselves as Adi-Andhra claiming, like the former, that they were the original sons of the soil and rulers of the region (Omvedt 1994: 117). They argued that Hinduism was not the ancestral religion of the aborigines who abhorred discriminatory scriptures like the Vedas and *Manusmriti*. The Vedic religion, its ideas and prejudices, the dalit leaders contended, had been forcibly thrust upon the non-Vedic aborigines by the invading Aryans.

A conference of dalits in Vijayawada in 1917, sponsored by the reformist Hindus, tentatively labelled as the First Provincial Panchama Maharaja Sabha, changed its name to the Adi-Andhra Maharaja Sabha at the insistence of radicals. The dalit delegates, who were showing signs of defiance, had trouble getting accommodation in the town, and the major temples there, fearing an attempted entry, closed down for three days (ibid.: 118). Subsequently, the Adi-Andhra conferences were held every year in different parts of the region. The movement had a mass base, and as the 1931 census indicated nearly a third of the Malas and Madigas of the Madras Presidency now claimed identity as Adi-Andhra (ibid.).

Bhagyareddy Varma (1888-1939), a Hyderabad dalit originally named Madari Bhagaiah, played a major role in organising the Andhra dalits and building a protest movement. Varma, who had been organising Adi-Hindu conferences since 1912, used the term Adi-Hindu in a radical way. 'Hindu' did not refer to religion but was used for the natives of the land, who were pushed down to the south by brahman outsiders (ibid.: 124). A strong votary of dalit autonomy, he was generally opposed to the temple-entry movements: at one instance, when the delegates of Adi-Andhra conference in 1938 in East Godavari were debating this contentious issue, Bhagyareddy Varma refused to preside until all there agreed not to support a bill for temple-entry then being introduced in the Madras provincial council by the dalit reformer M. C. Rajah (ibid.). Varma also had a profound interest in Buddhism. From his early life he greatly admired the Buddha, presenting him as one who fought brahmanical injustice and oppression. He organised a function on the occasion of the Buddha's birth anniversary in 1913 and again in 1937, two years before his death. During his last years when he became somewhat politically inactive, he gave his support to a new generation of radical Ambedkarites (ibid.).

A common theme running through the non-brahman movements, particularly dalit liberation struggles, was linkages between the oppressive present and the past history of the Aryan conquest and brahman exploitation through a pseudo-religion. Nowhere was this subversive construction more visible than Maharashtra, the land of Phule and Ambedkar. We have studied Phule's anti-caste movement in the previous chapter, and shall delve into Ambedkar's liberation struggle in the next one. Suffice it to say here that Phule's social radicalism was carried forward by many pre-Ambedkar dalit leaders of the region. One such leader, Kisan Faguji Bansode (1870-1946), gave expression, for instance, to growing dalit militancy in a 1909 article:

The Aryans – your ancestors – conquered us and gave us unbearable harassment. At that time we were your conquest, you treated us even worse than slaves and subjected us to any torture you wanted. But now we are no longer your subjects, we have no service relationship with you, we are not your slaves or serfs. . . . We have had enough of the harassment and torture of the Hindus. . . . If you don't give us the rights of humanity and independence, then we will have to take our own rights on the basis of our own strength and courage, and that we will do. (see Omvedt 1994: 110)

THE BATTLE IN THE NORTH:
ACCHUTANAND AND MANGOO RAM

In Uttar Pradesh, marginalised existence and low occupational experience of untouchable castes, especially in urban centres, created a context for the revival of the radical tradition of Kabir and Ravidas and the assertion of autochthon autonomy and equality (Gooptu 1993). The dalits began their liberation struggle at the turn of the twentieth century under the leadership of Swami Acchutanand (1879-1933) and Ram Charan (1888-1939). Their own life experiences were the main source of their estrangement from the brahmanical society and a driving force behind the construction of group identity. Like other subaltern leaders in the subcontinent, they advocated social justice and egalitarianism, and repudiated the Vedic-brahmanic trajectories on caste, culture, and society.

Acchutanand, a dalit ascetic from Mainpuri district, was the main ideologue of the dalit liberation movement in Uttar Pradesh. In the beginning of his public life, he had flirted for a while with the Arya Samaj, but soon became disillusioned with it by discovering a huge gap between its proclaimed ideals and its actions. He and his associates left the Arya Samaj after they realised that the Samaj aimed to 'make all Hindus slaves of the Vedas and the brahmans' (Gooptu 1993). No valorisation of the Vedas as the divine depositor of timeless truths was acceptable to them. For them, emphasis on the Vedas implied the divine sanction of caste hierarchy and a further fortification of caste distinctions. Alarmed by the 'army of high caste Hindus' built by the Arya Samaj, the dalits pointed out that its only intention was to rally the Hindu community against the Muslims, and that its attempt to uplift the lower castes was merely a part of this strategy (ibid.). They argued that the Samaj did not aim to abolish untouchability and that *shuddhi* was a cunning ploy to perpetuate the hold of the higher castes over the untouchables. 'Its professions of purification', declared Acchutanand, 'are a clever fraud and a clever verbal gimmick of the varna system.' He termed the programme of intercaste marriage led by the Samaj as an eyewash, challenging its leaders to arrange such marriages among the twice born and low born to vindicate their position (ibid.).

The dalit thinkers opposed birth-based social division of labour and labourers, arguing that this prevented occupational diversification resulting in the continued poverty, illiteracy, and subordination of the depressed classes. This anti-caste sentiment being spread by leaders like Acchutanand and Ram Charan gradually evolved into a popular movement spread across the state, especially in urban centres such as Kanpur, Lucknow, Allahabad, and Benaras (ibid.). The struggle for social equality was animated by the bhakti radicalism of Kabir and Ravidas, and an assertion of a supposed pre-Vedic egalitarian religion practised by the original inhabitants, whom they termed as the Adi Hindus, the ancestors of the dalit communities of India. Acchutanand argued that the immigrant Aryans conquered the Adi Hindus — Dasas and Dravidians — not by valour but by 'deceit' and 'manipulation', rendering the self-sufficient, pushing the aborigines into poverty and slavery. 'Those who ardently believed in equality were ranked, and ranked lowest. The Hindus and untouchables have since always remained poles apart' (Khare 1984: 85).

Importantly, the Swami and his ideologues emphasised the need to build their own knowledge-system to understand the problematic past and present — 'from Manu down to Gandhi' — in order to regain their freedom. Instead of toeing the reformist approach, they advocated a complete overhaul of the entire cultural order that bred social injustice and discrimination. Quoting their words, Khare has summed up their formulations thus:

The cobweb of Hindu scriptures, deities, incarnations, temples and Brahman priests is so intricate and pervasive that it has imprisoned the Hindu within his family and jatis, and consigned the Untouchable to the bottom. Since there have been no truths in this cobweb — from Manu down to Gandhi, the Untouchable has to take the lead on his own. And this means that he has to examine the Hindu social tactics very closely to get his freedom. The

Hindus have suppressed and destroyed all critical literature produced by the Untouchable intellectuals from ancient times until recently. Hence, the Untouchable must start rebuilding his knowledge, moving carefully from the recent to the remote past. At present, one knows little about anything other than the Hindu's side of the story. . . . . Marriage, commensality, occupation, Gita-Ramayana, and extended family are the five most important sacred domains where the Untouchables encounter maximum discrimination and resistance. The radical solution must therefore reject totally and exactly those reasons the Hindus accept and value. (Khare 1984: 85)

Emphasising the separate identity of dalits which became the fulcrum of their protest movement, Acchutanand formed the Adi Hindu Sabha in the 1920s. The Sabha soon spread its intense activities in the state through a network of vocal and articulate volunteers culled from the literate segments of town-based dalits (Gooptu 1993). Adi Hindu activists and preachers were regularly invited to address meetings of local caste panchayats and socio-religious congregations. Ravidasis and some sweepers of Kanpur hailed Acchutanand as their leader and invited him to address their meetings. In Allahabad and Lucknow, the Ravidasis proclaimed their support for the Adi Hindu movement and held public meetings to celebrate their 'separation from upper caste Hindus' (ibid.). The Kumbh Mela of 1928-9 at Allahabad witnessed the most strident proclamation of Adi Hinduism. At the mela, a *mahotsav* of all Adi Hindu devotional sects was held, in which Kabirpanthi, Ravidasi and Shivnarayani groups participated.

An important aspect of the Adi Hindu ideology of emancipation was education among the deprived masses. The Adi Hindu leaders stressed the role of education in social and cultural liberation and in the improvement of economic conditions (ibid.). They argued that illiteracy was the root cause both of the dalits' domination by the educated upper castes, and of the former's exclusion from economic opportunities and better jobs. Education was also necessary, they emphasised, for thinking-for-oneself and developing one's autonomous world-view, independent of brahmanical notions about life, religion, and culture. Critical thinking and introspection were encouraged as roads to *atmagyan* (self-realisation) and *sadgyan* (true knowledge) that 'would enable one to discern the difference between truth and falsity, which in turn would reveal the irrelevance and falsity of one's 'low' role in society' (ibid.). Interacting with fellow dalits, Acchutanand observed:

Real knowledge is the knowledge gained through introspection and which you have understood and realised on your own. For this reason, you will have to discern between good and evil, virtue and vice, auspicious and inauspicious, through your own introspection. This (introspection) is the path of self-realisation of the sants (saints and preachers). Self-realisation is the only touchstone against which you can test truth and falsity, high and low.
(Gooptu, ibid.: 291)

Underpinning this thinking was a clear-cut anti-caste ideology that stressed the fact that *varna* and *jati* divisions were neither divinely ordained, nor natural, nor grounded in truth. There was no justifiable basis, they asserted, for the low and menial jobs that the dalits were expected to perform as the servants of the upper castes. They argued that the shudras were forced to do dirty, impure, and menial jobs, and then, on the plea of ritual impurity, were accorded a low servile status. Underlining this in a speech in 1927, Ram Charan, the Adi Hindu leader of Lucknow, said:

The untouchables were made to do the most insulting and demeaning jobs, such as cleaning excreta and dirty clothes. They were repeatedly told that you are shudras and your work is to serve (gulami). Those who were thus made to serve (gulam or das) were then called untouchables. (ibid.: 291)

Adi Hindu ideologues created a counter-myth, an egalitarian golden past of their own, to debunk the Aryan-brahmanical myth of the Golden Age. There had been Adi Hindu kingdom, capital cities, forts, and a thriving civilisation, they claimed, which were destroyed by the invading Aryans through the treachery and brute force. The Aryan creation of the caste system and repressive social laws embodied in the Vedas and codified in the Dharmashastras, they contended, was motivated by their devious design to relegate the original inhabitants to untouchable status, and strip them of their civil and economic rights. They condemned Hinduism, and its caste system, as an expression of Aryan political manipulation. In the words of Ram Charan, 'The rule of making shudra was not a religious rule. It was naked politics' (ibid.: 292). By arguing that the caste system was a lethal political weapon to subjugate and enslave the shudras, the dalit leaders exhorted their fellow men not to tolerate this oppressive system which consigned and condemned them to a life of deprivation, illiteracy, and utter helplessness. The Adi Hindu leaders also attempted to build a positive self-image by presenting themselves as straightforward and honest people, inheritors of a glorious egalitarian tradition (ibid.: 293-4). They told their people that they had been treated as slaves for centuries after their capitulation to the barbaric Aryans, but now would come forward to reclaim their dignity and reassert their rights to education and power.

In Punjab, too, the movement against untouchability and injustice took the form of an autochthonous radicalism. Here, dalit leader Mangoo Ram, also a disillusioned Arya Samaji, founded Adi Dharma in 1925, and declared untouchables a separate *qaum*, an independent religious community similar to those of the Hindu, Muslim, and Sikh communities. They claimed that their *qaum* existed in the subcontinent long before the Aryan invasion which marked the beginning of their enslavement:

We are the original people of this country and our religion is Adi-Dharma. The Hindu qaum came from outside and enslaved us. When the original sound from the conch was sounded all the brothers came together – Chamar, Chuhra, Sainsi, Bhanjre, Bhil all the untouchables – to make their problems known. Brothers, there are seventy millions of us listed as Hindus, separate us and make us free. (Juergensmeyer 1982: 46)

The first item on the agenda of Mangoo Ram was to get the changed identity of depressed classes as the Adi Dharma community officially accepted. At his instance, more than four lakh dalits identified themselves as Adi-Dharmis in the 1931 census. Armed with an emancipatory vision and the might of numbers, the Adi-Dharmis entered the political fray. Like most dalit and lowered caste organisations elsewhere, the Adi-Dharmis opposed the 'brahmanical' Congress and Gandhi, and 'wanted no part of independence if independence meant government by upper caste Hindus' (see Aloysius 1997: 68). The movement presented a social vision in direct contrast to the closed and parochial caste society. It demanded social equality, dignity, and a representative share in economic and political spheres for the hitherto excluded communities as a necessary pre-condition for broader social integration. Invoking democratic principles, the Adi-Dharmis appealed to the upper castes to give up their devious ways and accept the egalitarian change with grace. Mark Juergensmeyer observes: 'Movements like Adi-Dharma have been separatist only to the extent that they have insisted on separating their followers from old ideas of social integration. They have tried to provide new visions of society in which the upper castes are also invited to play a role, albeit a more humble one than at present' (ibid.: 275). The Adi Dharma campaign was gradually absorbed into Ambedkar's movement in the late 1930s and 1940s.

Movements from Below Signal the End of Colonialism

The so-called nationalist leaders targeted only colonial exploitation — after colluding and collaborating with, and fattening themselves on, colonial rule for a century and a half. Their aim was to wrest power from the British, and they showed no commitment to overthrow the internal colonisation of lowered caste masses. The subaltern leaders in the subcontinent thus came forward to challenge their hegemonic politics. As we have seen in the study of Phule, Periyar, and other social radicals, and shall further explore in the next chapter while probing the conflicting views of Ambedkar and Gandhi on the nation and nationalism, the underclass leadership was left with little choice but to bypass the 'official' nationalism and charter a different course with a radical agenda for a new order where the dalit-subalterns would play a major role in nation-building. Not surprisingly, such movements became a thorn in the sides of the upper class national leadership as they posed a threat to the entrenched caste and class interests.

As Omvedt has argued, while some Marxists and Congress leaders, especially Gandhi and Nehru, later sought to appropriate in some measure both (elite-based and mass-oriented) nationalisms, still 'democracy' and 'humanity' for most of them were represented either by science, technology, and state, or the vision of self-sufficient village communities — in ways that never challenged caste inequality and exploitation. On the other hand, dalit-subaltern struggle based on vision of a casteless, democratic and modern society reflected the birth-pangs of the nation. Based on the values of equality, liberty, and fraternity, the movements from below were 'a crucial expression of the democratic revolution in India'.

The brahmanical mindset and models for the study of anti-caste movements tends to obscure the real issue at stake: democratic aspirations of the masses ranged against the social establishment. The nationalist discourse in fact provided an ideal mask for the caste-feudal and authoritarian structure of social and economic exploitation in Indian, especially Hindu, society. Whatever the description of the 'nationalist' school, it is quite clear that despite their diverse origins and differentially articulated philosophies, the central theme of all anti-caste movements was an outright rejection of brahmanical caste ideology as a prerequisite for social equality and national unity. Though uneven and multifarious in appearance, the anti-caste movements presented a uniform pattern:

> *The main figures of this larger anti-caste movement . . . all attacked the system of exploitation at all levels, culturally, economically and politically. They challenged the 'Hindu-nationalism' which was emerging as a consequence of the elite organising from the nineteenth century onward to define Indian society, and the majority of Indian people, as essentially 'Hindu': not only did they criticise distortions and 'excrescences', they attacked Hinduism itself by arguing that it was in essence Brahmanical, caste-bound and irrational. They asserted that Hinduism had not been the religion and culture of the majority but rather was an imposed religion; and that escaping exploitation today required the low castes to reject this imposition, to define themselves as 'non-Hindu' and take a new religious identity. Phule tried to formulate a new, theistic religion; Periyar promoted atheism; Ambedkar turned to Buddhism; others in the Tamil Nadu non-brahman movement tried to claim Saivism as an independent religion, Narayanswami Guru formulated 'one religion, one caste, one God' while his more radical follower Ayyappan proclaimed 'no religion, no caste, and no God for mankind'. Whatever the specificities, the rejection of Hinduism remained a feature differentiating the anti-caste radicals from the reformers.*
> (Omvedt 1994: 12)

The anti-caste movements had a radical agenda of economic and political emancipation of the masses:

They were also economic radicals, though from different points of view, identifying themselves not simply with low castes but with peasants and workers as such. Phule strongly attacked the exploitation of peasants by the bureaucracy; Ambedkar and Periyar both supported and helped organise movements of peasants against landlords and workers against capitalists; and Ambedkar unambiguously identified himself as a socialist. Politically they opposed the Indian National Congress as controlled by upper castes and capitalists . . . and sought for an alternative political front that would represent a kind of left-Dalit unity with a core base of workers and peasants. They (particularly Ambedkar) also insisted that this had to lead to the empowerment of Dalits and other exploited sections. In the language of the Dalit Panther's manifesto, 'We don't want a little place in Brahman alley; we want the rule of the whole country.' (ibid.: 12-13)

Thus, contrary to the nationalist position that the anti-caste movements were inspired and supported by the colonial rulers to divide and weaken the national unity, the beginning of equality-driven mass resistance signalled a democratic revolution and marked the beginning of the end of colonialism, both external and internal. In a ground-breaking study Aloysius contends that

The struggles of the hitherto excluded communities bear the special significance of signalling democratic revolution, however uneven and irregular, against the vested interests of the dominant, both native as well as foreign. The pact between the native and foreign dominant groups on which colonialism itself was founded, was indeed based on the premise that the status quo of power, resource and leadership distribution within the colonised country was to be maintained and that rule itself was to be indirect, through the medium of local dominance. The British imperialist policy of non-interference was not based on any goodwill or appreciation of Indian culture, but on compulsion, and they had no choice in the matter. In this situation, the lower class/caste struggles did have the unfortunate effect of upsetting the precariously balanced applecart of colonial power struggle and ideology. The British were certainly aware of this: the colonial educational policy, for example, was dictated by the realisation that if education descended from the higher to the inferior classes, it 'would lead to a general convulsion of which foreigners would be the first victim'. (Aloysius 1997: 90-1)

Thus the colonial rulers and Indian elites both were aware of the implications of mass emergence. Both feared that its cascading effect would intensify the democratisation process in every sphere of life. Both tried to prevent it in their pursuit of monopoly power. India's ruling classes were the main collaborators of the colonial rule, generously rewarded and protected for their services to the British. By virtue of being in charge of land revenue management as zamindars, and serving the Raj in various administrative capacities, the Indian elite played a pivotal role in ensuring legitimacy, safety, and continuance of the colonial regime. As their interests complemented each other they often united to suppress peasant and tribal struggles during the British rule. On socio-religious questions too, the British adhered to the no-interference policy upholding the custom and tradition of the Hindu upper castes. However, towards the end of the Raj, when the British were compelled to concede some demands for representation in job, education and legislative bodies from the lowered castes/classes, the Indian upper classes, now clamouring for total transfer of power, turned nationalist. They accused the British of pursuing a nefarious policy of divide-and-rule and tarred the movements from below with the same brush, as antinational or pro-colonial.

This was the hypocrisy of the nationalist leadership: Gandhi, Nehru, and many brahmanic Marxists were part of the 'nationalist' farce. The attempts of the lowered castes and classes to get their share of the educational-social-political spheres 'cannot but have the same application as those of the attempts of the upper castes, for instance, the aspiration to become civil servants under the Raj'. Pointing this out, a non-brahman leader of the south had wryly said: 'If we ask for a ministry, it is job-hunting, but if a Congressman asks for it, it is patriotism' (cited in Baker 1976: 360).

As a matter of fact, the lowered caste struggles were not only against the caste-feudalism and the traditional social order but also against the colonial regime. The appearance of collaboration with the colonial masters – to ensure some measures of social safety and economic welfare for the oppressed – was a tactical move necessitated by the highly antagonistic attitude of selfish Indian elites in the strategy to dismantle the structure of exploitation, both external and internal, and build a democratic society. But why did these widespread though scattered struggles fail to transform themselves into a pan-Indian form and upstage the elitist nationalism which successfully presented itself as an Indian response to the colonial regime? Aloysius has given a credible explanation:

The reasons for this are crucial – economic, cultural and ideological, the inherent difficulties of a generally traditional, subaltern and colonially dispossessed social position, particularly in the absence of widespread economic change, was the first. Secondly, these struggles were well-rooted in the vernacular, regional cultures and were a continuity of the alternate subcontinental tradition not only of power as resistance but also power as diversity which the colonial impact did much to damage. In this sense, the diversified, vernacularised and hence the rootedness of these movements were indeed an asset that could have led to a federal and de-centralised modern India. Thirdly, the antagonistic pan-Indianism of the nationalists towards this process of internal democratisation articulated from a traditional as well as colonially empowered social position is the ideological reason why mass emergence as the nation could not but be stopped from formally and verbally articulating the anti-colonial nationalist ideology. (ibid.: 92)

7

Nationalist Power Politics, Excluded Masses, and the Gandhi-Ambedkar Debate

> Patriotism in its simplest, clearest, and most indubitable signification is nothing but a means of obtaining for the rulers their ambitions and covetous desires, and for the ruled the abdication of human dignity, reason, and conscience, and a slavish enthralment to those in power.
>
> LEO TOLSTOY
> *Writings on Civil Disobedience and Non-Violence*, 1987: 103

Historians subscribing to the dominant nationalist discourse and Gandhian politics tend to portray Ambedkar as an unpatriotic reactionary for his 'politicisation of caste' and his insistence that the untouchables were a separate and legitimate social category, a subordinated one, and not part of brahmanic Hinduism. Ambedkar was indeed very vocal on this point, as he wanted dignity, equity, and justice for dalit-subalterns and not the condescension and charity that was being offered by the Gandhian nationalism. However, as we have seen in the previous chapters, even before Ambedkar's emergence on the scene there had been large scale dalit alienation and antagonism against the national movement led by the elite. It was seen as a movement for monopoly power in the name of patriotic unity and freedom. The censuses of 1901 and 1911 and the Congress leadership's opportunistic move to incorporate the untouchables in the Hindu fold to bolster their majoritarian claims are significant in this context. (Note that at this juncture Ambedkar had not even started his political career.)

Census Commissioner H.H. Risley's attempt in 1901 to classify castes in each region according to notions of 'social grade and precedence' on the brahmanical paradigm had generated a lot of heat marked by caste claims and counter-claims. It is not generally understood that the imperative to prove one's social pedigree in the caste hierarchy for census operations was the result of collusive acceptance – by the British and Indian ruling elites – of the brahmanical model of Hindu society. Livening up of the so-called 'caste-spirit' was heightened by the hegemonic character of elitist nationalism, which had excluded, except for the rhetoric and democratic numbers game, a vast majority of Indians – lowered castes, tribal people, and Muslim masses – from the national domain. Parallel to the nationalist power politics, the lowered castes were trying to organise themselves locally and regionally across the subcontinent into a multiplicity of socio-religious and politico-economic movements against the oppressive traditional order. In fact, anti-caste agitations – and tensions – had been building up in many parts of India well before the colonial design to conduct censuses on caste identities. The limited yet significant spread of political awareness and education and some economic opportunities brought about by the new times, had spurred a new consciousness among the toiling masses. The nationalist leadership, however, tended to uniformly deride the growing lowered caste assertions for social and economic rights as divisive and, hence, not in the 'national' interest. To safeguard their privileges and entrenched interests, the high caste nationalists retained their dogmas and traditional values under the garb of seamless national unity and anti-colonial struggle, repudiating the mass grievances and democratic aspirations of the caste-oppressed as unpatriotic and anti-national.

With democratic representation being conceded in principle under the Morley-Minto reforms of 1909, the 1911 Census Commissioner, E. A. Gait, sought to estimate the population of different religions amidst the controversy over inclusion of the untouchables in Hindu religion. He formulated a questionnaire – popularly known as the Gait circular – which spelt out the criteria for ascertaining the validity of a subject's statement of religious affinity. Gait defined the meaning of the term Hindu by suggesting omission from that category of those excluded from temples and priestly services or considered to be untouchable.[1] This invited strong protest from Hindu leaders as it established the fact that the Hindu population included millions who were denied entry into places of worship. Several lowered castes, whom many upper caste census enumerators of 1901 and 1891 did not acknowledge as part of Hindu society, were now being vehemently claimed as 'our Hindu brothers'. But there were several who did not consider themselves Hindu, and many 'objected to being so classed' (Gupta 1985: 36-70; Mendelsohn and Vicziany 2000: 26-9). Given the complexities of the exercise, it was promptly abandoned. Gait decided that the question of social precedence would not be reopened and ordered a return to an alphabetic classification. Yet this had created for a while a turbulence in the ranks of Hindu nationalists.

The great importance attached to numbers in the political and administrative calculations of the British jolted the high caste leaders out of their stupor. Adding to their consternation was the Muslim League, formed recently to represent the Muslim interests, which sought to argue that the Hindu population was being artificially inflated by the inclusion of the untouchables (ibid.). Compelled by the arithmetic of parliamentary representation, the self-styled leaders of Hinduism now woke up to the misery of their 'untouchable brethren'. Lajpat Rai, for example, noted with anxiety: 'They (the untouchables) are with us . . . but they are not of us, their fidelity is being put to a severe strain and unless we recognise the justice and humanity of their cause and recognise it in time, no blame could attach to them if they were to separate themselves from us and join the ranks of those who are neither with us nor of us' (Gupta 1985: 39). Rai's apprehensions grew with time. In 1915, he wrote: 'Indications are not wanting that many of them (the depressed classes) have already become conscious of the wretched position they hold in Hindu society. . . . It will be no wonder if a large number of them leave Hindu society with thoughts of retaliation and revenge' (cited in *Frontline*, 8 August 1997).

Hindu nationalist anxieties were not misplaced as the subordinated castes were showing signs of rebellious restlessness. Besides contemplating conversion to more egalitarian religions like Christianity, Islam, and Buddhism, there were determined attempts in many parts of the country for political mobilisation. Gopal Baba Walangkar and Shivram Janba Kamble represented the early stirrings among the Mahars of Maharashtra, the caste from which Ambedkar came. In 1904, a memorandum was sent to the Governor of Bombay on behalf of 15,000 Mahars, requesting the removal of restrictions in public schools, permission to join the police and the army, and admission to lower grades of public services. A similar and better written document was sent in 1910 by the Conference of Deccan Mahars to the then Secretary of State for India. Such small yet ambitious attempts were being made by emerging dalit leaders in other parts of the country as well. Above all, in early 1917, the Depressed Classes of Bombay had expressly asked the Congress to take on its agenda the issue of caste oppression and untouchability in exchange for their support. The dalit insistence was made in the same vein as that the Muslims had a year earlier successfully demanded during the Lucknow session of Congress as reflected in the 1916 Congress-Muslim League constitutional scheme. The writing on the wall was clear: if the Congress leadership wanted to establish its national credentials it could no longer afford to ignore the hopes and aspirations of the subordinated classes.

It was this compulsion – the census exercise, pressure of representative politics, the nationalist Hindu fear of losing the untouchables and a slow yet steady political awakening among the latter – which forced the Congress in 1917 to adopt a resolution underlining its commitment to remove various caste disabilities. This forced resolution, however, did not bring about any actual change in the Congress attitude towards the caste question. Tilak and other Congress leaders of the time continued their opposition to social reform. Their obscurantist nationalism was symbolised in Lajpat Rai's well-known formula 'reform is revival and revival is reform'. The show of solidarity with the caste-oppressed was a stage-managed affair, a matter of sheer political expediency, a fact that has been underlined by historian S. Natrajan:

The interest that the Congress showed after 32 years of neglect in social reform was intrinsically political in the worse sense of the term and its espousal of the cause of the depressed classes an expedient which was not seriously implemented. It is worth noting that from this half-hearted manoeuvre sprang the painful process by which the depressed classes passed into a mood of distrust. (see Aloysius 1997: 190)

A little later, it was under such circumstances that Gandhi entered national politics and addressed the question of untouchability, offering a highly convoluted critique of 'distorted' caste system while showing full faith and allegiance in the original – and wonderful – caste culture. In between making some politically correct noises on untouchability, Gandhi was consistently emphatic that an individual's caste was ascribed at the moment of birth, and not to live by one's caste was 'to disregard the law of heredity' because 'varnashrama is inherent in human nature and Hinduism (had) simply reduced it to a science.' Note that Gandhi was initially opposed even to the temple-entry demand from the depressed classes,[2] and even after his 'change of heart' on these issues, his position remained ambiguous.

How the Congress and Gandhi's politics of caste was determined by the numbers game of Hindu nationalism – in its political expediency to include the untouchables in the Hindu fold to form a Hindu majority – becomes obvious when one sees Gandhi's overanxiety to present the untouchability problem as an exclusively Hindu affair (and not a national one). Intervening during the Vaikkom temple agitation of the 1920s, where the caste-oppressed and social activists (including some local Syrian Christians) were fighting for the untouchables right to temple entry, Gandhi took pains to emphasise that the Vaikkom movement was a Hindu affair and that 'Hindus (alone should) do the work' (Menon 1994: 81). As untouchables would help the Hindus constitute the majority, he insisted that untouchability was a 'reproach to Hinduism' rather than to the national culture. Gandhi, on the one hand, insisted, reiterating the Congress resolution at Nagpur, that only the 'Hindu members' should be involved in this intra-Hindu affair, and on the other, he tried to present the issue as part of the national, not Hindu, reconstruction, thus making it amply clear that despite his occasional evocation of the secular basis of Indian nationalism, he also equated it with Hindu nationalism.

THE MYTH OF THE MAHATMA

A great panegyric myth has been created around Gandhi and his nationalist politics. In fact, much of what passes off as modern Indian historiography is but a hagiography of Gandhi and Gandhism.

This has been done with missionary zeal because Gandhi was one who, more than anyone else, defended – and validated – brahmanism when its legitimacy was being seriously challenged and its existence seemed precarious. Behind the glamour of seamless unity and patriotism, Gandhi's politics was unambiguously centred around tenacious – though highly imaginative – defence of caste and the whole socio-cultural paraphernalia associated with the brahmanic order. At the very beginning of his autobiography, while identifying himself as a bania, Gandhi, it may be noted, hastens to add that for three generations his forefathers had not practised the caste occupation but had served as prime ministers (traditionally, such jobs had been the preserve of the brahman) in several princely states in Kathiawad region of Gujarat. The region was a bastion of orthodoxy dominated by the wealthy merchant caste and its puritanical conservatism. Gandhi was an outstanding product of this orthodox milieu: he was a bania more brahmanised than brahmans; his world-view and life-philosophy were moulded and shaped by the age-old brahmanic values and way of life. While winning friends and influencing people through his seductive rhetoric of truth, non-violence, God, sin and punishment, he never gave up his basic belief in the brahmanic fundamentalism which is evident from his constant evocation of varnashrama, Ram-rajya and trusteeship – the three unmistakable status quoist concepts embedded in the traditional structure of hierarchy and exploitation – that represent his social, political and economic philosophies.

Before delving into Gandhi's politics on caste and untouchability, it would be in order to have a broad understanding of his highly successful but sinister synthesis of varna dharma, culture, and nationalism which, beneath the colourful appearance of integrity and humanity, was deeply brahmanic, hegemonic, and regressive. The essence of Swaraj, 'self-government' or 'freedom' – each time Gandhi spoke on the subject he gave a different definition of the word – was kept 'delightfully vague' (Nehru 1999: 76) which meant almost everything for everybody, without actually disturbing anybody or changing anything. The kind of nationalism that the Congress under Gandhian guidance established was the same one, perhaps a bit more nuanced and evolved as per exigencies of time, as visualised by the nineteenth century proponents of Vedic-brahmanic nationalism. Since the past model of caste-based 'organic' and 'harmonious' society was Gandhi's ideal, he was for strengthening, not weakening, the established order. Awash with religious symbolism, his nationalism was sharply opposed to the mass struggle for social and material change; whatever changes were to be effected had to come from above. The net result, of the real nature and impact of Gandhian nationalism, as Aloysius (1997: 170-213) has shown, was to 'deflect the course of political awakening from the hard world of the economic and political to that of the nebulous and mysterious'.

Criss-crossing the subcontinent and conquering the masses with the mesmeric straddling of religion and politics – made possible by material support from his wealthy castemen (Bombay industrialists and Ahmedabad millowners) and his unquestioned political leadership accorded by the grateful upper castes – Gandhi gave a body blow to the secular and political agendas of the lower classes and Muslim masses, which till now were gaining momentum through the subcontinent, and instead established an abstract, vacuous nationalism embedded in a conformist religiosity that negated the emergence of the masses into a newly aware political community. In short, the Gandhian synthesis meant little more than 'religion for the lower caste masses and politics for the upper caste nationalists', which in essence degraded both religion and politics.

Before Gandhi's arrival on the scene, as Aloysius has compellingly argued, political mobilisation was not only interest-based, but also a reflection of the horizontal divide between and the upper castes and the masses in general, a divide that had widened as a result of colonial policies and practices.

While this social disjunction, in the absence of large-scale industrialisation and social mobility, did not come anywhere near the Marxian concept of class, it did unambiguously point out the direction in which economy and politics were moving. Propertied classes in the subcontinent came to be perceived as upper casteist (with a handful of the Muslim elite thrown in, of course), and the shudra, Ati-shudras, tribals and Muslim masses represented the dispossessed. The class-like formation was clearly horizontal, cutting across so-called religious unities. Particularly remarkable was the fact that the Muslim masses, most of whom were converts from the lower

castes, stood within the social structure as near equals to their Hindu counterparts exhibiting unmistakable signs of unity of interest with them. Together they were antagonistically poised towards the upper castes/classes.
(Aloysius 1997: 182-3)

Gandhi, a champion of the presumed organic and inclusive nature of Hindu society where the lowered castes have for centuries been living in harmony with the upper castes, was alarmed by this subversive trend. The Hindu-Indian ethos, he insisted toeing the line of early Hindu nationalists like Dayananda and Vivekananda, was eternally spiritual and harmonious, unlike the materialist – and decadent – West. Those who were clamouring for social and material change, Gandhi gratuitously claimed, did not know the 'eternal India'. This basic Gandhian refrain was elaborated into an attractive patriotic ideology by an impressive array of 'nationalist' scholar-activists. It suited the political needs of the upper classes who lost no time in recognising their messiah, and happily handed over the reins of nationalist leadership to him. Gandhi's insistene on total adherence to what he called passive resistance and non-violence had indeed been very effective in restraining peasants and workers. The native elites wanted the masses to be roused only against British rule. They restrained them in their actions and struggles against internal exploitation.

Gandhi's first major agitation against the British – Non-Cooperation movement – was a case in point. Based on Khilafat, cow protection and anti-untouchability, it was not directed only against the British but also aimed at arresting and reversing the secular-political movement of the lower classes (ibid.). Gandhi gave the mass of 'Hindu' workers and peasants who aspired for material change, the issues of cow-protection and anti-untouchability, while his prescription for the Muslim masses who, like the Hindu lower classes, were agitating for education, social betterment, diversification of occupations, and such issues, was Khilafat (to restore the Caliphate in Turkey as the global Islamic head a la the Pope, when the Arabs and Turks themselves had turned their back on the Caliphate issue in favour of modern political establishment). The Khilafat, however, met the political aspirations of the Muslim elite who were looking for a separate constituency.

> In this project of the setting up of a vertical pan-Indian Muslim political community, under the leadership of the Ali brothers, Gandhian Khilafat and Non-Co-operation played a major, if not a decisive role. In several senses this coming into being of a pan-Indian Muslim political consciousness is a logical sequel and a necessity to the previous rise of pan-Indian Hindu political consciousness. (ibid.: 183)

Though preposterously aimed at bringing Hindu-Muslim unity, Non-Cooperation and Khilafat 'prevented the maturing of the masses into a whole in terms of secular politics', and instead fashioned a cosmetic and transitory unity of Hindu and Muslim elites in terms of symbolic religious categories. The first wave of Gandhian nationalist politics – using the idioms of all-India political identities based on religious categories – succeeded in rupturing the ongoing process of unity of the lower classes with the Muslim masses, and effectively brought them back under the traditional upper class leadership of their respective communities (ibid.: 184). 'This shift from the secular to the spiritual, politics to religion, was presumed to be in accordance with the Eastern genius and a part and parcel of the erection of the nationalist moral response to imperialism' (ibid.). In this nationalist paradigm the so-called liberal-democratic advocates of Hindu-Muslim unity (the so-called nationalist secularists) as well as the practitioners of communal (Hindu/Muslim) politics 'both had a remarkable identity of function: to prevent the nation from emerging. The autonomy of the lower caste masses was to be denied at all costs and their differential and modern political agenda to be submerged.' In the nationalist version, the nation was now 'composed of two vertical communities presumably run on the basis of the pre-modern social order, of course with the necessary expansion of power and a political role for the upper caste elite' (ibid.: 185).

The elite segments of both Hindu and Muslim communities grabbed the opportunity that Gandhi provided them to reassert their leadership on 'religious' lines, as it greatly helped them thwart the egalitarian aspirations of the common people. It was more than evident that the vested interests of both communities dreaded the socio-economic restructuring that secular politics would necessarily entail. The politics of religion, on the other hand, gave them the unique opportunity to conjure up an external threat – the Hindu threat to Muslims and the Muslim threat to Hindus – to divert attention from public pressure for socio-economic changes. This politics based on social immobility necessarily led to polarisation on communal lines and was shamelessly exploited by the elite not only to corner many colonial benefits and jobs in the name of representing their communities, but also in building their 'nationalist' credentials among their respective masses. Of course, it was in the British interest to fan suspicion between Hindus and Muslims, but the policy of divide and rule was also in the interest of the vested interests of both communities. With this reason, the Hindu and Muslim elites actively helped the British to succeed in their divisive design. In his autobiography, written in the 1930s, Nehru could see the sinister and quintessentially anti-national face of elite politics:

It is nevertheless extraordinary how the bourgeois classes, both among the Hindus and the Muslims, succeeded, in the sacred name of religion, in getting a measure of mass sympathy and support for programmes and demands which had absolutely nothing to do with the masses, or even the lower middle class. Everyone of the communal demands put forward by any communal group is, in the final analysis, a demand for jobs, and these jobs could only go to a handful of the upper middle class. . . . These narrow political demands, benefiting at the most a small number of the upper middle classes, and often creating barriers in the way of national unity and progress, were cleverly made to appear the demands of the masses of that particular religious group. (Nehru 1999: 138)

Obviously, this nationalism was symbiotically attached to the colonial politics of viewing Indians in terms of religious identities which the architects of the early phase of cultural nationalism – Dayananda, Vivekananda, Bankim, Tilak, Aurobindo – had followed. By overlapping nationalism with Hinduism, Gandhi only carried this tradition forward to its logical conclusion – Hindu-Muslim communalism and the ultimate partition of the country.[3] The bloody vivisection of the country, in which millions lost their lives in riots that accompanied the truncated freedom, was a disaster waiting to happen as in both versions of nationalism, political identities were based on religion.

Ambedkar's Revolt

Around the time when Gandhi had firmly established himself as the supreme leader of Hindu society and the national movement, B. R. Ambedkar (1891-1956) – an erudite, astute, articulate and audacious dalit, later to emerge as the representative of what he termed *Bahishkrit Bharat* (the excluded and marginalised India) – entered the public life of a doubly colonised society. The people for whom he was to wage a life-long struggle were not only socially and educationally backward, economically subservient, and culturally oppressed, but also, as Gore (1993) correctly stresses, regionally dispersed and divided into hundreds of castes and sub-castes. In the given circumstances, Ambedkar was left with only two alternatives – either to offer himself in a spirit of resignation to the reformist patronage of brahmanic Hinduism led by Gandhi, or to strike out in radical search of an alternative vision of society with emphasis on civic equality and the economic-political empowerment of the oppressed communities. While the first option was easy for a person like Ambedkar, whom the Gandhis of the world would surely have loved to parade as their dalit showboy, the second was hugely daunting. He would have to fight, without any material support, the immensely powerful forces of injustice and oppression.

It may be recalled that Ambedkar's struggle against the social establishment was both an extension and a modification of the shramanic ideologies and traditions of counter-culture that had, since the time of the Buddha, challenged the system of hegemony, hierarchy, and oppression. Ambedkar was emphatic about his ideological kinship with the egalitarian ethos of the Buddha, Kabir, and Phule – the three figures who inspired him. Notwithstanding the changing strategies of his movement in the face of extremely hostile circumstances, he never wavered from the broader vision and objectives of his movement which he set out with remarkable clarity in the very beginning of his social life. As Gore puts it, 'Self-esteem, liberation and the opportunity to develop one's potential was the goal. Politics and law were the means. Organisation and unity were necessary for success in political conflict. Education was important in itself, but also as a means to gain economic opportunity and administrative office' (1993: 214). With this vision, he gave the call to 'Educate, Agitate and Organise' which he subsequently elaborated in different ways and with newer emphasis throughout his life.

From his early days in public life in the 1920s to his conversion to Buddhism, the establishment of the Republican Party, and his death – all in 1956 – Ambedkar's life is a story of spirited struggle and total dedication to the wretched of the earth. To know and understand Ambedkar is to know and understand that one is not born but rather becomes a dalit – oppressed, broken, and grounded. His genius lay in the fact that he lost no time in realising – and brilliantly articulating – that the ignorance, humiliation, and inaction of the oppressed had been symbiotically related to the whole situation of their domination in the name of religion. Forcibly kept away from education for centuries, the depressed classes had not been allowed to know and respond to the situation that submerged them in a state of subjugation and slavery.

Ambedkar gradually emerged not merely as a champion of the dalits or Scheduled Castes – which he definitely was – but 'a national leader of all marginalised classes, with an alternative vision of society, nation, culture and politics'. His commitment and struggle made him a hero in the eyes of the deprived and the voiceless, who expected him to lead them in their battle for a life of dignity under the emerging civil society. As such, Ambedkar's alternative ideology of Indian culture and nationalism was not only his own but reflected the viewpoints of the entire spectrum of disadvantaged and marginalised classes (Aloysius 1997). It was a huge responsibility which Ambedkar wielded heroically, scripting in the process a liberation struggle which has few parallels in history. Ambedkar's contribution in humanising, rationalising, and modernising Indian society is yet to be analysed and appreciated in its historical perspective. His personality and ideology – which has been grossly distorted and suppressed in the dominant academia like that of the people he represented – were not only remarkably modern and creative, but also national in the truest sense. Ambedkar's crusade for the greatest happiness of the greatest number – *bahujana hitaya bahujana sukhaya* (to use his spiritual mentor Gautam Buddha's famous words) – as the foundation of all morals and legislations set him apart as a radical action-philosopher. A lawyer, a social scientist, an economist, an outstanding parliamentarian and the principal architect of the Indian Constitution, Ambedkar was an intellectual colossus, who ingeniously put to use his extraordinary erudition and talents for evolving a liberation theory rooted in the Indian soil.

Ambedkar thought deeply about the problems of casteism, untouchability, inequality, and deprivation. He showed how they were inter-linked, and in turn responsible for social strife, which hindered emotional integration and economic development. Laying bare the regressive world-view of Hinduism – which was to him a mere euphemism for brahmanism – Ambedkar systematically exposed the traditional monopoly of power and knowledge in Indian society. In a series of books, speeches, and editorials he developed a thesis that irrefutably illustrated why the Hindu discourse offered no route to liberation for the depressed classes. This was the 'original sin' committed by Ambedkar – 'the unredeemed sinner' – who was 'guilty' of being born in an untouchable caste. The brahmanical forces, which were now at the forefront of the nationalist power politics, lost no time in recognising the danger. Beverley Nichols, author of the controversial *Verdict on India*, who considered Ambedkar one of the six best brains in the India of the mid-twentieth century, has sketched the kind of upper caste treatment meted out to the dalit Ambedkar:

... a creature from whose touch the extreme orthodox must fly as though he were a leper, a monster whose slightest contact compels them to precipitate themselves into the nearest bath-tub, to soap and pray, and pray and soap, so that the filth of Dr. Ambedkar – (M.A. London) – the shame of Dr. Ambedkar – (high honours at Columbia University) – the plague and scourge of Dr. Ambedkar – (special distinction at Heidelberg) – should be washed for ever from their immaculate and immortal souls.
(Nichols 1946: 30)

Nichols, as if to give credence to his dramatic description, adds chillingly: 'We are not talking of the past, but of the year 1944. These are not legends, fairy tales, gypsy songs; they are news paragraphs, stop-press' (ibid.). As India was bracing itself to kick out the external colonialists, untouchability – 'history's most flagrant example of man's inhumanity to man' – was still deeply rooted in the Hindu social order. Thanks to the internal colonisers, nearly all attempts to abolish it had met with failure.

Ambedkar, who plodded his way through such insults and humiliations and who had to leave rental accommodation and jobs where high caste peons flung files at him, considered caste as anathema to the nation and nationalism. He went on to prove – through a series of brilliant writings including the classic *Annihilation of Caste* – that the degrading and dehumanising caste system has been the chief factor responsible for horrifying forms of bondage, deprivation, ignorance, and ultimate downfall of millions of people relegated as 'low' caste. He wanted human rights and dignity for them. He wanted equality, not patronage and charity. He wanted constitutional measures and legal safeguards, not Gandhian trusteeship. Ambedkar's endless clash with the Congress and Gandhi along with the kind of nationalism they envisioned and practised was precisely on these issues.

Ambedkar was a visionary yet an incorrigible realist, and his reading of the social scenario proved to be frighteningly true. When he spearheaded a peaceful campaign to ensure to dalits the right to draw water from a public tank at Mahad (Maharashtra) in 1927, bloody retaliation from upper-caste Hinduism was swift in coming. Interestingly, at about the same time, Radhakrishnan was waxing eloquent on the Hindu view of life, vindicating and glorifying the caste system at Oxford. When Ambedkar was burning the *Manusmriti* for handing down all kinds of humiliations to shudras and women during the Mahad struggle, Gandhi was defending varna order and trying to prove the unprovable that Hindu shastras and scriptures do not sanction social and gender discrimination. Jawaharlal Nehru, the high priest of socialism, was no different. Ambedkar had reason to suspect that Nehru's pride in his Pandit title and his deafening silence on caste oppression was not that innocent.[4] As we have seen in the Introduction, Nehru, in his *Discovery of India*, presents caste as a solution to the problem of organising the co-existence of different races and communities, and even warns against dismantling the caste structure that had, according to him, ensured social 'cohesiveness' and the 'stability' of India (Nehru 1996: 246-7).

In his historic Mahad speech on 25 December 1927, Ambedkar declared that the issue at stake was not merely to enable the untouchables to drink water from the prohibited lake (that water was not nector that would make us immortal, he jibed) but 'to assert that we too are human beings like others'. The real reason why the upper castes prevented the untouchables from drawing water, he stressed, was not because they would pollute it, but to show that castes declared inferior by the sacred tradition of shastras were not their equals. The struggle, therefore, was to set up the norm of equality. This could not be accomplished unless the edifice that supported the whole hierarchical and ascriptive structure was brought down (see Dangle 1992: 223-33). As he put it, the struggle was the beginning of a social revolution comparable to the French Revolution of 1789 which paved the way for the historic Charter of Human Rights for all French citizens. Ambedkar emphasised that the issue was not merely to remove untouchability but to radically reorganise Indian society on the principles of equality, fraternity, and liberty. 'We need to pull away the nails which hold the framework of caste-bound Hindu society together, such as those of the prohibition of intermarriage down to the prohibition of social intercourse so that Hindu society becomes all of one caste. Otherwise untouchability cannot be removed nor can equality be established' (Dangle 1992: 227-8).

As Gore has observed, in Ambedkar's ideology, identity was subordinate to human dignity. Advocating a recourse to resistance to upper caste high handedness and assertion of one's human rights, he said, 'We do not value Hinduism, we value human dignity' (Gore 1993: 97). Elsewhere, he reiterated the same point, 'We want equal rights in society. We will achieve them as far as possible while remaining within the Hindu fold, or if necessary, by kicking away this worthless Hindu identity' (ibid.: 91). He also stressed that the task of removing untouchability and establishing equality would be carried out not by others but by the sufferers of the system themselves. This would benefit the entire nation. The abolition of graded inequality was not only a movement for freedom but also an attempt to build bridges between people that would result in unifying them. Putting Ambedkar's Mahad struggle in a wider perspective, Gore has equated its significance with that of Gandhi's Dandi march:

The burning of a copy of the Manusmriti at Mahad was one way of symbolically rejecting the rules that it specified and the doctrine of inequality at birth on which the caste system was based. As a method of communicating a message to an illiterate following, this had the same significance as the making of salt at Dandi by Gandhi. They both symbolised a rejection of the premise on which authority was based and they both helped to break down the mystique of 'divine' dispensation. (1993: 199)

Ambedkar's famous statement 'the freedom which the governing class in India was struggling for is freedom that rules the servile classes in India' was not an endorsement of colonial rule as is made out by his opponents. It was a devastating – and quite justifiable – denunciation of the self-serving nationalist leadership. True, the question of dalits – their centuries-old social slavery and economic misery – was uppermost in Ambedkar's mind. But his struggle against internal colonialism does not contradict his opposition to the British rule which, he said categorically, did nothing to improve the life of the socially and economically suppressed classes. In the plenary session of the First Round Table Conference, Ambedkar made a major statement which clarified his political stance *vis-à-vis* the British government and the Hindu society. In his speech on 20 November 1930 'to put the point of view of the depressed classes', Ambedkar stated that the 'bureaucratic form of Government of India should be replaced by a government of the people, by the people and for the people'. Along with this, he demanded a unitary state and adult suffrage with reserved seats and legal safeguards for the depressed classes. Ambedkar stressed that the British government had not done anything about social evils and the oppression of the downtrodden classes as it had 'accepted the social arrangements as it found them'. The British, he said, had not been interested in removing exploitation of farm and industrial labour by landlords and capitalists. While asserting that the goodwill of the British was irrelevant, he also pointed out the danger from within:

We feel that nobody can remove our grievances as well as we can, and we cannot remove them unless we get political power in our hands. No share of this political power can evidently come to us so long as the British government remains as it is. It is only in a Swaraj constitution that we stand any chance of getting the political power in our own hands, without which we cannot bring salvation to our people. . . . We know that political power is passing from the British into the hands of those who wield such tremendous economic, social and religious sway over our existence. We are willing that it may happen, though the idea of Swaraj recalls to the mind of many the tyrannies, oppressions and injustices practised upon us in the past. (BAWS, vol. 2: 505-6)

Ambedkar was for freedom, but he certainly held the view – and this is the crux of the matter – that as no country was good enough to rule over another, no class or caste was good enough to rule over another. His concepts of freedom, nation, and nationalism were radically different from the ones envisioned and advocated by the Congress leadership. Ambedkar was sceptical of the high caste leaders who represented the power politics mainly of landlords, capitalists, and moneylenders but as leaders of all sections of Indian society. He resented the fact that the masses were drawn into the Congress only to be camp followers, with no say in policy.

Driven by the discriminatory philosophy of brahmanism, the governing classes in India had always been hostile to those outside the fold and, therefore, it did not sympathise with the masses, their wants, pains, or aspirations. The Congress did not favour the idea that the deprived masses should be educated and appointed to high office, and it opposed their movement to raise towards self-respect (BAWS, vol. 9: 235-6). Brahmans and banias[5] in the vanguard of the freedom project, he argued, were still guided consciously or sub-consciously by the inegalitarian brahmanism. The ancient tradition and its social ideology on which the high caste nationalists prided themselves so much, he elucidated with facts and compelling arguments, were grossly unjust and barbaric. Laying bare the structural reasons for the production of misery in brahmanical social ideology and religion, he exposed the 'sacred' law-books, which he termed the 'lawless laws', and brought out their horrors:

1. Graded inequality between the different classes;
2. Complete disarmament of the shudras and the untouchables;
3. Complete prohibition of the education of the shudras and the untouchables;

4. Ban on the shudras and the untouchables occupying places of power and authority;
5. Ban on the shudras and the untouchables acquiring property; and,
6. Complete subjugation and suppression of women. (BAWS, ibid.: 215)

The official doctrine of brahmanism, Ambedkar stresses, is inequality, whereby the suppression of the lower classes aspiring to equality had been systematically carried out by the upper classes. India was the only country where the intellectual class not only made education its monopoly but declared that the acquisition of education by the lower classes was a punishable crime. Exposing the double standards of the nationalist high caste leaders who took pride in the vicious tradition of suppression of a large number of their own countrymen and women but flailed the British – from a high moral pedestal – for outraging the dignity and human rights of Indians, Ambedkar argued:

The Congress politicians complain that the British are ruling India by a wholesale disarmament of the people of India. But they forget that disarmament of the Shudras and the Untouchables was the rule of law promulgated by the Brahmins. . . . If the large majority of people of India appear today to be thoroughly emasculated, spiritless, with no manliness, it is the result of the brahmanic policy of wholesale disarmament to which they have been subjected for the untold ages. . . . It would, however, be a mistake to suppose that only the wrongs of man are a religion to him. For the Brahmin has given his support to the worst wrongs that women have suffered from in any part of the world. Widows were burnt alive as suttees. . . . Widows were not allowed to remarry. . . . The record of the Brahmins as law givers for the Shudras, for the Untouchables and for women is the blackest as compared with the record of the intellectual classes in other parts of the world. For, no intellectual class has prostituted its intelligence to invent a philosophy to keep his uneducated countrymen in a perpetual state of ignorance and poverty as the Brahmins have done in India. (ibid.: 215-16)

In Ambedkar's opinion, the nationalism of high caste Hindus was not only not dissociated from, but constructed and nurtured on, such dubious and essentially immoral tradition. According to him, most nationalist stalwarts – and he included Tilak, Patel, and Nehru among them – were quite conscious that they belonged to the governing class and were destined to rule. Citing several examples from contemporary life and politics, Ambedkar went on to assert that the old regressive tradition was kept alive in both ideology and practice by the high caste nationalists. Tilak and his fellow Congressmen, he alleged, were not only very conscious and proud of their caste positions but also egregiously contemptuous of the lowered castes:

In 1918, when the Non-Brahmins and the Backward Classes had started an agitation for separate representation in the Legislature, Mr. Tilak in a public meeting held in Sholapur said he did not understand why the oil pressers, tobacco shopkeepers, washermen, etc. – that was his description of the Non-Brahmins and the Backward Classes – should want to go into the Legislature. In his opinion, their business was to obey the laws and not to aspire for power to make laws. (ibid.: 209)

Similarly, in 1942, when the Viceroy invited many Indians, including some members of the depressed classes, to support the war effort, Patel commented maliciously that the Viceroy sent for even Ghanchis (oil pressers) and Mochis (cobblers) (ibid.). Citing such examples, Ambedkar reveals how the means adopted by the Congress in its politics of boycott also reeked of its deep-dyed contempt for the lower classes. The Congress in its attempt to dissuade others from contesting elections took out processions in various states carrying placards,

Who will go to the Legislatures?
Only barbers, cobblers, potters and sweepers.

When the Congress found that this was not enough to deter many 'respectable' persons from standing for the elections, it went to the extent of putting up illiterate barbers, potters, sweepers, etc. and got them elected in order to make the legislatures objects of contempt and worthlessness:

. . . While on the one hand Congressmen were engaged in fighting for Swaraj which they said they wanted to win in the name and for the masses, on the other hand . . . they were committing the worst outrages upon the very masses by exhibiting them publicly as objects of contempt to be shunned and avoided. (ibid.: 211)

The mentality of these nationalists towards their unprivileged countrymen, he remonstrated, was as odious, if not more egregious, as that of the British for the colonised. These politicians in the name of Indian people and nationalism, Ambedkar said, just wanted to establish their monopoly power as they had no intention to give up their own privilege and end hierarchy and hegemonism. What is to be the fate of the servile classes of India under this governing class, he asked despairingly. The governing class, he warned, would not disappear by the magic wand of Swaraj, it would remain as it was and having been freed from the incubus of British imperialism, the Indian elite would acquire greater strength and vigour and capture power – as the governing classes in every country do – to serve its own interests (ibid.: 212).

THE MACHIAVELLI IN THE MAHATMA: THE TRUE STORY OF POONA PACT

The Second Round Table Conference and the subsequent MacDonald Award for separate electorates set the stage for a frontal confrontation between Gandhi and Ambedkar on the question of the depressed classes. Let us examine what was at stake. If the confrontation was inevitable, who exacerbated it? While giving shape to a proposed constitution, the first conference had agreed upon two disturbing things from the nationalist point of view – one, the powers left to the princely states or its 'federal' structure, and two, the provision of separate electorates for the minorities (Omvedt 1994: 169). Ambedkar's stand during the first conference – when he espoused universal adult suffrage and affirmative action for the weaker sections – should have been closest to the nationalist perspective. The Congress could have seized this opportunity to give a truly nationalist direction to the future constitution by forging an alliance with Ambedkar and social democrats like him. However, for reasons best known to Gandhi and his followers, the Congress did not oppose either the 'federal' structure or separate electorates for Muslim and Sikh minorities (ibid.). Not only did the Congress seem to have easily capitulated before the powerful Muslim lobby, it did not show any resolve to press for democracy in the princely states either. But the Congress was quick to cry foul at separate electorates for the untouchables. Gandhi would not accept the untouchables' claim for special protection within or outside Hinduism. Opposing any form of special representation involving reserved seats to the untouchables, Gandhi insisted that what they needed the most was social and religious acceptance by the upper castes, not the legal and political rights or safeguards.

By far the most exploited and vulnerable section among all those claiming special treatment, the untouchables' interests were not only different but in conflict with the material interests of the upper classes (ibid.). However, from the viewpoints of the untouchables, claiming and gaining special protection was not possible unless they established their separate identity as a social group. This situation amidst the Congress' growing impatience for transfer of power from the British to the Indian elite, forced Ambedkar to demand a separate electorate for the untouchables. Ambedkar was not opposed to the transfer of power – freedom – *per se*; his endeavour was to secure the arrangement that the freedom must be accompanied by such conditions and by such provisions that power would not fall to the privileged groups, whether Hindu or Muslim, and that the solution would be such that power shall be shared by all communities in a fair and democratic manner. As Gore writes, Gandhi's strategy, on the other hand, was to simply deny the untouchables a special identity and a separate electorate with the intent that once their demand for special representation was rejected there would be no discussion of special protective measures, except in so far as the Hindus wished to concede them of their own free will (1993: 135).

Not unexpectedly, Gandhi and Ambedkar clashed at the Second Round Table Conference. Before the conference, Ambedkar had met Gandhi in London in August 1931 in a surcharged atmosphere. It was a clash of the two titans.

According to B. C. Kamble's description, Gandhi treated Ambedkar with a lack of even normal politeness, while Ambedkar responded with a condemnation of the Congress, walking out after a scathing speech ending with the famous statement, 'Mahatmaji, I have no country'. This was not dialogue, but confrontation. They confronted each other again at the conference, each speaking with emotion and eloquence, with the self-assurance

> of leaders who can gather masses behind them. Each claimed to speak on behalf of untouchables. There was a vast difference in point of view, with Ambedkar stressing the need for political power for the Dalits, and with Gandhi arguing for reform and protection from above: 'What these people need more than election to the legislatures is protection from social and religious persecution.' But the emotional quality of the debate indicates an ever deeper clash. (Omvedt 1994: 170)

The conference ended inconclusively, and the representatives, including Gandhi, left the matter of separate electorates for the minorities to be decided by the British Prime Minister. Finally, in August 1932, the Prime Minister Ramsey McDonald announced the British policy on the issue. The British proposal, in nutshell, was that there would be a number of special seats for the depressed classes to be filled by election from special constituencies in which only the members of the depressed classes electorally qualified would be entitled to vote (Baxi 2000). The depressed classes would also be entitled to vote in the general constituencies. Reserved constituencies were to be formed in areas where the depressed classes were most numerous and, except in Madras, they should not cover the whole area of the Province. The arrangement was initially limited to twenty years. The British Premier also clarified in a letter to Gandhi that the number of special seats thus created 'will be seen to be small' and was just not intended to 'provide a quota numerically appropriate for the total representation of the whole of the depressed class population'. McDonald made it clear that this proposal was different from the idea of a 'communal electorate for the depressed classes', stressing that it was primarily intended to 'place them in a position to pick for themselves'. The method of creating legislative reservation of seats, the Prime Minister further clarified, was not considered helpful since it was unlikely to produce representatives who could genuinely represent the depressed classes 'because in practically all cases such members would be elected by a majority consisting of higher caste Hindus' (ibid.).

Gandhi thought this reasonable proposal to be dangerous to Hindu and national interests – 'calculated to destroy Hinduism' – and decided to oppose it with the threat of self-immolation. He began his fast unto death in Yeravada prison 'as a man of religion' and also as a leader of 'numberless men and women who had childlike faith in his wisdom'. Gandhi did not attempt to give reasons or counter arguments against the separate electorate for the depressed classes, except declaring that for him the matter was purely a religious one. 'For me the question of those classes is predominantly moral and religious. The political aspect, important though it is, dwindles into insignificance compared to the moral and religious one.'

Gandhi, however, revealed his real motive a day after he began his fast in a conversation with Sardar Patel. Mahadev Desai, the Mahatma's secretary, has recorded what he said to justify his threat of self-immolation:

The possible consequences of separate electorates fill me with horror. Separate electorates for all other communities will still leave room for me to deal with them, but I have no other means to deal with 'untouchables'. . . . It will create division among Hindus so much so that it will lead to blood-shed. Untouchable hooligans will make common cause with Muslim hooligans and kill caste Hindus. (see Zelliot 1998: 167)

From the time of the Gandhi-Ambedkar clash in London, a vicious political battle ensued in which the upper caste Congress leaders, in league with the 'nationalist' press, sought to hijack leadership of the depressed classes by organising meetings and producing untouchable spokespersons to sing praises of Gandhi and lambaste Ambedkar (Omvedt 1994: 172). By the time of Gandhi's fast, Ambedkar-bashing had reached a crescendo. Ambedkar was isolated and reviled in the filthiest of words for 'putting the Mahatma's life in danger'. Keeping his cool under most trying circumstances, Ambedkar responded to the challenge in his characteristic style:

It has fallen to my lot to be the villain of the piece. But I tell you I shall not deter from my pious duty, and betray the just and legitimate interests of my people even if you hang me on the nearest lamp-post in the street.
(Keer 1971: 209)

On the eve of Gandhi's fast, to begin on 20 September 1932, Ambedkar issued a long statement (*BAWS*, vol. 9: 311-17), clarifying his position on the issue and requesting the Mahatma to reconsider his decision to self-immolate and avert the 'terrorism by his followers against the depressed classes'. Gandhi's arguments, he said, were 'strange and incomprehensible', and if given a choice 'between Hindu faith and the possession of political power', the depressed classes would choose the latter, and thus end Gandhi's agony and fast. Remonstrating that 'he has staked his life in order to deprive the depressed classes of little they have got', he counselled Gandhi that his 'determination to fast unto death was worthy of a far better cause'. Responding to Gandhi's claim that the proposed electoral separation would arrest the 'marvellous work' of generations of Hindu reformers and give a jolt to the campaign for removal of untouchability, Ambedkar said:

There have been many Mahatmas in India whose sole object was to remove Untouchability and to elevate and absorb the Depressed Classes, but every one of them has failed in his mission. Mahatmas have come and Mahatmas have gone. But the Untouchables have remained as Untouchables.
(ibid.: 315)

Ambedkar argued that if separate electorates of Muslims and Sikhs would not split up the nation, there was no reason why separate electorate for the depressed classes, who were more in need of protection, should threaten national unity. Referring to the 'manufactured' opposition from some Congressmen (supporting joint electorates) who were being projected as the voice of untouchables, Ambedkar made it clear that they could vote in and contest from general constituencies; it was not compulsory for these – or any – members of the depressed classes to enrol in separate electoral rolls or to contest from separate constituencies if they so desired. Obliquely referring to Gandhi's supporters who were beating their breasts over the 'Mahatma's life in danger' due to 'this untouchable', Ambedkar asserted that he was not prepared to accept slavery for his people under such unholy histrionics:

I desire to assure the public that although I am entitled to say that I regard the matter as closed, I am prepared to consider the proposals of the Mahatma. I however trust the Mahatma would not drive me to the necessity of making a choice between his life and the rights of my people. For I can never consent to deliver my people bound hand and foot to the caste Hindus for generations to come. (ibid.: 317)

Meanwhile, politicians of various hues, mostly die-hard Gandhians, had gathered in Bombay to strike a compromise formula. They tried to break the deadlock by arranging a one-to-one talk between Gandhi and Ambedkar. After hard bargaining, the confrontation ended in an uneasy compromise known as the Poona Pact. Gandhi accepted reserved seats, Ambedkar acceded to a joint electorate with a provision for primary elections in which the depressed class vote would decide who would stand for the election. Ambedkar secured 148 seats – he wanted 197 – in the Provincial Assemblies for the depressed classes out of a total of 780, and 10 per cent of seats in the Central Assembly. However, Ambedkar's insistent demand for a referendum on the same after twenty five years – and not before – was set aside when a 'critically ill' Gandhi said with a tone of finality, 'Five years or my life' (Keer 1971: 214).

The pact gave dalits some reserved seats but robbed them of the crucial opportunity to elect their own leaders, which was what separate electorates should have meant. Now they were to vote in all constituencies – general as well as reserved – with the upper caste Hindus and others. Under this scheme, for all practical purposes, the non-dalit choice became crucial in selecting and electing dalit representatives in the reserved constituencies since there was no constituency in any state where dalits were more than 25-30 per cent of the electorate. In order to win, dalit candidates became critically dependent on their acquiescent relationship with non-dalit voters, which made the emergence of an independent dalit leadership almost impossible. This was the real implication of the Poona Pact and that is why Ambedkar had been adamant about a separate electorate. Not surprisingly, the militant among the dalits derided the compromise as a defeat, and so did Ambedkar soon after the customary exchange of pleasantries during the talk. The sense of betrayal was to deepen in subsequent years as the Congress leadership would not nominate able, educated and truly representative dalit candidates for reserved constituencies. In an incisive analysis of the 1937 elections, Ambedkar was to show later how and why the Congress selected the best educated candidates from the high castes, and preferred to field the least educated SC nominees from the reserved categories (*BAWS*, vol. 9: 217-24). Since then the duplicity – nominating weak, semi-literate and pliable SC/ST candidates — has been practised by all mainstream parties, making a mockery of Ambedkar's dream.

Dalits still debate the issue and curse Gandhi for falsely claiming to represent their 'cause' and their 'vital interests'. 'Gandhi who feared a political division . . . in the villages ignored the division that already existed; in his warning against the spread of violence, he ignored the violence already existing in the lives of the dalits' (Omvedt 1994: 172). Claiming to speak in the name of untouchables, Gandhi did not play the part of a national leader; he played the role of a typical [upper caste] Hindu (ibid.). In the words of Ambedkar's biographer Dhananjay Keer:

> At Yeravada, the politician in Gandhi became successful and the Mahatma was defeated! So effective and crushing was the victory of Gandhi that he deprived Ambedkar of all his life-saving weapons and made him a powerless man as did Indra in the case of Karna. (1971: 216)

Ambedkar himself considered the fast to be 'moral blackmail' since Gandhi's self-immolation would have provoked a bloody retaliation against dalits from upper caste Hindus. By pointing out that initially Gandhi was opposed to even the idea of reserved seats for dalits, Ambedkar saw in Gandhi a politician whose politics was directed in the interests of keeping dalits in the Hindu fold. 'There was nothing noble in the fast. It was against them (the untouchables) and was the worst form of coercion against a helpless people. . . . It was a vile and wicked act' (BAWS, vol. 9: 259).

Today, there is general agreement among dalit thinkers that the rejection of the demand for separate electorates and the constitution of joint electorates gave a body blow to the idea of independent political participation by dalits (and adivasis) in independent India. The brahmanical forces that Gandhi led, orchestrated the whole affair in a manner that ensured that only stooges could have come out of it. Kanshi Ram has assessed its ramifications in a blunt manner in The Chamcha Age (The Age of Stooges):

> Poona Pact made dalits helpless. By rejecting separate electorate, dalits were deprived of their genuine representation in legislatures. Several and various kind of chamchas were born in the last fifty years. As and when India's

high caste Hindu rulers felt the need of chamchas and when the authority of the upper castes got endangered by real and genuine dalit leaders, chamchas were brought to the fore in all other fields. (see Dubey 2001: 295)

On the other hand, elite historians have portrayed the hard power politics that underpinned the conflict between Ambedkar and Gandhi as a unique moral instance of Gandhi's ability to win over his opponent's heart! See how Ravinder Kumar, a 'progressive' historian, has tried to erase the sordid reality in his eagerness to glorify Gandhi and his politics:

Gandhi had thus achieved what as a true Satyagrahi he always strove for: He had won his opponent's heart! . . . The differences between the two leaders, one an untouchable by birth, the other an untoucha' ' by volition, were thus healed. . . . The agreement between the Mahatma and Ambedkar saved a society from turning into itself and committing collective suicide. Indeed, the Poona Pact was a victory won by Gandhi in the course of a struggle seeking to liberate Hindu society from a dangerous malformation lodged in the very core of its social being. It was, perhaps, the Mahatma's finest hour. (cited in Omvedt 1994: 175)

Such scholarly perception appears to be formed on the information provided by Gandhi's countless 'propaganda friends' whose sense of 'sacrifice for the country' was synonymous with beating the Mahatma's drum. What one such Gandhian, Rai Bahadur Mehrchand Khanna, said at a meeting of the untouchables at Peshawar on 12 April 1945, under the auspices of the Depressed Classes League, captures the sum and substance of the Congress chorus on the issue:

Your best friend is Mahatma Gandhi, who even resorted to a fast for your sake and brought about the Poona Pact under which you have been enfranchised and given representation on local bodies and legislatures. Some of you, I know, have been running after Dr. Ambedkar, who is just a creation of the British Imperialists and who uses you to strengthen the hands of the British Government in order that India may be divided and the Britishers continue to retain power. I appeal to you in your interests, to distinguish between self-styled leaders and your real friends. (cited in *BAWS*, vol. 9: 239)

Rubbishing the reading of the likes of Ravinder Kumar, Kancha Ilaiah, on the other hand, sees the Poona Pact as Gandhi's biggest blunder and Ambedkar's finest hour:

If the greatest blunder that Gandhi committed in his life was going on a fast against Dalit rights, this was also Ambedkar's finest hour. For if Gandhi had died in Yerawada Jail, the British Government would have washed off its hands as the fast was more against SCs, STs than against the British. In the event of his death massive caste riots would have broken out. . . . If Ambedkar were to yield to Gandhi's fast there would have been no constitutional safeguards for SCs, STs today. The SCs and STs know best what such safeguards mean in terms of reservations since, but for such safeguards, no SC or ST person would have come up in life. (Ilaiah 1997)

Two diametrically opposite interpretations of the Poona Pact is a classic example of how classes and masses – and their representative scholars – view the same event with vastly different perspectives. In sharp contradiction of the Vedic dictum *ekam sad vipra bahudha vadanti*, truths in general, and sociological/historical truths in particular, are not absolute; they are relative and hold different meanings for different strata of society. What was truth for Gandhi, especially on India's social reality, was a travesty of the truth for Ambedkar.[6] Indian historiography, like the nation and nationalism, has been a victim to the brahmanical tendency to perpetuate that truth that serves the self-interests of the upper castes and helps maintain their monopoly over knowledge and power.

The Anatomy of Gandhian Paternalism

Gandhi's 'moral' coercion, through the threat of self-immolation and a sanctimonious posturing witnessed during the Poona drama was nothing if not a total refutation of Ambedkarite ideology and politics. For Gandhi, the question of these classes was 'predominantly moral and religious', not political or economic as Amedkar was emphasising all along. Maintaining that the exploited untouchables were an element separate from the exploiter Hindus, Ambedkar went to the root of the problem, holding that the Hindus had much to lose by the abolition of untouchability. In a brilliant deconstruction of the Indian apartheid and Gandhian position on the issue,

Ambedkar argued that untouchabiltiy as an exploitative socio-economic system was even worse than slavery. In slavery, he said, the master had the responsibility to feed, clothe, and house the slave and keep him in good condition lest his or her market value fall; but in the system of untouchability the Hindu takes no responsibility for the maintenance of the untouchable. As an economic system, he insisted, untouchability permits unbridled exploitation without any obligation:

The system of Untouchability is a gold mine to the Hindus. In it the 240 millions of Hindus have 60 millions of Untouchables to serve as their retinue to enable the Hindus to maintain pomp and ceremony and to cultivate a feeling of pride and dignity befitting a master class, which cannot be fostered and sustained unless there is beneath it a servile class to look down upon. In it the 240 millions of Hindus have 60 millions of Untouchables to be used as forced labourers and because of their state of complete destitution and helplessness can be compelled to work on a mere pittance or sometimes on nothing at all. In it the 240 millions of Hindus have 60 millions of Untouchables to do the dirty work of scavengers and sweepers which the Hindu is debarred by his religion to do and which must be done by non-Hindus who could be no others than Untouchables. In it the 240 millions of Hindus have 60 millions of Untouchables who can be kept to lower jobs. . . . In it the 240 millions of Hindus have the 60 millions of Untouchables who can be used as shock-absorbers in slumps and dead-weights in booms, for in slumps it is the Untouchable who is fired first and the Hindu is fired last and in booms the Hindu is employed first and the Untouchable is employed last. (BAWS, vol. 9: 196)

Gandhi, on the other hand, having refused to see the untouchability problem in socio-economic terms and context, kept falling back on the same specious arguments. He bitterly contested Ambedkar's claim to represent the dalits. The onus was on Gandhi to prove his bona fides as the real leader of untouchables, and so he had to embark on *achchutoddhar*, 'uplift of the untouchables'. With paternalistic fanfare, Gandhi now rechristened the untouchables Harijans – 'children of God' – and formed an organisation called the Anti-untouchability League (which he later renamed as the Harijan Sevak Sangh) to do the *achchutoddhar*. The great irony was that Harijans themselves were marginalised in his Harijan campaign; the latter was basically intended as 'an expiation of upper castes' sins'. As Gandhi said, 'We have to obtain not the salvation of the untouchables but ours by treating them as equals' (see Keer 1971). Besides temple entry, Gandhian Harijan reformism consisted of a series of symbolic actions which centred on upper-caste reformers working among untouchables to inculcate in them temperance and discipline, and reforming their unhygienic ways, meat-eating, and alcoholism, seen as main reasons for their degradation. The approach was hegemonically integrationist.

The Harijan project neither intended to produce leaders from the dalit ranks to lead the liberation movement nor did it hide its strong opposition to any suggestion of structural changes in the age-old system. In stark contrast to the Ambedkarite spirit of constructive struggle against the iniquitous system, Gandhi's recipe veered around 'change of heart' and self-purification by the upper castes. He did not have any agenda of civil rights, political power, or economic opportunity for the deprived classes. In other words, Gandhi's approach was to create an 'ideal bhangi' who would continue to clean the excreta of others with the status of a brahman whereas Ambedkar's approach was to integrate the untouchables into mainstream society by giving them education and political rights.

Gandhi did not even bother to enter into a dialogue with Ambedkar and other dalits, solely concentrating on courting the upper caste Congressmen, who saw his anti-untouchability campaign as a political necessity, a fact Gandhi himself was aware of: 'Many Congressmen have looked upon this item (removal of untouchability) as a mere political necessity and not something indispensable' (cited in Aloysius 1997: 189). Swami Shraddhanand has reported that many high caste reformers who put the show of mixing with the untouchables in Gandhi's presence went and took a bath later, with their clothes on!

In a letter to A. V. Thakkar, General Secretary of the Anti-untouchability League (which later became Harijan Sevak Sangh), Ambedkar suggested that rather than dissipating its energies on symbolic gestures like temple entry, temperance, and discipline, the League should concentrate on campaigns to secure civil rights, equality of opportunity, and active social intercourse. Ambedkar's letter did not evoke any response – it was not even acknowledged.

Ambedkar refers to another interesting fact. To a deputation who waited on Gandhi requesting him to appoint untouchables on the managing committee of the Harijan Sevak Sangh, Gandhi was reported to have said:

The welfare work for the Untouchables is a penance which the Hindus have to do for the sin of Untouchability. The money that has been collected has been contributed by the Hindus. From both points of view, the Hindus alone must run the Sangh. Neither ethics nor right would justify the Untouchables in claiming a seat on the Board of the Sangh. (BAWS, vol. 9: 142)

The Gandhian approach, thus, was unmistakably paternalistic. In his scheme of things, the untouchables were to be the passive objects for the penance and practice of virtue by the upper castes. Gandhi was even against the untouchables giving up their traditional, degrading, and exploitative occupations like latrine cleaning, tanning, flaying, etc.: 'I do not advise the untouchables to give up their trades and professions.' One born a scavenger, Gandhi pontificated, must earn his livelihood by being a scavenger, and then do whatever else he likes. And then to give an air of sublimity to this sinister suggestion, he added fatuously, 'For, a scavenger is as worthy of his hire as a lawyer or your President. That, according to me, is Hinduism' (*Harijan*, 6 March 1937). He was also against their going on strike to demand better wages and working conditions. Chastising the sweepers of Bombay who went on strike in 1946, Gandhi wrote:

My opinion against sweepers' strike dates back to about 1897 when I was in Durban. A general strike was mooted there and the question arose as to whether scavengers should join it. My vote was registered against the (strike) proposal. . . . In spite of my close attachment to sweepers, better cause of it, I must denounce the coercive methods they are said to have employed. They will thereby be losers in the long run. City folk will not always be cowed down. . . . A Bhangi may not give up his work even for a day. (*Harijan*, 21 April 1946)

This statement is from a man who is greatly eulogised by his admirers for his supreme love – and sacrifice! – for scavengers. His acolytes never tire of citing his declaration: 'I may not be born again, but if it happens I will like to be born in a family of scavengers, so that I may relieve them of the inhuman, unhealthy, and hateful practice of carrying nightsoil' (*Young India*, 27 April 1921). The irony of the statement is generally lost on his admirers: had he been born in a family of scavengers, Gandhi of course would have struggled to relieve them of the sub-human task of handling the excreta of others; but the fact was, in his present avatar as an upper caste Hindu he was willing to do no more than pay lip-service to their cause. In the Gandhian orientation the functional equivalent of Harijan, 'the children of God', is the euphemism of their position as the 'helpless beings existing at the mercy of the upper castes'.

It is not difficult to see why Ambedkar was in total opposition to Gandhi's humbug on caste and untouchability. He critiqued Gandhi's insistence that poverty was soul-uplifting, and that all castes were equal and 'a scavenger has the same status as a brahman', as 'an outrage and a cruel joke on the helpless classes':

If Gandhism preached the rule of poverty for all and not merely for the shudra the worst that could be said about it is that it is a mistaken idea. But why preach it as good for one class only? Why appeal to the worst of human failings, namely, pride and vanity in order to make him voluntarily accept what on a rational basis he would resent as a cruel discrimination against him? What is the use of telling the scavenger that even a Brahmin is prepared to do scavenging when it is clear that according to the Hindu Shastras and Hindu notions, even if a Brahmin did scavenging, he would never be subject to the disabilities of one who is a born scavenger? For, in India, a man is not a scavenger because of his work. He is a scavenger because of his birth, irrespective of the question whether he does scavenging or not. If Gandhism preached that scavenging is a noble profession, with the objective of inducing those who refuse to engage in it, one could understand it. But why appeal to the scavenger's pride and vanity in order to induce him and him only to keep on to scavenging by telling him that scavenging is a noble profession and that he need not be ashamed of it? To preach that poverty is good for the Shudra and for none else, to preach that scavenging is good for the Untouchables and for none else and to make them accept these onerous impositions as voluntary purposes of life, by appeal to their failings is an outrage and a cruel joke on the helpless classes which none but Mr. Gandhi can perpetuate with equanimity and impunity. (BAWS, vol. 9: 292-3)

Gandhi's love for the spinning wheel and khadi, symbolising self-reliance, is well-known. He – and his foot soldiers – passionately spoke of it as a historic economic initiative that would provide mass employment and also affordable clothing for the millions. But khadi self-reliance, ironically, always survived on subsidies provided first by his rich friends and later by the governments of free India. In reality, he chiefly used it for political mobilisation. It is significant that at one point he was seriously considering spinning to be imposed as a pre-condition for Congress membership. But as Ambedkar has pointed out, Gandhi never ever thought of adopting a similar approach for the removal of caste disabilities. Between the transfer of power and the eradication of social discrimination, Gandhi apparently gave priority to the former and was in no mood to concede the depressed classes anything more than pious assurances and sanctimonious sentiments. Tearing into Gandhi's famed love for universal truth and justice, Ambedkar contended that Gandhi resorted to direct action against the British rule because it was founded on injustice, but was opposed to any such action against the Hindus who perpetrated worst kinds of social crimes against millions of their own countrymen. Gandhi, who was in the habit of going to fast on everything, did not ever go on a fast against upper-caste social oppression.

Abraham Lincoln, the American President, trapped in somewhat a similar situation during the Civil War in 1860s, refused to concede the demand of Confederate (Southern) slave states. In the teeth of opposition from the Southern states, bordering on secession, Lincoln in the Gettysburg Address (1863) declared the aims of preserving a 'nation conceived in liberty, and dedicated to the proposition that all men are created equal'. Our Gandhi, revered as the very embodiment of soul-uplifting spirituality, was made of a different stuff! His vacuous sympathy for the untouchables was not destined – or intended – to develop into an action plan.

Above all, Gandhi's anti-untouchability politics was embedded in his tenacious defence of everything Hindu. It is important that Gandhi's stout defence of varna system in *Harijan*, as a rebuff to Ambedkar's advocacy to abolish caste in his famous tract *Annihilation of Caste* (1936), came at a time when caste distinctions dominated everything, and due to caste millions of people were robbed of their rights. No matter what the Gandhiana and Gandhians say, Gandhi in fact did not consider his Harijan as a full human being born with natural and inalienable rights. A critical study of his fabled Harijan campaign leaves little doubt that it was a political charity, intended to integrate depressed classes into the Hindu fold, not as partners but as poor relations. Gandhi had once even asked a Christian missionary to pray for the Harijans but not to try to convert them as 'they did not have the mind and intelligence to understand what you talked. . . . Would you preach the Gospel to a cow?' (*Harijan*, 19 December 1936). This provoked even Jagjivan Ram, the rising Harijan mascot of the Congress, who registered a strong protest and described the Harijan Sevak Sangh as being 'erroneous in conception, faulty in emphasis, and halting in execution'. Jagjivan Ram had to be pacified with Gandhi clarifying that no ill-will was intended, for him the cow was 'a symbol of gentleness and patient suffering' (Zelliot 1996: 170).

Quite obviously, as many such instances of gross paternalism show, in Gandhi's concept of service to untouchables, there was hardly any scope for the educated, politically conscious untouchables struggling for civil rights. Not surprisingly, Ambedkar dismissed Gandhi's paternalistic gestures as hypocritical and his spirited defence of varnashrama as phoney religiosity.

Gandhi's support for the caste order – and, hence acquiescence in accepting inferior position of the lower classes – has been variously interpreted by historians. In order to save Gandhi's image as the messiah of the masses, some historians have argued that his views on caste were not that simple; they were, as they say, 'richly ambivalent'! Abusing their talents, these scholars have gone to the extent of portraying him as a crusader against caste. There are others who cook up the excuse that Gandhi as a mass national leader had to make compromises with upper-caste Hinduism. This, too, is a lame argument: in reality, Gandhi's views on caste mingled and converged with the world-view of brahmanic Hinduism. Those who cite isolated pontifications of Gandhi and try to glorify him by recording his 'soul's agony' and lamentation against untouchability tend to turn a blind eye to the fast-changing scenario of the time. It was no longer possible for brahmanical forces to openly justify the outrageous social practices as instances of protests were on the rise in many parts of the country.

Gandhi extracted a very heavy price from the lowered caste people for his symbolic opposition to the practice of untouchability. His excessive accent on temple entry which became the fulcrum of his anti-untouchability drive, in effect shifted attention from the vital question of socio-economic rights. Ambedkar, who initially supported temple-entry campaign as a way of restoring religious rights to untouchables, saw through the game and eventually came out against this 'side issue', asserting that the real issues were education, employment, and economic development. Even on this side issue Gandhi kept changing his position. He led a much-glorified campaign of temple entry for the untouchables in 1933, but had no hesitation to write in the *Harijan* of 23 February 1934:

I have absolutely no desire that the temple should be opened to Harijans, until caste Hindu opinion is ripe for the opening. It is not a question of Harijans asserting their right of temple entry or claiming it. They may or may not want to enter that temple even when it is declared open to them. But it is the bounden duty of every caste Hindu to secure that opening for Harijans.

Criticising such politics of piety with the disdain it deserved, Ambedkar described the temple entry as 'strange game of political acrobatics':

Mr. Gandhi begins as an opponent of Temple Entry. When the Untouchables put forth a demand for political rights, he changes his position and becomes a supporter of Temple Entry. When the Hindus threaten to defeat the Congress in the election, if it pursues the matter to a conclusion, Mr. Gandhi, in order to preserve political power in the hands of the Congress, gives up Temple Entry! Is this sincerity? Does this show conviction? Was the 'agony of soul' which Mr. Gandhi spoke of more than a phrase?
(BAWS, vol. 9: 125)

The man who considered the removal of untouchability as a most powerful factor in the process of attainment of Swaraj in 1919 had no qualms of conscience in championing the caste system. Writing in *Navjivan*, Gandhi saw the seeds of Swaraj in caste and argued that the Hindu society had been able to survive because it was founded on the caste system:

The seeds of Swaraj are to be found in the caste system. . . . A community which can create the caste system must be said to possess unique power of organisation. . . . The caste system is a natural order of society. In India it has been given a religious coating. Other countries not having understood the utility of the caste system . . . have not derived . . . the same degree of advantage as India has derived. (reprinted in the vol. II of the series called *Gandhi Sikshan*, cited in *BAWS*, vol. 9: 275-6)

Rebuffing those who advocated social democracy and wanted to do away with the principle of hereditary occupation, Gandhi asserted:

To destroy the caste system and adopt the western European social system means that Hindus must give up the principle of hereditary occupation which is the soul of the caste system. Hereditary principle is an eternal principle. To change it is to create disorder. I have no use for a Brahman if I cannot call him a Brahman for my life. It will be a chaos if everyday a Brahman is to be changed into a Shudra and a Shudra is to be changed into a Brahman. (ibid.)

Varna, he insisted in his tract *Varna Vyavastha*, is not a human invention but an immutable law of nature which 'reveals the law of one's being and thus the duty one has to perform, it confers no right, and the idea of inferiority or superiority is wholly repugnant to it' (1993: 218). After this specious argument, he gives this call: 'What is essential is that one must seek one's livelihood, and no more, from following the vocation to which one is born' (ibid.: 221). This pontification is from the alleged Mahatma who himself quit – and so did his forefathers – *tarajoo*, the scale, the duty of his ancestral calling in favour of the brahmanic professions such as practice of law and preaching the dharma.

Gandhi's construction of the ideal shudra that he visualised in perfect accordance with shastric injunctions is not only silly but also sinister. The shudra who serves the higher castes as a matter of religious duty and who will never own any property, who indeed has not even the ambition to own anything, Gandhi writes in *Varna-*

Vyavastha, is 'worthy of the world's homage. . . . The gods will shower their choicest blessings on him. One may not say this of the proletariat of the present day. They certainly own nothing, but I expect they covet ownership' (ibid.: 220). It was this regressive mindset which occasionally made Gandhi oppose the education of the masses which, he feared, might ignite their mind about the wretched conditions in which they lived:

What you want to gain by giving literacy to the children of the peasants? What comfort are you going to add to their life by educating them? Do you want to ignite discontent in his mind for his thatched hut and pathetic condition? . . . We are going to do excess when some preach for imparting education for all, without considering its pros and cons. (cited in Biswas 1998: 267)

Such ideas came naturally to Gandhi since he considered the caste system the natural order of society, perfected religiously in India. 'The caste system', according to him, 'has a scientific basis. Reason does not revolt against it. . . . I can find no reason for their abolition. To abolish caste is to demolish Hinduism.'

GRIME BEHIND THE GLAMOUR

Using religious and home spun idioms, Gandhi often spoke of the India of his dreams that would become a reality after Swaraj through swadeshi, Ram-rajya, trusteeship, self-sufficient villages, panchayat, cottage industries, etc. All these have been coherently crafted by a long line of hagiographer-historians into what is popularly known as Gandhism. This ideology has generally been interpreted as an indigenous recipe for a peaceful revolution, 'a clarion call for a new social order and a blueprint for New India' (Aloysius 1997). What is deliberately left unsaid by the pandits is the all-revealing fact that Gandhi's world-view, his social ideology, his economic thinking, his vague and vacuous concepts of swadeshi and swaraj were all embedded in traditional varna order. As we know, Gandhi was very conscious and proud of being a 'sanatani Hindu', and he himself said time and again that he believed in all the sacerdotal literature of Sanskrit, the concepts of avatar and rebirth, idol-worship, cow-protection, and above all, varna-vyavastha (*Young India*, 6 October 1921). In his reconstruction of the Indian past, Gandhi blithely equated the tradition of sanatani Hinduism with the Indian tradition. For he included, like other Hindu supremacists before and after him, all shramanic heterodox traditions like that of Buddhism and Jainism in his Hinduism.[7] His theme was the old, worn out formulation of the early nationalists, that Hinduism, founded on the varna ideology, had produced in the past a uniquely spiritual, homogeneous, holistic, and harmonious culture which made India intrinsically superior to the materialist West. Speaking in the cliched obscurantist language of a fundamentalist, he declared: 'What of substance is contained in any other religion is always to be found in Hinduism. And what is not contained in it is insubstantial or unnecessary' (*Young India*, 17 September 1925). Not surprisingly, his critique of the present and the status quo, far from a call for a new egalitarian order, was based on an appeal for a reversal to the status quo ante.

The edifice of Gandhi's socio-cultural philosophy was varna order which, he said, was built on the consensus of all concerned. In his analysis of varna, there was no inequality or exploitation rather a stricter 'fulfilment of the law would make life livable, would spread peace and content, end all clashes and conflicts, put an end to starvation and pauperisation, solve the problem of population and even end disease and suffering' (Gandhi 1993: 218). Here there was no antagonism between the brahman and the shudra, here his bhangi loved to clean excreta of others just as bania loved to amass wealth and brahman loved to acquire knowledge. He found the varna model of society worthy of export to the whole world. As he said, 'Though the law of varna is a special discovery of some Hindu seer, it has universal application. The world may ignore it today but it will have to accept it in the time to come' (ibid.: 219). Warning of the dangers of 'class wars and civil strife' unleashed by the ongoing – and in his view highly undesirable – process of modernisation, he gave the call to return to the varna purity to end 'the conflicting inequalities':

These wars and strife could not be ended except by the observance of the law of varna. For it ordains that everyone shall fulfil the law of one's being by doing it in a spirit of duty and service that to which one is born. Its due observance by a large part of mankind will end the conflicting inequalities and give place to an equality in diversity. (ibid.)

Quite clearly, the Gandhian way to meet modern challenges was to hark back to the imagined pure state of Hindu society characterised by the four-fold division of labour. Gandhi's visualisation of the Indian past is a gross distortion of the Indian tradition. His reconstruction of the tradition not only vehemently denies India's problematic, conflict-ridden and troubled past but also makes a mockery of its rich plurality, radical heterodoxy, and the egalitarian aspirations of the lower classes. In the words of Aloysius, 'Gandhi's construction of the ideal-typical tradition is composed of the worst elements of the subcontinental history, elements that kept the masses under social and cultural tyranny'. Laying emphasis only on the unifying and uniformising aspects of Indian culture, Gandhi conveniently cast aside diversification as an aberration. Unity and diversity in the context of the socio-cultural development of the subcontinent are highly dialectical terms loaded with socio-political significance:

Unity represents the dominant and uniformising culturo-ideological and mythical Brahminic factors and is thus oppressive: Vedic-Brahminic Hinduism as the only acceptable form of Hinduism, Sanskrit as the basis of all languages, Brahmins as the caste to be found all over the subcontinent, and Varnashrama Dharma as the traditional order, representing the dominant and oppressive, ideal social order of the ruling and vested interests. Diversity on the other hand, stands for the movement away from these uniformising factors, the tendencies of resistance of the subaltern and the locally rooted castes and communities in general; the growth of the vernaculars and their cultural communities, and the scores of attempts of creating culturally specific non-Brahminic myths and popular religions, are, in a sense, the defiance of the commoners against the imposition from above. Finally, the actual and attenuated realisation of the Varnashrama Dharmic ideal in the different regions of the subcontinent represent a history of resistance and uneven success. (Aloysius 1997: 186-7)

Viewed in this perspective, 'India's history, culture and inheritance are composed of both these distinct yet often dialectically united streams.' However, Gandhism as a particular mutant of the broader brahmanic construct of the Indian culture and the nationalism based on it, 'elevated only one trend and that too the oppressive one', thus sabotaging 'the political emergence of the social forces that historically represented the subaltern and the suppressed'. An essential component of Gandhian reconstruction of Indian tradition is to regard equalitarianism, or any form of protest against the ascriptive establishment as alien, foreign inspired, Western, and hence to be rejected in the 'national' interest (ibid.).

There was nothing new in Gandhi's call to return to the old order to get rid of the modern maladies. Ideologies of the dominant classes in the East as well as the West have always viewed transformative politics as subversive and counter-productive, while lower classes everywhere have aspired for change and revolution. What was remarkable about the Gandhi phenomenon was its phenomenal success. While earlier ideologues of brahmanic nationalism in India had failed in their endeavour to weld together diverse social forces in the subcontinent, Gandhi created a heavy cocktail of history, myth and religion, and used his carefully crafted saintly persona to win over or at least neutralise the recalcitrant masses. Behind his trademark simplicity lay concealed a sanatani mind of extraordinary shrewdness that could pursue its course with single-minded devotion. His goal was to expel the British, but freedom had to be won under the traditional ruling classes without any social change or upheaval. He was well aware of the veneration that the saintly figures receive from the Indian masses. Discarding western garb in favour of the loincloth, and using cultural symbols associated with the life of a holy man – austere living, fasts, the observance of days of silence, the demonstrative use of celibacy, holy books and prayer meetings – gave him the image of a saint. His deft use of religious forms to communicate with the masses absolved him of the need to lay out his plans and programmes in concrete terms. Claiming to represent the masses, he and his upper class followers exploited to the hilt his saintly image while indulging in power politics.

Gandhi's constant emphasis on the myth of Ram-rajya symbolising inclusiveness, interdependence and the harmony of varna society, was to offset the growing protest and stridence of the lower classes in the new political structure and emerging civil society. Gandhi and the entire upper class leadership were deeply disturbed by the intensifying rivalries between the landlords and tenants, capital and labour, higher castes and lower, all of which they attributed to modernity. Gandhi's essential advice to the masses was to accept the traditional leadership in order to make broad-based unity against the British. However, his attempts at reconciliation were not based on the promotion of the interests of all classes, especially those of the downtrodden. Gandhi's way of tackling social fissures was in the form of teaching the masses to follow the social higher-ups. Sermonising the tenants of the United Province who had risen against their landlords, he wrote, for example, in *Young India* of 18 May 1921:

While we will not hesitate to advise the kisans (cultivators) when the moment comes, to suspend payment of taxes to government, it is not contemplated that at any stage of Non-Co-operation we would seek to deprive the zamindars of their rent. . . . The kisans must be advised scrupulously to abide by the term of their agreement with the zamindar, whether such is written or inferred from custom.

Similarly, Gandhi advised workers to arrive at agreement with their employees/capitalists and not to resort to strike to improve their economic conditions because, as he wrote in *Young India* of 23 February 1922, 'India's history is not one of strained relations between capital and labour'.

VARNA SWARAJ: OBSCURANTIST CRITIQUE OF MODERNITY

Gandhi's ideology and advocacy of varnashrama-based Indian tradition not only targeted British rule but also tried to delegitimise and weaken the protest movements from below as untraditional or unIndian. He held the West-inspired modernity, industry, science, and reason as the biggest stumbling block in realising and retrieving the 'purity and simplicity' of the old order. With this understanding, Gandhi became a trenchant critic of modern civilisation and all that it represented – science, technology, railways, representative democracy, new secular institutions, modern judiciary, medicine, etc. He articulated these views in his *Hind Swaraj* (1908) which is a sort of an anti-modernity, anti-technology manifesto. Encompassing Gandhi's civilisational angst and anguish, *Hind Swaraj* is perhaps the most important tract to understand Gandhi as it represents his world-view at its coherent best.

Given his proneness to subjectivity and ability to emotionalise — by being responsible only to his inner voice — any debate and discussion, *Hind Swaraj* remains his most consistent exposition and caustic critique of modern civilisation, a theme to which he returned time and again through his life. Vividly reminiscent of the cliched images of *Kaliyuga*, conjured up by the brahmanic authors against the backdrop of problems and challenges mounted by the caste-oppressed from time to time, Gandhi here brands modern civilisation 'satanic', a 'disease' that must be totally shunned. He was not willing to understand that all traditional societies, in the absence of modernity, had been religious and there was nothing exceptional about India in this regard. He summarily set aside the fact that India down the ages had been a hugely diverse and pluralistic society, containing people from different backgrounds. He failed to recognise that Indian culture as all cultures the world over had always been open to, and considerably shaped by, influences from outside. The notion that Eastern as well as Western civilisations have evolved through the natural process by which cultures blend and form fresh ones was beyond Gandhi's understanding. He saw modernity in black and white, equating the West with the materialism which modernity promoted, and India with only spirituality.

While unravelling his vision of Indian Home Rule, Gandhi launched a polemic against modernity and all that it represented with the vehemence of a puritanical fanatic, seeing in it nothing but spectre of dangerous developments that would lead only to hell (Gandhi 1993: 3-66). Machinery was the 'chief symbol of modern civilisation' and a 'great sin'. In this satanic world, he says, 'Women, who should be the queens of households, wander in the streets or they slave away in factories'. He compared the British Parliament, 'which you consider to be the Mother of Parliaments', with a sterile woman and a prostitute, and pronounced: 'Parliaments are really emblems of slavery' (ibid.: 13-18). In his view hospitals were against all religious sanctions. 'Hospitals', he asserted, 'are institutions for propagating sins' because their existence encourages 'men (to) take less care of their bodies and immorality increases' (ibid.: 33-4).

Railways, the services of which Gandhi frequently availed both in India and abroad, too, attracted his wrath. They were the villainous facilitator of disease and disaster that is modern civilisation.

He held them responsible for the British hold on India and for spreading plague and famines (ibid.: 23-4).

Economic changelessness, educational purity or orthodoxy, and cultural insularity, the main products of the brahmanical ideology, along with religiously sanctioned social oppression and gender discrimination, had Gandhi's fulsome approval. True civilisation, he announces, brimming with moral fervour, can flower only in the traditional mode of living, in the absence of technological change and life-corroding competition.

We have managed with the same kind of plough as existed thousands of years ago. We have retained the same kind of cottages that we have had in former times and our indigenous education remains the same as before. We have had no system of life-corroding competition. Each followed his own occupation or trade and charged a regulation wage. It was not that we did not know how to invent machinery, but our forefathers knew that if we set our hearts after such things, we would become slaves and lose our moral fibre. (ibid.: 35)

And,

India's salvation consists in unlearning what she has learnt during the last fifty years. The railways, telegraphs, hospitals, lawyers, doctors and such like have all to go; and the so-called upper classes have to learn consciously, religiously and deliberately the simple pleasant life, knowing it to be a lifegiving true happiness.

Many have erroneously assumed that Gandhi's world-view and ideology underwent a major change after the *Hind Swaraj* phase and that he outgrew most of the obscurantist ideas contained therein. He has himself categorically dispelled such impressions. Writing in *Young India* (26 January 1921) he made it very clear: 'The booklet (*Hind Swaraj*) is a severe condemnation of modern civilisation. It was written in 1908. My conviction is deeper today than ever. I feel that, if India would discard modern civilisation she can only gain by doing so.' Gandhi held fast to the ideas expressed in the tract till the very end. He wrote to Nehru on 5 October 1945:

I have said I still stand by the system of Government envisaged in Hind Swaraj. These are not mere words. All the experience gained by me since

1908 when I wrote the booklet has confirmed the truth of my belief. (see Austin 2001: 39)

Besides his unwillingness or inability to diagnose the true nature of social malaise afflicting India, Gandhi also discounted the fact that only a transformed mentality and attitudinal change could bring about a desirable transformation. Despite his moral sermons invoking change of heart, which so impressed – and continue to overwhelm – his acolytes, Gandhi's orthodox views on most socio-religious issues not only hindered an attitudinal change in Indian society, but contrary to popular belief, his posturing and priorities gave a new lease of life to moribund brahmanism. His uncritical glorification – even deification – by the privileged classes despite having little faith in his anti-modernity and anti-technology mantras is mainly due to his tenacious fight to defend the basic tenets of brahmanic Hinduism.

No matter how strongly neo-Gandhian modernity-bashers such as Ashis Nandy might disagree, the fact is that Gandhi and his ilk fell into the trap laid by the European Indophiles who said exaggerated and flattering things about Indian culture, invariably pairing the latter with the other-worldly spirituality. Taking the 'romantic cult of the exotic East' too seriously, Gandhi in league with his kindred souls of both European and Indian origins believed that material aspects of life did not matter to spiritual Indians. The sanatani complex of Gandhi convinced him that the machine would bring about social change of such a magnitude that it would endanger varna-inspired spirituality. Fear of the new and the unfamiliar made Gandhi an ardent champion of the social and economic status quo, complete with his mythical notion of a Ram-rajya drenched in vacuous spiritual values and social harmony. While many eminent Indians of the earlier era – Jotiba Phule, Dadabhai Naoroji, M.G. Ranade, and Surendranath Banerjee – were keen to promote science, technology, and industrialisation for the progress of the country, the leader of the twentieth century India dismissed industrialisation as an unmitigated evil.

Gandhi's condemnation of technology, industry, allopathic medicine and his much-vaunted anti-capitalism was strange and full of irony. He frequently rode in railway trains and motor cars, and was a willing victim to what he termed 'medical tyranny' for most of his life. For example, he gave his consent to have himself operated upon for appendicitis in 1924, and was at all times an ideal patient under the safe care of allopathic physicians. Likewise, his 'constructive' projects and *ashram-vyavastha* at Sabarmati and Wardha were financed by the captains of industry like Ghanshyam Das Birla and Jamnalal Bajaj. Gandhi admitted in an interview with Louis Fischer that all expenditure incurred on him and his large following was borne by his rich friends. Should a man so dependent on the generosity of the rich – which must have spurred him to come up with his 'trusteeship' thesis – have fancied himself as the saviour of the poor? And did the Birlas and the Bajajs – who incurred his huge expenditure and went on to become India's top industrialists after Independence under a friendly Congress regime – share his anti-capitalist and anti-machine enthusiasm? Playing the double role of saint of the masses and champion of the propertied classes, Gandhi's hypocrisy was indeed staggering.

In fact, the whole Gandhian approach to the regeneration of India was part, and not solution, of the national problem. His politics which he claimed had its roots in religion was in the concrete context of subcontinental reality extremely helpful to the power-hungry politicians from dominant classes. The kind of association that he brought about between (Hindu) religion and politics was a receipe for disaster from the national viewpoint as such a combination only further marginalised the masses who aspired to script a new social order based on non-traditional religion:

Within the Gandhi-Event a running discourse on renunciation and moral regeneration is carried on with another, of ruthless pursuit of monopoly, political power. The elaborate agenda of wresting moral authority from the British is but a prelude to investing the same on a set of power-driven politicians. The different Ashrams as part of constructive programmes, though intended for moral regeneration of Hindu society at large, were also propaganda centres for Congress politics. (Aloysius 1997: 176)

Gandhi himself carried many of these contradictions in his person. His trademark poverty, as Sarojini Naidu once quipped pointing to the money that moved the Mahatma and his politics, cost fortunes to the Birlas and Bajajs. His discourse on the spiritual equality of all men was anchored in an unshakeable faith in the discriminatory varnashrama-dharma. He preached renunciation and a politics of powerlessness, but treated Congress as his personal fiefdom brooking no rivals in leadership. His posture of self-effacement was coupled with claims to exclusive access to the truth, and the careful cultivation of a large army of followers who took his every word like an article of faith.

Despite glaring contradictions and inconsistencies in Gandhi's proclaimed mission to make a better society, and a huge gap between what he preached and what he promoted, Gandhi often occupied the high moral ground spouting change of heart, trusteeship, purity of means to be adopted in the fight for a cause. This, perhaps, was the 'humble' Gandhian way to kill with kindness the social radicals who, by any computation, were no less morally serious than was the official apostle of truth and morality.

NEHRU AND AMBEDKAR ON GANDHISM

Quite a few, even among the upper caste nationalist ranks, made discordant notes with the frustrating paradox that is Gandhism. One such person was Jawaharlal Nehru, who posed in public as the greatest of Gandhi's disciples but almost wholly disagreed with the master's understanding of history and contemporary society. Though in his pursuit of power Nehru hypocritically staked claim to the Gandhian legacy, he has in his autobiography summarily written off the ideas contained in Gandhi's *Hind Swaraj* as 'utterly wrong . . . and impossible of achievement'. To Nehru, this was true of Gandhism in general. Contesting the ideas of trusteeship, change of heart, and making moral men in an immoral and unjust society, he sarcastically asserted that individuals and groups could be allowed to interpret ethics in accordance with their own interests, only at the cost of democratic principles and procedure (Nehru 1999: 543). He seriously questioned Gandhian moralism which envisioned that socio-economic justice could be resolved by ethical persuasion alone:

If there is one thing that history shows it is this: that economic interests shape the political views of groups and classes. Neither reason nor moral considerations override these interests. Individuals may be converted, they may surrender their special privileges, although this is rare enough, but classes and groups do not do so. The attempt to convert a governing and privileged class into forsaking power and giving up its unjust privileges has therefore always so far failed, and there seems to be no reason whatever to hold that it will succeed in the future. (ibid.: 544)

Nehru had fundamental problems with the politics of Gandhi. The Mahatma's constant evocation of peace and justice and his 'muddled humanitarianism', Nehru feared, would only strengthen the reactionary and status quo-ist forces:

For years I have puzzled over this problem: why with all his love and solicitude for the underdog he yet supports a system which inevitably produces it and crushes it; why with all his passion for non-violence he is in favour of a political and social structure which is wholly based on violence and coercion? Perhaps it is not correct to say that he is in favour of such a system but . . . he accepts the present order. (ibid.: 515)

It is another matter, however, that Nehru's own actions, when in power, were not consistent with this understanding. But he was indeed dismayed at times to find that Gandhi not only lacked reasonable intellect and insight into social reality, but also perhaps, an 'ethical attitude':

In spite of the closet association with him (Gandhi) for many years, I am not clear in my own mind about his objective. I doubt if he is clear himself. . . . Look after the means, and the end will take care of itself, he is never tired of repeating. Be good in your personal individual lives, and all else will follow. That is not a political or scientific attitude, nor is it perhaps an ethical attitude. It is narrowly moralist, and it begs the question: What is goodness? Is it merely an individual affair or a social affair. Gandhiji lays all stress on character and attaches little importance to intellectual training and development. Intellect without character is likely to be dangerous, but what is character without intellect? How, indeed, does character develop? (cited in Hiren Mukherjee 1991: 208)

After making such candid comments about Gandhism, Congress politicians like Nehru bend over backwards to outdo their rivals in singing hosannas and encomia to the great man. Gandhi of course was a remarkable and charming person. Such elitist deification has, however, often obscured the real face of his ideology.

One of the earliest and finest attempts at critiquing Gandhism was made by none other than Ambedkar in many of his writings. In his sociological classic *What Congress and Gandhi Have Done to the Untouchables?*, first published in 1945 (reprinted in *BAWS*, vol. 9), Ambedkar has deconstructed from the subaltern viewpoint, almost every aspect and dimension of Gandhi's philosophy – his social ideology, his anti-modernity, his trusteeship, his anti-untouchability drive, his moral cosmos, etc. Ambedkar comes to the conclusion that barring Gandhi's illusory campaign against untouchability, Gandhism is just another form of sanatanism, the ancient name for militant orthodox Hinduism. He asks rhetorically, what is there in Gandhism that is not to be found in orthodox Hinduism? (*BAWS*, vol. 9: 295-6).

All Gandhism has done, according to Ambedkar, is to find specious and deceptive arguments to justify Hinduism and its dogmas. Hinduism, he argues, is merely a set of rules which gives it the appearance of a crude and cruel system, and Gandhism supplies a philosophy to smooth its surface and give it the appearance of decency and respectability. The philosophy that Gandhi upholds is the philosophy which says that 'All that is in Hinduism is well, all that is in Hinduism is necessary for public good.' The Hindus like Radhakrishnan who eulogise Gandhi as 'God on earth', are pleased with Gandhian Hinduism, as 'it suits them and accords with their interest', but what does Gandhism mean, Ambedkar asks, to the caste-oppressed? Arguing with those who get carried away by Gandhi's noble-sounding but essentially fallacious differentiation between caste and varna, Ambedkar asserts that Gandhi is nothing if not an arch social reactionary who beguiles the unthinking Hindu with arguments which make no distinction between fair and foul. All the oppressive instruments – the sanctity and infallibility of the shastras and smritis, the iron law of caste, the heartless law of karma and the senseless law of the status of birth – which have mutilated and blighted the life of the lower orders are to be found intact and untarnished in the bosom of Gandhism (ibid.: 296-7).

Ambedkar analyses Gandhi's anti-modern exhortations and economics and finds them equally hopeless and fundamentally fallacious. The Gandhian diagnosis of economic ills, insofar as it attributes them to science, technology, and the civilisation built upon them, however, was not new. The arguments that machinery and modern civilisation caused monopolisation of wealth and resources in a few hands, and also death and environmental decay, have some merit, but they are all old and worn out theses propounded first by the likes of Rousseau, Ruskin, Carlyle, and Tolstoy, all of whom exerted influence on Gandhi. (The neo-Gandhians, postmodernist prophets of doom, and environmental radicals who regard the Mahatma's critique of modernisation as strikingly original and tend to portray it as a uniquely Eastern rejection of the colonialist West and its oppressive science and technology, fail to recognise this simple truth.) Ambedkar concedes that the excessive and indiscriminate machinisation have produced some evils, but these evils were not due to machinery but to 'wrong social organisation which has made private property and pursuit of personal gain matters of absolute sanctity'. If science and technology have not benefited everybody, the remedy is not to condemn it but 'to alter the organisation of society so that the benefits will not be usurped by the few but will accrue to all' (ibid.: 283).

Arguing that throughout history man's creative faculties have devised ways to make life easier through inventions and scientific breakthroughs, Ambedkar contends that the machine, by lessening human toil, produces the much-needed leisure for man and makes a life of culture possible. This, he insists, is especially necessary in a democratic society which must assure a life of leisure and culture to every citizen, not only to the privileged few. An undemocratic, deeply class-divided society, however, can afford to do away with machinery only by subjecting the majority to a life of toil and drudgery for the leisure and comfort of the few. Even with the spread of scientific ethos and democratic values, there are and will always be, to some extent, social cleavages and class differences. Yet Gandhism, Ambedkar stresses, makes the hierarchical structure of society and also the income structure sacrosanct, with the consequent distinctions of rich and poor, high and low as permanent parts of social organisation. Social consequences of such rigid social structure, he argues, are pernicious as the class divide psychologically sets in motion influences that are harmful to both the classes. As there is no common place where the privileged and the subject classes meet, there is no social interaction between them, and such segregation, he points out, not only dehumanises the lower order into slaves but also, though less perceptibly, brutalises the higher class:

The isolation and exclusiveness following upon the class structure creates in the privileged classes the anti-social spirit of a gang. It feels it has interests 'of its own' which it makes its prevailing purpose to protect against everybody even against the interests of the State. It makes their culture sterile, their art showy, their wealth luminous and their manners fastidious. Practically speaking in a class structure there is, on the one hand, tyranny, vanity, pride, arrogance, greed, selfishness and on the other, insecurity, poverty, degradation, loss of liberty, self-reliance, independence, dignity and self-respect. (ibid.: 285)

Ambedkar emphasises that consequences of hierarchies are disastrous for a democratic society and nation but Gandhism wants caste and class structure to function as a living faith. The Gandhian idea of trusteeship of the rich for the poor, he contends, is the most ridiculous, because in the conflict between ethics and economics the latter has always overpowered the former. Vested interests have never been known to have willingly divested themselves unless there was sufficient social and material force to compel them. Trusteeship, Ambedkar argues, is a silly theory to deceive the masses into believing that 'a little dose of moral rearmament to the propertied classes . . . will recondition them to such an extent that they will be able to withstand the temptation to misuse the tremendous powers that the class structure gives them over servile classes' (ibid.: 286).

Regarding Gandhi's advocacy of *Gram Swaraj*, which encompasses his idea of village democracy in which the traditional caste society is invested for discharging such functions as the spread of primary education or the settlement of disputes, Ambedkar reiterates the point that caste, which divides, is the worst possible instrument for the discharge of such functions. The Gandhian theory of the timeless beauty of the Indian village which valorises 'harmonious' rural culture against the ugly and competitive urban life is a myth; the reality, according to Ambedkar, is quite odious. Obviously, Ambedkar was not enamoured of Gandhi's obsession with the 'enlightened anarchy' and his enthusiasm for the Indian arcadia. In contrast to Gandhi's insistence that 'the blood of the villages is the cement by which the edifice of the cities is built', Ambedkar dismissed the antagonism between village and city as too simplistic.

Cautioning against the Gandhian utopia of a free India based on the 'beauty' and 'harmony' of the ancient village, Ambedkar underlined the iniquities and injustices of village life in a compelling speech before the Constituent Assembly. The love of the intellectual Indians for the village community, he said, is based on Metcalfe's romanticism of it as 'idyllic self-sufficient little republics' that have survived the vicissitudes of many eras. Survived it has, he conceded, but on a low and very selfish level. Far from the hub of freedom, independence, and creativity it is made out to be, the village, he said, has been 'a sink of localism, a den of ignorance, narrow-mindedness and communalism.' Ambedkar emphasised the need of speedy industrialisation along with development of the agricultural sector. Poverty in India, he argued, was due entirely to the dependence upon agriculture which has its roots in 'maladjustment of its social economy'. He said: '. . . population pressure is giving rise to an army of landless and displaced families as well. It can be stopped when agriculture is made profitable. Nothing can open possibilities of making agriculture profitable except a serious drive in favour of industrialisation. For it is industrialisation alone which can drain away excess of population into gainful employment other than agriculture.'

VISION OF THE NATION AS SOCIAL DEMOCRACY

Ambedkar wrote as early as 1920 in his journal *Mook Nayak* (Voice of the Voiceless) that it was not enough for India to be an independent country; India, he asserted, must become a state guaranteeing equal status in matters religious, social, economic and political to all classes, offering every individual an opportunity to rise in life and creating favourable conditions to his advancement. He stated that the swaraj wherein the depressed classes are not given opportunities to pursue careers of their choice or to lead a dignified life like others, would not be a swaraj to them. In the same article he argued that 'if the Brahmins were justified in their attack upon and opposition to the unjust power of the British Government, the Depressed Classes were justified a hundred times more so in their opposition to the rulership of the Brahmins in case the transfer of power took place' (Keer 1971: 41). Elsewhere, he wrote: If Tilak had been born among the untouchables, he would not have raised the slogan 'swaraj is my birthright', but 'annihilation of untouchability is my birthright' (ibid.: 81). While most historians depict Ambedkar as a spokesman of the depressed classes, they do not present the Congress and Gandhi as flag-bearers of the upper classes. Ambedkar himself had made this point repeatedly about the contradictory and often antagonistic views of (governing) class and (servile) mass.

Disentangling the odious reality from the nationalist rhetoric, Ambedkar noted with concern that far from sacrificing their privileges for nationalism, the higher castes were exploiting nationalism to preserve them. He said whenever the depressed classes asked for representation in the legislature, executive, or the public services, the governing class raised the bogey of 'nationalism in danger'. While opposing the demands of representation from the lower classes, the elites maintained that such measures were inimical to national unity, as they led to dissension in the national ranks. They also gave the impression that by insisting that every place of power and authority should be filled by none but the best man available, they were strengthening the nation built on meritocracy. Tearing into the fig-leaf of merit, Ambedkar asserted that 'the argument completely fails to carry conviction when in practice one finds that having regard to the historical circumstances of India every time the 'best man' is chosen he turns out to be a man from the governing class'. He asked in his usual combative style, who had determined the criteria of 'merit'. Had not the education for centuries been fraudulently monopolised by the governing class 'by sheer communalism'? Had not all strategic posts in the past been reserved for a particular class as per the injunctions of Dharmashastras like *Manusmriti*? Above all, could the 'best man' from the viewpoint of governing class be necessarily regarded the 'best man' from the point of view of the oppressed?

Nobody will have any quarrel with the abstract principle that nothing should be done whereby the best shall be superceded by one who is only better and

the better by one who is merely good and the good by one who is bad.
. . . But man is not a mere machine. He is a human being with feelings of sympathy for some and antipathy for others. This is even true of the best man. He too is charged with the feelings of class sympathies and class antipathies. Having regard to these considerations the 'best' man from the governing class may well turn out to be the worst from the point of view of the servile classes. The difference between the governing classes and the servile classes in the matter of their attitudes towards each other is the same as the attitude a person of one nation has for that of another nation.
(BAWS, vol. 9: 229-30)

Nationalism to Ambedkar, thus, was not merely protest against and eventual expulsion of the alien domination but also the termination of internal oppression. His main stress was on freedom of the people without which, he said, elitist nationalism was bound to perpetuate internal slavery, forced labour, and institutionalised exploitation of the poor and depressed classes. Challenging the Congress's claim of fighting for freedom, he raised the question, for whose freedom the Congress was fighting: was it fighting for the freedom of the governing class in India, or for the freedom of all the people of India?

For words such as society, nation and country are just amorphous, if not ambiguous, terms. . . . Nation though one word means many classes. Philosophically it may be possible to consider a nation as a unit but sociologically it cannot but be regarded as consisting of many classes and the freedom of the nation if it is to be a reality must vouchsafe the freedom of the different classes comprised in it, particularly those who are treated as the servile classes. (ibid.: 201-2)

The exploitative character and anti-democratic attitude of the governing class in India, Ambedkar stressed, would not disappear by the magic wand of swaraj. The Congress, he added, was speaking of making radical changes after Independence as political expediency, to win over the masses. For the Indian elites, swaraj meant preserving and strengthening the traditional brahmanical order, whereas for the non-elites, swaraj meant the demolition and destruction of that order. For this reason, he argued, the nationalism of the oppressed and humiliated communities stood in direct contrast to Congress nationalism as the former had a different vision and expectation of independence:

Speaking for the servile classes, I have no doubt that what they expect to happen in a sovereign and free India is a complete destruction of Brahmanism as a philosophy of life and as a social order. If I may say so, the servile classes do not care for social amelioration. The want and poverty which has been their lot is nothing to them as compared to the insult and indignity which they have to bear as a result of the vicious social order.
(ibid.: 212-13)

Ambedkar's nationalism, therefore, rested on questioning, attacking and ultimately destroying the traditional social order in order to build a new, open, non-hierarchical, modern and democratic society, while Gandhi's project, as we have seen, was to preserve the hierarchical social structure in the name of tradition and patriotism. This tradition was so dear to Gandhi that all his saintly sublimeness could not convince him of the stark truth that the caste system has a dehumanising face, that the notion of purity and impurity, and the practice of segregation and untouchability had religious sanctity under Hinduism, that the birth-based cleavages in the Indian society was incompatible with the idea of nation. A nation was founded, Ambedkar insisted, on egalitarianism and fellow feeling between citizens.

If this was the attitude of 'the greatest Indian of his generation', one can well understand the callous indifference of the lesser nationalist heroes, the Nehrus and the Rajgopalacharis, to the caste question. Going by the form and substance of the Congress politics for freedom, Ambedkar was not unduly suspicious that once India got independence, the dalits and lowered castes would once again be subjected to the brahmanic discrimination though in vastly different and modernised garb. Ambedkar, therefore, believed that India needed a social and cultural revolution to destroy the traditional value system.

Ambedkar was compelled to stand apart from the hegemonic national movement. He had little option but to oppose the national luminaries, most of whom were openly lauding caste as a superior form of social organisation, while others were supporting and practising it in private and the remaining few were pretending as though the problem did not exist. His struggle against brahmanical hegemony was denounced in the nationalist circles as anti-patriotic and pro-British because any attack on caste was seen as an attack on Indian society and culture.

To the dalit-subalterns who were trying through both individual as well as organisational efforts to break free from caste-based occupational, religio-cultural and educational restrictions and liabilities, the political plank and banner of the upper classes – protection of ancient culture and tradition in the name of nationalism – within the existing socio-economic conflict seemed to be plainly a call to reinforce the old caste order (Aloysius 2002). Not surprisingly, the domain of the national came to be increasingly identified with upper caste exclusivism. Congress-led nationalism in general, and Ambedkar's ideology of nationalism in particular, are to be situated and analysed within this broader framework where the upper and lower classes were locked in an irreconcilable conflicts of interests (ibid.).

Undoubtedly, the nation and nationalism which Ambedkar championed and which find eloquent, emotive expression in his writings and speeches was not meant to serve the special interests of India's privileged classes. His nationalism was embedded in a radical vision of social reconstruction, and as such was symbiotically attached to the hopes and aspirations of those who have been at the receiving end of a systematic dehumanisation over the centuries. It was based on a vibrant, participatory democracy where everyone irrespective of class, caste and gender could get a fair deal and justice. This nationalism was not the upper caste cultural nationalism rooted in the mythical Hindu land of milk and honey where some people speak *devbhasha* – Sanskrit – and the rest thank the Almighty for being given the opportunity to serve the *devbhasis* blessed with the divine knowledge of their 'inherent' and 'genetic' superiority. As Ambedkar said:

Nationality is a social feeling. It is a feeling of corporate sentiment of oneness which makes those who are charged with it feel that they are kith and kin. (BAWS, vol. 8: 31)

Nationality, he professes, is a 'consciousness of kind' which binds together those who have it. In other words, nationalism for Ambedkar is a social democracy.

Democracy is not merely a form of government. It is primarily a mode of associated living, of conjoint, communicated experience. It is essentially an attitude of respect and reverence towards fellowmen. (BAWS, vol. 1: 57)

As Ambedkar argues, 'There cannot be a caste in the single number. Caste can exist only in the plural number. Caste to be real can exist only by disintegrating a group. The genius of caste is to divide and disintegrate' (BAWS, vol. 5: 211). One could not be more categorical about the antagonistic relationship between caste and nation. In Ambedkar's opinion, anti-social spirit of caste makes common activity and associated living impossible, as various castes have an innate tendency to develop their own interests and do injustice or mischief to others. Caste distinctions based on birth or on occupation provide a breeding ground for mutual distrust and animosity. It is hard for each section to recognise the equal rights of the other. He sees the caste system not only as an assortment of castes, but as several warring groups living for themselves in an insular environment with their selfish ideals (BAWS, vol. 1: 52). The existence of caste and caste-consciousness, he stresses, has also served to keep the memory of past feuds alive preventing solidarity between various groups as equal citizens of a common nation. Holding caste-consciousness as the mother of communalism, he argues that nationalism necessarily implies negation of caste-spirit which is nothing but a deep-rooted communalism. 'Caste has killed public spirit. Caste has destroyed the sense of public charity. Caste has made public opinion impossible. Virtue has become caste-ridden, and morality has become caste-bound' (ibid.: 56).

In short, Ambedkar enunciates that castelessness essentially means equality, which is the principal prerequisite for a nation to emerge. Equality, though it may not avert conflict of interests between communities, helps each section of society to understand the mind of the others, and creates a general opinion in favour of the nation. He also implicitly negates, as Aloysius (1997) underscores, the notion that equality as a modern political theory is peculiar to the Western world. It is not Western or Eastern, it is to be found everywhere as aspirations of the lower classes and as Ambedkar points out certainly within the shramanic/Buddhist/heterodox traditions in India.

Ambedkar's opposition to the kind of nationalism conceived and promoted by upper caste leaders can only be read and understood in this perspective. He had basic differences with the Congress-led movement for freedom. It was a principled and consistent approach which he carried from the beginning of his public life right up to the end, except for short periods of issue-and-programme-based collaboration with the Congress leadership. That is why, as early as 1930 during the First Round Table Conference, he advocated for independence but at the same time insisted on special protection and reservations in legislatures and public services for the victims of institutionalised and prolonged discrimination. It is important that the elites who were deriding Ambedkar for his advocacy of affirmative action for the weaker sections were conspicuously silent on the nomination of princes and feudal lords in the legislatures in the British India. It was Ambedkar who had forthrightly opposed the nominations of *raja-maharajas* during the First Round Table Conference and had pleaded for the nomination of representatives of the depressed communities.

Even Jawaharlal Nehru, perhaps the most liberal and democratic among the nationalists and the darling of many Marxists in India, did not give heed to Ambedkar's critique of the Congress brand of nationalism. Nehru's Fabian socialism was fiery rhetoric; it had very little substance. Considered a visionary and a radical by many, Nehru, who succeeded his father Motilal as the Congress president in 1929 in a feudal manner, went on to lay informally the foundation of his dynasty when he anointed his daughter Indira as the Congress president while he was the Prime Minister. This visionary could not foresee that the Congress would become the dynastic bequest of his daughter and grandsons. It is not possible to overlook the difference between Nehru's brave rhetoric and reality. Consider, for example, this case: an important part of the rhetoric of Nehru and 'radicals' within the pre-Independence Congress was to alter the rural property order. However, acknowledging the Congress' dependence on the landed upper castes, Nehru and his comrades ensured that the Constitution limited the Centre's ability to change the rural property order. It left the question of social and economic reform, whose importance Ambedkar was constantly underlining during the debate in the Constituent Assembly, to the state legislatures, where the rural landed gentry could bring local pressure against redistributive measures. This is not an isolated instance; Nehru remained loyal to the rich and the privileged while pretending to serve the poor. Invoking universal principles of justice and rights from time to time to win over the masses in the emergent democratic dispensation, the Congress government under Nehru and his successors ignored the interests of the poor.

The ideological and social hiatus between the Congress leadership and Ambedkar was immense. The Congress leaders' mocking speeches and vitriolic writings (C. Rajagopalachari's *Ambedkar Refuted* is a case in point) all bear testimony to their hatred for and resentment against Ambedkar. As a dignified and self-respecting person, Ambedkar resented the offensive tone of Congress leaders who tried to belittle him as a self-appointed representative of the untouchables. Referring to his humiliating marginalisation, Ambedkar said, during a debate in the Constituent Assembly, 'I am not one of your national leaders. The utmost rank to which I have risen is that of a leader of the untouchables. I find even that rank has been denied to me. Thakkar Bapa very recently said that I was only the leader of the Mahars' (*BAWS*, vol. 8: 346). Ambedkar suspected, not without reason, that a conspiracy was hatched by the Congress to divide untouchables along caste and sub-caste lines. Besides promoting spineless, incompetent Harijan leaders with the lure of offices, 'silver bullets' through the nationalist press, as he said, were freely used for creating divisions in the ranks of the dalit-subalterns. It must have been under such provocation that Ambedkar had famously asserted that his loyalty to the dalits came first and to India next. In the circumstances, he was left with no option but to fight independently for the rights of the oppressed classes. In 1935, he made it clear that he wanted a total break with oppressive Hinduism. In 1936, he founded the Independent Labour Party with radical socio-economic objectives. In 1942, he established the Scheduled Castes Federation, and three years later he set up People's Education Society dedicated to the spread of higher education amongst depressed classes.

RADICAL REALISM AMIDST EUPHORIA OF FREEDOM: THE CONSTITUTION AND THE HINDU CODE BILL

Ambedkar's radicalism in the 1930s as a political agitator-organiser who demanded swaraj was replaced in the first half of 1940s by his tactical co-operation with the British. His decision to join the Viceroy's Executive Council as Labour Member appears to be in retaliation to the utter indifference of the nationalist leadership to the question of marginalised millions. Obdurate and obstructionist methods employed by orthodox Hindu elements who dominated the national scene, to the burning social issues forced Ambedkar to forge a temporary alliance with the British. Apparently the mutual antagonism between Ambedkar and the Congress leadership had by then become irreconcilable. There was no love lost between Ambedkar and Gandhi. Ambedkar was inpatient for structural change while all Gandhi could offer him was assurances of a 'change of heart'.

So even at the height of the Quit India movement, Ambedkar remained aloof from the nationalist agitation and concentrated his efforts on benefits for the poor and marginalised in the given circumstances. As a member of the Viceroy's Council he authored a labour legislation which became the model on the subject for much that followed after Independence. Ambedkar constituted a Labour Conference to consider matters like the formation of a Joint Labour Management Committee and an Employment Exchange, and initiated measures to institute social security for industrial workers. Likewise, his pioneering work on water resources development – particularly in the context of Damodar Valley and Mahanadi basin – proved to be of significance and had a powerful bearing on the water management strategy in independent India.

However, the rapidly changing political situation in the 1940s and imminent independence from the British forced Ambedkar to change his strategy and to co-operate with the Congress for a brief while. But this co-operation was issue-based, and even in this hour of bonhomie Ambedkar did not succumb to the nationalist rhetoric and posturing. His principal concern then was to ensure the best possible deal for the marginalised in the wake of Independence. To safeguard their rights, at least in the theoretical framework, he joined the Nehru cabinet as Minister of Law. On the strength of his brilliant work at the Round Table Conference, his membership of the Joint Committee on Indian Constitutional Reform, and, his participation in the Constituent Assembly, Ambedkar was also elected Chairman of the Drafting Committee for a new Constitution.

Ambedkar's interest in the Constitution-making process was not only due to his commitment to get the depressed classes essential safeguards in the Draft Constitution which his participation made possible. He took up this back-breaking job which required a rare degree of legal expertise also because 'he had a wider vision of the kind of society and polity that should be brought into existence in India' (Gore 1993: 183). He wanted nationalisation of industries and land, and a time-bound scheme for social and economic empowerment of the weaker sections of society. He wanted insurance to be a state monopoly and every adult Indian to be compelled to have life insurance. When his social scheme as well as many other provisions in his programme were set aside, he tried to make the Directive Principles of State for social welfare as rigorous as possible. He, however, was aware, as Gore has pointed out, that a constitution is like a pledge one makes to oneself. Its accomplishment lies in one's sincerity and ability to live up to it. He said the problem was not that the laws were prejudicial to the interests of the masses but it was the lack of implementation due to 'bad administration'. As there were very few people belonging to the weaker sections in the government, the administration was dominated by the classes who practised 'tyranny and oppression' against the weak. The remedy, he argued, was to make members of the marginalised communities part of the various organs of governance and civil services.

Summing up his arguments in the Constituent Assembly on 25 November 1949, just before the Draft Constitution was adopted for the Republic of India, Ambedkar said many prophetic things in a forceful manner. He warned – even in the hour of euphoria – of the dangers both to India's independence and her democratic constitution. First, he advised constitutional and democratic methods of self-government:

If we wish to maintain democracy not merely in form, but also in fact, what must we do? The first thing in my judgment we must do is to hold fast constitutional methods of achieving our social and economic objective. It means we must abandon the bloody methods of revolution. (BAWS, vol. 13: 1215)

Second, to make democracy strong with a vibrant civil society, Ambedkar felt the need for vigilance against hero-worship which leads to dependency and servitude:

The second thing we must do is to observe the caution which John Sturat Mill has given to all who are interested in the maintenance of democracy, namely, not to lay their liberties at the feet of even a great man, or to trust him with powers which enable him to subvert their institutions. (ibid.)

Cautioning against the creation of messiahs, Ambedkar said, 'There is nothing wrong in being grateful to great men ... but there are limits to gratefulness. ... Bhakti in religion may be a road to salvation of the soul. But in politics, bhakti or hero-worship is a sure road to degradation and to eventual dictatorship.'

Third, Ambedkar advocated the conscious fostering of social and economic equality so that the democracy that the country has embraced after centuries of wilderness could become real social democracy:

We must make our political democracy a social democracy as well. Political democracy cannot last unless there lies at the base of it social democracy. Social democracy ... means a way of life which recognises liberty, equality and fraternity as the principles of life. These principles ... form a union of trinity in the sense that to divorce one from the other is to defeat the very purpose of democracy. Liberty cannot be divorced from equality, equality cannot be divorced from liberty. Nor can liberty and equality be divorced from fraternity. Without equality, liberty would produce the supremacy of the few over the many. Equality without liberty would kill individual initiative. Without fraternity, liberty and equality could not become a natural course of things. (ibid.: 1216)

He then pointed out the in-built inequality in a caste-based society. Indian society, he said, had not recognised the values of equality and fraternity and 'on the economic plane, there are some who have immense wealth as against many who live in abject poverty'. Equality in principle and widespread inequality in practice, he stressed, would create a dangerous situation for the new democracy:

On the 26th of January 1950, we are going to enter into a life of contradictions. In politics we will have equality and in social and economic life we will have inequality. In politics we will be recognising the principle of one man one vote and one vote one value. In our social and economic life, we shall, by reason of our social and economic structure, continue to deny the principle of one man one value. How long shall we continue to live this life of contradictions? . . . We must remove this contradiction at the earliest possible moment . . . (ibid.)

Ambedkar also cautioned against the illusion that India was already a nation. It was fragmented into thousands of castes, which was a menace to the emerging nation:

I am of (the) opinion that in believing that we are a nation, we are cherishing a great delusion. How can people divided into several thousands of castes be a nation? The sooner we realise that we are not as yet a nation in the social and psychological sense of the word, the better for us. For then only we shall realise the necessity of becoming a nation and seriously think of ways and means of realising the goal. (ibid.: 1217)

The remedies, he said, may not be very pleasant to some as in this country the political power had for too long been the monopoly of a few, but the long-suppressed people were tired of being governed, they were impatient to govern themselves.

Independence is no doubt a matter of joy. But let us not forget that this independence has thrown on us great responsibilities. By independence, we have lost the excuse of blaming the British for anything going wrong. If hereafter things go wrong, we will have nobody to blame except ourselves. There is great danger of things going wrong. Times are fast changing. People including our own are being moved by new ideologies. . . . If we wish to preserve the Constitution in which we have sought to enshrine the principle of Government of the people, for the people and by the people, let us resolve not to be so tardy in the recognition of the evils that lie across our path and which induce people to prefer Government for the people to Government by the people, nor to be weak in our initiative to remove them. This is the only way to serve the country. I know of no better. (ibid.: 1218)

Ambedkar's role as a member of the Union cabinet was

secondary during the constitution-making period. After that, party differences between the Congress and non-Congress in the Cabinet over several policy matters cropped up. Ambedkar saw that there was an inner-party caucus that took decisions on important issues before they were placed before the cabinet. Congress politics and priorities upset Ambedkar but he continued in the Cabinet until September 1951. As Law Minister, he introduced and steered through Parliament the Representation of People Bill. But his heart was set on the Hindu Code Bill, which he regarded as an indispensable part of his commitment to social reform. The Bill included, among other things, Hindu women's rights to inheritance and property. The conservative Hindu elements, including many top Congress leaders, raised a hue and cry. Their stiff opposition put spokes in the passage of the Bill, and Nehru too, who was seen as favouring the Bill, could not do much as the Congress refused to issue a whip in favour of the Bill. A vicious campaign was orchestrated against the Bill and Ambedkar was targeted for personal attack. Jere Shastri, one of the Shankaracharyas, was not the only one to abuse Ambedkar as 'an untouchable who dared to interfere with orthodox Hindu practices'.

Ambedkar was also aggrieved that despite Nehru's promise to give him charge of an administrative portfolio in addition to law, he had not only been denied this but even shut out from the policy-making Cabinet Committees. This was a serious thing because the Cabinet worked mostly in committees and these committees 'worked behind an iron curtain' so that 'others who are not members have only to take joint responsibility without any opportunity of taking part in the shaping of policy'. Ambedkar resigned from the Cabinet. He was not allowed even to read out his resignation statement in the House and he had to issue a Press brief in explanation. He repudiated all suggestions that he had resigned on the grounds of ill-health. The Government's decision to drop the Hindu Code Bill, the betrayal of the Scheduled Castes, a ruinous Kashmir policy, and the fiction of Cabinet responsibility were the reasons he gave for his resignation. As a person dedicated to the uplift of the lower classes, Ambedkar was deeply distressed over non-serious approach of the Nehru government to this issue. He challenged Nehru to issue a public statement detailing what the government had done or intended to do for the downtrodden.

8

Epilogue: Institutionalised Discrimination from the Past to the 'Democratic' Present

> He who would confine his thought to present time will not understand present reality.
>
> JULES MICHELET

> Freedom without opportunity is a devil's gift, and the refusal to provide such opportunities is criminal.
>
> NOAM CHOMSKY

Despite resistance to caste and brahmanism, beginning with shramanic heterodoxies and Buddhism, followed by various streams of Bhakti movements, Sikhism, Sufism, similar lesser known campaigns and ideologies and anti-caste egalitarian movements in modern India, caste consciousness and brahmanic mindset persist in their modernised, metamorphosed avatar, defying and denying democratic ideals. As a result, India remains one of the most iniquitous and unjust societies on earth. True, post-1947 India has made spectacular progress in many fields as claimed by sarkari economists and peddlers of 'India as the emerging superpower'. But 'who has collared them, and in what proportion?' Was discriminatory development not inherent in the brahmanic DNA of the cultural nationalism and process of growth adopted by Central governments since Nehru's time?

Since the days of the national movement, as in the earlier periods, here a small minority consisting mainly of upper castes and classes, guided by self-interest, have subverted the democracy and goal of an egalitarian society. The privileged and educated Indian 'has always seen democracy more as a means of voicing his demands, or asserting his rights, or registering his protests, and less as a system of accepting community obligations, or restricting unreasonable interests, or tempering freedom with responsibilities' (Varma 1998: 149). As a result, hundreds of millions are denied the basic minimums of life. India has, of course, changed in fifty years. Life expectancy, literacy, and education levels are higher than in 1947. There have been improvements and benefits. But, as P. Sainath asks, would that satisfy you if you were one of those who did not benefit?

If you draw a baseline in the last Ice Age, everyone's conditions have improved. . . . Knowing this won't satisfy the poor. Likewise, the concept of the 'poverty line' has a role and place. But crowing about a 'decline' in poverty from 39 per cent to 21 per cent is silly. If you belong to those just above the line, you don't know it – not from the quality of life. And anyway, those doing the counting are always from the top 10 per cent of the population. (Outlook, 19 October 1998)

India has the dubious distinction of entering the twenty-first century with the largest numbers of absolute poor. One out of every three persons in the world lacking safe drinking water is an Indian. Every fourth person in the globe dying of water-borne diseases is an Indian. Illiteracy envelops one in every two in a country whose elite prides itself on its glorious intellectual traditions. Tens of millions suffer malnourishment; one out of two children is malnourished. India has the highest numbers of people suffering from blindness, hepatitis-B, tuberculosis, leprosy and AIDS. It has the highest number of occupational casualties. It shares with the sub-Saharan countries the highest infant mortality rates. There is one doctor (mostly unavailable) for 25-odd villages or over 25,000 people in parts of the country while a large chunk of the health budget goes to urban hospitals. All this in a 55-year old republic, which Constitution (Article 47) declares, 'The State shall regard the raising of the level of nutrition and the improvement of public health as among its primary duties.'

Who are the inhabitants of this 'other India'? Around 40 per cent of the Indian poor are landless labourers. Another 45 per cent are marginal farmers. Of the remaining, close to 10 per cent are rural artisans. Their brothers and sisters who are migrating to urban centres in search of employment make up the rest. Save a few thousands, almost all these 'disenfranchised' people are dalit, adivasi, other backward classes and Muslim masses. What do the privileged strata which made most out of the modern Indian state think about the 'other India'?

As I talk to my friends, my relatives, my professional colleagues today, I get a feeling of total ignorance of the other India. When in fact they are forced to take note, such as when they walk through the pavements on which people are sleeping, there is a feeling of revulsion, of rejection, of contempt, not of compassion, empathy and least of all of any sense of guilt. (Rajni Kothari, The Times of India, 27 April 1986)

Speaking of the two Indias that are increasingly less and less in touch with each other, Kothari notes with anxiety that the other, non-modern and 'vernacular' India is 'not just getting marginalised and pushed to the peripheries of socio-economic and political systems; they are also being pushed to the peripheries of our consciousness' (ibid.). The policies and priorities of the ruling elite have been driving a wedge between the two Indias deeper and wider. The recent policies of economic liberalisation and the whole thinking on modernisation in essentially technological terms, policies in respect of education, health and nutrition, housing and provision of basic amenities leave little doubt that the welfaristic aspects of State are withering away and the interests of the poor and marginalised are driven out of policy framework. On the other hand, India is 'shining' for a tiny minority as globalisation has opened a world of possibilities for the privilegentsia. Exulting in the heady atmosphere of optimism generated by the economic 'reforms', one commentator crows:

New technologies, new ventures, new jobs are being introduced as never before. Industry is booming as never before. Most of all, there is a palpable hope in the air. People are doing lucrative deals, getting well-paid jobs, travelling and vacationing, convinced that India is at last over the hump.

The privileged class nurtures the illusion that what is good for it is also good for the country as a whole. For those looking forward to 'well-paid jobs', 'travelling and vacationing' as never before, the other India – the deprived India, the India of hunger, illiteracy, disease and diarrhoea – simply does not exist. The government policies and attitudes are making the gap and the schism more fool-proof of 'quarantining the elites and their cahoots and facilitators from the rest, effectively depriving the latter of their minimum rights of citizenship and many among them of their right to live' (Kothari, op. cit.).

It is the kind of horror that haunted Ambedkar both before and after Independence. Unmasking the ugly, hypocritical universe that existed behind that soul-stirring phrase 'Freedom Struggle', he had pointed out that the kind of freedom the elite-oriented nationalist movement was striving for was not the freedom to emancipate the masses but the freedom to perpetuate the discrimination and exploitation. It is futile to argue that Ambedkar's agenda was less patriotic, less relevant in the colonial period than Gandhi's. The real point is a contemporary one: Ambedkarite agenda of human rights and dignity, education, health care, and equality of opportunity remain largely unrealised, though the major Gandhian agenda was accomplished in 1947 with the attainment of freedom. If we are indeed sincere to engage with the 'other India', we will have to engage with Ambedkar, the 'other' of nationalist thought and practice represented by Gandhi and Nehru.

Ambedkar's insight into Indian reality, his socio-economic thoughts, especially his critique of caste and cultural oppression, can help us understand why Adam Smith's fabled 'hidden force' is not coming to the rescue of those trapped in poverty. Why and how the underclass continue to be exploited and excluded from the portals of knowledge and power despite the 'deepening' democracy? Why and how are they systematically barred from any economic channels or opportunities, while a tiny upper caste-class minority boarding onto the 'national' bandwagon are creating islands of unprecedented wealth through monopolising almost all space in the liberalised, globalised economy? Why there is hardly any presence of dalits, adivasis, other backward classes in the booming market economy, industries, print and electronic media, television, film and music industries?

Is it all fortuitous or does the continuing hold of brahmanical mindset, indignity of labour and patriarchy have something to do with the growth without social justice? Are those who slog in fields and factories, who interact with instruments of production and services, still not treated as 'inferior beings', despised as 'good-for-nothing' shudras and ati-shudras? And, is there no link between the rising tide of fundamentalism, the growing affluence of the rich and acute poverty of the majority? Is any substantial change and transformation possible in Indian society without evolving a cultural agenda to deconstruct the brahmanic mind? Had Ambedkar been alive today, would he have chosen to bask in the 'glory' of his elitist co-option in the pantheon of great Indians? Or would he have stepped off his pedestal, shrugged off the empty elitist adulation and walked out onto the streets, in villages and towns, to rally his people once more?

Even some affirmative action for the weaker sections in academic institutions and government services that Ambedkar, Periyar and others had to wrung out of the unwilling hands of the power elite have been rendered ineffective by insincere and hostile attitude of the governing classes. In any case, the government jobs are increasingly dwindling in the wake of liberalisation, and the private and corporate sectors which dominate the economy have very few openings for the non-elites. As Omvedt argues, various kinds of influence and access to power – which are so vital to set up even small industries and businesses – available to the dominant class in addition to the advantage of coming from families and castes who have as background generations of education, intellectual and entrepreneurial orientation and the economic resources to back it up, become direct or indirect factors of discrimination against the traditionally deprived castes and communities. The industrialists who talk about 'level playing field' for Indians in the global business, who seek support to compete with multinationals, do not want to discuss the issue of how company ownership and company employment works in India.

While the sociological data on caste and economic achievement is rather minimal, what studies we have show a heavy domination of upper castes. Strikingly, brahmans seem to be outdoing even the traditional 'bania' groups in industry today! . . . A study by Santosh Goyal of the caste composition of top corporate officers in 1979-80 showed that out of 2000 whose caste could be identified (of a total of 3129), 858 or 41.2 per cent were brahmans;

khatris and vaishyas were a poor second and third with 18.5 per cent and 17.9 per cent. Only 4.2 per cent were 'shudra' of any type. (Omvedt, *The Hindu*, 1 June 2001)

With the coming of knowledge and information-based industries and technologies, the gap between the brahman and allied castes and the rest is getting wider at the national, corporate and individual levels. However, the glaring difference in 'intelligence' and 'achievements' between upper and lowered castes is manufactured by social factors, it is not 'natural' or 'biological'. In the absence of human resources, particularly lack of education, no community, no individual has ever made any economic progress anywhere. As J. K. Galbraith once said, 'In this world there is no literate population that is poor, no illiterate population that is other than poor.' The difference is due to factors like poverty, lack of education and health care, and caste-induced social humiliation that have served to smother the abilities and potentials of people from lowered castes, dalits and adivasis. Omvedt says, 'This situation means that there is a vast wastage of human resources in India. It should be of concern not only to dalits and OBCs themselves, but to any true nationalist.'

In the absence of any sort of affirmative action in the private sector, new jobs and opportunities continue to be beyond the reach of not only dalits and adivasis but also majority of the other backward classes and Muslim masses. There is no simplified division between public and private; any sector that is regulated and/or funded by the government is open to government directives. In the United States most affirmative action programmes, in fact, work in the private sector, including educational institutions (Omvedt 2001). India, on the other hand, does the opposite: it subsidises the quality education of the rich and the resourceful at the cost of primary education of the poor!

A large number of schools in India are privately owned. Their funds, though, come from the public. As much as 60 per cent of government expenses on schools goes in grants to privately owned institutions. In fourteen major Indian states, education claims 32 per cent of all subsidies on social services. Much less than half of this is spent on primary education. Paucity of funds does not seem to cripple institutes of higher learning run by and for the elite. (Sainath 1996: 52)

Such dubious policy has resulted in a few Indians doing exceedingly well – speaking flawless, fluent English, storming the Silicon Valley and replicating the same in places like Bangalore and Hyderabad – while for the majority, education only means identifying 'vernacular' letters; in fact, in the villages, the illiterate as well as the 'literate' don't even manage that. India's literacy rates is no better than the sub-Saharan Africa, the most undeveloped region of the world:

Literacy rates in India are much lower than in China, lower than literacy rates in many east and south-east Asian countries at the time of their rapid economic expansion thirty years or so ago: They are lower than the average literacy rates for 'low-income countries' other than China and India, and also no higher than estimated literacy rates in sub-Saharan Africa. (Dreze and Sen 1998: 114)

Why India is doing no better than sub-Saharan Africa in the field of basic education appals Professors Sen and Dreze because, as they point out, unlike many countries of sub-Saharan Africa, India has been relatively protected from the calamities of political instability, military rules, divisive civil wars, and recurring famines since its Independence. The persistence of endemic illiteracy appears odious also in view of its impressive record in higher education and scientific research. Enormous educational disparities, in fact, have its roots in enormous social and economic inequalities. In many respects, economic, social and gender inequalities are more acute in India than the world's most undeveloped regions and countries. 'These inequalities, aside from social failures on their own, also imply much lower levels of well-being for disadvantaged sections of the population than the country and regional aggregate suggests. Gender inequalities, for instance, tend to be larger in India than in sub-Saharan Africa, and are responsible for extremely high levels of female deprivation in India' (ibid.: 31).

The power elite in India still seem to hold that their prosperity, knowledge and power have to be derived from poverty, illiteracy and exploitation of the lower orders. The brahmanical mindset has always valorised and promoted this tradition. In the words of

Omvedt, 'While much has changed in the structures and functioning of caste, old attitudes still persist and affect children of Bahujan and Dalit families – education is not for you. . . . Traditional attitudes coming from without produce active discrimination, and traditional attitudes internalised within the family make it difficult for children of the so-called 'low' caste to see themselves as people who can be good at intellectual pursuits'. Such attitudes, unfortunately, have been strengthened by no less a person that the 'Father of the Nation'. Gandhi praised 'the shudra who only serves the higher castes as a matter of religious charity, who has nothing to call his own and who has no desire for ownership.' One wonders: had Gandhi not indulged in brahmanical obscurantism, would he have been made the 'Mahatma' and deified as the 'Father of the Nation'?

Modernisation and technological advances without attitudinal changes have, in fact, heralded a neo-brahmanic dominance. The technology and electronic gadgets cannot become an instrument of people's empowerment unless the brahmanic mind is systematically deconstructed. Without 'brick and mortar', as Kancha Ilaiah says, the game of 'click and mouse' will continue to belong to the chosen few. The need is to thoroughly de-brahmanise socio-economic values that still pervade all aspects of life, culture and economy in India. Poverty is being perpetuated by the co-existence of caste distinction with modern technology. Ilaiah cites a specific example: billions of rupees that circulate in the name of temple economy do not benefit a single dalit family at a time when Hindu religion has been operating in an inter-connected manner with advanced technology. 'Today more computers are being used to modernise the images of Hindu deities than for computing the nature of caste-class inequalities and the number of atrocities taking place on dalits and women' (Ilaiah 2004: 175).

Caste and corruption are symbiotic in India and tend to feed and prosper on each other. Even the judiciary, the supposed citadel of justice and human rights, suffers from the caste virus, and has in its own way contributed to subvert the egalitarian goal enshrined in the Constitution. A Parliamentary Committee on the Welfare of Scheduled Castes and Scheduled Tribes headed by Karia Munda in its second report in September 2000 shows how the judiciary and the bar in the higher courts is 'neither sympathetic nor unbiased to the cause of backward classes'. It points out that the members of the judiciary have so far been drawn from the very section of society which is 'infected by ancient prejudices and is dominated by notions of gradations in life. . . . The internal limitation of class interests of such judges does not allow them full play of their intellectual honesty and integrity in their decisions. These judges very often betray a mindset more useful to the governing class than the servile class' (see Munda 2000). Lamenting that there were only 15 SC and 5 ST judges among the 481 High Court judges in the country and there was no judge from this social group in the Supreme Court as on 1 May 1998, the Committee reports: 'Judges take oath that they (will) uphold the Constitution and the laws. But the Supreme Court and a few high courts by claiming power over the Constitution, practise untouchability and are disobeying the Constitution with regard to Articles 16(4) and 16(4a)' (ibid.)

The Committee scoffs at the notion that the judiciary is a 'super speciality' service with 'merit' as its bedrock: 'To argue that only those with merit have found a berth in the judiciary is specious. . . . This presupposes that those from the weaker sections do not have enough merit.' Citing the observation of Justice P. B. Sawant in a landmark judgement in the early 1990s, in which Sawant had argued how in the name of 'merit' and 'national interests' . . . 'all aspects of life are controlled, directed and regulated mostly to suit the sectional interests of a small section of the society which numerically do not exceed 10 per cent of the total population of the country', the panel contends:

How can 10 per cent of the population represent the 'national interest' and is not the so-called merit the result of the cumulative advantages on social, educational and economic fronts enjoyed by a select social group? The Supreme Court which is the nation's last court of appeal, cannot afford to appear unjust in its own domain. But unfortunately that seems to have happened over the years. Judges have, of course, the power, though not the right, to ignore the mandate of a statute and render judgments despite it.
(see Munda 2000)

If this is the state of affairs in judiciary, then one can well imagine the plight of dalits and adivasis in other areas of national life. In fact, the 'classical tradition' of excluding the masses from knowledge, learning and power is embedded in the psyche of the Indian elite. The salient feature of the Indian culture, as Kosambi said, is its continuity and the main vehicle of this continuity has been the caste system which Berreman describes as 'institutionalised inequality', which 'guaranteed differential access to the valued things in life'. As he says, 'The human meaning of caste for those who live it is power and vulnerability, privilege and oppression, honour and denigration, plenty and want, reward and deprivation, security and anxiety' (Berreman 1991: 88).

Various facets of modernisation – industrial and technological developments, liberal-democratic ideals and legislatures enshrined in the Constitution, modern educational institutions, etc. – have not been able to offset the continued dominance of caste. The resilient caste structure has taken economic and technological breakthrough in its stride, and 'this transition, not transformation, has been quite smooth in as much as the skilled human resources with education, training and experience (as a result of monopolies of the high castes over them since the beginning of Indian society) have taken control of the new developments and as such only they have been the beneficiaries' (Chatterji 1998: 34-48). The various elements of the brahmanical socio-cultural order, though traditional, are still functional as instruments of distribution of power excluding an overwhelming majority from acquiring important positions in any walk of life.

The tradition of egalitarian castelessness is still very much relevant because Sita (forbidden from acquiring knowledge and power), Shambuk (eliminated for daring to acquire spiritual knowledge), Karna (treacherously deprived of his life-saving device), and Eklavya (robbed of his thumb for his 'illegitimate' prowess in archery) are still clamouring for their rightful place in society. The greatest sports award in India is still given in the honour of Arjuna, and not Karna or Eklavya, both of whom, according to legend, were greater archers. And the best coach award has been instituted in honour of Dronacharya, the perfidious guru who forced Eklavya to cut off his thumb as the *guru-dakshina* (teacher-tribute) in order to make Arjuna the best archer of his time. How can a country whose moral foundations are based on bricks of deceit and double standards excel in social democracy?

Notes

CHAPTER 1: HISTORICAL ROOTS OF DOMINANCE

1. The oft-quoted *Purusha-sukta* in the *Rigveda* provides a supernatural origin of the castes:
   *When they divided the Man,
   into how many parts did they divide him?
   What was his mouth, what were his arms,
   what were his thighs and his feet called?
   The brahman was his mouth,
   of his arms were made the warrior,
   his thighs became the vaishya
   of his feet the shudra was born.* (Basham 1991: 243)

2. To keep erring shudras firmly in their place, Manu has prescribed exemplary punishments. Here are some instances. 'If a shudra hurls cruel words at a brahman, his tongue should be cut out, for he was born from the rear-end. If he mentions their name or caste maliciously, a red-hot iron nail ten-fingers long should be thrust into his mouth. If he is so proud as to instruct brahmans about their duty, the king should have hot oil poured into his mouth and ears' (VIII.270-2) '. . . If a shudra injures a man of the higher castes with some particular part of his body, that very part of his body should be cut off. If he raises his hand or a stick, he should have his hand cut off; if in anger he strikes with his foot, he should have his foot cut off. If a man of inferior caste tries to sit down on the same seat as a man of superior caste, he should be branded on the hip and banished, or have his buttocks cut off. If in his pride he spits on him, the king should have his two lips cut off; if he urinates on him, the penis; if he farts at him, the anus' (VIII.279-82). The list of such vicious instructions runs long and is shared and suggested by other leading law-givers as well.

   Women, too, are the target of the most odious, vituperative attacks from Manu and other brahmanical authorities. Manu condemns all women to eternal surveillance by their male masters. This is what he says about women in general: 'Good looks do not matter to them, nor do they care about youth; "A man!" they say, and enjoy sex with him, whether he is good-looking or ugly. By running after men like whores, by their fickle minds, and by their natural lack of affection these women are unfaithful to their husbands even when they are jealously guarded here. Knowing that their very own nature is like this, . . . a man should make the utmost effort, to guard them. The bed and the seat, jewellery, lust, anger, crookedness, a malicious nature, and bad conduct are what Manu assigned to women. There is no ritual with Vedic verses for women; this is a fairly established point of view. For women, who have no virile strength and no Vedic verses, are falsehood; this is well established' (IX.14-18).

3. Shraman (*Saman* in Pali) is derived from the word *shram*, 'to exert'. Initially, shraman was used for practitioner of religious exertions. A shraman was a religious striver. Of the two earliest references to the word *shraman* in the Vedic literature, one is found in the *Brihdaranyaka Upanishad* where it is used in the same sense denoting a class of mendicants. Later the word *shraman* came to be referred to a member of the heterodox orders of monks. In the Pali Buddhist scriptures, we frequently meet the compound word shraman-brahman, the former denoting all kinds of mendicants including the Buddhists, and the latter the upholders of the Vedic tradition. The Buddha is called a great shraman, addressed frequently as 'Shraman Gautam', and members of his order are referred to as the shramans. In the Jain texts, Mahavir, too, is called a shraman, a term by which the practitioners of Buddhism and Jainism as well as all those opposed to the Vedic religion came to be identified.

CHAPTER 2: BUDDHIST INDIA

1. The Buddha's speeches, sayings, conversations and discourses, though initially handed down orally, were compiled just after his death, but had been given their present content in all probability in about Ashoka's time. Preserved in Pali, Buddhist hybrid Sanskrit and classical Sanskrit, the total literature of Buddhism – despite the fact that a major and authentic portion of it is lost, and in many cases wilfully destroyed by opponents like the king Pushyamıtra Shunga – is enormous, with various Buddhist schools such as Hinayana and Mahayana having their own versions of the scriptures. The original literature of most Buddhist sects has been lost, or only survives in Chinese or Tibetan translations. However, the earliest, most complete and authoritative canon of undivided and early Buddhism – the Pali *Tipitaka* – has been preserved in Sri Lanka. According to some scholars, Pali was either Magadhi Prakrit or an amalgam of various Prakrit dialects of the region corresponding to the modern south

Bihar and eastern Uttar Pradesh. The Buddha spent most of his time in this region, and delivered his speeches in Pali which, in all likelihood, he fashioned by mixing various dialects of the region he visited in order to be effectively communicable to a wider audience. It is but natural that the early Buddhist literature was composed in the language which the master himself spoke. The Pali canon, known as the *Tipitaka* – the Three Baskets – comprises *Vinaya, Sutta,* and *Abhidhamma Pitakas.* The *Vinaya Pitaka* contains the rules of conduct of the Buddhist order of monks and nuns. The *Sutta Pitaka* is the most important; it contains doctrinal expositions, discourses and conversations attributed to the Buddha, divided into five sections, namely the *Digha Nikaya* (the Long Collection containing long discourses); the *Majjhima Nikaya* (the Medium Collection with shorter discourses); the *Samyutta Nikaya* (the Connected Collection, containing brief pronouncements on related topics); the *Anguttara Nikaya* (the Progressive Collection, short passages arranged in eleven sections); and the *Khuddaka Nikaya* (the Minor Collection, containing various works of varying type, including the exquisitely poetic *Dhammapada,* the 'Way to Righteousness', and *Udana.* The third basket, the *Abhidhamma Pitaka* (the Supplementary Doctrines), is a collection of work on Buddhist psychology and metaphysics.

2. There is no mention of the word *dharma* in Vedic literature; its use in Sanskrit literature became popular only after the Buddha's time. Brahman priests and grammarians may well have fashioned the word in imitation of the Pali term, *dhamma* (see HaBir Angar Ee's *Pali is the Mother of Sanskrit*).

3. There is one known instance in the *Digha Nikaya* as well as *Khuddaka Nikaya* in which brahmans are reported to have attempted to harass the Buddha and his companions by throwing garbage in a well.

CHAPTER 3: MEDIEVAL MUKTI MOVEMENTS

1. According to the brahmanical legend, Kabir was so desperate to become a follower of Ramananda that he had to resort to trickery. He stretched himself across the stairs leading to the Ganga in Benaras where Ramananda came for his bath in the pre-dawn darkness. As expected, Ramananda tripped over Kabir's body and cried out his mantra 'Rama! Rama!' Kabir then claimed that the magical mantra had been transmitted to him, tricking the reluctant Ramananda into accepting him as a disciple.

2. He is referring here to the famous *Purusha-sukta* – the Creation

Hymn – of the *Rigveda*. At this, Kabir jeers: Why do you, O! brahman, who believe in the infallibility of the Vedas, come into this world as a shudra does?

3. It is not without significance that Phule and Ambedkar, two heroes of the oppressed in nineteenth- and twentieth-century India, came from the Kabirpanthi background. Phule and his friends were great admirers of Kabir's poetry which inspired them to found the Satyashodhak Samaj to fight the forces of evil and injustice (see the Chapter 5). Ambedkar's father was a staunch Kabirpanthi. Kabir was in Ambedkar's blood – so close was he to the radical poet that on his last night after a frugal meal he sang the song of Kabir *'Chala Kabir tera bhava sagar dera'* and, singing, he went to bed and never woke up. Ambedkar had accepted Kabir as one of his three gurus, along with the Buddha and Phule. Both Phule and Ambedkar had recognised the social radicalism of the Bhakti movement. Ambedkar's *The Untouchables* is dedicated to Nandnar, Ravidas, and Chokhamela, born among the untouchables.
4. Dhedh is the name of an untouchable caste in Maharashtra. The word *dhedh*, like the names of all untouchable castes, is an insult – here thrown at Namdev by the brahmans.

CHAPTER 4: COLONIALISM AND NATIONALISM

1. The brahmanic Hindu mind tends to blame the prolonged Muslim domination of medieval India for all that was wrong with the Hindu society, ignoring the fact that Muslim rule itself was established due to treacherous conspiracies of many Hindu rulers, made worse by the social disunity and distrust between castes. Probably, the people oppressed by caste-feudalism, especially the lower classes, had welcomed the Muslim invaders as deliverers and emancipators. According to M. N. Roy (1937: 96), Mohammad Ibne Kassim – the first Muslim warlord who triumphantly entered India in AD 712 – 'conquered Sindh with the active assistance of the Jats and other communities oppressed by the brahman rulers'.
2. David Kopf (1969: 103) has shown in his study of British Orientalist scholarship that in Fort William College, the earliest and premier centre of study of culture, language and literature of India, the young scholars under H. T. Colebrook and William Carey 'seemed to identify India with Hinduism and regarded Muslims as intruders'.
3. Vivekananda seriously believed that Max Müller was a reincarnation of Sayana: 'My impression is that it is Sayana who is born again as

Max Müller to revive his own commentary on the Vedas. I have had this notion for long. It became confirmed in my mind, it seems after I have seen Max Müller' (*The Complete Works of Swami Vivekananda*, vol. VI: 495).

4. Sumit Sarkar in his analysis of the built-in limits of a strategy of reform 'from within' has shown how the shastric method had a tendency to create problems for reform agendas. Pointing out deep and disturbing contradictions in a leading reformer's advocacy against polygamy, he writes: 'Vidyasagar sought to eliminate one kind of polygamy which Manu had permitted (marrying a woman of lower caste) by emphasising that in *Kaliyuga* intercaste marriage was strictly prohibited. His polemic against Kulinism also used the argument that it often led to delayed marriages for girls in the absence of suitably high-status bridegrooms – and this, Vidyasagar emphasised, clearly contradicted the shastric command that marriage had to be consummated before the first menses. Perhaps it was this passage in his own earlier writing that contributed to Vidyasagar's surprising ambiguity on the Age of Consent issue, when his opinion was officially asked for shortly before his death' (1997: 269-70).

5. Prose rendition of the Upanishadic verse (*Chandyoga Upanishad*: V.X.7) upholding human hierarchy on the basis of good or bad conduct in previous birth equates a low born person with a beastly creature: 'Those whose conduct has been good, will quickly attain some good birth – the birth of a brahman or a kshatriya, or a vaishya. But those whose conduct has been evil will quickly attain an evil birth – the birth of a dog, or a hog or a chandala'. It is to be noted that Chandyoga is among the Upanishads considered most important because it is derived from the *Samaveda* which has been given the most exalted place by Krishna declaring, 'I am the *Samaveda* among the Vedas' (*Gita* X.22).

CHAPTER 5: PHULE'S STRUGGLE

1. See Gail Omvedt 1994: 23; G. P. Deshpande's Introduction in *Selected Writings of Jotirao Phule* (2002); Uma Chakravarti 1998, 2002.
2. Literally, atishudra means those beyond the shudras. In contemporary language, shudras and atishudras would be 'other backward classes' and dalits respectively. But Phule generally also included women, adivasis, Muslims and all others who are at the receiving end of the brahmanical order in his notion of the shudratishudras.
3. Later, Ambedkar too identified his struggle with this tradition. He

considered Phule as one of his three masters, along with the Buddha and Kabir (Keer 2000: vii; 139). Ambedkar came from a Kabirpanthi background – both his parents were Kabirpanthis. It is well known that the Buddha was his favourite historical figure and he regarded Buddhism as an antithesis to ascriptive Hinduism, which is why towards the end of his life he embraced Buddha's religion with his followers. Phule was another inspirational figure for Ambedkar who saw his own work as the continuation of that started by Phule. Dedicating his book *Who were the Shudras?* (1946) to Mahatma Phule, Ambedkar has underlined his revolutionary contribution. In his last days, Ambedkar was very keen to write a biography of Phule which he could not do due to his deteriorating health (Keer 2000).

4. Quoting Pinjan's letter to M. Patil, O'Hanlon has underlined the strong influence of Kabir's ideas on Phule and his colleagues which led to the formation of Satyashodhak Samaj (1985: 229-30). See also (in Hindi) Dr. Sadanand More's *Mahatma Phule Ka Vicharatmak Gathan* (Ideological make-up of Mahatma Phule) in Hari Narke, ed., *Mahatma Phule: Sahitya Aur Vichar* (1993: 53).

5. Phule's appreciation of robust democratic ideals is remarkable. Deshpande has commented (2002: 3) that with the exception of Phule, all other social reformers/revolutionaries of the time were greatly enamoured, and therefore constrained, by the English liberalism – best represented by thinkers like Mill and Spencer – which was a rather weak branch of European liberalism.

6. Kosambi (1992: 171) has lucidly explained the *hiranya garbha* (golden womb) ceremony, by which kings and aspiring rulers – coming from lower castes or casteless tribal societies – acquired kshatriya status, agreed to maintain the caste order, and convert the rest of the tribe into subject peasantry.

7. Contrary to the popular historiography, Shivaji had to undertake a bitter struggle with the entrenched brahmanical hierarchy of the time. The story of Shivaji's coronation as *Chhatrapati* after his brilliant military exploits, documented by Jadunath Sarkar and G. S. Sardesai, is a sordid tale of how even a man who saw such spectacular success and popularity had to hunt down a brahman priest from Benaras to perform the 'purification' and thread ceremony that could effect legitimacy on his coronation. Pandits from the Deccan and south were strongly opposed to the grant of kshatriya status to the fabled Maratha warrior. Shivaji, therefore, had to engage one Gagabhat, a brahman of Benaras, who declared, after receiving staggering monetary largesse and fabulous gifts that the Bhosale's family could claim a

direct line of descent from the Sisode Rajput kings of Udaipur. Most local brahmans boycotted the coronation ceremony, and those who attended demanded (and got) enormous sums of money which virtually emptied Shivaji's coffer. Jadunath Sarkar (1973) has contended that though Shivaji was installed as *Chhatrapati*, he was not allowed to recite the *Gayatri Mantra*, the holiest of Vedic text. The ambiguity over the varna status of Shivaji and his descendants was to give birth in later years the bitter conflicts between the brahman Peshwas and Shivaji's successors.

8. Regarding the position of women, particularly widows, in Hindu society, Ramabai and Vivekananda had diametrically different views, and as Uma Chakravarti (1998: 333-7) has delineated at great length, they clashed over the issue – though without referring to each other directly – in America in the 1890s. Ramabai had went to America in 1886 and stayed there for two years during which she travelled a great deal, addressed hundreds of meetings and also authored a bestseller, *The High Caste Hindu Woman* as part of her effort to collect money for the suffering women in India. She was the first public figure from India to seek financial assistance for social work back home. A few years later, following his much-celebrated pyrotechnics on Hindu spirituality at Chicago (1893), Vivekananda did the same but used a very different strategy. While Ramabai appealed to the American women as women to help the oppressed widows in India, Vivekananda, in his zeal to create an image of India in uniquely spiritual mould, painted Hindu women as chaste, self-sacrificing goddesses wallowing in material misery. Regarding the question of widows, he argued they voluntarily chose to lead an austere life in deference of their departed soulmates. In a lecture on womanhood, he dramatically asserted that though Hindu women disdained material aspects of life, they had enjoyed, unlike their American counterparts, property rights for thousands of years. This contention was challenged by the followers of Ramabai in America, while the Swami's disciples pointed fingers at Ramabai whose 'unpatriotic' position on the women's issues, they alleged, was spoiling India's image abroad. Being a widow herself and having travelled to Benaras, Mathura and Brindavan, Ramabai knew how the widows were oppressed, neglected and sexually exploited without any 'Mahatma championing their cause'. In a letter from India, she appealed to the 'learned brothers and comfortable sisters' of America to take a good look, beyond the poetry, into the prose of women's lives and decide for themselves the nature of the fruits of the 'sublime philosophies' (ibid.: 336).

9. The Sarvajanik Sabha was a public association of brahman reformers and liberals founded in Pune in 1870, whose members set themselves up as middlemen between the government and people in the region.

CHAPTER 6: GURU, IYOTHEE, PERIYAR, ACCHUTANAND

1. Rao's source is a Malyalam article (1968) by K. R. Narayanan. This rebellion against ritual exclusivism, as Aloysius points out, took place 125 years before the Gandhi-led Congress was reluctantly drawn into the temple-entry agitation. The same temple at Vaikkom became the classic site of tussle in 1925 in which Narayana Guru's followers and Periyar, who had come all the way from Tamil Nadu, defiantly entered the temple, while Gandhi kept appealing for a compromise formula. The 'nationalist' hagiographers, however, tend to present the agitation as a Congress-Gandhi affair.
2. Pre-modern Kerala society was structured hierarchically with all the rigours of varna. Rules of purity-pollution, which included not only untouchability but also distance pollution, were maintained with utmost severity. The Nambudiri brahmans, at the top of social hierarchy, were considered purity personified, while the rest of the castes and their worth was measured in terms of their distance from the Nambudiris. 'The Ezhavas had to keep between 20 to 36 feet away from the Nambudiris, the Cherumas and the Pulayas 64 feet; and the Nayadis 72 feet. There were also some tribes whose mere sight polluted the Nambudiris; but only a touch of a Nayar polluted them. The Nayars were the bridge between the Nambudiris and the category of castes that polluted from a distance' (Rao 1979: 24).
3. The antiquity and glory of Dravidian culture and literature was discovered in the nineteenth century by a long line of Indian researchers and British Indologists. P. Sundaram Pillai (1855-97) and Robert Caldwell were among the earliest scholars who revealed that the Dravidian language and culture had originated independent of Aryan-Sanskrit influence, and that the former was more ancient than Sanskrit. Pillai also extolled the virtues of the native Ravana as against Rama who was portrayed as leader of the invading Aryans, who debased the Dravidian culture and demoralised the Tamils. The brahmanical priesthood, caste system and Sanskrit scriptural tradition were held to be responsible for destroying the 'superior' culture and civilisation of the Dravidian people. The recovery of their egalitarian past thus became entwined with the struggle for establishment of their rights in the present, paving the way for a popular non-brahman movement in the region.

4. It is only recently that Iyothee Thass' uniquely modern work has caught the attention of some scholars. V. Geetha and S. V. Rajadurai and G. Aloysius have done pioneering work in this regard. Geetha and Rajadurai's outstanding work on the Dravidian movement, *Towards a Non-Brahmin Millennium: From Iyothee Thass to Periyar* (1998), explores the writings of Iyothee Thass and the rise of dalit consciousness in colonial Tamil Nadu. Aloysius' *Religion as Emancipatory Identity: A Buddhist Movement Among the Tamils Under Colonialism* (1998) is a penetrative sociological study of the socio-religious movement in which Iyothee Thass played a pioneering part. Aloysius' two-volume collection of the dalit scholar's articles in Tamil *Iyothee Thassar Sinthanaigaal* (The Thoughts of Iyothee Thassar), recently published by Folklore Resources and Research Centre, Polayamco-Hai, Tamil Nadu, is the first such attempt.

CHAPTER 7: THE GANDHI-AMBEDKAR DEBATE

1. Gait issued a preparatory circulation – detailing exact criteria – to his provincial commissioners on the question of drawing the border between Hindus and those communities/tribes who could be regarded as such. The circular contained six questions to resolve the issue:
   a. Do the members of the caste or tribe worship the great Hindu Gods?
   b. Are they allowed to enter Hindu temples or to make offerings at the shrine?
   c. Will good brahmans act as their priests?
   d. Will degraded brahmans do so? In that case, are they recognised as brahmans by persons outside the caste, or are they brahmans only in name?
   e. Will clean castes take water from them?
   f. Do they cause pollution, (a) by touch; (b) by proximity?

   (*The Tribune*, 12 November 1910, see Mendelsohn and Vicziary 2000: 28)

2. For a long while Gandhi himself was opposed to untouchables entering temples, saying, 'How is it possible that the Antyajas (untouchables) should have the right to enter the existing temples? As long as the law of caste and ashram has the chief place in Hindu Religion, to say that every Hindu can enter every temple is a thing that is not possible today' (*Gandhi Shikshan*, vol. II: 132; cited in *BAWS*, vol. 9: 107).

3. As British imperialism was then the main enemy of nationalism,

communalism was set aside by the Congress as diversion from the nationalist ideal of wresting power from the colonialists. But after Independence – with the creation of Pakistan – Indian nationalism is defined more and more in terms of anti-Pakistan – as the Islamic state is projected as the main threat to India's integrity and security. This explains why the Congress' brand of secularism erected on the class interests of the Hindu and Muslim upper classes which prevented the masses of both communities to enter politico-economic mainstream is seriously challenged by the rank communal outfits led by the RSS and its progeny the Bharatiya Janata Party (BJP) which now parades as the main carrier of Indian nationalism. The RSS family now lays claim to the legacy of the national movement and has appropriated all the national icons to its pantheon. For example, Venkaiah Naidu, the BJP president, asserted on 26 December 2002: 'Our nationalism is what was preached by the likes of Mahatma Gandhi and Jawaharlal Nehru in pre-Independence days. The post-Independence Congress does not have it. We have inherited it' (*Frontline*, 28 February 2003).

4. Many are 'under the impression that Pandit Nehru is a socialist and does not believe in caste', Ambedkar says and quotes Pattabhi Sitaramayya from the latter's introduction to the *Life of Pandit Jawaharlal Nehru* (written by Y. G. Krishnamurti), 'Pandit Nehru is very conscious of the fact that he is a Brahmin'. Nehru's sister, Vijaya Laxmi Pandit, is equally proud, he informs, of her caste identity. 'At the All-India Women's Conference held in Delhi in December 1940, the question of not declaring one's caste in the Census Return was discussed. Ms. Pandit disapproved of the idea and said she did not see any reason why she should not be proud of her Brahmin blood and declare herself as a Brahmin at the Census.' He has quoted this from *Sense and Nonsense in Politics* by J. E. Sanjana (see *BAWS*, vol. 9: 208-9).

5. Ambedkar argues that the brahman is the principal governing class in India on the basis of (a) his most elevated – even sacred – position in the caste society, and (b) preponderance in administration. The brahman, he holds, has always – and assiduously – cultivated others as his allies provided they are prepared to carry out the work with him in subordinate position. In ancient and medieval times, he says, the brahman made such an alliance with the sword-wielding kshatriya and together as ruling classes they controlled and exploited the masses. However, in the modern age dominated more by money than the sword, the brahman, he contends, has left the kshatriya and bonded a relationship with the class with money, that is, the bania.

Huge money required to run political machinery could come only from the bania who on his part has 'realised that money invested in politics gives large dividends'. This class – led by the Ahmedabad millowners and Bombay businessmen – was financing the Congress largely because Gandhi, who hailed from this class, could be trusted to represent its interests. Ambedkar has quoted Gandhi who himself admitted – in an interview with Louis Fisher on 6 June 1942 – that the Congress was almost totally financed by 'rich friends'. As Fisher writes in A Week with Gandhi:

I said I had several questions to ask him about the Congress Party. Very highly placed Britishers, I recalled, had told me that Congress was in the hands of big business and that Gandhi was supported by the Bombay millowners who gave him as much money as he wanted. 'What truth is there in these assertions', I asked.

'Unfortunately, they are true', he declared simply, 'Congress hasn't enough money to conduct its work. We thought in the beginning to collect four annas (about eight cents) from each member per year and operate on that. But it hasn't worked'.

'What proportion of the Congress budget', I asked, 'is covered by rich Indians?'

'Practically all of it', he stated. 'In this ashram, for instance, we could live much more poorly than we do and spend less money. But we do not and the money comes from our rich friends.' (see BAWS, vol. 9: 208)

6. Jabbar Patel, author of a remarkable cinematic biography of Ambedkar, who intensely researched on the Gandhi-Ambedkar tussle to ensure that everything filmed was historically accurate, especially since the film was funded by a Gandhi-deifying government, holds that Gandhi behaved like 'a cunning, selfish politician always anxious to outwit Ambedkar. . . . That is why Ambedkar felt so slighted. Ambedkar tried his best to explain his point of view but Gandhi was not ready to listen. Gandhi pushed him to the edge by refusing to listen to him. That comes out clearly if you look at the historical evidence.' (interview with Pritish Nandy, *The Times of India*, New Delhi, 29 June 2000).

7. 'I do not regard Jainism or Buddhism as separate from Hinduism', Gandhi wrote in *Young India* of 20 October 1927.

Bibliography

Alam, Javeed, 'Tradition in India Under Interpretative Stress: Notes on Its Growing Social Irrelevance', in Indu Banga and Jaidev, eds., *Cultural Reorientation in Modern India*, pp. 66-79 (Shimla: Indian Institute of Advanced Study, 1996).

Ali, Daud, ed., *Invoking the Past: The Uses of History in South Asia* (Delhi: Oxford University Press, 2002).

Aloysius, G., *Nationalism without a Nation in India* (Delhi: Oxford University Press, 1997).

——, *Religion as Emancipatory Identity: A Buddhist Movement among the Tamils under Colonialism* (Delhi: New Age International Publishers, 1998).

——, 'Caste in and above History', in S. L. Sharma and T. K. Oommen, eds., *Nation and National Identity in South Asia*, pp. 151-73 (Delhi: Orient Longman, 2000)

——, 'Caste Against Nation in Ambedkar', *The Radical Humanist*, February and March 2002.

Altekar, A. S., 'Buddhism and Indian Culture', *The Journal of the Bihar Research Society*, Buddha Jayanti spl. issue, vol. 2, 1956.

Althusser, Louis, 'Ideology and Ideological State Apparatuses', in idem, *Lenin and Philosophy and Other Essays*, pp. 121-73 (London: New Left Books, 1971).

Ambedkar, B. R., *Dr Babasaheb Ambedkar: Writings and Speeches (BAWS)*, vols. 1-15, ed. Vasant Moon (Bombay: The Education Department, Govt. of Maharashtra, 1987-97).

——, *The Problem of the Rupee* (1923); *The Evolution of Provincial Finance in British India* (1925), in *BAWS*, vol. 6.

——, *Annihilation of Caste* (1936), in *BAWS*, vol. 1.

——, *Pakistan or the Partition of India* (1940), in *BAWS*, vol. 8.

——, *What Congress and Gandhi Have Done to the Untouchables* (1945), in *BAWS*, vol. 9.

Ambedkar, B. R., *Who were the Shudras?* (1946); *The Untouchables* (1948), in *BAWS*, vol. 7.

——, *The Buddha and His Dhamma* (1957), in *BAWS*, vol. 11.

——, *The Revolution and Counter-Revolution in Ancient India*, unfinished work (1956), in *BAWS*, vol. 3.

Amin, Shahid, 'Gandhi as Mahatma', in Ranajit Guha, ed., *Subaltern Studies III, Writings on South Asian History and Society* (Delhi: Oxford University Press, 1996).

Anderson, Benedict, *Imagined Communities* (London: Versa, 1983).

Angar Ee, HaBir, *Pali is the Mother of Sanskrit* (Nagpur: Tarachand Chavhan, 1994).

Austin, Granville, *The Indian Constitution: Cornerstone of a Nation*, 1964, rpt. (Delhi: Oxford University Press, 2001).

Awaya, Toshie, 'Some Aspects of the Tiyyas' Caste Movement', in H. Kotani, ed., *Caste System, Untouchability and the Depressed*, pp. 139-68 (Delhi: Manohar, 1999).

Baird, Robert D., ed., *Religion in Modern India*, 4th revised edn. (Delhi: Manohar, 2001).

Baker, C. J., *The Politics of South India 1920-37* (Delhi: Vikas, 1976).

Ball, Terence and Dagger, Richard, *Political Ideologies and the Democratic Ideal*, 5th edn. (New York: Pearson Longman, 2004).

Bali, Arun P., 'The Virasaiva Movement', in S. C. Malik, ed., *Indian Movements*, pp. 67-100 (Shimla: Indian Institute of Advanced Study, 1978).

Bandyopadhyay, Sekhar, *Caste, Politics and the Raj: Bengal 1872-1937* (Calcutta: K. P. Bagchi & Co., 1990).

Banga, Indu and Jaidev, eds., *Cultural Reorientation in Modern India* (Shimla: Indian Institute of Advanced Study, 1996).

Bapat, P. V., ed., *2500 Years of Buddhism* (Delhi: Publications Division, Govt. of India, 1997).

Basham, A. L., *The Wonder That Was India*, 1954, rpt. (Delhi: Rupa, 1991).

——, ed., *A Cultural History of India*, 1975, rpt. (Delhi: Oxford University Press, 1985).

Basu, Shamita, *Religious Revivalism as Nationalist Discourse: Swami Vivekananda and New Hinduism in Nineteenth-Century Bengal* (Delhi: Oxford University Press, 2002).

Basu, Tapan et al., *Khaki Shorts and Saffron Flags: A Critique of the Hindu Right* (Delhi: Orient Longman, 1993).

——, ed., *Translating Caste* (Delhi: Katha, 2002).

Batchelor, M. and K. Brown, eds., *Buddhism and Ecology* (Delhi: Motilal Banarsidass, 1994).

Baxi, Upendra, 'Emancipation as Justice: Legacy and Vision of Dr. Ambedkar', in K. C. Yadav, ed., *From Periphery to Centre Stage: Ambedkar, Ambedkarism and Dalit Future*, pp. 49-74 (Delhi: Manohar, 2000).

Bayly, C. A., *Origins of Nationalism in South Asia* (Delhi: Oxford University Press, 2001).

Bayly, Susan, *Caste, Society and Politics in India: From the Eighteenth Century to the Modern Age* (Cambridge: Cambridge University Press, 2000).

Bazaz, Premnath, 'The Role of the Bhagavad-Gita in Indian History', *The Radical Humanist*, August 2002.

Berlin, Isaiah, *The Crooked Timber of Humanity: Chapters in the History of Ideas* (London: Pimlico, 2003).

Berreman, Gerald D., 'The Brahmanical View of Caste', in Dipankar Gupta, ed., *Social Stratification*, pp. 84-92 (Delhi: Oxford University Press, 1991).

Bhattacharyya, N. N., *Buddhism in the History of Indian Ideas* (Delhi: Manohar, 1993).

Bipan Chandra et al., *India's Struggle for Independence* (Delhi: Penguin, 1989).

Biswas, A. K., *Social and Cultural Vision of India* (Delhi: Pragati Publications, 1996).

Biswas, Oneil, *Dalits after Partition* (Delhi: Blumoon Books, 2001).

Biswas, Swapan K., *Gods, False Gods and the Untouchables* (Delhi: Orion, 1998).

Bloch, Marc, *The Historian's Craft*, tr. Peter Putnam (New York: Vintage Books, 1953).

Bose, Nemai Sadhan, *Swami Vivekananda* (Delhi: Sahitya Akademi, 1994).

——, 'Swami Vivekananda and Challenge to Fundamentalism', in William Radice, ed., *Swami Vivekananda and the Modernisation of Hinduism*, pp. 281-99 (Delhi: Oxford University Press, 1999).

Bougle, C., 'The Essence and Reality of the Caste System', in Dipankar Gupta, ed., *Social Stratification*, pp. 64-73 (Delhi: Oxford University Press, 1991).

Carrithers, Michael, *Why Humans Have Cultures* (Oxford: Oxford University Press, 1992).

Carus, Paul, *The Gospel of Buddha*, rpt. (Chennai: Samata Books, 1997).

Casolari, Marzia, 'Hindutva's Foreign Tie-up in the 1930s: Archival Evidence', *Economic and Political Weekly*, 22 January 2000.

Chakravarti, Uma, *The Social Dimensions of Early Buddhism* (Delhi: Munshiram Manoharlal, 1996).

——, *Rewriting History: The Life and Times of Pandita Ramabai* (Delhi: Kali for Women, 1998).

——, 'Whatever Happened to the Vedic Dasi? : Orientalism, Nationalism, and a Script for the Past', in Kumkum Sangari and Sudesh Vaid, eds., *Recasting Women: Essays in Colonial History*, pp. 27-87 (Delhi: Kali for Women, 1989).

——, 'From Exclusion to Marginalisation? Hegemonic Agendas and Women's Writing', in Sujata Patel et al., eds., *Thinking Social Science in India*, pp. 115-32 (Delhi: Sage, 2002).

Chandrashekhar, S., *Colonialism, Conflict and Nationalism: South India: 1857-1947* (Delhi: Wishwa Prakashan, 1995).

Chatterjee, Partha, *Nationalist Thought and the Colonial World* (Delhi: Oxford University Press, 1986).

——, *The Nation and its Fragments* (Princeton: Princeton University Press, 1993).

Chatterji, S. K., 'Some Emerging Issues in Independent India', in Sebasti L. Raj, SJ, ed., *Fifty Years After Freedom* (Delhi: Indian Social Institute, 1998).

Chattopadhyaya, D. P., *Lokayata: A Study in Ancient Indian Materialism*, 1959, rpt. (Delhi: People's Publishing House, 1992).

——, *What is Living and What is Dead in Indian Philosophy*, 1976, rpt. (Delhi: People's Publishing House, 2001).

Chaudhuri, Nirad, *Scholar Extraordinary: The Life of Friedrich Max Müller* (Delhi: Orient Paperbacks, 1974).

——, *The Autobiography of an Unknown Indian*, 1951, rpt. (London: The Hogarth Press, 1987).

Chaudhuri, Nirad, *The Continent of Circe*, rpt. (Bombay: Jaico, 1999).

Chomsky, Noam, *Powers and Prospects* (Delhi: Madhyam Books, 1996).

Crook, Nigel, ed., *The Transmission of Knowledge in South Asia* (Delhi: Oxford University Press, 2001).

Dangle, Arjun, ed., *Poisoned Bread: Modern Marathi Dalit Literature* (Bombay: Orient Longman, 1992).

Das, Arvind N., *Agrarian Unrest and Socio-Economic Change in Bihar 1900-1980* (Delhi: Manohar, 1983)

Datta, B. N., *Studies in Indian Social Polity*, 1944, revised edn. (Calcutta: Nababharat Publishers, 1983).

Deshpande, G. P., ed., *Selected Writings of Jotirao Phule*, with Introduction, pp. 1-21 (Delhi: LeftWord, 2002).

Delany, Sheila, ed., *Counter-Tradition: The Literature of Dissent and Alternatives* (New York: Basic Books, 1971).

Desai, A. R., *Social Background of Indian Nationalism*, 5th edn. (Bombay: Popular Prakashan, 1991).

Dhani, S. L., *Politics of God: Churning of the Ocean* (Panchakula: DD Books, 1984).

Dharma Theertha, Swami, *History of Hindu Imperialism*, 1941, rpt. (Madras: Dalit Educational Literature Centre, 1992).

Dharmaveer, *Kabir ke Aalochak*, in Hindi (Delhi: Vani Prakashan, 1997).

Dirks, Nicholas B., *Castes of Mind: Colonialism and the Making of Modern India* (Delhi: Permanent Black, 2002).

Doniger, Wendy and Brian Smith, eds., *The Laws of Manu*, with Introduction, pp. xv-lxxviii (Delhi: Penguin, 1991).

Dreze, Jean and Amartya Sen, *India: Economic Development and Social Opportunity* (Delhi: Oxford University Press, 1998).

Dube, Siddharth, *Words Like Freedom* (Delhi: HarperCollins, 1998).

Dubey, A. K., 'Anatomy of a Dalit Power Player', in Ghanshyam Shah, ed., *Dalit Identity and Politics*, pp. 288-310 (Delhi: Sage, 2001).

Dumont, Louis, *Homo Hierarchicus: The Caste System and Its Implications*, revised English edn. (Delhi: Oxford University Press, 1998)

Durkheim, Emile, *The Elementary Forms of Religious Life*, 1912, tr. Carol Cosman (Oxford: Oxford University Press, 2001).

Dutt, R. C., *A History of Civilisation in Ancient India*, based on Sanskrit Literature, vols. 1-3 (Calcutta: 1889-90).

Dutt, R. Palme, *India Today*, 1940, revised edn. (Calcutta: Manisha, 1989).

Dwivedi, H. P., *Kabir*, in Hindi, 1940, rpt. (Delhi: Rajkamal, 1999).

Easwaran, Eknath, tr., *The Dhammapada* (London: Routledge & Kegan Paul, 1986).

Edwards, David, *The Compassionate Revolution: Radical Politics and Buddhism* (Delhi: Viveka Foundation, 2001).

Edwardes, Michael, *British India 1972-1974*, 1967, rpt. (Delhi: Rupa, 1999).

Embree, A. T., Hay, Stephen, eds., *Sources of Indian Tradition*, vols. I & II, 2nd edn. (Delhi: Penguin, 1991).

Fanon, Frantz, *The Wretched of the Earth*, tr. Constance Farrington (New York: Grove, 1963).

Farquhar, J. N., *Modern Religious Movement in India*, rpt. (Delhi: Low Price Publications, 1999).

Foucault, Michel, *The History of Sexuality*, vol. I (London: Penguin, 1990).

——, *The Foucault Reader*, ed. Paul Rabinow (London: Penguin, 1991).

Freire, Paulo, *Pedagogy of the Oppressed*, 1970, new revised edn., tr. Myra Bergman Ramos (London: Penguin, 1996).

Frykenberg, Robert Eric, 'The Emergence of Modern Hinduism', in G.-D. Sontheimer and Hermann Kulke, eds., *Hinduism Reconsidered*, 1989, revised edn., pp. 82-107 (Delhi: Manohar, 2001).

Fukuzawa, Hiroshi, *The Medieval Deccan: Peasants, Social System and Status 16th to 18th Centuries* (Delhi: Oxford University Press, 1998).

Gandhi, M. K., *The Complete Works of Mahatma Gandhi*, vol. I (Delhi: Publications Division, Govt. of India, 1979).

——, *The Penguin Gandhi Reader*, ed., Rudrangshu Mukherjee, includes *Hind Swaraj* (1909) and *Varna Vyavastha* (1934) (Delhi: Penguin, 1993).

——, *What is Hinduism?* (Delhi: National Book Trust, 1994).

——, *The Story of My Experiments with Truth*, 1927, rpt. (Ahmedabad: Navajivan Publishing House, 1996).

Gavaskar, Mahesh, 'Colonialism Within Colonialism: Phule's Critique of Brahmin Power', in S. M. Michael, ed., *Dalits in Modern India* (Delhi: Vistaar Publications, 1999).

Geetha, V. and S. V. Rajadurai, *Towards a Non-Brahmin Millennium: From Iyothee Thass to Periyar* (Calcutta: Samya, 1998).

Gellner, Ernest, *Nation and Nationalism* (Oxford: Basil Blackwell, 1983).

George, K. M., *Kumaran Asan* (Delhi: Sahitya Akademi, 1991).

Ghurye, G. S., *Caste and Race in India*, 1932, 5th edn. (Bombay: Popular Prakashan, 2000).

Golwalkar, M. S., *We, or Our Nationhood Defined* (Nagpur: Bharat Prakashan, 1939).

Gooptu, Nandini, 'Caste, Deprivation and Politics: The Untouchables in U.P. Towns in the Early Twentieth Century', in Peter Robb, ed., *Dalit Movements and the Meanings of Labour in India*, pp. 277-98 (Delhi: Oxford University Press, 1993).

Goyal, D. R., *Rashtriya Swayamsewak Sangh*, 2nd revised edn. (Delhi: Radhakrishna, 2000).

Gore, M. S., *The Social Context of an Ideology: Ambedkar's Political and Social Thought* (Delhi: Sage, 1993).

Govinda, Anagarika, *The Psychological Attitude of Early Budhhist Philosophy* (London: Rider & Company, 1961).

Gramsci, Antonio, *Selections from the Prison Notebooks*, tr. Quintin Hoare and Geoffrey N. Smith, rpt. (Chennai: Orient Longman, 1996).

Grewal, J. S., 'Ideas Operative in Early Sikh History', in J. S. Grewal et al., eds., *The Khalsa Over 300 Years* (Delhi: Tulika, 1999).

Gupta, Dipankar, ed., *Social Stratification* (Delhi: Oxford University Press, 1991).

Gupta, S. K., *The Scheduled Castes in Modern Indian Politics: Their Emergence as a Political Power* (Delhi: Munshiram Manoharlal, 1985).

Guha, Ranajit, *Elementary Aspects of Peasant Insurgency in Colonial India* (Delhi: Oxford University Press, 1992).

Guru, Gopal, 'The Dalit Movement in Mainstream Sociology', in S. M. Michael, ed., *Dalits in Modern India* (Delhi: Vistaar Publications, 1999).

Haq, Jalalul, *The Shudra: A Philosophical Narrative of Indian Superhumanism* (Delhi: Institute of Objective Studies, 1997).

Hawley, J. S. and Mark Juergensmeyer, eds., *Songs of the Saints of India* (New York: Oxford University Press, 1988).

Hess, Linda and Shukdev Singh, tr., *The Bijak of Kabir*, includes Introduction by Hess, pp. 3-37 (Delhi: Motilal Banarsidass, 1986).

Ilaiah, Kancha, *Why I am Not a Hindu* (Calcutta: Samya, 1996).

——, 'The God of Little Men', *Biblio*, November 1997, pp. 7-8.

——, *God as Political Philosopher: Buddha's Challenge to Brahminism* (Calcutta: Samya, 2000).

——, *Buffalo Nationalism: A Critique of Spiritual Fascism* (Calcutta: Samya, 2004).

Inden, Roland, *Imagining India*, 1990, rpt. (London: Hurst, 2000).

Irschick, Eugene, *Politics and Social Conflict in South India* (Berkeley: University of California Press, 1969).

Ishwaran, K., *Religion and Society among the Lingayats of South India* (Delhi: Vikas, 1983).

Iyengar, K. R. S., ed., *Guru Nanak* (Delhi: Sahitya Akademi, 1994).

Jaffrelot, Christophe, *The Hindu Nationalist Movement and Indian Politics* (Delhi: Penguin, 1999).

——, *India's Silent Revolution: The Rise of the Low Castes in North Indian Politics* (Delhi: Permanent Black, 2003).

——, 'The Ideas of the Hindu race in the writings of Hindu nationalist ideologues in the 1920s and 1930s: A concept between two cultures', in Peter Robb, ed., *The Concept of Race in South Asia*, pp. 327-54 (Delhi: Oxford University Press, 1997).

Jaini, Padmanabh, ed., *Collected Papers on Buddhist Studies* (Delhi: Motilal Banarsidass, 2001).

Jaiswal, Suvira, *Caste: Origin, Function and Dimensions of Change* (Delhi: Manohar, 2000).

Jatava, D. R., *Social Philosophy of B. R. Ambedkar* (Jaipur: Rawat, 1997).

Jha, D. N., *Ancient India in Historical Outline* (Delhi: Manohar, 2001).

Jordens, J. T. F., 'Medieval Hindu devotionalism', in A. L. Basham, ed., *A Cultural History of India*, pp. 266-80 (Delhi: Oxford University Press, 1985).

Joshi, Barbara, *Untouchable! Voice of the Dalit Liberation Movement* (Delhi: Select Books Service Syndicate, 1986).

Joshi, T. Laxmanshastri, *Jotirao Phule* (Delhi: National Book Trust, 1992).

——, *Critique of Hinduism and Other Religions* (Bombay: Popular Prakashan, 1996).

Juergensmeyer, Mark, *Religion as Social Vision: The Movement agaisnt Untouchability in 20th-Century Punjab* (Berkeley: University of California Press, 1982).

Kadam, K. N., *Dr B. R. Ambedkar: The Emancipator of the Oppressed* (Bombay: Popular Prakashan, 1993).

Kailasapathy, K., 'The Writings of the Tamil Siddhas', in K. Schomer and W. H. McLeod, eds., *The Sants: Studies in a Devotional Tradition of India*, pp. 385-411 (Delhi: Motilal Banarsidass, 1987).

Kalupahana, David J., *Buddhist Philosophy: A Historical Analysis* (Hawaii: University Press of Hawaii, 1976).

Keer, Dhananjay, *Mahatma Jotirao Phule: Father of Indian Social Revolution*, 1964, rpt. (Bombay: Popular Prakashan, 2000).

——, *Dr. Ambedkar: Life and Mission*, 1954, rpt. (Bombay: Popular Prakashan, 1971).

Kejariwal, O. P., *The Asiatic Society of Bengal and the Discovery of India's Past* (Delhi: Oxford University Press, 1988).

Ketkar, S. V., *History of Caste in India*, 2 vols. (New York: Ithaca, 1909).

Khare, R. S., *The Untouchable as Himself: Ideology, Identity and Pragmatism among the Lucknow Chamars* (New York: Cambridge University Press, 1984).

Kochhar, Rajesh, *The Vedic People: Their History and Geography* (Delhi: Orient Longman, 2000).

Kopf, David, *British Orientalism and the Bengal Renaissance: The Dynamics of Indian Modernisation 1793-1835* (Berkeley: University of California Press, 1969).

Kosambi, D. D., *Myth and Reality*, 1962, rpt. (Mumbai: Popular Prakashan, 2000).

——, *The Culture and Civilisation of Ancient India in Historical Outline*, 1965, rpt. (Delhi: Vikas, 1992).

——, *An Introduction to the Study of Indian History*, 1956, rpt. (Bombay: Popular Prakashan, 1999).

Kosambi, Dharmanand, *Bhagwan Buddha: Jeevan aur Darshan*, in Hindi, rpt. (Allahabad: Lokabharati Prakashan, 2000).

Kothari, Rajni, *Caste in Indian Politics*, 1970, rpt. (Hyderabad: Orient Longman, 1991).

——, 'Flight Into The 21st Century', *The Times of India*, 27 April 1986.

Kriplani, Krishna, *Dwarkanath Tagore* (Delhi: National Book Trust, 1981).

Kuber, W. N., *Ambedkar: A Critical Study*, 2nd revised edn. (Delhi: People's Publishing House, 2001).

Kumar, Arun, *Rewriting the Language of Politics: Kisans in Colonial Bihar* (Delhi: Manohar, 2001).

Kunhappa, Murkot, *Sree Narayana Guru* (Delhi: National Book Trust, 1988).

Lal, Shyam et al., eds., *Ambedkar and Nation-Building* (Jaipur: Rawat, 1998).

Lannoy, Richard, *The Speaking Tree: A Study of Indian Culture and Society*, 1971, rpt. (Delhi: Oxford University Press, 1999).

Lingat, Robert, *The Classical Law of India*, tr. J. D. M. Derrett, 1967 (Delhi: Oxford University Press, 1998).

Lorenzen, David, *Praises to a Formless God* (New York: State University of New York Press, 1996).

Louis, Prakash, *The Emerging Hindutva Force: The Ascent of Hindu Nationalism* (Delhi: Indian Social Institute, 2000).

——, *Political Sociology of Dalit Assertion* (Delhi: Gyan Publishing House, 2003).

Lucacs, Georg, *History and Class Consciousness: Studies in Marxist Dialectics*, tr. Rodney Livingstone, rpt. (Delhi: Rupa & Co., 1993).

MacGuire, Randall and Robert Paynter, *The Archaeology of Inequality* (Oxford: Blackwell, 1991).

MacMunn, George, *The Indian Social System*, rpt. (Delhi: Discovery Publishing House, 1984).

MacPherson, Stewart, *Social Policy in the Third World* (Sussex: Wheatsheaf Books, 1982).

Madan, T. N., ed., *Religion in India* (Delhi: Oxford University Press, 1991).

Mani, Lata, 'Contentious Traditions: The Debate on Sati in Colonial India', in K. Sangari and S. Vaid, eds., *Recasting Women: Essays in Colonial History*, pp. 88-126 (Delhi: Kali for Women, 1989).

Manickam, S., *Slavery in the Tamil Country: A Historical Overview* (Madras: The Christian Literature Society, 1993).

Marshall, P. J., ed., *The British Discovery of Hinduism in the Eighteenth Century* (Cambridge: Cambridge University Press, 1970).

Mehrotra, S. R., *The Emergence of Indian National Congress* (Delhi: Vikas, 1971).

Mencher, Joan, 'The Caste System Upside Down', in Dipankar Gupta, ed., *Social Stratification*, pp. 93-109 (Delhi: Oxford University Press, 1991).

Mendelsohn, O. and M. Vicziany, *The Untouchables: Subordination, Poverty and the State in Modern India* (Delhi: Cambridge University Press, 2000).

Menon, Dilip, *Caste, Nationalism and Communism in South India: Malabar 1900-1948* (Cambridge: Cambridge University Press, 1994).

Metcalf, Thomas, *Ideologies of the Raj* (Delhi: Cambridge University Press, 1998).

Michael, S. M., ed., *Dalits in Modern India* (Delhi: Vistaar Publications, 1999).

Mishra, B. B., *The Indian Middle Classes: Their Growth in Modern Times* (Delhi: Oxford University Press, 1983).

Mookerjee, R. K., *Ancient India* (Allahabad, 1956).

Moya, Paula, et al., *Reclaiming Identity: Realist Theory and the Predicament of Postmodernism* (Hyderabad: Orient Longman, 2001).

Müller, F. Max, ed., *Dhammapada* and *Sutta Nipata*, in *The Sacred Books of the East*, vol. X, rpt. (Delhi: Motilal Banarsidass, 1998).

——, ed., *Vinaya Texts*, in *The Sacred Books of the East*, vol. XIII, rpt. (Delhi: Motilal Banarasidass, 1982).

——, *India: What It can Teach Us* (London: Longmans Green, 1892).

Mukherjee, Hiren, *Gandhiji: A Study* (Delhi: People's Publishing House, 1991).

Mukherjee, Prabhati, *Beyond the Four Varnas: The Untouchables in India* (Delhi: Indian Institute of Advanced Study/Motilal Banarsidass, 1988).

Mukherjee, S. N., 'The Social Implications of the Political Thought of Raja Rammohun Roy', in R. S. Sharma and Vivekanand Jha, eds., *Indian Society: Historical Probings*, 1974, rpt., pp. 356-89 (Delhi: People's Publishing House, 1993).

Mukta, Parita, *Upholding the Common Life: The Community of Mirabai* (Delhi: Oxford University Press, 1997).

Munda, Karia, et al., *2nd Report of Parliamentary Committee on the Welfare of Scheduled Castes and Tribes* (Delhi: Govt. of India, 2000).

Murthy, B. S., *Depressed and Oppressed* (Delhi: S. Chand, n.d.).

Nanda, B. R., ed., *Essays in Modern Indian History* (Delhi: Oxford University Press, 1980).

Nanda, Meera, *Breaking the Spell of Dharma and Other Essays* (Delhi: Three Essays, 2002).

——, *Prophets Facing Backward: Postmodernism, Science, and Hindu Nationalism* (Delhi: Permanent Black, 2004).

Nandy, Ashis, *The Intimate Enemy: Loss and Recovery of Self Under Colonialism* (Delhi: Oxford University Press, 1983).

——, *At the Edge of Psychology: Essays in Politics and Culture* (Delhi: Oxford University Press, 1983).

Narke, Hari, ed., *Mahatma Phule: Sahitya Aur Vichar*, in Hindi (Bombay: Govt. of Maharashtra, 1993).

Narasu, Lakshmi, *The Essence of Buddhism*, rpt. (Delhi: Winsome Books, 2004).

——, *Religion of the Modern Buddhist*, G. Aloysius, ed. (Delhi: Wordsmiths, 2002).

Nayak, Radhakant, ed., *The Fourth World* (Delhi: Manohar, 1997).

Narayan, Badri, *Documenting Dissent* (Shimla: Indian Institute of Advanced Study, 2001).

Narayanan, M. G. S., 'Historical Perspectives on Ancient India', *Social Scientist*, no. 39, October 1975, pp. 3-11.

Nehru, Jawaharlal, *The Discovery of India*, 1946, rpt. (Delhi: Nehru Memorial Fund/Oxford University Press, 1996).

——, *An Autobiography*, 1936, rpt. (Delhi: Nehru Memorial Fund/Oxford University Press, 1999).

Nemade, Bhalchandra, *Tukaram* (Delhi: Sahitya Akademi, 1997).

Nichols, Beverley, *Verdict on India* (Bombay: Thacker & Co., 1946).

Nietzsche, F., *Thus Spoke Zarathustra*, 1883, tr. R. J. Hollingdale (Harmondsworth: Penguin, 1974).

——, *The Anti-Christ*, 1895, tr. R. J. Hollingdale (Harmondsworth: Penguin, 1968).

Noorani, A. G., *The RSS and the BJP: A Division of Labour* (Delhi: LeftWord, 2000)

O'Hanlon, Rosalind, *Caste, Conflict and Ideology: Mahatma Jotirao Phule and Low Caste Protest in Nineteenth-Century Western India* (Cambridge: Cambridge University Press, 1985).

——, *A Comparison between Women and Men: Tarabai Shinde and the Critique of Gender Relations in Colonial India* (Delhi: Oxford University Press, 1994).

Oldenberg, H., *Buddha: His Life, His Teachings, His Order* (Calcutta: 1927).

Omvedt, Gail, *Cultural Revolt in a Colonial Society: The Non Brahman Movement in Western India 1873-1930* (Bombay: Scientific Socialist Education Trust, 1976).

——, *Dalits and the Democratic Revolution: Dr Ambedkar and the Dalit Movement in Colonial India* (Delhi: Sage, 1994).

——, *Dalit Visions* (Delhi: Orient Longman, 1995).

——, 'Reservation in the Private Sector', *The Hindu*, 22 January 2001.

——, 'Reservation in the Corporate Sector', *The Hindu*, 31 May & 1 June 2001.

——, *Buddhism in India: Challenging Brahmanism and Caste* (Delhi: Sage, 2003).

Orsini, Francesca, *The Hindi Public Sphere 1920-1940* (Delhi: Oxford University Press, 2002).

Pandey, Gyanendra, 'Hindus and Others: The Militant Hindu Construction', *Economic and Political Weekly*, 28 December 1991.

Pandian, J., *Caste, Nationalism and Ethnicity* (Bombay: Popular Prakashan, 1987).

Panikkar, K. N., *Culture, Ideology, Hegemony: Intellectuals and Social Consciousness in Colonial India* (Delhi: Tulika, 1998).

Pankratz, James N., 'Rammohun Roy', in Robert D. Baird, ed., *Religion in Modern India*, 4th revised edn., pp. 373-87 (Delhi: Manohar, 2001).

Patil, Sharad, *Dasa-Shudra Slavery* (Delhi: Allied Publishers, 1982).

Paz, Octavio, *In Light of India* (Delhi: Rupa & Co., 1997).

Phule, Jotirao, *Collected Works of Mahatma Jotirao Phule*, vols. I & II, tr. P. G. Patil (Bombay: Educational Department, Govt. of Maharashtra, 1991).

Phule, Jotirao, *Selected Writings*, ed., G. P. Deshpande, includes *Slavery (Gulamgiri* 1873), *Cultivator's Whipcord (Shetkaryacha Asud* 1883) (Delhi: LeftWord, 2002).

———, *Mahatma Jotiba Phule Rachanavali*, in Hindi, ed., L. G. Meshram Vimalkirti, includes *Tritiya Ratna* (1855), *Sarvajanik Satya Dharrma Pustak* (1890) (Delhi: Radhakrishna Prakashan, 1996).

Pinch, William R., *Peasants and Monks in British India* (Delhi: Oxford University Press, 1999).

Prasad, R. C., tr., *Tulsidas' Shri Ramacharitamanasa* (Delhi: Motilal Banarsidass, 1990).

Prashad, Vijay, *Untouchable Freedom* (Delhi: Oxford University Press, 2000).

Quigley, Declan, *The Interpretation of Caste* (Delhi: Oxford University Press, 1999).

Radhakrishnan, S., *Indian Philosophy*, vol. 1 (London: George Allen and Unwin, 1962).

———, tr., *The Bhagvadgita*, rpt. (Delhi: Oxford University Press, 1992).

Radice, William, ed., *Swami Vivekananda and the Modernisation of Hinduism* (Delhi: Oxford University Press, 1999).

Rai, Alok, *Hindi Nationalism* (Delhi: Orient Longman, 2001).

Rangarajan, L. N., ed., *Kautilya: The Arthashastra* (Delhi: Penguin, 1992).

Rao, M. S. A., *Social Movements and Social Transformation* (Delhi: Manohar, 1979).

———, *Social Movements in India* (Delhi: Manohar, 2000).

Ray, Himanshu P., *The Winds of Change: Buddhism and the Maritime Links of Early South Asia* (Delhi: Oxford University Press, 1994).

Ray, Niharranjan et al., eds., *A Sourcebook of Indian Civilisation* (Calcutta: Orient Longman, 2000).

Rhys Davids, C. A. F., *Psalms of the Early Buddhists* (I. Psalms of the Sisters; II. Psalms of the Brethren), 1909, rpt. (London: The Pali Text Society, 1980)

Rhys Davids, T. W., *Buddhist India*, 1902, rpt. (Delhi: Motilal Banarsidass, 1981).

———, *Dialogues of the Buddha*, vol. 1., 1899, rpt. (Delhi: Motilal Banarsidass, 2000).

Rhys Davids, T. W. and C. A. F. Rhys Davids, *Dialogues of the Buddha*, vols. 2 & 3, 1910 and 1921, rpt. (Delhi: Motilal Banarsidass, 2000).

Robertson, B. C., *Raja Rammohun Roy* (Delhi: Oxford University Press, 1999).

Rodrigues, Valerian, ed., *The Essential Writings of B. R. Ambedkar* (Delhi: Oxford University Press, 2002).

Roy, Arundhati, 'Gujarat, Fascism and Democracy', in Chaitnya Krishna, ed., *Fascism in India* (Delhi: Manak, 2003).

Roy, M. N., *Gandhism; Nationalism; Socialism* (Calcutta: Bengal Radical Club).

———, *The Historical Role of Islam* (Bombay, 1937).

Rude, George, *Ideology and Popular Protest* (London: University of North Carolina Press, 1995).

Said, Edward, *Orientalism: Western Conceptions of the Orient* (London: Penguin, 1978).

Sainath, P., *Everybody Loves a Good Drought* (Delhi: Penguin, 1996).

———, 'Dregs of Destiny', *Outlook*, 19 October 1998.

Sangharakshita, *Ambedkar and Buddhism* (Glasgow: Windhorse Publications, 1986).

———, 'Buddhism', in A. L. Basham, ed., *A Cultural History of India* (Delhi: Oxford University Press, 1985).

Sankrityayan, Rahul et al., *Buddhism: The Marxist Approach* (Delhi: People's Publishing House, 1990).

Saradmoni, K., *Emergence of a Slave Caste: Pulayas of Kerala* (Delhi: People's Publishing House, 1980).

Sardar, G. B., 'Saint-Poets of Maharashtra: Their Role in Social Transformation', in S. C. Malik, ed., *Indian Movements*, pp. 101-38 (Shimla: Indian Institute of Advanced Study, 1978).

Sardesai, S. G., *Progress and Conservatism in Ancient India*, rpt. (Delhi: People's Publishing House, 1994).

Sarkar, Jadunath, *Shivaji and His Times* (Delhi: Orient Longman, 1973).

Sarkar, Sumit, *Modern India 1885-1947* (Delhi: Macmillan, 1983).

———, *Writing Social History* (Delhi: Oxford University Press, 1997).

Sastri, Nilkanta and Srinivasachari, *Advanced History of India* (Delhi: Allied Publishers, 1980).

Satish Chandra, *Historiography, Religion and State in Medieval India* (Delhi: Har-Anand, 2001).

Satyamuthy, T. V., ed., *Region, Religion, Caste, Gender and Culture in Contemporary India* (Delhi: Oxford University Press, 1996).

Savarkar, V. D., *Hindutva – Who is a Hindu?*, 1923, 7th edn. (Mumbai: Savarkar Rashtriya Smarak, 1999).

Savitri Chandra, 'Dissent and Protest in Hindi Bhakti Poetry', in S. C. Malik, ed., *Indian Movements*, pp. 139-58 (Shimla: Indian Institute of Advanced Study, 1978).

Schomer, Karine and W. H McLeod, eds., *The Sants: Studies in a Devotional Tradition of India* (Delhi: Motilal Banarsidass, 1987).

Schouten, J. P., *Revolution of the Mystics: On the Social Aspects of Virashaivism* (Delhi: Motilal Banarsidass, 1995).

Sen, Amiya P., *Hindu Revivalism in Bengal 1872-1905* (Delhi: Oxford University Press, 1993).

Shah, Ghanshyam, *Social Movements in India: A Review of the Literature* (Delhi: Sage, 1990).

——, ed., *Dalit Identity and Politics* (Delhi: Sage, 2001).

Sharma, Arvind, 'Swami Dayananda Saraswati', in Robert D. Baird, ed., *Religion in Modern India*, pp. 388-409 (Delhi: Manohar, 2001).

Sharma, R. S., *Perspective in Social and Economic History of Early India* (Delhi: Munshiram Manoharlal, 1983).

——, *Material Culture and Social Formations in Ancient India*, 1983, rpt. (Delhi: Macmillan, 2001).

——, *Indian Feudalism*, 2nd edn. (Delhi: Macmillan, 1980).

——, *Shudras in Ancient India*, 1958, 3rd revised edn. (Delhi: Motilal Banarsidass, 1990a).

——, *Ancient India* (Delhi: NCERT, 1990b).

——, *Aspects of Political Ideas and Institutions in Ancient India*, 1959, revised edn. (Delhi: Motilal Banarsidass, 1991).

Shirer, William, *The Rise and Fall of the Third Reich*, rpt. (London: Mandrin, 1991).

Shyam Chand, *Saffron Fascism* (Delhi: Hemkunt Publishers, 2002).

Simeon, Dilip, 'Communalism in Modern India', *Mainstream*, 13 December 1986, pp. 7-17.

Singh, Darshan, *A Study of Bhakta Ravidasa* (Patiala: Publication Bureau, Punjab University, 1996).

Singh, Iqbal, *Rammohun Roy: A biographical inquiry into the making of modern India*, vols. II & III (Bombay: Asia Publishing House, 1987).
Sircar, D. C., *Inscriptions of Asoka*, 1957, rpt. (Delhi: Publications Division, Govt. of India, 1998).
Srinivas, M. N., *Caste in Modern India*, 1962, rpt. (Bombay: Media Promoters, 1985).
Sunil, K. P., 'And Justice for All . . .', *The Illustrated Weekly of India*, 8-14 June 1991, pp. 16-19.
Szasz, Thomas, *The Second Sin* (London: Routledge and Kegan Paul, 1974).
Talwar, Vir Bharat, *Hindu Navjagaran ki Vichardhara, Satyarth Prakash: Samalochana Ka Ek Prayas*, in Hindi (Shimla: Indian Institute of Advanced Studies, 2001).
Thapar, Romila, *The Past and Prejudice* (Delhi: National Book Trust, 1975).
——, *Ashoka and the Decline of the Mauryas*, 1961, rpt. (Delhi: Oxford University Press, 1999).
——, *A History of India*, vol. I, 1966, rpt. (Harmondsworth: Penguin, 1984).
——, 'Syndicated Hinduism', in G.-D. Sontheimer and H. Kulke, eds., *Hinduism Reconsidered*, 1989, revised edn. (Delhi: Manohar, 2001).
——, 'The Tyranny of Labels', in K. N. Panikkar, ed., *The Concerned Indian's Guide to Communalism* (Delhi: Viking, 1999).
Turner, Bryan S., *Religion and Social Theory* (London: Heinemann, 1983).
Upadhyaya, B. S., *Feeders of Indian Culture* (Delhi: People's Publishing House, 1989).
Varma, Pawan, *The Great Indian Middle Class* (Delhi: Penguin, 1998).
Varma, V. P., *Studies in Hindu Political Thought and its Metaphysical Foundations*, 1954, revised edn. (New Delhi: Motilal Banarsidass, 1974).
——, 'The Origins of Buddhism', *The Journal of the Bihar Research Society*, Buddha Jayanti spl. issue, vol. 2, 1956.
Vaudeville, Charlotte, *Myths, Saints and Legends in Medieval India*, 1996, rpt. (Delhi: Oxford University Press, 1999).
——, *A Weaver Named Kabir*, 1993, rpt. (Delhi: Oxford University Press, 1997).
Vishwanathan, E. S., *The Political Career of E. V. Ramaswami Naicker* (Madras: Ravi and Vasanth Publishers, 1983).

Vivekananda, Swami, *The Complete Works of Swami Vivekananda*, vols. 1-8 (Calcutta: Advaita Ashrama, 1989-92).

——, *Caste, Culture and Socialism* (Calcutta: Advaita Ashrama, 1988).

——, *The Nationalistic and Religious Lectures*, ed. Swami Tapasyananda (Calcutta: Advaita Ashrama, 1998).

Voigt, Johannes H., F. M. *Max Müller: The Man and his Ideas* (Calcutta: Firma K. L. Mukhopadhyaya, 1967).

Walker, Benjamin, *Hindu World*, vols. I and II (Delhi: Munshiram Manoharlal, 1983).

Weil, Simone, *Oppression and Liberty*, 1955, tr. Arthur Wills and John Petrie (London: Routledge, 2001).

Woodward, F. L. and E. M. Hare, *Anguttara Nikaya*, vol. I (London, 1932).

Zelliot, Eleanor, *From Untouchable to Dalit: Essays on the Ambedkar Movement* (Delhi: Manohar, 1996).

Index

aborigines/non-Aryans 17ff.
Acchutanand, Swami 38, 39, 299, 333-7
adharma 56
Adi-Andhra 331
Adi-Dharma/Adi-Dharmis, in Punjab 294, 337-8
Adi-Dravida/Adi-Dravidians: *see* Dravidian movement
Adi-Hindu movement, in Andhra 332
Adi Hindu movement, in Uttar Pradesh 333-7
adivasis (original inhabitants) 24ff.; and egalitarian culture 198, 368
agrahara 157; see also *brahmadeya*
Ajivika sect 73, 83
Ajita Keshkambal 87
Akbar Shah II 210
Akhil Bharatiya Brahman Mahasabha 221
Alberuni 84
Allopanishad: see Upanishad(s)
Alvars 156-7
Althusser, on ideological indoctrination 14
Ambedkar, Bhimrao Ramji 15, 20, 29, 37, 38, 39, 40, 43, 44, 98, 113, 114-15, 149, 239, 241, 292, 295, 299, 313, 320, 323, 326, 330, 332, 338, 339, 340, 343, 346, 353-77, 390-405, 409, 410; and Gandhi: contestation over caste and untouchability 370-9, and the separate electorate 362-70, 426n; and nationalism: his critique of elitist 358-62, his vision of 393-400; and shramanic ideology 353; and the Constitution and Hindu Code Bill 401-5; and the Mahad struggle 356-8; *Annihilation of Caste* 356, 375; his vision and struggle against caste 353-62; mass conversion to Buddhism 113-16; *The Buddha and His Dhamma* 98, 113; *The Revolution and Counter-revolution in Ancient India* 20, 125-7; *What Congress and Gandhi Have Done to the Untouchables?* 390-3
Ananda 111
anuloma marriage 125, 163
anti-caste ideology/movement(s) 17-18, 36-9, 224, 225, 251, 286, 291-342; as nationalism/anti-imperialism from below 296, 340-2; education as focal point of 40, 295-6; *see also* Phule, Iyothee Thass, Narayana Guru, Ambedkar, Periyar, Acchutanand, Mangoo Ram
Apabhransha 141
Apastambh Dharmasutra 58
arajaka (anarchy) 80
Aranyakas 46, 51, 53, 76
Arjuna 60, 62, 66, 415
Arthashastra: see Kautilya

Aryadeva 117
Aryan/Indo-Aryan 17, 46, 47, 52; battles with indigenous people 46; immigration 17
Aryan race theory 31-2, 190, 192-3, 195, 234, 241; *see also* Orientalism
Arya Samaj: *see* Samaj-es
Aryavarta 30, 212
Asan, N. Kumaran 299, 304, 305, 306-7
Ashoka 35, 40, 76, 118, 119, 121-3, 130; his edicts and inscriptions 83, 123, 124; his dhamma 123; uniformity in law 124
Ashvaghosha 121
astika-nastika, real meaing of 82-3
asura 22, 75
asura-views 75
Asuropanishad 87
Atman, Upanishadic 55; and Brahmana 97, 101
Attenborough, Richard 28
Aughars 82
Aurobindo Ghosh 33, 63, 64, 211, 216, 232, 238, 352
avarna, and *savarna* 52-3
avatar (incarnation) 28, 29, 63
Ayyankali 299, 311-12
Ayyappan, K. 38, 299, 304, 308, 309-10, 311, 312, 339

Babri mosque, demolition of 25
Bagul, Baburao 292
Bajaj, Jamnalal 387
Banerjee, Surendranath 208, 287, 386
Bankimchandra Chatterjee 33, 211, 228, 231, 237, 352
Bansode, Kisan Faguji 332-3
Bali Raja 265, 270; Bali-rajya 269
Basava: *see* Mukti

begar 298
Bengal Brahman Sabha 223
Bentinck, William 204
bhadralok 201, 210, 221, 223, 227
Bhagvad Gita, critique of 59-68
Bhagyareddy Varma 299, 332
bhakti (devotion): *see* Mukti
Bhakti movements: *see* Mukti
Bhalekar, Krishnarao 283
Bhandarkar, R. G. 203, 218
Bharati Dasan 327-8
Bhave, Vinoba 64
Bhattacharya, Jogendra Nath 222
Bhima Bhoi 298
bhudeva/bhudevata 55, 72
Birla, Ghanshyam Das 387
Bodhisattva: *see* Buddhism
Brahma 55, 74, 86, 97, 107
Brahma-bhoj 55
brahmadeya 55, 129, 157
Brahma-hatya 55
Brahmana (the Supreme Spirit) 55, 66
Brahmanas (Vedic texts dealing with sacrificial ritual) 46, 51, 53, 55, 76; *Shatapatha Brahamana* 48, 55, 99
brahman(s) 16ff.; etymology of 55; nexus with kshatriyas 69, 70, 142, 143; *see also* caste and brahmanism
brahmanism: hegemonic ideology, power politics, and symbiosis with caste hierarchy and patriarchy 15-22; and communalism 22-6; attack on Buddhism 81, 82, 124-9, 142; colonial knowledge and rule, collusion with 31-4, 289-90; neo-brahmanism/neo-Hinduism 24, 36, 196-200, 284; revival of, and massive forgeries for

brahmanisation of Indian culture 129-33
Brahmi script 121
Brahmo Samaj: *see* Samaj-es
Brihadratha 124
Brihaspati 74; *Brihasapatisutra/Lokayatasutra* 87
Buddha, the 35, 40, 41, 254, 266, 353, 354; and *bahujana hitaya* 102; and *bodhi hradaya* 100; and caste 102-9; and Krishna 90; and Vedic-brahmanic epistemology 97-100; and women 111-12; definition of good and bad 98; life 88-9; political philosophy 116-18; pragmatic rationalist 91, 101; theory of dependent origin (*paticca samuppada*) 95-6, 100; *see also* Buddhism
Buddhism/Buddhist(s) 18, 24, 41, 61, 63, 65, 73, 83, 85-133, 136, 141, 142, 143, 332, 380, 399, 406; *Aggannasutta* 106, 116; *Ambalatthika-Rahulovadasutta* 98; and brahmanism 81, 82, 83, 97-8; and caste 102-9; *anicca* and *anatta(vada)* 96, 99; ascendancy and achievements of 118-23; *Assalayana-sutta* 103; *Atthangika Magga* 94; Bodhisattva, concept of 95, 127; backlash against and role of brahman-Buddhists in decline of 124-9; dhamma 89, 97, 98, and dharma 97, 98, 418n; *Dhamma-cakka-ppavattana* 95; *Dhammapada* 92, 93, 100; Dharmakirti: *Pramanvarttika* 109-10; dialectics of: *paticca samuppada* 95-6, 99, 100; hegemonic Hindu critique of 96-7; and the myth of Upanishadic influence on 97, 99; Hinayana 128; *kamma* 110, 127; *Mahaparinibbana-sutta* 90, 109; *Mahasammata*, theory of 116-17; Mahayana school 127-8; *majjhima patipada* 94; neo-Buddhism 113-16; *nibbana* 94, 101, 102, 110, 127; Pali canon 89, 91, 417-18n; people from lower strata in sangha 108-9; *Sabba-sutta* 91; sangha system, democratic basis of 117-18; spread of 119-20; suffering, idea of, and compassion (*Mettasutta*) 92; *Theragatha* 108; *Therigatha* 108, 111-12; unorthodox religion 89-90; *Vasala-sutta* 104; *Vasettha-sutta* 103; *vipassana* 95; women (bhikkunis) in sangha 108-9, 111-12

Carlyle, Thomas 391
caste/varna: system of, symbiosis with brahmanism 15-17, 51-4, 56-8; and colonialism 188ff.; and Dayananda 212-14; and patriarchy 16, 51, *see also* women; and social mobility 86; epistemic violence against shudras and women 16, 48-63, 68-73, 416-17n; history of 19; mythical origin of, in *Rigveda* 47, 52, 416n; 'nationalist' glorification of 219, 220-3; patronage by ruling groups 70; resilience/persistence of 16-17, 21, 406ff.; *see also* Ambedkar, Gandhi, and Nehru
censuses, of 1901 and 1911 343-5; and Gait circular 344-5, 424n

Chaitanya 183
Chanakya: see Kautilya
Charvaka(s): see Lokayata
Chatterjee, Bankimchandra: see Bankimchandra Chatterjee
Chetty, Thyagaray 316, 317
Chhotu Ram 299
Christ, Jesus 264
Christianity 24, 25, 139, 197, 217; conversion to 38, 279, 293; Nietzsche's attack on 242
Christian(s)/missionaries 25, 230, 259, 376
Chokhamela: see Mukti
Chola dynasty 157
Colebrooke, H. T. 193
colonialism/colonial: nexus with native elites and brahmanism 189-99, 256-7, 292-3, 299, 340-1; knowledge/Orientalism 31-3, 189-99
communalism, brahmanic basis of 22-6; and conflation with cultural nationalism 237-40, 241-50
conversion, dynamics of 345
Communist Manifesto, the 252
counter-culture, definition of 13
cultural nationalism, the myth of 233-7, 291-2; see also Phule, Iyothee, Periyar, and Ambedkar
culture of silence 19, 295
dalit/dalit-bahujan 18-20, 24; ideology of 19, 20
Dalit Panther's manifesto 340
danda 50, 71, 72, 78, 79; brahminical dandaniti 68-73, 122; and rajadharma 71-2
dasa/shudra/ati-shudra/chandala 18ff.
Dayananda Saraswati 20, 42, 210, 218-19, 233, 251, 350, 352; Satyartha Prakash and the

Aryan-Vedic revivalism 212-17; and shuddhi 214
Delhi Sultanate 143, 144
demonisation/rakshasisation 23
Desai, Mahadev 365
Devanagari script 121
dharma, origin of 56, 68
Dharmashastras 18, 19, 22, 39, 54, 56, 57, 70, 78, 129, 163, 220, 268, 275, 336, 394
dominance and resistance, dynamics of 13-15, 17; ideology, role of 14-15; Marxian-Gramscian dialectic 15
Dravidian people/culture/ languages/ literature 52, 131, 157, 423-4n; see Dravidian movement; Aryanisation/Sanskritisation of 157-8; see also Tamil Siddhas in Mukti
Dravidian movement 312-30
Dronacharya 39, 66, 67, 415
Durkheim, Emile 115
Dutt, R. C. 33, 222
dwija 162, 213; and Tagore 235

East India Company 188, 190, 200
Eklavya 39, 67, 415

Fa Hsien 119
Fanon, Franz 14, 188
feudalism/feudal forces 129, 136, 143; caste-feudalism 26, 27, 142, 202, 298, 299, 339, 341
Fischer, Louis 387, 426n
Foucault, Michel 251
French Revolution, the (of 1789) 258, 357

gahapati 105
Galbraith, J. K. 411

Index

Gandhi, Mohandas Karamchand 20, 21, 26-9, 33, 63, 64, 65, 192-3, 216, 233, 238, 240, 320, 321, 325-7, 334, 337, 338, 341, 343, 347-52, 356, 362-93, 401, 409; and Ambedkar: see Ambedkar; and caste 26-7, 223, 347-8, 376-9, 380; and modernity, sanatani critique of 383-8; and untouchability 370-7; deification of 27, 28, 347, 413; Gandhism: Ambedkar's critique of 390-3, Nehru's critique of 388-9; historio-cultural vision of 381-3; politics of 347-52, 379-83; varnashrama/brahmanism, defence of 326, 378-83
Gauri 59
Gautama Dharmasutras 58
Gayatri Mantra 261
gender/patriarchy: see women
Ghosh, Aurobindo: see Aurobindo Ghosh
Gita: see *Bhagvad Gita*
Godse, Nathuram 64, 248, 327
Gokhale, Gopal Krishna 232, 238
golden age, notion of the 252
Golwalkar, M. S. 245-6, 248
Gorakhnath 142, 171
Gorakh-Gita 171
Gramsci, and hegemony 14
Grihyasutras 220
Gulamgiri (Slavery): see Phule
Gupta, Ishwar Chandra 211
Gupta period 129, 133
Guru Chanda 297, 299; and the Namashudras 297
Guru Ghasi Das, and his son Balak Das 297
Guru Gobind Singh 154
Guru Nanak 35, 40, 207: see Mukti

Guru Granth Sahib/Adi Granth 140, 153
Gyaneshwar 63, 64; see also Mukti
Gyanoba Krishnaji Sasane 254

Harappan culture: no connection with Indo-Aryans 46
Hari Chanda Thakur 299
Harijan/Harijan Sevak Sangh 371-3, 374, 376, 400; see also Gandhi
Harischandra, Bhartendu 237-8
Harshavardhan 81, 82, 120, 121
Hastings, Warren 190, 191
Hedgewar, K. B. 238, 245, 248
heterodoxies: see shramanic tradition
Hindi movement 237-8; Hindi-Hindu-Hindutan 238, 330
Hinduism/Hindus 24, 26, 42, 56, 137, 147; folk Hinduism 135, 198, 217; neo-Hinduism, construction of 196-200
Hindu backlash, the myth of 25-6
Hindu communalism, historical relations with European fascism 244-8
Hindu secularists/the Hindu Left 22, 232
Hindutva 23, 244, 246; see also RSS
Hindu nationalism: see Hindutva and cultural nationalism
Hindu-Muslim antagonism 26
hiranyagarbha (the golden womb) 70, 71, 260
history, writing of: nationalist 30, 31; colonial 31; Orientalist 32
History and Culture of the Indian People, The 220
history from below 18
Hitler, Adolf 23, 241, 243-5
Hsuan Tsang 81, 83, 120; attempt on life by brahman fanatics 81

Indian National Congress: see political parties
Indian renaissance/reforms/national awakening of the nineteenth century, the myth of 199-211
Indo-European(s) 46
intellectuals, collusive role in dominance 15
Islam: see Muslim
itihas-purana (brahmanical texts claiming to refer to events of the past) 183, 268
Iyengar, Srinivasa 321
Iyothee Thass 38, 113, 224, 225, 299, 307, 313-16, 424n; on brahmanic culture and epistemology 315

Jagannath temple, identification with Buddhism 298
Jagatguru 55
Jagjivan Ram 376
Jain/Jainism 88, 141, 142, 191, 198, 314, 380
Jataka stories 121
jati: see caste
Jatibhed-Viveksar, by Tukaram Tatya Padwal 260
Jogendranath Mandal 299
Jones, William 189, 191-2
julahas (weavers) 143-4
Justice Party: see political parties

Kabir 35, 38, 40, 207, 254, 265, 333, 353; see also Mukti
Kali 59
Kalinga war 121
Kaliyuga (the degenerate age) 60, 68, 72, 80, 384; and varna-samkara 78, 79, 80; Kabir's definition of 147; and Tulsi 184, 186

Kalidasa: *Abhijnanshakuntalam* 192
kallumalai 311
Kamble, Shivram Janba 345
Kanishka 119, 121
Kanshi Ram 368-9
Kapalikas 82
karma 56, 57
karmakanda 73
Karna 66, 67, 368, 415
Katha-sarita-sagar, attributed to Somadeva 132
Kautilya: *Arthashastra* 72-3, 79, 122
Kautsa 74
Kavsheya 75
Kayastha Pathashala 221
Khilafat movement 350-1
Krishna 59, 60, 61, 62, 63, 64, 65, 66, 67, 183
Krishnan, C. 308
kshatriya: see caste
Kumaril Bhatta 142

Lajpat Rai 33, 235, 345, 346
Lincoln, Abraham 375
Lingayata/Virashaiva movement: see Mukti
Lokahitavadi/Gopal Hari Deshmukh 256, 257, 267
Lokayata, Lokayatika(s)/ Charvaka(s) 74-5, 87, 88
Lokhande, N. M. 283
lowered castes 18ff.

Macaulay, Thomas Babington 199
Madhavan, E. 309
Madhavan, T. K. 304, 308, 311
McDonald, Ramsey 364
Mahabharata 50, 54, 69, 71, 77, 79, 129, 130, 131, 184, 219; see also *Bhagavad Gita*
Mahabodhi Society, the 120
Mahaparinibbana-sutta: see Buddhism
Mahasammata: see Buddhism

Mahavir, Vardhamana 74, 85, 88
Mahayana: see Buddhism
Mahendra 119
Makkali Gosala 87
Mangoo Ram 244, 299, 337
Manu 16, 23, 52, 54, 57, 71, 125, 186, 189, 204, 226, 334, 416-17n
Manusmriti 16, 54, 57, 58, 69, 71, 79, 125, 126, 129, 203, 205, 331, 394; burning of 325, 356, 357-8; colonial resurrection of 189, 191
Marx, Karl 14
materialist philosophy, in ancient India: see Lokayata
matsyanyaya 50
Masilamani 313
Maurya(s) 73, 77, 124; see also Ashoka
Megasthenes 83
Menander 119
metta: see Buddhism
middle path: see Buddhism
Mirabai: see Mukti
mleccha 22, 25, 54
Morley-Minto reforms (1909) 344
Muddaliar, S. Muthiah 322
Muktabai 272
Mukti (Bhakti) movements 134-87; and brahmans 135, 139, 140, 169; and Eknath 169, 181-2; and Gyaneshwar 138, 139, 169, 171, 181-2; and Ramananda, the myth of 139-40; and Ramdas 182; and Tulsi 138, 183-7; link to shramanic heterodoxies 135, 141-2; and Buddhism 136, 166; *nirguna* 137, 140, 145, 146, 160, and *saguna*, conflict of 183-4; non-brahmanic God, creation of 135, 137; opposition to caste and brahmanic dominance 135ff.; peoples' languages preferred to Sanskrit 138-9, 168, 181; religion, new vision of 137-8; respect for labour 138, 183; secular and egalitarian agenda 136-7; Tamil Siddhas/Sittars 155-62; Varakaris 168-82; Virashaivas 162-8; women, subaltern, and decaste saint-poets: Allama 165; Bahinabai 179; Basava 135, 162-66; Chokhamela 135, 170, 174-6; Dadu Dayal 134, 136, 141, 151, 183; Darya Saheb 152; Dhana 139; Dharmdas 152; Gora 136, 174, 181; Haralayya, and Madhuvayya, martyrdom of 163-4; Janabai 174; Joga Paramananda 174; Kabir 134, 136, 137, 138, 139, 140, 141, 143-9, 153, 154, 156, 161, 162, 175, 183, 185, 187, 418n, 419n; Madar Cannayya 165; Mahadevi 135, 166-7; Mirabai 136, 154-5; Muktayakka 166; Namdev 135, 140, 141, 149, 170, 171, 172-4; Nanak 134, 136, 138, 141, 152-4, 183, 185; Nandnar 156; Narhari Sonar 174, 181; Pambatti Sittar 134, 136, 160-1; Pipa 139; Ravidas 134, 136, 138, 139, 141, 149-51, 153, 154, 174, 175, 183, 186, 187; Sadhana 139; Savata Mali 136, 174, 181; Sena 136, 139; Siddharama 166; Sivavakkiyar 136, 159-60; Tirumular 136, 155, 158, 161; Trilochan 149;

Tukaram 135, 136, 137, 170, 176-81, 183, persecution of 179-80; Yari Saheb 152
Müller, Max, 31, 32, 34, 193, 194, 195, 241, 286, 419-20n
Muslim(s)/Islamic (religion or rule) 22, 23, 25, 26, 135, 143, 144, 145, 147, 191, 197, 201, 207, 217, 219, 222, 230-1, 234, 264-5, 294, 346, 362, 363, 366, 419n; invasions 126, 136

Nagpur, Maharashtra, the birthplace of the RSS 239, 248; the mass conversion to Buddhism 115
Naidu, Sarojini 387
Naidu, M. V. 317
Nair, T. M. 316, 317
Namashudras 297
Namdev: see Mukti
Nandas, dynasty of 73
Nandnar: see Mukti
Naoroji, Dadabhai 287, 386
Narada Smriti 79
Narasu, Lakshmi 328
Narayana Guru 38, 295, 299, 339; and Gandhi 303-4, 310, 311; the SNDP movement 300-12
nastika: views against brahmanism 82-3, 86-7; *nastiko vedanindakah* 58, 83
Nathpanthi(s)/Nath-Siddhas 141, 142, 143, 158, 171
nationalism, elitist 20; brahmanic basis of 24, 291-2; and caste 20
Nayanars 156
Nazi Germany 32, 243-4
Nehru, Jawaharlal 20, 26, 231, 338, 341, 352, 356, 360, 385, 388-9, 399-400, 405, 409; brahmanic vision of history in *The Discovery of India* 29-36; and caste 20, 26, 29, 30, 356, 396, 425n; *see also* Gandhi
Nehru, Motilal 399
neo-Gandhians 391
nibbana (nirvana): *see* Buddhism
Nietzsche 23, 32; and Manu 241-4
Niggantha Natputta 87
nirguna: *see* Mukti
niyoga (levirate) 215-16
Non-Cooperation movement 350-3
non-brahman movements: *see* anti-caste movements

Orientalism/orientalists 31-3, 189-99, 229; Asiatic Society of Bengal 191; Asiatic Society of Bombay 191; Asiatic Society of Great Britain 191
other backward classes (OBCs) 25, 239, 249, 408, 411, 420n

paap-yoni (born of sin) 53, 61
Pal, Bipin Chandra 33, 217, 235
Pala dynasty 82
Pali 18, 128, 131, 417n; Buddhist-Jain texts in 80, 83, 84, 108, 120
Pali Buddhist canon 108, 417-18n
Pallava dynasty 157
Palpu, Dr 299, 301, 304, 305
Panini 47
Parashara 205
Parashuram 269
paribbajaka (parivrajaka) 87
Parshva 88
Pashandas 73
Patanjali 83, 88, 124; on shraman-brahman antagonism 83
Patel, Vallabhbhai 360, 361, 365
peasantry 280-3, 298; revolts 299

Periyar, Ramaswami Naicker 37, 38, 40, 292, 299, 320-30, 338, 339, 340; and Ambedkar 326, 330; and Gandhi 325-7; *Kudi Arasu* 325; on nationalism 321; on non-brahmanism 324, 410
Peshwa(s)/Peshwai 255-6, 259, 270, 271
Phule, Jotirao 36, 37, 38, 39, 40, 42-3, 149, 177, 221, 224, 225, 238-9, 251-90, 292, 293, 295, 299, 320, 324, 332, 338, 339, 340, 353, 386; a new religion, vision of 265-6; and brahmanical patriarchy 275-80; support for Ramabai and Tarabai Shinde 278-80; and Ranade 266-7, 288, 290; and shramanic tradition 254; campaign for education 252, 262, 271-5, 276; caste and brahmanism, critique of 251-2, 259-62, 268-9; colonialism, criticism of 289-90; community of the oppressed, notion of 263-4; *Gulamgiri* 261-2, 269, 273; history from below, attempt at 267-70; life 253-4, 257-9; on nation and nationalism 284-90; Satyashodhak Samaj 262ff.; brahmanic backlash 263, 270; struggle for peasantry and labour 280-4
Phule, Savitribai 266, 276, 277
political parties: Bharatiya Janata Party (BJP) 24, 25; Communist parties/Marxists 329, 341, 399; Congress/Indian National Congress 24, 221, 240, 287, 289, 290, 294, 310, 311, 316, 320, 321, 322, 329, 337, 387, and caste 346, see also Ambedkar and Gandhi; Justice Party 316-20, 323, 324, 325, 329, 330, and the Non-Brahman Manifesto 316; Muslim League 345
Politics, by Aristotle, and Kautilya's *Arthashastra* 73
ponga pandit/Babaji 80
Poona Pact 362-70
Poona Sarvajanik Sabha: see Samaj-es
Prakrit 18, 121, 131, 132, 133, 181
Prakuddha Katyayana 87
Prarthana Samaj: see Samaj-es
pratiloma marriage 163-4
Princep, James 130, 191
punarjanma (rebirth) 56, 198
Puran Kassapa 87
Purusha-sukta 47, 52, 77, 416n
Pushyamitra Shunga 124-7, 129; persecution of Buddhists 124-5

racial theory/racism 234, 241
Radhakant Deb, Raja 204, 209-10
Radhakrishnan, S. 21, 30, 96-7, 356, 390
Rajagopalachari, C. 63, 64, 67, 396, 400
Rama 59, 183, 185-7, 313, 325
Ramabai, Pandita 278-9, 422n
Ram Charan 299, 333, 334, 336-7
Ramakrishna Mission 226
Ramakrishna Paramhans 223, 224, 228, 279
Ramananda: see Mukti
Ramayana 75, 130, 131, 132, 183, 185, 219, 313; *chora* (thief) for the Buddha in 77, 132; *Ramacharitamanasa*, by Tulsidas 183-7

Ranade, Mahadev Govind 33, 139, 168, 170, 232, 236, 238, 240, 266-7, 287, 288, 290, 386
Rashtriya Swayamsevak Sangh (RSS) 24, 25, 238-40, 244-50
Ravidas 38, 333; see also Mukti
Republic, by Plato, and Kautilya's Arthashastra 73
reservation/affirmative action 318-19, 322-3, 331, 410, 411; and the Constitution, first amendment of 323
Rigveda: see Vedas
Romain Rolland 34
Round Table Conference, London 358, 362
Rousseau, Jean-Jacques 391
Roy, Raja Rammohun 20, 42, 195, 217, 251, 275; and the bhadralok movement, the myth of 199-211
Ruskin, John 391

sacrifice, system of 48, 49
saguna: see Mukti
Sahajiya/Sahajyani Buddhism 141, 171
Sakyas, tribe and territory to which the Buddha belonged 73, 106, 107, 116
Said, Edward: Orientalism 194-6, 251
samadharma, Dravidian vision of 328-9
Samaj-es (societies): Adi-Andhra Maharaja Sabha 331; Adi-Hindu Sabha 335; Arya Samaj 205, 212ff., 224, 286, 333-4; Brahmo Samaj 205, 206, 209-10, 286; Dharma Sabha 209-10; Hindu Mahasabha 244, 247; National Social Conference 236, 287; Poona Sarvajanik Sabha 286, 423n; Praja Mitra Mandali 331; Prarthana Samaj 205, 286; Sahodara Sangham 309-10; Satnami Mahasabha 297; Satyashodhak Samaj 238, 320, see also Phule; Self-Respect League 320-30; Sree Narayana Dharma Paripalana Yogam 305-12; Swatantra Samudayam 309; Tribeni Sangh 298; Veda Samaj 205; Virashaiva Mahasabha 331; Vokkaliga Association 331
Sanjaya Belathaputta 87
Sanghamitra 119
Sanskrit (language and literature) 47, 54, 59, 76, 77, 78, 80, 81, 120, 121, 129, 136, 138-9, 163, 177, 181, 190, 191, 225, 397; and Hindi 237; and Vedic language 47; forgeries/interpolations in 76, 77, 130-3; genesis of literature in 131
Sanskritisation 21, 129-33
sati 202-4, 209, 275, 276
Satyashodhak Samaj: see Phule
Savarkar, Vinayak Damodar 20, 21, 33, 244, 245
savarna, and avarna: see avarna
Sayana 23, 194, 419-20n
Schopenhauer 32, 34, 243
Self-Respect movement: see Periyar
Sen, Keshab Chandra 33, 192, 212
Separate electorate: see Poona Pact
Shahu Maharaj 299
Shaivism 38
Shambuk 39, 40, 187, 313, 415; story of 185
Shankara 51, 63, 64, 75, 77, 142, 180; and mayavada 128-9; his attack on Buddhism 128-9, 230

Shashank 82
Shiva/Adinath 59, 171, 302
Shivaji Bhosale 255, 260, 270, 421-2n
shlokas/subhasitaanis/suktis 58
shoonyavada (nihilism) 127, 128
Shraddhanand, Swami 372
shraman (saman)/shramanic tradition 35, 41, 73ff., 127, 196, 399, 406; and Ambedkar 353, 421n; and Gandhi 380, 426n; and Mukti movements 134-5; and Phule 254; contestation with brahman(ism) 83-4, 86-7, 134; eminent leaders besides the Buddha and Mahavir in the sixth century BC 87; origin and meaning of 417n
shudra: see caste
Siddhas 82, 135, 143, 171; see also Nathpanthis
Siddhartha Gautam: see Buddha
Sikhism/Sikh(s) 24, 152-4, 191, 198, 207, 366, 406
Singaravelu, M. 328, 329
Sita 40, 183, 186, 415
Smith, Adam 409
Smith, Vincent 33
social Darwinism 71
Sonadhar Senapati 299
South Indian Buddhist Association: see Iyothee Thass
Subramania Bharathi 162
Sufi(ism) 82, 135, 43, 158, 406
Sugatan, R. 308
swaraj, notion of 284, 322
'syndicated Hinduism' 197

Tagore, Debendranath 210, 218
Tagore, Dwarkanath 206, 210
Tagore, Prasanna Kumar 210
Tagore, Rabindranath 162, 235, 240

Tamil/Tamilian: see Dravidian
Tamizhan 314
Tarabai Shinde 278-80; Stri-Purush Tulana 279-80
Thakkar, A. V. 372, 400
theendal 300, 310, 423n
the 'other India'/the two Indias 407-9
Thomas Paine 258, 259, 265
Tilak, Bal Gangadhar 20, 21, 33, 63, 64, 232-3, 235-7, 267, 270, 271, 287, 346, 352, 360, 361, 394
Tipu Sultan 188
Tiruvalluvar: Kural 156
Tolstoy, Leo 391
Tukaram 254; see also Mukti
Tukaram Hanumant Pinjan 254
Tulsidas 42; see also Mukti

Upali 108
Upanishad(s)/Upanishadic ideology/ metaphysics (Advait/Vedanta) 34, 46, 50, 51, 55, 70, 75, 96, 97, 101, 420n; Allopanishad 99; Brihadranyaka Upanishad 90, 99; Chandyoga Upanishad 75, 420n; composition of 99; Katha Upanishad 49

Vajrayana 82
Vaikkom (temple) agitation 311, 347
Varma, Bhagyareddy: see Bhagyareddy Varma
vaishya(s): see caste
Vallabhacharya 183
varnashrama-dharma 16, 25, 73, 142, 152, 165, 321, 376, 388
varna system: see caste and varnashrama-dharma
Veda(s)/Vedic 31, 32, 33, 45, 46,

57, 58, 74, 75, 76, 82, 83, 86, 88, 265, 331, 336; composition of 46; interpolations and redactions 47; *Vaidiki himsa himsa na bhavati* 76; Vedic ideology 48-50
Vidyasagar, Ishwarchandra 205, 208, 217, 223-4
Vidyapati 183
Virochana 87
Vithoba, at Pandharpur 170, 174, 178
Vivekananda, Swami 20, 33, 42, 194, 216, 223, 224-33, 251, 279, 350, 352; and caste 226-7; and gender 228, 422n; diatribe against Christianity, Islam, and Buddhism 230-2
Voltaire 139
Vratya(s) 53

Vrishala(s) 73, 79
Walangkar, Gopal Baba 345
women/gender/patriarchy 16, 22, 56, 57, 141, 202, 320, 325, 412, 413; and Ambedkar 360, 405; and caste 16; and Phule 275-80; and the reform movements 199-209, 215-16, 218-19; in Buddhist sangha: *see* Buddhism; in the medieval movements: *see* Mukti; of brahman caste forge unity with shudras and vaishyas 79; the Age of Consent Bill 236

Yajnavalkya 16, 79, 226; and Gargi 90, 91; *Yajnavalkya Smriti* 58

zamindar(s)/landlords 28, 189, 200, 294, 298, 341